A COMPANION TO THE *AENEID* IN TRANSLATION

Volume 1

A COMPANION TO THE *AENEID* IN TRANSLATION

Volume 1

INTRODUCTION AND INDICES

Christopher Tanfield

BLOOMSBURY ACADEMIC

LONDON • NEW YORK • OXFORD • NEW DELHI • SYDNEY

BLOOMSBURY ACADEMIC
Bloomsbury Publishing Plc
50 Bedford Square, London, WC1B 3DP, UK
1385 Broadway, New York, NY 10018, USA
29 Earlsfort Terrace, Dublin 2, Ireland

BLOOMSBURY, BLOOMSBURY ACADEMIC and the Diana logo are trademarks of Bloomsbury
Publishing Plc

First published in Great Britain 2025

Library of Congress Cataloging-in-Publication Data
Names: Tanfield, Christopher, author.
Title: A companion to the Aeneid in translation / Christopher Tanfield.
Description: London ; New York : Bloomsbury Academic, 2025. | Includes
bibliographical references and index. | Contents: v. 1. Introduction
and indices – v. 2. Commentary to books 1-6 – v. 3. Commentary
to books 7-12.
Identifiers: LCCN 2024019924 (print) | LCCN 2024019925 (ebook) | ISBN
9781350499492 (v. 1 ; paperback) | ISBN 9781350499485 (v. 1 ; hardback)
| ISBN 9781350157118 (v. 2 ; paperback) | ISBN 9781350157125 (v. 2 ;
hardback) | ISBN 9781350499546 (v. 3 ; paperback) | ISBN 9781350499539
(v. 3 ; hardback) | ISBN 9781350499508 (v. 1 ; ebook) | ISBN
9781350499515 (v. 1 ; pdf) | ISBN 9781350157132 (v. 2 ; ebook) | ISBN
9781350157149 (v. 2 ; pdf) | ISBN 9781350499553 (v. 3 ; ebook) | ISBN
9781350499560 (v. 3 ; pdf)
Subjects: LCSH: Virgil. Aeneis. | Virgil–Translations into
English–History and criticism. | LCGFT: Literary criticism.
Classification: LCC PA6825 .T26 2025 (print) | LCC PA6825 (ebook) | DDC
873/.01–dc23/eng/20240801
LC record available at https://lccn.loc.gov/2024019924
LC ebook record available at https://lccn.loc.gov/2024019925

ISBN: HB: 978-1-3504-9948-5
         PB: 978-1-3504-9949-2
         ePDF: 978-1-3504-9951-5
         eBook: 978-1-3504-9950-8

Typeset by RefineCatch Limited, Bungay, Suffolk
Printed and bound in Great Britain

To find out more about our authors and books visit www.bloomsbury.com
and sign up for our newsletters.

To my mother, late father and aunt Maria, each omnis curae casusque levamen

CONTENTS

Volume 2: Commentary on Books I–VI (available separately)
Volume 3: Commentary on Books VII–XII (available separately)

PREFACE

'If you take from Vergil his language and metre, what do you leave him?'

Coleridge[1]

Every new book on Virgil must start with its apologia. This one's is that, as the *Aeneid* is more and more often read in English, Coleridge's question needs an answer beyond the bare translation. In 1985, R. D. Williams produced a slim commentary on the rendition of C. Day Lewis, but his remit did not allow him to go very far; other translations have since been provided with notes of their own that go further. Nevertheless, when teaching the *Aeneid* in English, I missed something comparable to P. Jones' commentaries on the *Iliad* and the *Odyssey* for readers in translation; surely the *Aeneid*, an epic rooted in literary tradition and national history, deserved similar treatment? I waited expectantly, confident that others would be making good the omission; but nothing was forthcoming. Meanwhile, as a teacher of the *Aeneid* in Latin, able to give detailed attention to only one book at a time, I found myself like the blind man reporting on his prescribed part of the elephant: to gain some grasp of the whole, pupils would have to read the rest in translation straight through (or much more likely a synopsis), and this did little justice to the ideas worked out through the tapestry of the whole poem.

So, the aim of this *Companion* is to encourage a deeper appreciation of the text of the *Aeneid* in its entirety – for teachers and students but also for that mythic creature, the 'general reader'. They could all, of course, consult commentaries on the Latin, but for one not concerned with (or equipped for) the language of the original, its prosody or the textual criticism of the manuscripts essential to its transmission, this could feel like going on a scenic drive with one's head under the bonnet. Likewise the books and articles on the *Aeneid*, or on specific aspects of it, bulk vast enough to intimidate the most intrepid – it is hard to know where to start, especially since one can never finish, or hope to be up-to-date; addressing it can feel like trying to embrace an octopus.

I have tried to structure the *Companion* to cater for varying levels of curiosity: the introductory essays are designed to support the commentaries on the individual books but can also be read independently; they cover, however cursorily, many of the topics most earnestly debated; they do not peddle my own views, even if these cannot help intruding; and with the footnotes they offer a set of library steps up to the shoulders of giants, with an inkling of the view from the top. For anyone minded to research further, this is a good time to make that ascent, especially if you have access to digital resources: by consulting a database of journals and some of the books in the Select Bibliography, you will quickly be taken towards the scholarly horizon. Equally, there has never been wider availability in online translation of the cited Latin or Greek works (see the Select Bibliography for guidance): the *Aeneid* affords a rabbit-hole into Augustan Rome, most vividly experienced through the voices that could be heard there.

The commentary on the individual books (referred to using Roman numerals, e.g. 'Book IV', to distinguish them from books in other epics, though line numbers are given as conventionally, e.g. '4.135') is based upon the most purchased prose (West) and verse (Fagles) translations. It breaks the text up into self-contained sections; each section is given its own higher-level set of remarks (in a shaded box) before the line-by-line analysis, West cited in bold font and Fagles in bold italics. (My own emphases are underlined.) The Index allows another point of entry into these notes, as well as to the introductory essays. In short, users of the *Companion* should be able to find what they are seeking, if it is there, while avoiding as much as possible of the rest.

This book was largely written during the Covid pandemic, when libraries were closed; my profound gratitude to the London Library for its postal loans can well be imagined. My editors, Alice Wright and Lily McMahon, and their team have been endlessly accommodating, and I am much indebted to the readers they recruited for their comments. Martin Kauffmann and Lesley Smith have been sources of encouragement, practical assistance and wisdom at every turn. Sheila Wood provided me with Cyclopean foundations for the index, Joshua Benjamins with invaluable guidance on the superstructure.

Virgil's prestige has waned since Quintilian endorsed[2] him as 'second to Homer, but closer to first place than to third'. Even so, many Virgilian introductions conclude with his capacity for perpetual relevance – regrettably, since his themes are melancholy ones. After Covid's exile, as prophecies on the environment sound more insistently, when war has broken out in Gaza to add to the wars in Ukraine and elsewhere, it is hard not to feel Virgil's, or his narrator's, 2,000-year-old urgency and indignation at the strain required to found the Roman race (1.33). These, too, lie at the genesis of this *Companion*.

Christopher Tanfield
4 March 2024

CHAPTER 1
HISTORICAL BACKGROUND

The *Aeneid* is, among other things, the story of Rome's foundation, even if the poem ends some 300 years before it (753 BCE 1.263–6 note). Rome, the city and its people (which by Virgil's day included the whole of Italy), is in the foreground from the outset. The short Proem mentions it by name twice, including at its close (line 33), while Aeneas, although the focus of the first ten lines, is not named at all. Thereafter it seldom recedes for long; its future history is the subject of prophecy, vision and even depiction (Jupiter in Book I; the pageant in Book VI; the shield in Book VIII); its countryside is described and lovingly evoked (especially in Book VII – the mouth of the Tiber; the landscapes of the catalogue); the ancestry of Roman society is hinted at, from the great families (the captains in Book V's boat race) to the salt-of-the-earth common stock (the ethnography of Book VII) and the links with Greece (Epirus, Book III; Evander's Arcadians, Book VIII); Roman customs and rituals hatch fully fledged throughout the narrative (forms of worship in Book III; the performance of the *lusus Troiae* in Book V; the opening of the Temple of Janus in Book VII); the landmarks of eventual Rome are glimpsed in their primordial state (Evander's tour of Pallanteum in Book VIII). Fate makes Rome inevitable and Rome by its greatness imparts purpose to Fate. Not without reason has Rome been called the real hero of the *Aeneid*.[1]

1.1 Rome's origins: Rival traditions

Foundation stories are invented or elaborated to fit an identity that develops long after the 'foundation' itself.[2] What the story brings out will depend on who is elaborating it and why – an inhabitant of the United States of America could point to any of the influx of people across the Siberian land bridge, the first European settlers, the Pilgrim Fathers, the American Revolution or the signing of the constitution as moments of 'foundation', and in doing so highlight, for instance, the primacy of the indigenous, the value of immigrants, the links with Europe, the independence from Britain, religious toleration or humanitarian principles.[3] By Virgil's time there had come to be a plethora of different traditions for the foundation of Rome, many of which probably originated in the fourth or third centuries BCE among Greek historiographers.[4] His contemporary, Dionysius of Halicarnassus, gives a flavour of their variety[5] and their agenda:[6] to make Rome trace its ultimate origin to the Greeks and Aeneas a Johnny-come-lately. As Rome shook itself free from deference to Greek culture, however, from the end of the third century BCE onwards, two accounts came to prevail: the literary one of Aeneas and the oral tradition of Romulus and Remus, an Italic homegrown legend. Each served a different purpose: Aeneas represented heroic ancestry that owed nothing to Greece[7] and a mission that propelled Italy towards union; Romulus and Remus a rootedness in the Italian countryside and bond with specifically Roman traditions. Livy, the early books of whose history predate Virgil's work on the *Aeneid*, begins by scurrying through a narrative of Aeneas'

Italian campaign in two chapters, then turns to his expatiation on Romulus first with and then without Remus, signalling it by the words, 'But the Fates had, I believe, already decreed the origin of this great city and the foundation of the mightiest empire under heaven.'[8] And whereas Dionysius of Halicarnassus had preferred a version in which the twins were sent to Gabii to be educated in Greek,[9] Livy presents them as young men who 'did not neglect their pastoral duties … their special delight was roaming through the woods on hunting expeditions.'[10]

Virgil restores Aeneas to pride of place (see also *Introduction* – 3.2.2 Aeneas between the *Iliad* and the *Aeneid*: The Aeneas legend). Although it is a mistake to view Aeneas as a proto-Augustus (10.260–86 note), as figure-head and leader[11] he certainly provides an exemplar for Augustus the (re)founder (6.788–94 note). And the final settlement Virgil engineers between Jupiter and Juno (12.834 ff.) allows the Italians to absorb the Trojans, in keeping with Romans' sentimental autochthony[12] and Augustus' policy of opening the opportunities of the capital to citizens from wider Italy.[13]

1.2 Rome's origins: Archaeology

The extent to which the history of early Rome is artificially constructed is brought out by comparing it to sober archaeological evidence. The Capitoline hill shows signs of settlement in the Bronze Age (i.e. before 1000 BCE; ancient authors date the Trojan War variously from the mid-thirteenth to the beginning of the twelfth century BCE[14]). These pottery sherds are of the local, Apennine, type. Pottery from Mycenae reached central Italy in the thirteenth and twelfth centuries but contact between western Italy and the outside world seems otherwise to have been limited to Sicily and the copper mines of Sardinia (in which the Phoenicians might have had a hand; they did later). The Apennine people of Rome's hills 'may be envisaged as living in scattered farmsteads and gathering from time to time at sanctuaries generally associated with springs and caves.'[15] Towards the end of the Bronze Age, urns containing cremated remains begin to be found and, at the start of the Iron Age, the offerings buried with them, a model table service or a lance in miniature, which are unique to Rome and the Alban Hills, confirm the link forged by mythology between Alba Longa and Rome. But of Aeneas and the Trojans, not a trace.[16] The settlements in Latium, with the possible exception of Rome (its early remains have been too damaged to judge), remained small and dominated by the Etruscan towns to the north and south that flourished in the eighth century (hence the importance of the Etruscans to Aeneas).[17] Greek colonies arrived in southern Italy from the eighth century onwards and reached as far north as Ischia, in the Bay of Naples. They used the Tiber as a conduit for trade. A graffito of one Kektos on a Corinthian vase suggests that Greeks were living in Rome (on the Esquiline Hill) by the seventh century. But this hardly amounts to Evander at Pallanteum in the twelfth. A map of the pre-Roman peoples of Italy based on archaeological evidence produces a mosaic.

Such was Rome's extraordinary rise that the history of these peoples was written by Roman and Greek authors; even the names they have been given may not be their own. And when Virgil revives their memory in the catalogues of Book VII and Book X, they belong to an exotic past.

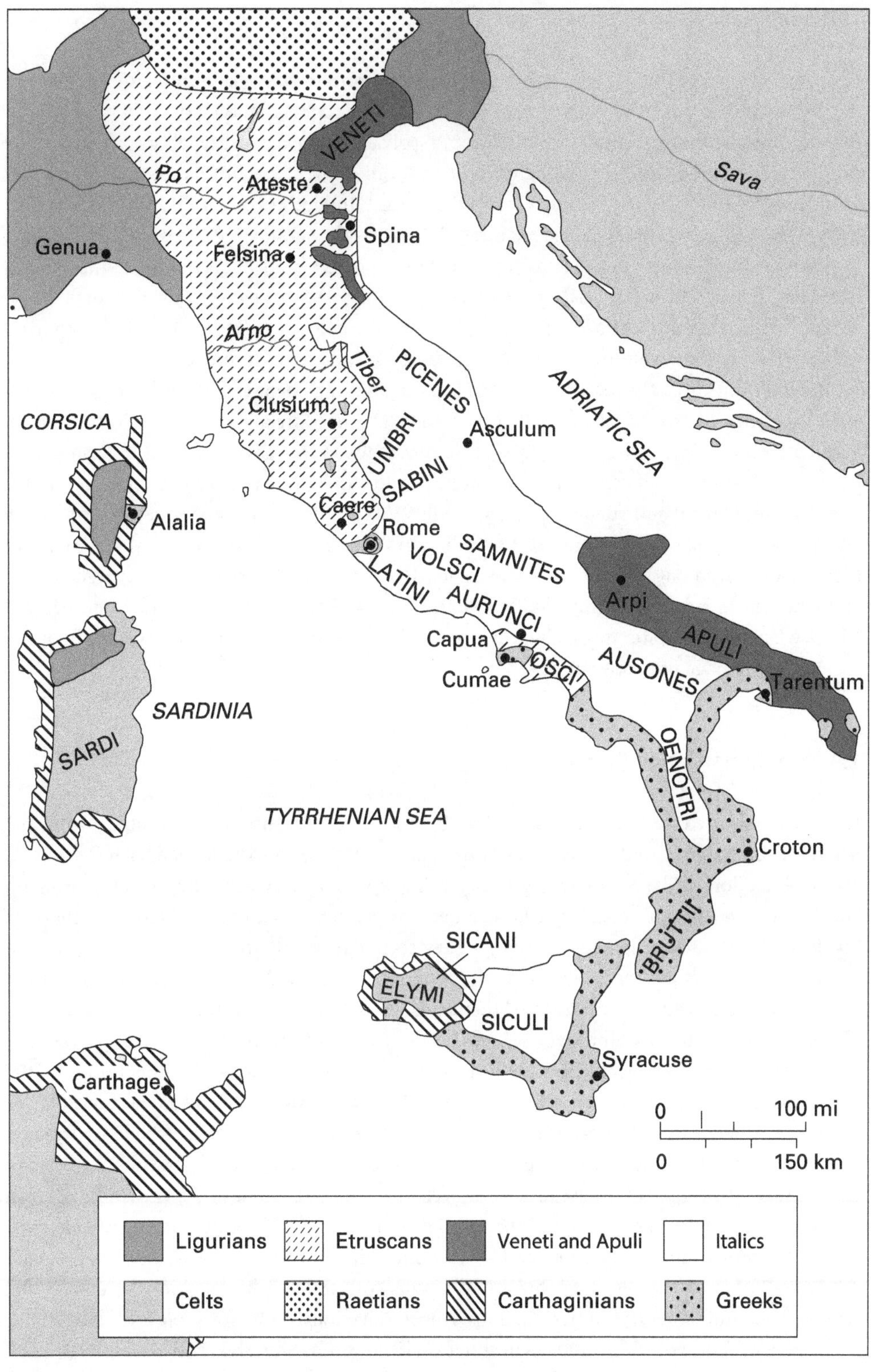

Ancient Italic peoples (*Encyclopaedia Britannica*, 2012).

1.3 From Aeneas to Romulus: The Alban kings (to 753 BCE)

For Rome's Iron Age there was scant written evidence from the city itself until after the siege of the Capitol by the Gauls, in 390 BCE (8.652-62 note; Livy claims that the little that there was 'in the pontifical commentaries and public and private archives nearly all perished in the conflagration of the City'[18]). Through this haze loomed the conventional date for Romulus' foundation of Rome itself, given by Varro as 753 BCE.[19] Jupiter's summary in Book I (1.263 ff.) defines the gap between the Trojan War and this date – though he is 100 years short, seduced by his own numerology: after Aeneas' tenure at Lavinium (3 years) and Ascanius' at Alba Longa (30 years) there follows the series of Alban kings, who last 300 years (6.767–70 note). These chronological shims[20] achieve dim individuality in Anchises' pageant (6.760 ff.), offering examples of piety and valour; they expand Alba Longa's sphere of influence.[21]

The last of the line, Numitor (6.768), the legend has it, was deposed by his brother Amulius who also killed his sons and compelled his daughter, Rhea Silvia, to become a Vestal Virgin. Virgil incorporates the twins, Romulus and Remus, to whom she gave birth (1.272–7 note) into a scene on Aeneas' shield (8.630 ff.): on Amulius' orders they were exposed in a floating cradle, but then were found and suckled by a she-wolf.[22] Virgil passes over the sequel, how the boys when grown up deposed Amulius, restored their grandfather Numitor to rule Alba Longa and themselves moved out to establish a larger city. They quarrelled over what it was to be called and who was to rule it – Romulus killed Remus and so 'Rome', not 'Reme', came into being.[23] Virgil, when he has Jupiter foreseeing the two brothers giving laws to their city (1.292 f.), turns them into an image of cooperation.

1.4 The Roman kings (to 509 BCE)

Romulus bolstered his infant foundation by in some measure amalgamating with the neighbouring Sabines, under their king Titus Tatius.[24] This seems to be factual basis for the tale of the abduction of the Sabine women (8.635 ff.). Romulus also, according to Livy, drew up laws and created a small senate, of 100 members, very much under the thumb of the king.[25] At his death Romulus was deified (6.779 f.) – Livy seems discreetly to prefer the theory that he was assassinated by the senate to the public pronouncement that he had been snatched up to heaven by a whirlwind.[26] An 'interrex' then took up temporary control; Romulus' successor was elected by popular assembly, the senate subsequently ratifying its decision.[27] The kings that follow, similarly chosen by election, are little more than hazy outlines – Virgil mentions (6.809 ff.) Numa Pompilius, Tullus Hostilius (the executioner of Mettus, 8.642 ff., responsible for absorbing Alba Longa into Rome[28]), Ancus Marcius and then the Tarquins. The latter were an Etruscan family whose ambition appeared to be to set up an Etruscan dynasty. (Archaeology substantiates the arrival of Etruscan ideas as well as artefacts in Rome at the end of the seventh century.) According to Livy,[29] when Tarquinius Priscus was murdered, his (non-Etruscan) son-in-law, Servius Tullius, seized power (Virgil omits him); he in turn was murdered by the Tarqinius known as Superbus ('The Proud'), who consolidated his position by culling the senate. This and other tyrannical actions (most notoriously his son's rape of Lucretia, a noblewoman[30]) provoked L. Junius Brutus to expel Tarquinius Superbus and his family (6.818), in 510/509 BCE. From this event stemmed the Roman aversion to monarchs, and the Republican structure of government by an empowered senate and two consuls.[31] Senators were known as *patres* ('fathers') and election to their ranks remained the preserve of a few families, the patrician *gentes*; Aeneas is frequently given the epithet *pater* (e.g. 1.580).

1.5 The early Republic (to 133 BCE)

The banished Tarquinius, after several foiled manoeuvres to return to Rome, took refuge with Lars Porsenna, king of the Etruscan city of Clusium, and persuaded Porsenna to reinstate him on his throne. The resulting siege of Rome inspired the bravery of Horatius Cocles and Cloelia (8.646–51 note); and although Porsenna seems to have captured the city, he did not restore Tarquinius Superbus, who eventually died in exile at Cumae (in 496 BCE). After the defeat at Aricia (in 506 BCE) of Porsenna's son by an alliance that modern historians name the 'Latin League' (7.59–63 note),[32] Rome grew in strength, taking on the Latin League, the Aequi and the Volsci (see 7.706-22 note for a map). The Roman reversal against the Etruscans at Veii (in 479 BCE) unleashed a display of typically Roman persistence – A. Cornelius Cossus slew the Veian king Tolumnius in battle (*c.* 426 BCE; 6.841) and M. Furius Camillus eventually captured Veii itself after a twenty-year siege (in 396 BCE; 6.825).[33] The Etruscan cities, worn down by war (the last act of defiance was when Volsinii was besieged and captured in 264 BCE), were eventually absorbed into Rome's sphere of influence. The *Aeneid*, by contrast, portrays an amicable alliance between Aeneas and the Etruscans from the first (10.153 f.).

The start of the fifth century saw significant social change. The office of tribune of the people was created to represent the interests of the *plebs* (6.824, 6.842), which were soon protected by the set of laws known as the Twelve Tables (449 BCE); further offices, of chief priest and sole ruler with emergency powers were created at this time (though the titles *pontifex maximus* and *dictator* came later). The functions of the king, as performed by Aeneas, were divided up. Neither this nor Rome's creeping subjugation of neighbouring tribes provides matter for Virgil: he is aware of popular politics (as uprisings – 1.148 ff., 5.654 ff., 7.585 ff., or in the deeds of the Drusi and Gracchi as tribunes of the people – see above) but not interested in the structures that sustained them; and although the catalogue of Book VII (7.647) demonstrates his ethnographic curiosity, Jupiter's settlement (12.834, 12.838), speaking as it does of 'Ausonia' (3.170–1 note), is a smooth and instant coalescence of a great tranche of Italy – four centuries of struggle elided.

Nor was Italy left to sort out its affairs in isolation. Crossing the borders from about 650 BCE onwards, Gauls, who had for centuries been importing merchandise from the Greeks and Etruscans, were settling in the north of Italy in what was to become known as 'Cisalpine Gaul' (= 'Gaul this side of the Alps').[34] They continued to encroach on the local population, who did their best to resist. In 391 BCE, a Celtic army led by the Senones attacked Etruria; the next year they came back for Rome.[35] After defeating the Romans at the Battle of Allia (390 BCE), they captured Rome and razed it; layers of burnt debris illustrate their systematic pillaging. They were not aiming at conquest, however, and were soon bought off – leaving room for face-saving anecdotes, as of the goose-guardians (6.825, 8.652 ff.). (The Senones eventually lost their taste for marauding and made peace with Rome in 331 BCE.)

In reaction to its defeat, Rome built walls round the city and reformed the army. This did not prevent its neighbours, including the Etruscans, from taking up arms. The Romans beat off assaults by the Etruscans and by members of the Latin League, but there ensued decades of warfare, until Rome first took hegemony of the League and then, after the League rebelled (6.824-5 note, **Decii**, **Torquatus**) converted it in 338 BCE into alliances between itself and individual members, cemented in many cases by citizenship or citizenship without voting rights. In 343 BCE, Rome broke a treaty with the Samnites, the Oscan-speaking inhabitants of the Apennines north-east of Campania, initiating three long-drawn-out wars. Only in 295 BCE did Rome win a decisive victory, at the Battle of Sentinum (6.824-5 note, **Decii**), against a daunting coalition of Samnites, Senones, Umbrians and Etruscans. The Samnites remained hostile, but the most troublesome sequel came when Tarentum, a Greek colony on the sole of Italy's foot, resentful of Rome's intrusion into its sphere of influence during and after the Third Samnite War, called in its ally, Pyrrhus of Epirus – a formidable general and willing adventurer. Again, Rome finally triumphed against the odds, at the Battle of Beneventum (in 275 BCE)[36] but only after a mighty tussle (6.841-6, **Fabricius**; 6.824-5 note, **Decii**). With this in mind, Aeneas' pledge of unity between Italy and Epirus (3.503) sounds forlorn; it eventually (in 167 BCE) became part of the Roman province of Macedonia.

Having by now gained dominion over most of Italy (except the north), Rome's attention turned seawards, more by accident than imperialism. At the time Carthage (1.13 note), as befitted a Phoenician city, was the dominant mercantile power in the Mediterranean; its empire comprised territory in North Africa, southern Spain and – uncomfortably close for Rome – Corsica, Sardinia and western Sicily. It was a city in eastern Sicily, Messana, that set Rome and Carthage by the ears:[37] in 264 BCE, its local rulers asked the Romans to flush out the Carthaginians who had come to their assistance but overstayed their welcome. Twenty-five years later, after its naval victory over the Carthaginians off Drepanum (northwest Sicily) in 241 BCE, Rome, now a sea power (6.841-6 note, **Serranus**), took over the whole island except for Syracuse. (Aeneas' stop-overs in Book III and establishment of Segesta in Book V are in part a homage to the importance of this first province.) The following year Rome seized Corsica and Sardinia, a provocation that rankled.[38] Nevertheless, the Carthaginians compensated for their losses not by retaliation but by extending their lands in Spain northwards. Meanwhile the Romans faced an invasion of Gauls in 225 BCE; this was roundly trounced but triggered a six-year campaign by which Rome gained control of north Italy (6.858 note). In 221 BCE, however, the town of Saguntum, on the west coast of Spain, invited the Romans to arbitrate in a dispute between rival factions, one of them pro-Carthaginian. The situation resembled that of Messana; Rome's interference gave an excuse for Hannibal to lay siege to the city, and so began the Second Punic War. Hannibal's invasion of Italy via the Alps preceded massacres at Lake Trasimene (217 BCE) and Cannae (216 BCE); Rome was prostrate, but survived through the strategy of its dictator, Fabius Maximus 'the delayer' (6.845): guerrilla attacks on the Carthaginian supply lines, made more effective by the refusal of many Italian cities to go over to Hannibal. The war was decided when, in 203 BCE, the Roman general P. Cornelius Scipio (later 'Africanus'; 6.843 f.) crossed to Africa, threatening Carthage; the Carthaginians recalled Hannibal, but Scipio defeated him the following year at the battle of Zama. The terms of settlement handed Spain and north Africa to Rome but left Carthage itself intact. This did not satisfy the veteran of the Punic War, M. Porcius Cato (6.841), Cato the Elder, who is alleged to have concluded any speech of his in the senate with the words, 'Carthage must be destroyed.'[39] Eventually the Roman general P. Cornelius Scipio Aemilianus (6.843) obliged by wiping out the city, in the Third Punic War (149–146 BCE) – but too late for Cato, who had died in 149 BCE.

Jupiter in the *Aeneid* mentions the Punic Wars cursorily (10.12 f.); much more powerful is the aetiology for them that Virgil creates in Dido's resounding curse (4.625 ff.). When Aeneas' shield looks forward to future conflict ('Rome's wars in the order fought', 8.629), it is Actium, not the Punic Wars, that provides the climactic repulse of alien attack: the appeal to his listeners' personal experience is paramount, and the battle's centrality implies that no such attack will occur again.

Rome's gravitational pull in the poem relegates its other campaigns of the second century, in Macedonia, Asia Minor and Spain, to the sidelines of the *Aeneid*; Jupiter refers to the conquest of Greece alone (1.283 ff.), this being the ultimate retribution of Troy on its conquerors. It is left to Vulcan, portraying Augustus' triple triumph after Actium on Aeneas' shield (8.724 ff.), to probe (and exaggerate) the range of Rome's influence to the north, south and east.

1.6 The late Republic (from 133 BCE onwards)

Thanks to its land confiscations in Italy after the Second Punic War and its conquest of Cisalpine Gaul, Rome found itself with large acreages at its disposal. These it allocated in small parcels to individuals. As the second century progressed, however, many smallholders were drawn into military service abroad or life in the capital; they sold their land to proprietors of much larger estates, run on slave labour. In 133 BCE, the noble Tiberius Gracchus[40] (6.842) was elected as tribune of the people on a platform of reversing this tendency (his motives are still debated); in doing so he antagonized the senate and was clubbed to death by a mob from its ranks. Undeterred, his younger brother Gaius (also 6.842) as tribune of the people ten years later took up Tiberius' reforms and extended them to include regulation of the corn supply and changing the composition of juries. This time the senate used political means to oppose him, but its supporters and the Gracchan faction before long resorted to force; Gaius too was killed. A rift had opened between senate and people that was only to widen in the first century, as the labels *optimas* and *popularis* became current; discord in the Roman Republic had deep roots.

C. Marius does not feature in the *Aeneid* but occupies a key place in the history of the late Republic.[41] A 'new man' (i.e. not from the old senatorial families), on the back of military commands in North Africa (108–4 BCE) and against the Germanic tribes invading north Italy (104–100 BCE) he turned the army from a force of self-funded conscripts to a professional body loyal to the general who paid and pensioned it; and as consul five years in a row (during his second tour of duty against the Germanic tribes) he showed how power could again be concentrated in a single person. The ingredients of a warlord were now at his, and at others' (most notably Julius Caesar's), disposal.

Before they could be combined again, however, the Italian allies of Rome rebelled (91 BCE); they had, under the terms of their alliance, provided troops for Rome's wars but did not receive equitable treatment in service, in the redistribution of land or in their access to political office.[42] The four years of grinding conflict that ensued,[43] the so-called Social (= 'of allies') Wars, brought to prominence L. Cornelius Sulla as a military rival to Marius.[44] Their aftermath also saw the Italians fully enfranchised: the conditions for Jupiter's settlement of Book XII were 'realized' at last. Indeed, one way of taking the *Aeneid* is as a promotion of this pan-Italian Romanness that in Virgil's own day was still raw (see note to the Catalogue, 7.641-817).[45]

Without interruption, Rome plunged itself into its first civil war (88–83 BCE), between the factions of Marius and Sulla, during which Rome was marched on and captured three times. Sulla emerged triumphant; the senate and popular assembly appointed him dictator, an office supposedly limited to six months, with unlimited duration – he held it from 82 to 79 BCE, when he stepped down and went into retirement; another precedent had been set.

What might have appeared a comparative domestic lull while international campaigning resumed during the 70s and 60s BCE was a period of fevered individual power-broking. Among the losers was Catiline (8.668), an impoverished noble who in 64 BCE stood for the consulship of 63 relying on the support of other nobles, similarly impoverished. When he failed, he hatched a desperate plot to seize control of the city; Cicero (one of the election winners) was informed and stamped it out.[46] In the senate's debate on punishing the conspirators, Caesar argued for mercy (life imprisonment) while M. Porcius Cato, great grandson of his namesake, advocated the death penalty (8.670).

By mid-century,[47] the great rivals were Caesar and Pompey. Pompey, a soldier whom Sulla had hailed as 'The Great' (in emulation of Alexander) when he was only twenty-five, espoused the title without any concession to modesty.[48] He served as the senate's commander, in Spain, in the Mediterranean (mopping up pirates) and in Asia Minor, between 77 and 63 BCE; yet, after he came back to Italy in 62 BCE and disbanded his army – to the senate's relief – found himself cold-shouldered by it. So to circumvent the senate he made common cause with Caesar, marrying his daughter Julia (a genuine love-match – she died in 54 BCE). Caesar, consul in 59 BCE, then spent ten years in the conquest of the rest of Gaul (only the far south was already incorporated in the Roman Empire).[49] Apprehensive of the power base he was building there, Caesar's enemies engineered his recall, wooing Pompey to their side; Caesar returned in 49 BCE, but at the head of an army of seasoned veterans. (A glimpse of Pompey and Caesar's uneasy amity, before Caesar's arrival across the Alps, is offered in 6.826-31.)

In the civil war that followed,[50] Caesar's legions defeated the senate's, under Pompey, at Pharsalus in 48 BCE. Once in Rome Caesar, like Sulla before him, secured his nomination as dictator, but for life - that is, without any intention of resigning. This evoked memories of the kings and precipitated his assassination, in 44 BCE, by a confederacy of conspirators that included M. Junius Brutus (6.817–23 note), a descendant of L. Junius Brutus, expeller of Tarquinius. Caesar's assassins did not meet with the popular acclaim they had anticipated, and the resulting power vacuum was filled first by M. Antonius (Mark Antony), Caesar's lieutenant, and then by the youth C. Octavius, known as Octavian, Caesar's great-nephew, named by him in his will as adopted son and heir: the future Augustus. They cemented an alliance known as the 'Second Triumvirate' in 43 BCE (with M. Aemilius Lepidus, somewhat in their shadow) and together defeated the tyrannicides Brutus and Cassius at Philippi in 42 BCE. Rather as Pompey and Julia's marriage had sealed a political collaboration, so Antony married Octavian's sister, Octavia, in 41 BCE. At the same time, the triumvirate partitioned military control – to Octavian the west (Spain and Gaul), to Lepidus the south (Africa) and to Antony the east (Greece and Asia). Octavian was now occupied with quelling opposition from Antony's wife Fulvia and brother Lucius, holed up in Perusia (Antony was otherwise occupied – see further), and in counteracting the naval stranglehold on Rome of Pompey's son, Sextus Pompeius.

Antony had first met Cleopatra when,[51] in 41 BCE, touring the eastern provinces to fill his war chest for a campaign against the Parthians,[52] he overwintered at her invitation in Alexandria. He did not see her or the twins she bore him again until four years later; by then his incursions into northern Persia had gone badly and he had been forced into an ignominious retreat. Cleopatra joined him at Antioch in 36 BCE, Octavia having been sent home the previous year. After a foray into Armenia, Antony was in Alexandria again in 34 BCE. There he celebrated a sham of a triumph for dethroning the Armenian king. According to Dio Cassius and Plutarch,[53] at it he and Cleopatra sat on golden thrones; Antony declared Caesarion (Ptolemy Caesar, Caesar's son by Cleopatra) the legitimate heir of Caesar (one in the eye for Octavian) and distributed his own eastern dominions, as well as lands over which he had no nominal control, between Caesarion and Cleopatra's now three children by him. At some point before 33 BCE, and the year before he divorced Octavia, he became Cleopatra's consort under Greek law. It seems less like a precursor to the story of Aeneas, Creusa and Dido than a nightmarish rehash of it.

The end of that year, 33 BCE, marked the legal term of the Second Triumvirate (five years renewed in January 37 BCE). As consul in 31 BCE, Octavian obtained from the senate a declaration of war against Cleopatra. The Battle of Actium (see 8.675–713 and note for its depiction on Aeneas' shield) was followed by the suicides of both Antony and Cleopatra; Octavian made Egypt a Roman province. He celebrated a triple triumph, for Dalmatia and Alexandria as well as Actium, in 29 BCE (8.714–28 and note). In 27 BCE, the senate decreed him the title 'Augustus'[54] to honour him for having, in his own words, 'transferred the Republic from my own control to the will of the senate and the Roman people'[55] (see also 6.808–12 note). He avoided the taint of his predecessors' mistakes, holding neither the dictatorship (Sulla, Caesar) nor, after 23 BCE, multiple consulships (Marius),[56] but founded his authority instead on his theoretical command of the whole army[57] and on 'tribunician power'[58] (Tacitus called[59] it 'the title of highest rank'); the latter forestalled popular or seditious agitation through actual tribunes. He also controlled the appointment of the most important officials. Decades of strife subsided – the return of Saturn's golden age, according to Anchises (6.894 f.); a 'cheerful acceptance of slavery', according to Tacitus.[60] The picture Anchises also gives, of a globe-trotting Augustus expanding the empire (6.794–805 – cf. Jupiter at 1.286 ff.) belies Augustus' not so much foreign policy as opportunism abroad;[61] and after Actium and the follow-up expedition from Egypt into Syria,[62] his military campaigning in person was restricted to northern Spain for three years up to 24 BCE, when he fell ill and withdrew to Tarragona.[63] Tacitus portrays[64] Augustus' advocates as claiming that he had 'fenced' the empire by the ocean or distant rivers – in other words, extended it to defensible borders. Augustus himself was proud of the peace he achieved in Rome's dominions, as symbolized by the closures of the Temple of Janus (1.291 – see 1.291–6 note) and the Ara Pacis ('altar of peace'). The condition of that peace was autocracy; the Republic had ended at the moment of its revival.

Decades of civil wars made it plain, even early on in Augustus' principate, that he could not leave the transfer of power to 'fate' and a possible descent into discord. Keeping the family powerful was a patrician principle; Augustus in trying to do so need not have been planning a dynasty. In any case, he could not, since he lacked a male heir. His hand was forced when, in 23 BCE, he lay at death's door; he passed his signet ring to Agrippa, the admiral who had secured victory for him at Actium (8.682). On recovering, however, he arranged a marriage between his nephew M. Claudius Marcellus (6.883; 6.854–92 note) and his daughter Julia; Agrippa withdrew on a tour of the eastern provinces, only for Marcellus to die the same year of the disease that had afflicted his uncle. Augustus married Julia to Agrippa on the latter's return to Rome, in 21 BCE, but that did not settle the matter: Agrippa died in 12 BCE and it was

Julia's third husband of 11 BCE, Tiberius Claudius Nero, who was designated Tiberius Caesar Augustus and, in 14 CE, succeeded Augustus as emperor.

1.7 Augustus in the *Aeneid*

Virgil's presentation of Augustus in the *Aeneid* is not so much historical as adulatory, in the mouths of Jupiter (1.286 ff.) and Anchises (6.791 ff.) or the metals of Vulcan (8.678 ff.). The panegyric in each case has its narrative motive: Jupiter is reassuring Venus, Anchises encouraging his son and Vulcan turning the eyes of the audience as well as of Aeneas' enemies to an unwritten future (8.714–28 note). (Since Virgil was penning the *Aeneid* when Augustus was still relatively young – he died when Augustus was forty-four– he was bound to hint at further achievements; as it turned out, Augustus was less than a third of the way into his reign.) In the action of the *Aeneid* as opposed to its prophecy, Virgil, like Jupiter and Anchises, plots a march through time, of Rome before its foundation; and like Vulcan, he records battles, those that made the foundation possible. His Aeneas, the lone leader forging Rome's destiny from Troy's hot iron, is in part a paradigm for Augustus (3.525–7 note, 8.617–23 note), lone refounder of the Republic out of civil war; viewed in that light Augustus becomes not the terminus of Jupiter's, Anchises' and Vulcan's visions but a new point of departure. But a paradigm only in part: Aeneas' dalliance with Dido (Book IV), savagery (Book X) and ultimate outburst of wrath against Turnus (Book XII) are not held up as examples, unless protreptic ones. And Augustus, in Marcellus (6.868 ff.), is pointedly not immune to tragic bereavement; one link between Aeneas and Augustus that the *Aeneid* wants to make are the uncertainties with which they have to deal, the imminent threat of loss.[65]

1.8 Literary sources for Roman history

The following are the main authors cited in the introduction and commentary.

1.8.1 Polybius

Polybius (*c.* 200–118 BCE), a Greek from Megalopolis in the central Peloponnese, served as a diplomat and politician in Arcadia before being deported to Rome. There he became an associate of Scipio Aemilianus and witnessed the latter's sack of Carthage in the Third Punic War; he also crossed the Alps in Hannibal's footsteps. His *Histories* covered period from the First to the Third Punic Wars; of the 40 books, the first five are complete and we have fragments from many of the others.

Polybius examined the causes behind Rome's rise to power by taking a broad and long-term view of events;[66] he was discerning and analytical towards his source material.[67] He commented in polemical vein, 'As a living creature is rendered wholly useless if deprived of its eyes, so if you take truth from history what is left is but an idle unprofitable tale.'[68]

1.8.2 Livy

Titus Livius (59 BCE–17 CE), from Padua, wrote a monumental annalistic history of Rome, *From the City's Foundation*, in 142 books down to 9 BCE. Of these, 35 books survive, while the remainder have come down in summary form (the *Periochae*, omitting Books 136–7; another Oxyrhynchus epitome exists for some books). He probably started work on the first books before Virgil began the *Aeneid*; Virgil may well have seen or heard them. Augustus took an interest in the project.[69]

Livy's style is narrative and his method not unduly critical; his purpose is overtly moral. He does not set out to glorify the times under which he is writing, however; indeed, he reflects the disillusionment after protracted conflict:

> Here are the questions to which I would have every reader give his close attention—what life and morals were like; through what men and by what policies, in peace and in war, empire was established and enlarged; then let him note how, with the gradual relaxation of discipline, morals first gave way, as it were, then sank lower and lower, and finally began the downward plunge which has brought us to the present time, when we can endure neither our vices nor their cure.[70]

1.8.3 Diodorus Siculus

From Agira in Sicily, Diodorus wrote a universal history in 40 books (15 survive, with many other bits and pieces) between 60 and 30 BCE, his 'Library of History'. It ranges in time from mythical prehistory to 60 BCE (though the end has been lost), and in space from Egypt and North Africa to Arabia and India. As the name suggests, it houses a magpie assemblage of material from a multitude of Greek sources.

1.8.4 Dionysius of Halicarnassus

A rhetorician as well as a historian, Dionysius was active in Rome from 30 BCE. His *magnum opus* was a 'Roman History' from foundation to the First Punic War; it began circulating in 7 BCE. The first 10 of its 20 books survive and form a useful complement to Livy, drawing on Greek historical traditions. It is particularly useful because it is the only prose account that has come down to us of Aeneas' travels and Italian wars and,[71] being roughly contemporary with Virgil, contains material that might have been familiar to him.

1.8.5 Strabo

A Greek geographer and historian from Asia Minor (*c*. 64 BCE–*c*. 24 CE), Strabo travelled widely and, in his *Geography* (mapless), tours the empire with forays further afield (Persia, India), setting down history, ethnography and topography (plus some geology). Like Dionysius, he is a useful repository of information current in Virgil's lifetime.[72]

1.8.6 Res Gestae

In his will (of 14 CE), Augustus ordained[73] that an inscription cataloguing his achievements, the text of which he provided, be published on bronze tablets standing outside his mausoleum. Copies of this long text (35 paragraphs) were erected at temples to 'Rome and Augustus' around the empire; the most complete one, in both Latin and Greek, was found at Ankyra, in

Turkey. Its omissions have been made good from other copies, also in Turkey (Apollonia and Antioch). Although a piece of self-aggrandisement, Augustus' list challenged refutation by its sheer accessibility. It is also a statement of the values for which Augustus, at the end of his reign, wished posterity to remember him.

1.8.7 Velleius Paterculus

A soldier of many campaigns who served under Tiberius, also a quaestor and praetor, Velleius (*c.* 19 BCE–30 CE) turned to writing his *Roman Histories* late in his career. The first of its 2 books has largely been lost; what remains is a very cursory account of Greek and Carthaginian history up to 146 BCE; the second book slows in pace to cover from 146 BCE up to his own time and is the only extant uninterrupted account of that period. It smacks of the enthusiastic amateur.

1.8.8 Pliny the Elder

The naval commander and polymath C. Plinius Secundus (23/4–79 CE – he died at the eruption of Vesuvius) wrote on history and, in his last work, the *Natural History* in 37 books, a virtual encyclopaedia, on a bewildering range of other topics. These incorporate historical information, but more importantly compile a cabinet of curiosities that can be consulted on almost any aspect of Roman culture in his time.

1.8.9 Tacitus

In his two major works Cornelius Tacitus (*c.* 56–*c.* 117 CE) recounted first, in the *Histories*, the period from the year of four emperors (69 CE) to the death of Domitian (96 CE) and then, turning back on himself in the *Annals*, the period from the death of Augustus (14 CE) to the death of Nero (69 CE). As a successful lawyer and politician (he was suffect (= replacement) consul in 97 CE and later became governor of Asia, he brings a forensic and dramatic intensity to what he records; his Latin is concentrated and corrosive. In a densely written retrospect at the start of the *Annals* he provides a 'for' and 'against' on Augustus; elsewhere he sheds occasional light on the more distant past.

1.8.10 Suetonius

C. Suetonius Tranquillus (*c.* 69–121 CE) held a series of secretarial posts at the imperial court (as a tutor then in charge of libraries and correspondence) until dismissed by Hadrian in 121/2 CE. When he set about writing the lives of the twelve Caesars, from the Deified Julius to Domitian, he had access to court documents such as the correspondence of Augustus. This seems to have ceased with his departure. In each *Life* he interrupts chronological order to explore particular behaviour or characteristics, which, when compounded with a taste for salacious gossip, reduces his historical worth but not his ability to entertain.

1.8.11 Appian

A lawyer and administrator from Alexandria, Appian (1st–2nd century CE) wrote in the mid-second century a Roman History in 24 books, organized geographically. Much of the first

5 books (early Italy, Gaul, Sicily and the islands) and the last quarter (Egypt, Dacia and Arabia) have perished; Books 12–17, which are intact, provide the most comprehensive account of the civil wars available, from the Gracchi down to 36 BCE. Appian had access to much material no longer available, including the memoirs of Augustus.

1.8.12 Plutarch

A native of Chaeronea in Boeotia, L. Mestrius Plutarchus (<50–120 CE), was a writer on philosophy and a biographer; he travelled regularly to Athens, Egypt and Rome, but for the last thirty years of his life was a priest at Delphi, some 35 miles from Chaeronea. His *Parallel Lives* pair famous Greeks and Romans (Alexander the Great and Julius Caesar, for instance) over a vast chronology, and vividly retell events and anecdotes with variable reliability but in chronological order.

1.8.13 Dio Cassius

A suffect consul under Septimius Severus (possibly 205 CE) and a full consul under Alexander Severus (in 229 BCE) as well as a provincial governor, L. Cassius Dio compiled and wrote, over twenty-two years, an annalistic history of Rome from its origins to the reign of Elagabalus (229 CE). Of its 80 books, 36–54 (68–10 BCE) are fully preserved, 55–60 (9 BCE–46 CE) in abbreviation and 17 and 79–80 in part. He seems to have followed Livy and his sources as well as referring to other annalist traditions but lacks an understanding of Republican institutions.

CHAPTER 2
VIRGIL'S LIFE AND WORKS

The proclaimed 'death of the author'[1] cannot stamp out an abiding interest in the biographies of writers. In the case of the *Aeneid*, any clues Virgil's life story might promise to understanding the poem, however debatable, are made more tenuous by lack of evidence. Even so, the regular intrusion of the narrator's own voice in the poem, starting with the first line, gives Virgil peculiar status within it.

2.1 Life

'Publius Vergilius Maro[2] was born on the ides of October in the consulships of Cn. Pompeius Magnus and M. Licinius Crassus' (15 October 70 BCE.) So begins the second paragraph of Aelius Donatus'[3] life of the poet, written in the fourth century and the earliest extant biography, though substantially based on the lost earlier one by Suetonius.[4] It is one of the few universally accepted statements that it contains – despite the absence of census records and an open field for speculation, there has never been another date to jostle with it. It places Virgil's birth in the midst of the political turmoil as the Republic collapsed. The rest of Donatus' life is more or less open to question,[5] as fabrication (1) of the kind conventional in the genre, or (2) derived from Virgil's own works, or (3) to defend the poet against criticism. Thus, (1) the day before she delivered her son in a ditch, Virgil's mother dreamed of bringing forth a laurel branch that instantly took root and bore a variety of fruit;[6] (2) his father was a beekeeper (from *Georgics* Book 4)[7] and Virgil's property was exempted from the confiscation and distribution among army veterans after the Battle of Philippi[8] (from Eclogues 1 and 9); lastly; (3) the *Aeneid* was composed to a prose outline but piecemeal and in no particular order, the poet moving on and leaving sections incomplete, propped up with lightweight verses until the solid columns arrived[9] (unfinished sections, inconsistencies and incomplete lines are certainly to be found[10]). Donatus (or Suetonius) is not averse to gossip, however cumulatively implausible: Virgil was known as Parthenias ('virginal'), loved boys, and his friend and fellow-poet L. Varius Rufus, who might be expected to know his proclivities, offered him his wife (or mistress – Virgil declined).[11] Donatus' life is fascinating for what it reveals of succeeding generations imagining Virgil; in the thrall of the poem they filled out the life of the poet, but not because the poem itself requires it.

What can tentatively be salvaged from Donatus' life is substantially what can be confirmed from other sources contemporary with Virgil or from names dropped within the texts themselves. That Virgil was from Mantua explains the prominence he gives it in both the *Aeneid* and the *Georgics*.[12] He progressed to Rome (via Cremona and Milan, the life claims) and there studied, as well as the inevitable oratory, possibly under the Epicurean philosopher Siro (not in the Life).[13] He moved in the circle of poets that included Asinius Pollio (Eclogues 3, 4 and 8), and Cornelius Gallus (Eclogues 6 and 10)[14] – also of Horace,[15] who calls Virgil 'half of my being';[16] Virgil and L. Varius Rufus had introduced him to Maecenas, major patron of poets and Octavian's friend and political adviser;[17] Virgil and Varius joined Horace and Maecenas on a trip to Brundisium (possibly in 37 BCE):[18]

> The next day's sunrise brings great joy: since Plotius,
> Varius and Virgil, meet us at Sinuessa: no more
> Shining spirits did earth ever bear, and no one
> Could be more dearly attached to them than I.
> O what embraces there were there, and what delight! …
> Then to Capua, where the mules shed their loads early.
> Maecenas is off for sport, Virgil and I for sleep:
> Those ball-games are bad for sore eyes and stomachs.

(Trans. Kline)

Maecenas, the formal addressee of each book of the *Georgics*, a work that he commissioned,[19] is said to have composed a 'Symposium' in which Virgil and Horace were fellow drinkers.[20] That Virgil benefited from the subsidy of both Augustus and Maecenas[21] is corroborated by Horace, who reminds[22] Augustus of his gifts to his favourites, Virgil and Varius. The poet Propertius also knew Virgil, and of the *Aeneid*'s gestation – Donatus quotes:[23]

> Give way, Roman writers; give way, Greeks:
> Something greater than the *Iliad* is being born.

Propertius in the preceding lines (not quoted) speaks of the poet commemorating Actium, which hints temptingly at a date around 31 BCE for the first stirrings of the *Aeneid*.

In establishing a chronology, Donatus goes through Virgil's opus, accepting as authentic early works what is now called the *Virgilian Appendix* (2.2) and treated substantially as later imitations; so we have to use internal indications to establish a start date for Virgil's first major work, the *Eclogues*, of 42–1 BCE;[24] Donatus allocates three years for their composition, then seven for the *Georgics* and eleven for the *Aeneid*.[25] If we allow Virgil no respite, this does not quite take us to his death in 19 BCE, but is a plausible distribution. (Demarcations are in any case less than clear-cut – what counts as 'starting'? Is the first distribution of the text 'ending'?)

On Virgil's method of composition the anecdotes found in Donatus are attractive not least because, true or not, they fit what we find. Speaking of the *Georgics*, Donatus says that Virgil would dictate many lines with great fluency[26] in the morning then whittle them down to a very small number by evening, like a bear licking its offspring into shape;[27] Virgil's verse at its finest in the *Aeneid* also has a watchmaker's precision and, over eleven years, he could have written a comfortable average of three lines per day. On the *Aeneid*, continues Donatus, he liked to keep up momentum,[28] and, as has already been mentioned, tackle different parts of his outline as the fancy took him.[29] This might account for some of his self-echoes (see *Introduction* – 8.1 Intratextuality: Self-allusion). It would also account for a poem that is complete in its extent but uneven in its polish;[30] and although Donatus' assertion, that Virgil had decided to retire to Greece and Asia Minor and spend three years on revision, is suspect (why abandon Rome? why did he foresee three years?), he must have been revising the poem when he died – on 21 September 19 BCE, at Brundisium, says Donatus,[31] also accepted as fact. His will, according to

Donatus, included Augustus and Maecenas (it was customary to remember benefactors and patrons) as well as his literary executors Plotius Tucca and L. Varius Rufus – Donatus cites[32] verses by one Sulpicius of Carthage (possibly Sulpicius Apollinaris, second century CE), telling how they were charged with destroying the poem (Donatus adds,[33] should anything befall Virgil); but incompatibly he notes[34] that they were only forbidden to publish what he had not revised (had Virgil revised nothing? how would they know what he had finished?) – and no mention of burning the rest. Surer ground is what Donatus also records, that Varius (without Tucca) published the whole with minimal alteration and under Augustus' instruction[35] – which means, at the very least, without any obstruction from Augustus. Virgil was buried near Naples, having quite possibly lived there; Donatus quotes his epitaph:[36]

> Mantua gave birth to me, the Calabrians snatched me away, now holds me fast
> Parthenope [=Naples];[37] I sang of pastures, fields, and princes.

On Virgil's literary relationship with the princeps, Donatus' *Life* maintains that their friendship began after the release of the *Eclogues*;[38] that Virgil recited the entire *Georgics* to Octavian, who is addressed in Book 1 and admired in Book 3,[39] over four days[40] (not a taxing programme – it could be done in as many hours); that the by-now Augustus 'jokingly entreated him in his letters, with threats as well as prayers, "that you send me" (to employ his own words) "your first sketch of the *Aeneid*, or any section you please, it does not matter which"';[41] and that Virgil, much later, read Books II, IV and VI to Augustus and his sister Octavia (see 6.854–92 note).[42] Macrobius seems to have preserved[43] Virgil's reply to that early encouragement:

> I am receiving letters from you regularly … If I had anything worthy of your ears, I would gladly send it to you; but the undertaking is so massive that I wonder if I have not tackled it almost out of a failure of good sense, especially because, as you know, I am putting in extra and much more demanding efforts to realise it.

Since the letters of the famous were circulated,[44] this sequence of events has a plausible ring. Notably it does not include a commission from Augustus for the *Aeneid* (it is no more than surmise that there was one), and it shows Augustus cajoling, not compelling, Virgil – for although Donatus' 'threats as well as prayers' smacks of iron hand as well as velvet glove,[45] the poet slides courteously from its grip. Augustus' interest did not pass unnoticed – Ovid, writing with a certain envy to Augustus from his exile in Tomis, speaks of 'that happy author of your *Aeneid*';[46] but everyone with a taste for poetry was interested (like Propertius, previously mentioned) and Ovid need not imply that the whole project was Augustus' from start to finish.

2.2 *Virgilian Appendix*[47]

This works grouped under this title purport to be Virgilian juvenilia. The Appendix has contracted from its contents as listed in the Middle Ages, now confining itself to poems mentioned by Donatus:[48]

- *Culex* ('The Gnat') – a miniature epic (*epyllion*[49]) and pastoral parody on a gnat that, by biting a sleeping shepherd, wakes him up and though swatted saves him from being

> bitten by a snake; the gnat appears to him in a dream, tells him of its experiences in the underworld and reproves him for ingratitude; the shepherd builds the gnat a cenotaph, makes offerings and affixes an inscription.

- *Ciris* ('The Sea-Bird') – another *epyllion*, telling the story of Nisus of Megara and his daughter Scylla.[50]

- *Dirae* ('Curses') – a poem not unlike an Eclogue and probably dating from soon after that collection, in which a dispossessed farmer curses his farm.

- *Catalepton* ('Trifles') – a collection of fifteen epigrams of assorted lengths and metres, sometimes obscure.[51]

- *Aetna* ('Etna') – a long (636 lines) Lucretian attempt to give a physical account of Etna's behaviour.

On stylistic grounds modern scholars consider the great majority of these 'Virgilian' poems spurious – with the possible exception of *Catalepton* 5 and 8, on Siro the Epicurean. Other than the Dirae, they seem to date from the first century CE.

2.3 *Eclogues* (or *Bucolics*[52])

This series of ten short poems, averaging 83 lines in length (the longest is 111 lines) was probably written between 41 and 38 BCE. They are in the same hexameter metre as the *Aeneid*, and of a type we would consider quintessentially pastoral,[53] with a cast of lovelorn musical shepherds (really poets in disguise),[54] nymphs and satyrs, flocks and flowers, set in alternating dialogues (the first at Eclogue 1) and third-person narratives (Eclogue 8, an account of a singing contest like Eclogues 3 and 7, is a hybrid). The emotions, though stylized, range from ecstatic prophecy (Eclogue 4, a new Golden Age ushered in by a child – later taken by Christian authors to foretell the coming of Christ[55]) to the pangs of love (Eclogues 2, 8 and 10) and the pain of loss (a friend, Eclogue 5; land, Eclogues 1 and 9), and take in a chaffing exchange between two shepherds sitting on the grass (Eclogue 3), casting a spell (Eclogue 8) and the song of the satyr Silenus (Eclogue 6). Their point of departure is the Alexandrian Theocritus (see *Introduction* – 8.4.4 Alexandrian poetry and epic: Callimachus, Theocritus, Apollonius of Rhodes, Lycophron) but, unlike the latter's Idylls, the *Eclogues* cohere as a group,[56] often being analysed in nested pairs:

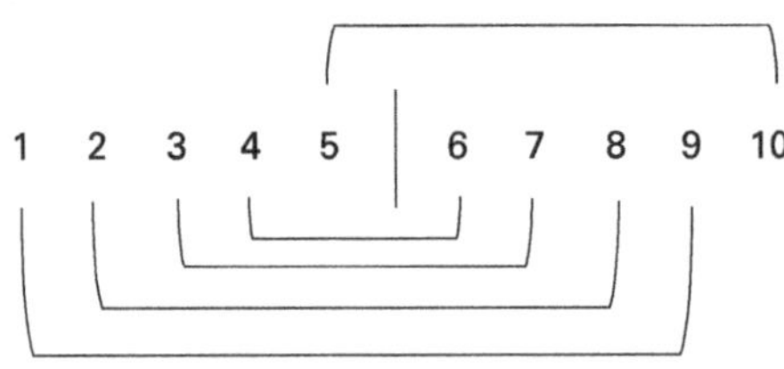

They are set in an Arcadian[57] Italy that, even taking land-grabbing soldiers into account, is a figment of Virgil's imagination, where shepherds live at ease under a summer sun (winter and the hardships of husbandry intrude only rarely, as if out of a misty background). The poems are self-reflexive, vignettes of bards in the process of composition and proud of their artistry – 'tender and graceful' are Horace's adjectives.[58] At their centre, Eclogue 6 begins (in a conscious echo of Callimachus – see *Introduction* – 8.4.4 Alexandrian poetry and epic: Callimachus, Theocritus, Apollonius of Rhodes, Lycophron):

> My first Muse was fit to play Sicilian[59] measures,
> and never blushed at living in the woods.
> When I sang of kings and battles the Cynthian[60] grasped
> my ear and warned me: 'Tityrus, a shepherd
> should graze fat sheep, but sing a slender song.'
> Now (since there are more than enough who desire to sing
> your praises, Varus,[61] and write about grim war)
> I'll study the rustic Muse on a graceful flute.
> I don't sing unasked.

(Trans. Kline)

Tityrus we meet at the opening of Eclogue 1, piping under a spreading beech tree; there Servius, hedging his bets, remarks, 'We should assume that Tityrus stands for Virgil – not that this is everywhere the case, but when it makes sense.' If we accept Servius' invitation,[62] we might detect behind the poet's conventional refusal to take on war epic (so-called *recusatio*,[63] again clearly modelled on Callimachus[64]) a certain willingness to be encouraged. And the tenth and final Eclogue, in which the real-world Gallus dismisses poetry as a source of solace in love,[65] concludes with the owner of the first-person voice (not identified) signing off as he sits and weaves a basket out of mallow:

> Let's rise, the shade's often harmful to singers,
> the juniper's shade is harmful, and shade hurts the harvest.
> Hesperus is here, home you sated goats: go home.

(Trans. Kline)

Apollo's command, to feed the herd fat, has been fulfilled.

2.4 *Georgics*

If in the *Eclogues* Virgil had turned the countryside into an escape from war and the songs of war, in the *Georgics* he plunged his hands into the soil and ran it through his fingers. Its four books, composed between roughly 38 and 31 BCE,[66] are in the guise of instructions for farmers, such as Hesiod had addressed to Perses in his *Works and Days* (the influence is strongest in Book 1). But as a manual it is whimsical[67] – it devotes many paragraphs to the vine but remarks only in passing on the olive (in Book 2); it ignores the pig completely and, almost completely, the dog (in Book 3); Book 4 expatiates on bees at length and then segues into the story of Aristaeus, never to return – Varro, who in his *On Farming*[68] provided Virgil with much of his technical content, in that work's last book wrote not just on bees but also on poultry, fish and dormice, and told no tales. Nor is any task ever explained so that you could perform it. What, then, is this avowedly didactic poem teaching?

A brief synopsis brings out both how difficult this question is to answer and in what ways the poem anticipates the *Aeneid*, both its themes and its similes. (Set-piece digressions are indicated by 'D...')

- **Book 1**

  After invoking the gods and Augustus as soon to be among them (and lord of countryside as well as cities), Virgil looks at the duty of the farmer to learn about his terrain and its climate, then at the tasks of working it: (**D1**) Jupiter has brought the age of Saturn to an end to make man's life hard; man uses his ingenuity and industry to render the earth productive again:

  > ... toil conquered all,
  > Remorseless toil, and poverty's shrewd push
  > In times of hardship.[69]

  > (ll. 145–6, trans. Greenough)

  This toil against pests and hostile conditions, likened to a war, must be unremitting, or else crops will fail and the farmer starve: the rower, if he stops rowing, will be swept away by the current. (So much for the leisured world of the *Eclogues*.)

  The calendar of the agricultural year is followed by a description of the best times for various activities. The farmer must above all show reverence to the gods and observe the signs in the sky and nature. If he does, he need never be caught unawares by adverse weather (there is a fearsome description of a storm). The sun in particular can warn of imminent violence: at Caesar's death it hid its face in a rusty fog. (**D2**) The book concludes with the other portents that accompanied the civil wars and with a lament for Rome's condition – 'Long enough now have we paid in our blood for the promise Laomedon[70] broke at Troy' (ll. 501 f., trans. Day Lewis). The city is running out of control, like a chariot whose driver tugs helplessly at the reins.

  The farmer, in his microcosm with its own struggles, is vulnerable also to the struggles of the wider world. And yet, just before bemoaning the sickles beaten into swords (7.601–40 note), Virgil pictures the aftermath:

  > Surely the time will come when a farmer on those frontiers [near Philippi]
  > Forcing through the earth his curved plough
  > Shall find old spears eaten away with flaky rust ...
  > And marvel at the heroic bones he has disinterred.

  > (ll. 493 ff., trans. Day Lewis)

  The farmer, like the epic poet, survives the blood-stained past and from it excavates the memories of heroes – or at least of victims fallen in a traumatic civil war. The ploughshare outlasts the spearhead.

- **Book 2**

  Virgil now invokes Bacchus, god of wine, inviting him to take off his buskins and paddle in grape must. Before turning to the vine, however, Virgil enumerates species of tree and where they grow best. This leads to a hymn of praise to Italy (**D3**), its fertility, resources, towns and peoples: 'Hail, great mother of harvests! O land of Saturn, hail! Mother of men!' (ll. 173 f., trans. Day Lewis). After considering different types of soil, Virgil comes to planting vines (with a meditation on spring, **D4**) and tending them, harvesting and dressing them. The amount of labour is daunting: 'Admire a large estate if you like, but farm a small one' (ll. 412 f., trans. Day Lewis). Moreover, after a passage on other trees of use to the farmer, Virgil rounds on Bacchus – he has done much deserving blame, such as infecting the Centaurs with *furor* and then killing them. The book, however, ends with a euphoric catalogue of the blessings of the farmer's simple life[71] (**D5**):

> Oh, too lucky for words, if only he knew his luck,
> Is the countryman who far from the clash of armaments
> Lives, and rewarding earth is lavish of all he needs!

> (ll. 458 ff., trans. Day Lewis)

He and his fellows were the last to be deserted by Justice before the age of bronze (8.306–36 note); they are spared the city-dweller's cares and pretensions; they are far from the paraphernalia of government; they are not tempted by desire for loot to forsake their homes and go soldiering. Instead they enjoy nature's bounty as in the age of Saturn, at last keeping holiday in a meadow with wine, a barbecue, wrestling and target shooting. (The poetry contests of the *Eclogues* are not reconvened.)

- **Book 3**

The briefest of preambles promises Apollo the shepherd[72] and Pales, the Roman god of livestock, their due. But then Virgil launches into a statement of more exalted ambition (**D6**), to erect a temple in Mantua to Octavian, on whose doors would be depicted Rome's victories over the Indians, Egyptians, Asians, Armenians and Parthians; whose statues would represent the Trojan descent from Jupiter; and on which somehow represented would be the tortured of Tartarus (Envy, i.e. envious men; Ixion – 6.601 note; Sisyphus – 6.616–20 note).[73] For now, he will stick to rustic matters, Maecenas' commission:

> Yet soon will I stir myself
> To tell of Caesar's furious[74] battles, to give him fame
> For as many years as divide his day from the birth of Tithonus[75].

> (ll. 46 ff., trans. Day Lewis)

Then fine descriptions of cow and horse upstage the farmer – as does an evocation of a chariot race (**D7**). Aspects of breeding, care and training lead into a discourse on sexual desire (**D8**), which drives creatures in its thrall to aggression and folly, both bringing destruction in their wake:

> All manner of life on earth – men, fauna of land and sea,
> Cattle and coloured birds –
> Run to this fiery madness [*furiae*]: love is alike for all.

> (ll. 242 ff., trans. Day Lewis)

Virgil enriches the ensuing discussion of pasturage with cameos of Libyan (far south) and Scythian (far north) herdsmen. Then he passes on to the threats to the flock (thieves, snakes) and diseases; this in turn ushers in a set-piece finale, an account of a plague in Latium (**D9**), alternately repellent and poignant; it seems to afflict all animals other than man – until the very last lines.

- **Book 4**

At its outset this book proposes bees as its only subject, but makes of them an ethnography in themselves: 'customs, pursuits, peoples and battles' (line 5). Virgil begins by locating and constructing the hive, then becomes fascinated by, and anthropomorphizes, apian behaviour – swarms and war ('epic struggles . . . quashed by a handful of dust', ll. 86 f.), and the role of the 'king' (i.e. queen). He diverges onto beautiful gardens, and one in particular, belonging to an old man at Tarentum (**D10**), before looking at two of the most remarkable bee characteristics: their communal spirit ('children in common, a city united beneath one roof . . . established laws . . . a native country . . . hearth and home', ll. 153 ff.); and their spiritual essence ('they do not breed by sexual union . . . but collect their young in their mouths from leaves and sweet herbs', ll. 198 ff.; some maintain they have a share in divine intelligence and do not die but are reabsorbed by it – ll. 219 ff.). This elevated theme, interrupted for a moment by practical reflections on collecting honey and protecting the insects against illness, returns with instructions on how to replace a lost swarm through apparently spontaneous generation out of a rotted calf (*bougonia*).

Virgil seeks the divine source of this knowledge (rather as he seeks the causes of Juno's wrath at the start of the *Aeneid*); this is the cue for the tale within a tale (**D11**) that concludes the whole poem: the narrative of Aristaeus' visits,[76] first to his mother Cyrene and then to Proteus,[77] embeds the *epyllion* of Orpheus[78] and Eurydice. Proteus reveals to Aristaeus that he had lost his swarm because of Orpheus' vengeful ire: Aristaeus had been pursuing Orpheus' beloved Eurydice when she, fleeing him, trod on a snake and died. Orpheus, grief-struck, descended to the underworld to retrieve her but, on the journey up again, could not prevent himself from turning round to look at her – which Proserpina had stipulated he should not do. As Eurydice is reclaimed by the darkness, she laments, 'What great madness (*furor*) has destroyed us?' (ll. 494 f. – see 2.705–44 for the parallels with Aeneas' loss of Creusa). Orpheus' inconsolable mourning by the river Strymon (in Thrace) provoked the Bacchants there into dismembering him. Having heard Proteus' story, Cyrene instructs Aristaeus to sacrifice to the nymph companions of Eurydice; this sacrifice becomes the *bougonia*.

The coda to the book constitutes the poem's *envoi*:[79]

> Thus of agriculture and the care of flocks I sang
> And forestry, while great Caesar fired his lightnings and conquered
> By deep Euphrates,[80] and gave justice to docile peoples,
> Winning his way to the Immortals.
> This was the time when I, Virgil, nurtured in sweetest
> Parthenope, did follow unknown to fame the pursuits

Of peace, who dallied with pastoral verse, and by youth emboldened,
Tityrus, sang of you in the shade of a spreading beech.'

(ll. 559–66, trans. Day Lewis)

Virgil recalls the first line of the first Eclogue to contrast himself with Octavian; he implies that his 'dalliance' with the countryside, in both *Eclogues* and *Georgics*, is over; what comes next he does not here disclose but his juxtaposition with Octavian is suggestive.

The *Georgics*, although in hexameters, seems barely to qualify as 'epic' – it contains no named hero and, until its last book, no narrative. Its staple is not great deeds but everyday farming existence, whether harsh or contented, given worth by rapt description and, as at the end of the poem, by its ramifications into the divine. It does, nevertheless, pave the way to the *Aeneid* – even if Virgil, at the start of Book 3 and the end of Book 4, appears himself to have had only vague ideas of what was coming next (the *Aeneid* is far, far more than battles, family genealogy and the underworld):

- From the exiguous summary above, it can be seen that the books alternate between 'dark' and 'light', in their emphasis on the woes or joys of farming. This is particularly brought out by the digressions (dark: **D1, D2, D8, D9**; light: **D3, D4, D5, D10, D11**). The dark books are not unrelieved (**D6, D7**), but the contradictory perspectives are left unreconciled, for the audience to make of them what it will. Thus Otis takes the *bougonia*, with some qualifications, as symbolic of the redemptive power of celestial order, counteracting the effects of the plague;[81] Ross treats it as fantastical embroidery on a world where conflict is the ultimate reality;[82] more recent criticism accepts the tension between opposites.[83] The similar challenge, to net off the darkness and light in the poem or to maintain them in some form of equilibrium, presents itself in the *Aeneid* (*Introduction* – 9.5 The twentieth and twenty-first centuries: Re-evaluation).

- Some of the virtues of the farmer in the *Georgics* – above all vigour, robustness and persistence in the face of hardship – prefigure those of the native Italians, above all as schematized by Numanus Remulus (9.603 ff.). (Other virtues in the *Georgics*, such as understanding the land and ingenuity in tackling the problems it throws up, have no place in the martial epic.)

- In the bees we are presented with a simulacrum of ordered human society that thrives on unity of purpose (see especially 4.153 ff.). Even if a monarchy and prone to wars, this is what Dido has founded and Aeneas intends to found (*Aeneid* 1.421 ff., where the Carthaginians toil like bees to build their city and Aeneas looks on in awe). The farmer is a founder of hives (4.8 ff.) but is relieved to remain aloof from urban stress and strain himself (**D5**); so bee society remains both exemplary and inhuman. Its wars, unlike human wars, are quickly halted – Jupiter in the *Aeneid* scatters no pacifying dust.

- The *furor* of love is held up as destructive of individuals (humans as well as animals – 3.258 ff.); its fatal eruption forms the climax of the Orpheus story and becomes an ostinato in the *Aeneid*.

- Virgil's exploitation of his literary predecessors is rich and varied – he may use them for technical background (the prose authors Cato,[84] Varro; in Greek Aristotle,

Theophrastus[85]); for ideas and their exposition (Hesiod, Lucretius,[86] various Alexandrian scholar-poets[87]); for turns of phrase (Lucretius; Catullus and the other innovators of his circle, the so-called 'neoterics' – *Introduction* – 8.4.7 Latin lyric and love poetry before Virgil); or, at the end of Book 4, for storytelling (Homer, Catullus). As in the Aeneid, Virgil alludes to other poets to add nuance to his own context – it is no homage of imitation for its own sake (see *Introduction* – 8.2 Intertextuality, narrow sense: External allusion).

- The Aristaeus episode in Book 4 looks both back to Catullus[88] (the tale within a tale) and Alexandrian narrative, as in Apollonius of Rhodes (the detached style of the consultation of Proteus); and forward to the subjective narrative style of the *Aeneid* (the tragedy of Orpheus and Eurydice; see *Introduction* – 7.3.2 Focalization).

To return to the question, 'What do the *Georgics* teach?': since they portray man in conflict with nature (Book 1) and in collaboration with her (Book 2), harnessing her (Book 4) but ultimately part of her and therefore subject to her (Book 3), there is no single standpoint from which either she or the farmer can be regarded; but each standpoint is valid at one time or another. Seeking definite lessons must be confined to (inadequate) tips on when to plant and which animals to mate; for the rest, it must suffice that nature will ensure the survival of the farmer over the warrior, the Old Man of Tarentum, 'in his soul as wealthy as a king' (4.132, **D10**).

2.5 A planned career?

In the thirteenth century, the links Virgil overtly made between the three major poems were schematized into equivalences at various levels (the *rota Virgilii*, or 'wheel of Virgil'[89]), which implied a purposeful progression from the humble style (*Eclogues*) to the middle and serious styles (*Georgics* and *Aeneid*). This has provided a model in career planning for other poets (e.g. Milton and Spenser[90]).

This view has largely been abandoned for one of natural evolution, in which Virgil remained faithful to various themes, such as exile, the return of the Golden Age, the bane of love, pastoral beauty and apotheosis, however different the contexts. As one critic writes,[91] 'we may be invited by <Virgil's> epitaph to read the three canonical works as one poetic space, in terms of an aesthetic and thematic coherence that unites them'. But Virgil did not prophesy for himself as he did for Aeneas.

CHAPTER 3
MAIN CHARACTERS

This section confines itself to humanity; for the characterization of the gods, see *Introduction – 4.5 Gods in particular*.

3.1 Characterization in the *Aeneid*

Virgil's characterization in the *Aeneid* is prone to be measured against Homer's and found wanting.[1] As Lyne puts it,[2] 'It is, I think, vain to pretend that Vergil characterizes with the sure vividness that Homer manages.' He goes on to say:

> This is the necessary introduction to the following statement: Vergil can characterize admirably: not like Homer, but admirably, exploiting action and word. It is an important point to establish. We shall then be properly placed to assess puzzles that the figure of Aeneas, who can seem curiously uncharacterized,[3] presents.

Heinze is harsher, deeming Aeneas no exception to a general rule:[4]

> What is true of Aeneas is just as true of the other characters in the work. Not a single person is depicted with a unique set of characteristics as a man who once walked on this earth, once and once only; nor is any of them drawn from real life. On the contrary, Virgil depicts character by starting from an ideal, and one person is distinguished from another by the degree to which he has progressed towards this ideal; he is characterized not by the qualities which he possesses, but by those which he lacks.

Lyne and Otis explain otherwise – for Lyne, 'a text so densely reflective cannot present characters with the requisite objectivity – leaving them sufficiently alone – for them to stand on their own feet.'[5] Otis, on the speeches of Dido and Aeneas, writes similarly:[6]

> The line between them and the empathetic narrative is often very thin indeed; both speeches and narrative are set within the same editorial frame. This does not mean that Dido is not a real character or individual, or that we cannot sympathize with her. But the fact is that we only see her through Virgilian spectacles.

These explanations seem partial truths: from what 'ideal' might Heinze say that Juno or Camilla starts? It may sometimes be hard to separate the emotion Virgil portrays in his characters from his own, as Otis would have it (see *Introduction – 7.3.2 Focalization*), but this is not a universal law. Does the grip Lyne and Otis see Virgil keeping on the audience's view of his characters never relax? There are counterexamples: Dido's sister Anna seems to think and act on her own terms; one of the reasons why Evander's narrative of Hercules and Cacus is unsettling is its cartoon-like violence, set against the violence of Virgil's battles, which however codified is viscerally felt.

Ancient literary criticism, although it does not go far in analysing characterization, does provide a useful corrective to modern assumptions on what to expect. For Aristotle, characterization is a form of imitation (epic imitates admirable people), it is secondary to action (people possess certain qualities in accordance with their character, but they achieve well-being or its opposite on the basis of how they act; you can have an epic or tragedy without character, but you cannot have one without action); an agent must act appropriately ('it should be necessary or probable that this kind of person says or does this kind of thing').[7] Virgil was bound by absolutely none of these precepts, if he ever read them, but, in the *Aeneid*'s story, where both events and characters are governed by Fate (the primacy of plot), he could be said to abide by them – except, perhaps, the very first one (in debating heroism, Virgil is also debating what counts as 'admirable'). In some ways he abides by them more closely than Homer: the *Iliad*, for example, shows two enemy warriors stopping in the middle of battle to converse about the guest-friendship between their families and to swap armour; one of them is Diomedes, whose slaughter of enemies had filled the previous book.[8]

When to the supremacy of plot is added the speed with which it must advance (Virgil allowed himself twelve books to Homer's twice twenty-four), economies are inevitable. As Heinze observes,[9] one of these is conversation, 'the best means of showing traits, individual qualities, and the differences between people'. Virgil was capable of writing dialogue (half of the *Eclogues* are in that form) but exchanges in the *Aeneid* tend to be briefer and less involved than in Homer: there is nothing in the *Aeneid* to match the cut and thrust of the assembly in Book 1 of the *Iliad*.[10] Outside assemblies, conversations are never as protracted as, for example, that between Odysseus and Eumaeus in the latter's hut.[11] And the moments in the *Aeneid* when stand-and-deliver speech-making, or emotional outburst, yield to something more every-day or intimate are (regrettably) rare – Anna with Dido (4.30 ff.), Turnus and Juturna (12.632 ff.), Mezentius one-sidedly[12] with his horse (10.861 ff.); it is no accident that these moments are some of the most human in the poem[13]. And they are not, strictly, required by the plot (see also *Introduction* – 7.6 Speeches).

Even if Virgil rations conversation, his range of techniques for granting psychological insight is not narrow. These techniques, and their limitations, are perhaps best appreciated through an example – the major minor-figure of Pallas – which from his behaviour at particular moments coalesces across episodes into a believable adolescent:

- (8.102 ff.) When Aeneas arrives, Evander is feasting with his son Pallas. The latter is not described as a personality at all – but he remains unafraid at the sight of the strange craft on the river; he respects the religious occasion; he is aware of the danger (taking up a weapon); when he shouts questions to the ships, he betrays a naïve openness. He is instantly awe-struck at the mention of Dardanus, in words and handclasp warmly welcoming – but he is canny enough to defer to his father and, by calling Aeneas a 'guest' (4.10–11 note), place him under the code of hospitality (and the implicit threat of the wrath against any treachery from Jupiter, hospitality's guardian deity).

- (8.308 ff.) On Evander's tour of Rome, Pallas comes with them: the father / son / *in loco parentis* triangle. But we hear nothing of Pallas' reaction to it all.

- (8.585 ff.) Evander's emotional farewell to Pallas contrasts with Pallas' implicit exhilaration as he leaves Pallanteum in Aeneas' cavalcade, clad in 'decorated armour'. The morning-star simile highlights how Venus' family has all but adopted him; he seems to know it, riding in the midst of the Trojan column.

- (10.160 ff.) Sailing back from Caere by night, Pallas is quizzing Aeneas with palpable excitement on the technicalities of navigation and all his adventures. We are left to imagine Aeneas' patience, impatience, or mixture of the two.

- (10.362 ff.) Suddenly Pallas is on his own, in combat and on hostile terrain. His speech to hearten his troops surprisingly bears all the hallmarks of an experienced leader. Near the start of it, however, he not only appeals to the name of his father Evander but also admits his own ambition to rival him – an old-fashioned Homeric hero in the making. He charges into the thick of battle where, dealing death right and left he inspires his men – they are like a front of summer fire sown by a shepherd in the woods and fields (a measure of Pallas' effectiveness and authority). He fells Halaesus with a prayer and promise to dedicate the spoils: a proper respect for the gods.

- (10.441 f.) After Turnus has dismissed his comrades and confronted Pallas alone, Pallas freezes at the sight of his massive opponent – we follow his gaze – and tries to make a defiant speech to Turnus, though he admits the possibility of his own glorious death and claims hollowly – a hollowness he, we and Turnus (ll. 443, 491 f., 11.152 ff., 12.934) detect – that Evander would be indifferent to it.

- (10.457 ff.) Pallas, seeing Turnus coming for him, is aware of his own inferiority and decides to make the first move – praying to another of his father's guests, Hercules, and boosting his own morale by incorporating into his prayer an image of himself looting the moribund Turnus. The prayer is not heard; his spear cast is wasted; Turnus' hits home and Pallas, as if in denial, tears the missile from his breast, pouring forth his life-blood and falling, in the Homeric fashion, to the soil. He has learned what being a Homeric hero can entail.

- (10.505 ff.) Pallas' comrades lament him, as does Virgil himself (addressing Pallas – so-called 'apostrophe') for the honour and pain he will bring his father.

- (10.515 ff.) Aeneas, driven wild by the news of Pallas' death, recalls the hospitality and pledges given by both Evander and Pallas.

- It gradually sinks in that Pallas has been playing Patroclus to Aeneas' Achilles. This structural parallel reinforces Pallas' warmth, impulsiveness and bravery – but also that Aeneas has not known Pallas long, that Patroclus unlike Pallas is an experienced warrior[14] and that Achilles unlike Aeneas gives detailed instructions (as well as lending armour) to his friend.[15]

- (11.42) Aeneas bemoans the loss of the 'boy to be pitied'.

- (11.68 ff.) The simile comparing Pallas on the bier to a wilted cut flower adds him, impersonally, to the accumulation of doomed young men.

- (11.152 f.) Evander remembers his son agreeing to be careful when he goes into battle; he knew the promises would be swept aside.

Most of this repertoire of devices (action, speech direct and indirect, effect on other people, their views of the character, retrospect, focalzation – *Introduction* – 7.3.2 Focalization) are familiar enough from other literature; the use of similes, the author addressing his character (apostrophe), epithets (though Pallas is not given one)[16] and allusion, especially allusion to other literary characters,[17] are more idiosyncratic. Striking, too, is the paucity of direct description of emotion or thought by the *Aeneid*'s narrator – the protracted evocation of Turnus' mental torment at 12.665 ff. is exceptional; what there is (e.g. Pallas' emotions on seeing Turnus opposed to him) is condensed and susceptible of different interpretation. (Yes, in the case of Dido the poet does describe her emotions, but in preparation for the anguish of her Book IV speeches; as a tragic figure she stands almost outside epic protocol.) Pallas emerges as an impetuously friendly adolescent brimming with heroic aspirations and precociously able to realize them – until Turnus; Virgil spells none of this out, except in the adjective *audax* ('bold', at 8.110 – also much used of Turnus, 3.3 further). Because he does not, the portrait vacillates between vulnerable boy and promising fighter; and how we judge Aeneas' leaving him to his own devices (10.362 ff.) depends on where we put the emphasis.

Such ambivalence in characterization can sometimes feel lumpy and inconsistent, perhaps the result of composition by episode (see *Introduction* – 2 Virgil's Life and Works).[18] Ascanius is an obvious example of this (see 3.5); Aeneas in his speech to Evander (8.127 ff.) is another, when its diplomatic expediency, even if motivated by desperate circumstances, comes as a surprise after his previous (apparent) sincerity. But so many characters evoke contradictory reactions at different points in the poem (Dido, Turnus, Mezentius are only the most obvious) that Virgil can give the impression of deliberately confronting us with unsettling lurches (see last two paragraphs of *Introduction* – 9.5 The twentieth and twenty-first centuries: Re-evaluation).[19]

3.2 Aeneas

3.2.1 Aeneas in the Iliad

Aeneas, though not in the foreground of the *Iliad*, emerges intermittently from the background:

- (*Il.* 2.819 ff.) Aeneas is introduced as commander of the Dardanians, along with the two sons of Antenor (1.242–9 note).

- (*Il.* 5.171 ff.) When Diomedes, wounded by the archer Pandarus and revived by Athena, resumes his *aristeia* (series of solo killings), Aeneas takes Pandarus in his chariot to assail Diomedes. Diomedes goes to meet them on foot and sets his sights on Aeneas' horses, of divine pedigree; he kills Pandarus and, when Aeneas defends the body, hurls a huge rock at him, hitting his hip. Aeneas collapses. Aphrodite embraces him and hides him with her robe. While Diomedes' charioteer Sthenelus leads Aeneas' horses away, Diomedes pursues and wounds Aphrodite. Apollo hides Aeneas in a dark blue cloud and, despite Diomedes' continued assault (*Il.* 5.431 ff.), bears him away to his temple on Troy's citadel, forming a phantom Aeneas for the Greeks to tussle over. Ares, in disguise, urges the Trojans to fend them off, calling Aeneas 'a warrior we honour in the same breath as godlike Hector'. Apollo then (*Il.* 5.513) brings Aeneas back to the front, having 'filled this shepherd of the people with new determination'.

Aeneas slays Crethon and Orsilochus ('two of the best among the Greeks') before turning on Menelaus himself, but Antilochus takes his stand beside Menelaus and Aeneas gives ground.

- (*Il.* 6.77 ff.) Helenus praises Hector and Aeneas as the two who bear the brunt of the fighting and as never having failed the Trojans in battle or in the council chamber. He urges them to rally the Trojans so that Hector can steal an opportunity to return to the city and commission a sacrifice to Athena. Homer implies that during Hector's long absence Aeneas manages to keep the resurgent Trojans solid against the Greeks.

- (*Il.* 13.459) Deiphobus, seeking help to ward off the Greeks from the corpse of Alcathous, finds Aeneas loitering behind the lines: he was bearing a grudge against Priam for showing him so little respect. Aeneas obliges and makes for Alcathous' killer, Idomeneus – amassing troops behind him who, 'like sheep following the leader of the flock from the pasture to drink at a stream, delighted the shepherd'. They succeed in forcing Idomeneus back. Aeneas stabs Aphareus in the throat.

- (*Il.* 15.332) In the rout of the Greeks at their ships, Aeneas picks off Medon and Iasus.

- (*Il.* 17.322 ff.) As the armies are locked in struggle over Patroclus' corpse, Apollo in the form of a herald of Anchises inspires Aeneas to harangue Hector and the other Trojans into making a vigorous stand. At their forefront, Aeneas kills Leiocritus. Later (*Il.* 17.483 ff.) Hector asks Aeneas to join him in attacking Automedon and Alcimedon, both in Achilles' chariot – Automedon calls to the two Ajaxes and Menelaus for assistance against 'Hector and Aeneas, who are the best of the Trojans'. Hector and Aeneas retreat before the Ajaxes.

- (*Il.* 20.79 ff.) As Achilles rampages against the Trojans and Zeus permits the gods to take sides, Apollo, now in the form of one of Priam's sons, approaches Aeneas and urges him to fulfil the boasts made in his cups to take on Achilles. Aeneas objects that he has already had a narrow escape from Achilles at the sacking of Lyrnessus and Pedasus and has no stomach to take him on now, unless a god gives him protection. The disguised Apollo reminds him of his divine ancestry and breathes 'tremendous energy into this shepherd of the people'. As the gods look on, the armies advance. Aeneas and Achilles, 'their two greatest champions', meet in the intervening space. Achilles hails Aeneas, reminding him of their encounter at Lyrnessus when, says Achilles, Zeus protected him – as he will not do any longer. Aeneas retorts at great length by tracing his lineage on the male side back to Zeus. Suddenly he cuts himself short with the words (*Il.* 20.246 ff.):

> We could sling plenty of insults at each other – enough to sink a ship. Man's tongue is glib. There are words of all sorts at its command. They cover a wide range, one way or another. You get the kind of answer you have asked for.

> (Trans. Rieu – Jones)

- Their spear casts do impressive damage; Aeneas is hoisting a large rock to throw at Achilles when Poseidon intervenes on his behalf, as he foresees the demise of 'this innocent man, who has always given the most gratifying offerings to the gods'. Poseidon urges action to save the line of Dardanus, most beloved of Zeus' mortal children. After Priam's fall, 'mighty Aeneas shall rule over Troy and be followed by his children's children in time to come' (see 3.97–8 note for Virgil's 'augmentation' of this; we assume no migration from Troy). With Hera's grudging consent, Poseidon himself scoops Aeneas up, removes him from the battlefield and gives him a stern talking-to: he should avoid Achilles, and only return to the front line after Achilles' death. No other Greek would kill him.

- In the *Homeric Hymn to Aphrodite*,[20] the goddess promises Anchises that Aeneas will rule among the Trojans, and his children's children.

Virgil was able to annex some of this Homeric Aeneas – the warrior who takes down his man and the leader whose summons is answered ('shepherd of men' is an epithet largely applied to kings[21]); showing piety and a distrust of the spoken word. His mother's protectiveness, however, manifested in a way unimaginable within the *Aeneid*, highlights a problem. For all the comments that put him on a level with Hector, Aeneas has the dubious distinction of being the most rescued hero in the *Iliad*; and he bows out when confronted by the Ajaxes. Virgil sets about reversing this image: from Troy Aeneas rescues his family (or most of it) himself (Book II); Diomedes is reinvented as a chastened man who bows before Aeneas' military prowess (*Aeneid* 11.281 ff.); when a dummy Aeneas makes its appearance in Book X (*Aeneid* 10.636 ff.), it decoys and thereby saves not Aeneas but Turnus; and Virgil, who first strove to equate Aeneas with Hector,[22] once Turnus has tried to do the same (9.742), gradually makes him shade into Achilles (see 6.88–90 note).

3.2.2 Aeneas between the Iliad *and the* Aeneid: The Aeneas legend

It is a long way from Poseidon's prophecy to the *Aeneid*, and in the interim a tangle of stories about Aeneas knit themselves covering:[23]

- the escape from Troy (see Book II, Literary sources);
- the Trojans' voyage to Italy (see Books III, V and VI Literary sources);
- the war they then waged there (see 7.45–80 note);
- Aeneas' posterity (see 6.760–6 note).

The detail fermenting in the background can be glimpsed in various references to Aeneas' *pietas*. The Greek historian Xenophon wrote,[24] 'Aeneas saved the gods of his father's and his mother's family, and with them his father himself; as a result he achieved fame for his piety.' (No mention of wife or child.) The Alexandrian poet Lycophron claimed[25] that Aeneas chose the household gods over his wife and children. Before the Roman period Aeneas' rescue of the gods is depicted on an Etruscan gem, and that of Anchises frequently, notably on vases found in Etruria. By the early first century, Aeneas was a by-word for *pietas* – a textbook on rhetoric cites[26] as an example of sarcasm 'calling some undutiful (*impius*) man who has beaten his father "Aeneas"'.

Virgil's great epic forerunners, Naevius and Ennius (see *Introduction* – 8.4.5 Early Roman epic and drama) had created their own versions of the Aeneas legend, both now lost. What can be reconstructed from fragmentary quotations, however, shows a very different storyline to that of the *Aeneid*:

- In Naevius, Anchises was endowed with prophetic powers by Venus.[27] Anchises and Aeneas both leave Troy with their wives.[28] There is a storm scene shared with the *Aeneid* (1.81 ff.), after which, as in the *Aeneid*, Venus complains to Jupiter and he reassures her with a prediction.[29] This scene may also have preceded a landing in Africa and encounter with Dido (see Book IV – Literary sources). Aeneas' daughter was the mother of Romulus.[30]

- In Ennius, Anchises was gifted with prophecy by Venus (as in Naevius);[31] he seems to have been the moving spirit behind the family's evacuation,[32] with encouragement from Venus.[33] Aeneas allied himself with the unnamed king of Alba and,[34] it can be assumed with his daughter, sired Ilia. Ilia became mother of Romulus (as in Naevius[35]). (No mention of a son to Aeneas in the sparse remains of the text – but since Alba, according to Ennius, already existed, he would have had nowhere to found.) Ennius too seems to have included a scene with Romulus, Remus and their wolf nurse.[36] Juno meanwhile continued hostile to the Trojans/Romans until the second Punic War.[37]

Despite Virgil's verbal homages to Ennius (and possibly to Naevius, though too little of his work survives to prove the indebtedness), the plot-master of the *Aeneid* took a red pencil to the versions of the Aeneas legend he found in them. Virgil's Anchises is no prophet – he is even a fallible interpreter of others' prophecy (Apollo's, 3.102 ff.) – until, that is, he is looking forth from the underworld. (In Naevius and Ennius, Anchises probably reached Italy.) More significantly, neither Naevius nor Ennius is interested, as Virgil most definitely is, in presenting the origin of the Julian dynasty (Iulus).

But then the Julian family itself had, since Naevius and Ennius, taken a hand in the matter[38]. Between 135 and 125 BCE, Sextus Julius Caesar minted coins on which Venus Genetrix was shown riding a chariot; Lucius Julius Caesar represented Venus on a coin of 94 BCE. Julius Caesar himself continued this publicity in a series of coins showing Venus on the obverse in 48 and 47 BCE – one such on the reverse displayed Aeneas bearing Anchises on his shoulder and the Palladium in one hand;[39] more followed in 44 BCE, though Venus was displaced to the reverse and on the obverse was a head of 'Caesar *imperator*'.[40] From the start of his career he had promoted the Venus connection – in 69 BCE, when he was quaestor, he delivered the funeral oration for his aunt Julia. Suetonius quotes from it:[41]

My aunt Julia is descended from kings on her mother's side and related to the immortal gods on her father's. For the Marcii Reges, her mother's name, are of the stock of Ancus Marcius, while the Julii, of which our family is a branch, are of the stock of Venus.

He made 'Venus' his password at the battle of Munda in 45 BCE, as he had at Pharsalus in 48 BCE;[42] Dio Cassius, writing of the year 45 BCE, notes[43] that Caesar wore footwear . . .

. . . after the style of the kings who had once reigned in Alba, for he claimed that he was related to them through Iulus. In general he was absolutely devoted to Venus, and was anxious to persuade everybody that he had received from her a kind of bloom of youth. Accordingly he used also to wear a carven image of her in full armour on his ring and he made her name his watchword in almost all the greatest dangers.

(Trans. Loeb, 1916)

Before Pharsalus, he vowed her a temple to her if she brought victory[44] and when victorious built one to dominate his forum; he consecrated it on 26 September 46 BCE,[45] though it was only finished under Augustus.[46] For the festivities, Caesar reintroduced the *lusus Troiae* (see 5.545 ff. and 5.545–603 note).[47] All this was advertising that Virgil could not, and did not, ignore.

Virgil's task in reducing his mythological and political inheritance to some sort of artistic order was immense. So he made a virtue out of political near-necessity when choosing a genealogy for the sons of Aeneas, a Julian line descended from Iulus and his grandmother Venus, though he has not purged his account of inconsistencies (see 6.760–6 note: was Silvius or Iulus the ancestor of the Alban kings?). Here as elsewhere, rather than carelessness, it is tempting to imagine Virgil preferring when it suited him to retain some of the contradictions in his sources than to rehearse a spurious certainty.[48]

3.2.3 Aeneas in the Aeneid: Filling in the blanks

Of all the characters in the poem, it is Aeneas himself who arouses most controversy (see, for example, 1.378–80 and 4.331–61 notes for, respectively, a damning overall verdict and a low moment; H. W. Garrod tersely described him as 'the wrong man in the wrong place';[49] Robert Graves called him 'a cad to the last'[50]): is he flat (Virgil's fault), unattractive (his fault) or misunderstood (our fault)? Would he have made a different impression on a Roman audience than he does on us? How did Virgil intend him to come across? Each question is harder than the previous one.

First of all, 'flatness'. Aeneas' emotions and actions cover a wide compass, especially in the first half of the poem when we see most of him and in the most varied circumstances. To make an arbitrary selection: in Book I he crosses from despair in the storm to decisive leadership when he encourages his men; the thwarted affection he feels with his mother turns to a simultaneous grief and awareness of compassion before the decorations in the Temple of Juno; and he ends in admiration and gratitude towards Dido. In Book II he tells of his horror at ravaged Troy, then his determination to resist at any cost, then his acceptance of the duty to save his family followed by his tragic failure in losing Creusa; in Book III he describes the weary succession of halts as he longs for his destination, his dependence on Anchises and the frustrating pursuit of prophecies ill-recalled or misinterpreted;[51] Book IV lets slip glimpses of a man happy in love but then homes in on the conflicting loyalties that he is unable to express as he abandons it; in Book V he is the genial president of the games until plunged into despondency by the burning of fleet, after which he is coaxed back into confidence again; Book VI depicts him absorbing the Wunderkammer of the underworld and yet afterwards oblivious of it; in Book VII he is reassured by the omen of eating tables and makes cautious overtures to Latinus, only for these to be wrecked by Juno; his dismay and helplessness at this in Book VIII is alleviated by Tiberinus and he is determined himself to woo support from the Etruscans – Venus' armour boosts his morale; with it in Book X he returns to relieve his encampment and proves what he can do on the battlefield, where his extreme ferocity at the death of Pallas is softened to compassion at the death of Lausus; then his mourning for Pallas and his dead comrades in Book XI is replaced by a stern resolve to fight Turnus in Book XII, and his consternation at the broken truce makes him increasingly implacable, until he flares up against his enemy in the final duel.

If 'flatness' is taken as 'lack of dynamic range', then, it is a misdiagnosis. What then is missing? There are several parallel answers to this question:

- Aeneas is a man on a mission not of his own making. This does not deprive him of self-determination (he is not, like Dido or Turnus, usurped by a deity) but it does mean that he can only want what is in keeping with that mission (see 1.1-7 note). His epithets, *pius* (see 1.8-11 note, **famous for his piety**) and *pater* ('father'), emphasize responsibility for others.

- He is shown in the company of his men but there is only one instance of one of them speaking to him (Achates, 1.584 ff., four lines) and of conversation with them (Achates again, 6.158 ff.; see 3.1 above; 1.102, 120–1 note). Thus Aeneas seems permanently isolated; he is locked inside his view of events, as when, looking at the scenes in Juno's temple, he addresses Achates (1.459 f.) but does not stay for a reply.

- He never has an exchange of any intimacy with anyone close to him – Venus,[52] Ascanius, Creusa, Anchises,[53] Dido (the last three of whom he loses); when the opportunity for one occurs, it is truncated before it can develop; and when Aeneas attempts to make an opportunity, it is too late (Dido in the underworld).[54] To judge from Aeneas' farewell to Ascanius (12.432 ff., 12.411–40 note), this more profound isolation is Virgil's intention: in Virgil's model, Hector takes off his helmet to embrace his little son who had been frightened by it; Aeneas keeps his helmet on and somehow kisses his son through the metalwork. He feels, but his emotion is trapped.

- We long to hear Aeneas' thoughts but often there is a deafening silence – what went through his mind when, thanks to Anchises, he was fired with love for his prospective glory (6.899)? Was he simply indoctrinated, or did he reflect on what he had been shown, possibly inquire about it? But providing such detail is not how Virgil's characterization works (3.1 above).

These answers go some way to explain Aeneas' remoteness on the page. They do not quite address the ways in which, where he does come alive, he can seem unattractive to a modern audience – his tone of self-pity when describing his misfortunes to Venus (1.372 ff.);[55] his lack of sympathy towards Dido (4.333 ff.);[56] his bloodthirstiness in action (10.521 ff.). Here a defence is available on grounds that he has not been understood as a Roman might have understood him – his speech to Venus contains the rhetoric that a Roman could admire in his situation (1.378–80 note); his unromantic declaration of rupture to Dido is in keeping with at least one Roman attitude to all-conquering love ('a source of immorality and irresponsibility'[57]); and his deeds in war are sanctioned by epic convention[58] and Roman lack of squeamishness.[59] Which does not disprove that Virgil might have intended to make aspects of his hero unattractive.

And even if it did, one can never be argued out of an impression. A different route to reconciliation with Aeneas is to go some way towards him ourselves. We might consider him as embodying the extreme sacrifices an individual must make who is dedicated to a communal, or rather national, goal:[60] the emotional, spontaneous captain of Book I becomes the hard-bitten commander, introvert *avant la lettre*, of Book XII. This does not get us very far because it treats the blanks in Aeneas' portrayal as genuine voids. Instead we could view them as in invitation for us to fill them in for themselves: 'Aeneas is left empty for us to inhabit.'[61] We would be free to insert sentiments at home in tragedy or lyric, or neither, rather than epic – and if we bother (it presupposes a degree of goodwill) we invest something of ourselves in the hero.

Although it is impossible to decide how Virgil intended Aeneas to come across, this last proposal just might be the challenge he wanted to set: then the point would not be whether Aeneas is flat or attractive, or even whether we fully understand him, but that we should try. Aeneas is not a stand-in for Augustus (10.260–86 note); but a readiness to enter into the cares and conflicts of a founder could transfer from one to the other and be of more service in tempering judgement on them both than any amount of panegyric.

3.2.4 Aeneas in the Aeneid: *Character development*

Part of the controversy over Aeneas is whether or not his character could be said to develop.[62] The idea of development is particularly seductive for those who would espouse the *Aeneid* as a piece of Roman didactic:

> Virgil took a single character . . . representing him as the typical Roman as conceived . . . by the Romans of the Augustan age and of the Stoic persuasion.
>
> I regard the change in the hero as Virgil's deliberate and considered design. In that case, we should not regard Aeneas as an ideal hero, perfect from the very beginning, but as a man who learns how to become a hero in the school of fate.

So Heinze,[63] who makes the pivotal change in Aeneas occur with Anchises' apparition at the end of Book V (5.746 ff.). Otis places it at the end of Book VI:[64]

> The *pius* Aeneas is thus the ideal man or hero of Virgil's Augustan ideology. But Virgil could not have shown him to be such had he presented him to us already formed and compete. His *pietas* had to be an achievement, or it would not have been truly *pietas*: hence Virgil's epic had to deal with his hero's formation, his attainment of *pietas*, as well as with his mature performance.

But to maintain that Aeneas' character develops you require a rather different synopsis of his emotional vicissitudes from that above (3.2.3) – in particular, the *furor* Aeneas displays in Books X and XII must be downplayed, as it seems if anything a decline from the self-knowledge, admittedly *furor* recollected in tranquillity, of Book II (2.314 ff.). Such changes as we see in Aeneas' behaviour can be explained otherwise, as by Camps:[65] 'The story of Aeneas' experience is narrated in three phases . . . quest, arrival, victory . . . In this development of events there is a corresponding change not indeed of the hero's character – there is no probable indication of that – but of his situation and consequently of his attitude.' Pöschl suggests,[66] 'The difference between the Aeneas of the last third of the poem and that of the first third lies not in his greater courage but in his greater experience and in his being more deeply pervaded by Roman attitudes.' What develops in Aeneas is his understanding of his mission. This allows the *Aeneid* an admixture of Roman homily without turning it into a *Bildungsroman*.[67]

3.2.5 Aeneas in the Aeneid: *A Stoic hero?*

Heinze (3.2.4) raises the importance of Stoicism to the Augustan period and therefore to the *Aeneid*. Evidence of Augustus' own adherence to Stoic doctrine is circumstantial – he had two Stoic tutors (Athenodorus Canaanites[68] and Arius Didymus[69] – the former is said to have advised him, in case of anger, to recite under his breath all the letters of the Greek alphabet[70]). But there are clear signs of Stoicism in the *Aeneid* – Fate is a Stoic notion, contrary to Epicureanism (see *Introduction* – 5.5 Stoicism, Epicureanism and the *Aeneid*); Aeneas is obedient to his mission rather than the pleasure that would distract him from it.[71] Certain turns of phrase echo Stoic terminology (e.g. 3.182 note) or were subsequently adopted by its proponents (5.709–10 note; 6.103–5 note). Nevertheless, it requires severe contortions to make of Aeneas a rigorously Stoic hero[72] or of the *Aeneid* a rigorously Stoic poem. His *furor* at the end of it does not qualify for the Stoic escape clause on anger, that it can be a motivator in battle (12.919–52 note, **ira**). Then there is his most unStoical 'sensitivity to tragedy'[73] – 'pity' (*misericordia*) is a Stoic vice, according to Seneca:[74]

> Pity is a disorder of the mind caused by the sight of other men's miseries, or it is a sadness caused by the evils with which it believes others to be undeservedly afflicted: but the wise man cannot be affected by any disorder: his mind is calm, and nothing can possibly happen to ruffle it. Moreover, nothing becomes a man more than magnanimity: but magnanimity cannot coexist with sorrow. Sorrow overwhelms men's minds, casts them down, contracts them ...

> (Trans. Stewart)

To this vice Aeneas repeatedly succumbs – towards Dido in the underworld (6.476) or towards Lausus (10.823), to cite just two occasions. Virgil's narrator is equally vulnerable (9.465, 472, 475, 484, 495) and even his gods, however callous, are not immune – **In the halls of Jupiter the gods pitied the futile anger of the two armies** / *The gods in the halls of Jove are filled with pity, feeling the futile rage of both great armies* (10.758 f.).

3.3 Turnus

Turnus seems much easier to read than Aeneas, partly because his inner life is usurped from the start by a higher power, in a process that we witness (7.445 ff.). This also creates a problem because, unlike Dido or Amata, who we also see being taken over by higher powers (1.712 ff., 7.346 ff.), Turnus does not come on stage before the usurpation[75] – we meet him first at midnight in his dreams when he encounters Allecto disguised as Calybe. This is not the easiest starting-point from which to estimate his previous character. He is certainly disrespectful towards her and arrogant (in his conviction of Juno's favour), but he also dismisses her bellicosity; the torch that she uses to raise his temperature does not necessarily imply that his blood was already hot (see 7.406–44 note[76]).

What we see of him after that is a polarized portrait – on the one hand the warrior of audacity (the adjective *audax* in Latin has both positive and negative connotations, 7.409 note) who sees himself, with some reason,[77] as an Achilles (9.742; 6.88–90 note), changes into the poem's first human embodiment of *furor impius* (see 9.691 ff.) and is the subject of a series of animal images (9.47–76 note); over against this, the tragic young lover who is manipulated by the gods, cornered by his political rival (Drances, Book XI) and made Jupiter's as much as Aeneas' victim (at the end of Book XII). This duality is captured in the decorations of his helmet (fire-breathing Chimaera) and shield (Io, recently transformed into a heifer by Jupiter or Juno) before he enters battle (7.784-802 note[78]) and his brutality continues almost to the end of the poem,[79] even as the tragic note sounds more and more insistently. In Book XII he recalls Dido[80] – at the start of that book the simile of the wounded lion reflects the opening of Book IV when Dido's love-wound is described; he clings to his honour as Dido to her love; at the moment of crisis he confides in his sister (12.632 ff.) as Dido in Anna (4.478 ff.);[81] Dido has nightmares (4.465 ff.) and Turnus lives one, or rather we live one through him (12.908 ff.). And although the two move in opposite directions, Dido from love to defiant hostility, Turnus from defiant hostility to submission, both face a death which seems to them inevitable (4.475 – Dido's choice; 12.676 – Turnus' reading of Fate).

Turnus is thus a human foil for Aeneas – one who seeks personal honour (against fate) versus one who promotes a common good (in accordance with it); he is the seething pot (7.462 ff.) to Aeneas' glinting pail (8.22 ff.). While Aeneas struggles with his *furor* and loses to it (12.938 ff.), Turnus encourages his (12.680); Turnus' *furor* steals his opportunity to win the war when he fails to open the Trojan camp gates (9.756 ff.), Aeneas' relieves the Trojan camp from the Latin stranglehold (10.604 f.). For Aeneas *pietas* means strict adherence to divine law, for Turnus it means not infringing it[82] – Aeneas strives to rescue the truce in Book XII while Turnus takes advantage of its breach (12.311 ff., 12.324 f.); Aeneas sets up a trophy from Mezentius' armour while Turnus wears Pallas' baldric. But what makes Turnus more than a symbolic anti-Aeneas who must be expunged to make way for the new order is precisely his abrupt humanity: when he shows tenderness to his sister and a clear appreciation of his prospects (12.632 ff.) he seems to have come to himself – to a character we have never so far seen – and acquires a private voice to go with his public one. His death at the end of the poem is not, as Drances would have it, an easy solution to a political problem.[83]

3.4 Dido

If we are largely deprived of Aeneas' and Turnus' private voices, then the opposite applies to Dido – we are immersed in hers. Not only is she a tragic figure, but the telling of her story takes on the structure, concentration and expression of a Greek tragedy, amenable to Aristotelian analysis. Virgil seems to invite us to think of it in those terms when he has her imagining herself on the stage, as Pentheus or Orestes (4.469 ff.). The formal elements of Dido's tragic drama could be summarized:

- Prologue: Venus introduces Dido to Aeneas and audience (1.335 ff.)
- First episode: Dido and Aeneas meet (1.579 ff.); after the interlude of Aeneas' narrative (Books II and III) there is a unity of action,[84] where every episode drives towards Dido's downfall and suicide
- Anna as confidante (4.8 ff. – see 4.1–30 note) – all the exchanges from now on are between two actors
- The set piece of the hunt, as if reported by a messenger (4.128 ff.)
- Dido's treatment of the liaison in the cave as marriage (4.172) could be considered her fatal error, Aristotle's *hamartia*[85] (4.160–72 note)

- Rumour then Iarbas as travesties of a chorus, observing and commenting on events (4.173 ff.; Rumour glimpsed again at 4.666)

- The reversal (*peripeteia*[86]) in Dido's fortunes when Mercury orders Aeneas to leave (4.265 ff)

- Dido's recognition (*anagnorisis*[87]) of what is happening (4.408 ff.)

- The clash (*agōn*, or 'contest'[88]) between Dido and Aeneas (4.304 ff.); in Homeric epic such a verbal clash would be between warriors (as in *Iliad* Book 9, the embassy to Achilles)

- The suffering (*pathos*[89]) of Dido's decline and death, including a descent into magic and nightmare, captured above all in speeches, whether to Anna or monologues

Parts of the narrative, inevitably, do not conform to a Greek tragic schema – Aeneas and Achates concealed in mist as they see Dido arrive and eavesdrop on Ilioneus (1.494 ff.); the banquet (1.695 ff.); the divine machinery (1.657 ff., 4.90 ff., 4.219 ff.; and to a lesser extent, because more like a dream, 4.553 ff.); and the depictions of Dido's inner state (as at 4.450 ff.). These parts nevertheless contribute to the tragic build-up – establishing Dido's stature[90] and augmenting the 'pity' and 'fear' we feel on her behalf.[91] One episode, however, falls outside the tragic schema completely: the epilogue in the underworld (6.450 ff.), which under this analysis, becomes all the more unexpected and troubling – Dido's silence has the last word.

That epilogue also highlights the different view of Dido that emerges from each book: Book I gives us the strongest sense of personality, of a charismatic and capable ruler made vulnerable by her warmth and generosity; Book IV almost obliterates that character in overpowering emotion[92] – she becomes Medea abandoned by Jason,[93] or a blend of Hippolytus and Phaedra.[94] In Book VI, Dido has moved beyond characterization – she has become part of Aeneas' emotional fabric (6.450–76 note).

Why this interpolation of tragedy into epic? One reason may be that it allows Virgil to expose the twists and turns of anguish over time. (Thus a different set of sensibilities again, of tenderness and intimacy, is mobilized through allusion to lyric in the episode of Nisus and Euryalus – see 9.176–449 note.) Another reason may be that tragedy is more than 'the heroic individual struggling for self-determination'; it is also 'the locus of contesting roles within the structures of gender, household and city'.[95] Dido as founder and ruler, a woman playing what was then a man's part, is the embodiment of Carthage; her death is compared to the city's destruction (4.669); her love and longing for family (4.328 f.) blinds her to her civic role just when Aeneas is jolted out of such blindness. Tragedy provides the means for exploring the contrast between them. The disproportionate attention paid to Dido compared to Aeneas sets her as if in a different perspective within the same picture – but Virgil seems deliberately to adapt his approach from one character to another.

3.4.1 Dido as an Epicurean

Just as it is tempting to regard Aeneas as in some measure an embodiment of Stoic ideals (3.2.5 above), so there are Epicurean facets to Dido (*Introduction* – 5.5 Stoicism, Epicureanism and the *Aeneid*):[96] her minstrel sings of an astronomy, zoology and meteorology that makes no mention of gods (1.742 ff.); she listens to Anna's arguments that the dead pay no heed to the living (4.34); and when Aeneas protests his divine mission she is sceptical of the gods' interest in human affairs – these would not impinge on divine **tranquillity** / *repose* (4.379). On the other hand, she is steeped in an un-Epicurean luxury (1.723–7 note), sacrifices to the gods (4.56 ff.; with a degree of subterfuge, 4.509 ff.) and contradicts Anna's assertion of the dead's indifference when she threatens to haunt Aeneas (4.386). She is therefore no rigid disciple of Epicurus. Even so, in Dido and Aeneas Virgil sets up the opposition between self-fulfilment (Epicurean) and social obligation (Stoic); the two philosophical schools illuminate the characters, but the characters are anything but philosophical mannequins.

3.5 Ascanius

In a poem preoccupied with family continuity (look at the entry of Marcellus, 6.883), Ascanius might be expected to steal more limelight than he does; instead he appears intermittently in scenes that trace his babyhood, boyhood and an impressive early adolescence, all laden with significance for the future,[97] but – and here he differs from Pallas – lacking the thread of a clear personality to string them together. His alias of Iulus, used only slightly less frequently than Ascanius, points both back to Troy / Ilium and forward to the Julian dynasty (1.267 f.).

Thus at Troy he is barely a toddler (2.674 – Creusa offers him to Aeneas; 2.724 – Aeneas takes him by the hand) but also an omen (2.682). On the journey he is Andromache's stand-in for her baby Astyanax (3.489) while, at Carthage, when he should be about ten years old,[98] his double on Dido's lap stirs a fatal maternal longing in her (1.718) – and then *propria persona* he frisks at the hunt on his pony, spoiling for a big trophy (4.166 ff.). At Anchises' memorial games his horseplay takes a serious turn when he leads the *lusus Troiae*, a link to Augustan Rome (5.570), and, when the women burn the ships, he makes a dramatic and effective appeal to their sense of parental duty before Aeneas comes up in support (5.667 ff.). No longer the frivolous child, it would seem, except that once arrived in Italy, he drops an impish quip (7.116) that takes the wind out of Celaeno's menacing prophecy (3.257). He is out hunting again when Allecto sabotages his sport and he kills Silvia's pet stag (7.479 ff.), sparking a skirmish that leads to war. Left behind while Aeneas goes upstream to Evander, he encourages Nisus and Euryalus in their sortie with ill-judged largesse (if one rashly attempts a strict reckoning, he can only be about eleven years old – 9.258 ff.) and is overwhelmed by the grief of Euryalus' mother, and his own (9.501 f.). His battle career, an extension of his hunting, begins and ends with his bowshot at Numanus Remulus (9.653 ff.), but only after he has shown *pietas* in praying to Jupiter (9.625 ff.) and a soldier's capacity for scorn (9.634 ff.). As some consolation for being confined to quarters by Apollo he joins in the sortie from the camp and pursuit of the routed Latins at 10.604 f.. He cries by the side of wounded Aeneas (12.399) and listens to what come across as Aeneas' final instructions to him (12.435 ff.), with what emotions we can only guess.

He is, like Aeneas, Fate's instrument, a shaper of events but also a hapless cause of events he does not intend. We do not see him returning any affection he is given – his grandmother cares so much for him (1.678 ff.) she spirits him away unconscious; Dido, offstage, presents him with a horse (5.570 f.); of the occasions when Aeneas warmly embraces him, on the first (1.715 f.) it is not the real Ascanius that Aeneas is embracing and on the second (12.432 ff.) Aeneas is wearing full armour. Within the compass of the *Aeneid* he is protected but, when Aeneas in the underworld is confronted by a rival line of descent – one with which Virgil's audience would have been familiar – there is a hint of potential discord (6.760–6 note). In the end, unlike the rest of the procession of doomed youth (Marcellus, Pallas, Lausus, the Danaids' victims ...), he survives. That, to ensure family continuity, is his most important challenge.

When Virgil's Ascanius is compared to the Ascanius in Cato, Livy and Dionysius of Halicarnassus (7.45–80 note), his development has obviously been arrested in Book IX (9.638–71 note); there is no hint of the afterlife he has in those other authors. The justification for this may be political – if Ascanius is the future, then the Latins have really lost to the Trojans (9.590–620 note[99]). Thus Ascanius' ascendancy is curtailed.

3.6 Anchises

Anchises affords an example, if not of character development, then of character progression:[100] the resolutely – and courageously – defeatist invalid at Troy (2.596, 4.599; 2.647 ff.), persuaded by a double portent to abandon the city (2.701 ff.), takes on the role not just of *pater familias*[101] but also of expedition high priest, at first fallibly (he sends the Trojans from Delos to Crete, 3.103 ff.) but with more and more confidence (most conspicuous in the approach to and arrival in Italy, 3.528–60); his death on Sicily is commemorated by games during which the omens (the snake, 5.84 ff.; the flaming arrow, 5.525 ff.) appear to indicate his incorporation among the gods – he acts as Jupiter's emissary to Aeneas in a vision (5.722 ff.); in the underworld's Elysium he is correspondingly exempt as one of the elect from the cycle of rebirth (6.743 ff.) and has privileged foreknowledge of the destiny of the souls to be reincarnated and of his son's future in Italy (6.756 ff., 6.890 ff.). The helpless Anchises of Book II had elicited the *pietas* of a son towards a vulnerable father (2.707 ff.); the transfigured Anchises of Book VI arouses awe (6.854).

3.7 Latinus and Evander

There are several cases in the *Aeneid* where pairs of characters exist in antiphony, sometimes at close quarters, sometimes at one remove. Pallas and Lausus, matched in age, handsomeness and doom (10.434 ff.) who by their deaths have diametrically opposed effects on Aeneas, are examples of the former; examples of the latter are Turnus and Mezentius, Aeneas' most formidable opponents on the battlefield, whom he meets separately (Mezentius substitutes for Turnus in Book X) but whose parallel ends, each first wounded then dispatched by him, provide utterly different cadences to two books (X and XII).

Latinus and Evander invite comparison with one another:

	Latinus	**Evander**
Place of origin	Latium	Arcadia, Greece
Ancestry	Latin born and bred, though by what descent is not entirely clear – 7.47 ff. and 7.191 ff. make him son of Faunus and Circe, grandson of Picus and Marica	Grandson (?) of the Arcadian Pallas (8.51)

	Latinus	**Evander**
Location	His city is never named and only its palace is described (7.170 ff.) – a great assembly hall serving as a primitive senate house, temple and refectory	Pallanteum (8.54), the future site of Rome, which Aeneas tours with him (8.306 ff.): the sites of future landmarks are rural vistas and his 'palace' a modest house (8.366)
Immediate family	His wife Amata has a mind, and passions, of her own (7.56 f.); the oracle of Faunus has predicted (7.96 ff.) that their only child (7.52), Lavinia, will marry a foreigner (Aeneas) – she is above all the prize in the contest of succession and Latinus' perpetuation	His Sabine wife (8.510) has died (11.159); his only son and successor (8.581) is Pallas, whom he already considers as his deputy (8.123 f., 8.308, 8.510) and for whom his love is abundantly clear (8.584); Pallas becomes Aeneas' comrade; at his death Evander's line dies out
Character	He is a frail ruler beleaguered at home and outside, who does not hesitate to betroth his only daughter to a stranger but shows determination, as well as naivety, in his efforts to achieve harmony.[102]	His hearty and garrulous hospitality does not hide a warlike bloodthirstiness, accentuated by hints of the fantasist (as in his vivid reimagination of the encounter between Hercules and Cacus); he overrides caution to entrust his only son to a relative stranger.[103]

For all the primitive simplicity, as a Roman would see it, of Latinus' and Evander's (contrasted) settings, they represent distinct strands in Rome's pre-history: Latinus the Italian continuity that will absorb the Trojans, Evander the Greek influence on Italy whose continuity will be broken and that Rome will displace. And the tragedy each suffers[104] comes about from opposite reasons (appeasement in Latinus' case, pugnacity in Evander's).

3.8 Amata

Another significant pairing is that of Amata and Dido: both are manipulated by the gods (Amata by Allecto and Dido by Venus), both are possessed by a love (turning to *furor*[105]) that fate opposes; and both commit suicide. The parallel is reinforced by verbal echoes – when Amata pleads with Turnus not to go out to face the Trojans, she reprises phrases Dido had used to Aeneas (12.62-3 note[106]).

Dido, however, also serves to bring out the questionable side of Amata's attachment. Before Cupid interfered, Dido had been impressed by Aeneas (the description of the dash he cuts when he steps forth from the cloud at 1.588 ff. is focalized through her as well as the other onlookers – hence her astonishment, 1.613); but it would be premature to say she was 'in love'. Amata, by contrast, if her Bacchic frenzy in the mountains (7.385 ff.) is any indication, is considerably younger than her husband Latinus (**by this time an old man /** *already old*, 7.46; even before Allecto sets the serpent upon her in a piece of repugnant sensuality (7.346 ff.), she is already displaying 'remarkable affection' in promoting Turnus' suit for Lavinia (7.57). In fact, Allecto had found her **seething with womanly anger and disappointment at the arrival of the Trojans and the loss of the wedding to Turnus** / *seething with all a woman's anguish, fire and fury over the Trojans just arrived and Turnus' marriage lost* (7.344 f.). This is not language that would be applied to a mother who simply had the best interests of her daughter at heart; thus her arguments to Latinus, that he will lose his daughter rather than gain a son-in-law and that Turnus after all (and it is rather late to say so) is the foreigner he is looking for (7.359–64, 7.365–72 notes), smack of Allecto-fired desperation. At the start of Book XII when, in rare agreement with Latinus, she attempts to stop Turnus from going out to fight the Trojans, she seems for a moment to have recovered from her feigned Bacchic rampage (7.385 ff.); but the passionate devotion of her entreaty recalls, as well as Dido, both Hecuba and Andromache (mother and wife) addressing Hector – particularly Andromache (see 12.1–53, 12.62–3 notes). When she kills herself, it is under the illusion that Turnus is already dead (12.598 f.) and in fulfilment of her earlier promise to share his fate (12.61 f.); news reaching Turnus of the death of the queen, **who placed all her trust in you** / *whose trust lay all in you*, is one of the list of catastrophes that convinces him to face Aeneas (12.659 f.).[107]

Yet at her death, the Dido parallel brings out Amata's profound misfortune: Dido commits suicide acutely aware of the dishonour she has brought on herself (4.653 ff.) and with her curse on the Trojans still ringing (4.612 ff.); her death is like the fall of a great city (4.669). Amata pathetically condemns herself for being the **fountainhead of all these evils** / *source of disaster* (12.600) – surely too severe or, as Virgil says, 'deranged' (12.599). The worst that can be said of her is that she removed Lavinia, for a while, from the scene (7.387) and added to the (already considerable) pressure for war on Latinus (7.580 ff.). She hangs herself ignominiously (12.593–611 note); Lavinia disfigures her face in grief, ahead of the general mourning (12.605 f.), a gesture which seems much more than conventional.

3.9 Lavinia

If proof were wanting that Virgil in his characterization did not abhor a vacuum, behold Lavinia.[108] She is passive and mute throughout the poem but her importance is patent in its second line: **the shores of Lavinium** / *Lavinian shores*. Creusa foretells her existence (2.783) and the Sibyl declares she will be **the cause of all this Trojan suffering** / *the cause of this, this new Trojan grief* (6.93). When the narrative reaches Italy, however, and her family is introduced (7.51 ff.), she is the anonymous object of questing suitors. She reacquires a name when she becomes an unprepossessing omen (7.71 ff.), at her father's side tending the altar with 'chaste torches', the very paragon of a 'daughter of the family':[109] her hair is caught up in a conflagration, smoke, glare and flames filling the palace – it may only singe her ornaments but it is far more menacing than Ascanius' comparatively gentle illumination (2.682 ff.). In obedience to the prophecy (7.96 ff.) that she must marry a foreigner, and almost clutching at a 'solution', her father bestows her on Aeneas before meeting him (7.268 ff.). (Fate, as it happens, is on his side – 7.314.) Any chance of Lavinia's encountering Aeneas is forestalled when Amata sweeps her off to the woods (7.387). She returns at some point before Latinus' assembly, at which Drances speaks of her hand in marriage as the seal on an eternal peace (11.355 f.) – but when hostilities resume she accompanies her mother to Athena's temple (11.479 f.), her eyes downcast, as if aware that she is what Virgil calls her, **the cause of all this suffering** / *cause of all their grief* – the Latin replicates precisely the words of the Sibyl above (6.93). (They are truer of her than of Amata, 12.600, but Lavinia can hardly be blamed.)

Then, at a meeting of Turnus with her parents (we do not see Lavinia without at least one of them), this virtual doll who will give birth to the most important Roman dynasty blushes – a blush on which the poet dwells over six lines including two similes (12.64 ff.). It is little short of explosive: firstly it prompts a wealth of speculation on why she blushes (12.54–80 note), on her relationships with her mother Amata and with Turnus, and on her feelings towards her father and towards the unmet Aeneas; secondly it injects her with a fleeting humanity. The next and final time we see her she is tearing at the cheeks that blushed, after her mother's suicide (12.606), the blush accentuating the impact of that freeze-frame.

As the demure and compliant daughter of a king in search of a successor, Lavinia is the very antithesis of Dido: Lavinia's past is as nothing compared to her future, the sequel to the *Aeneid*, in which she is to give her name to a city (12.194) and, according to Anchises, bring up her son Silvius in the forests (6.764). What Virgil does in the moment of that blush is endow her with the emotional possibilities she has been denied in her role as marriage object. At the final duel her presence is implied in the simile of the fighting bulls, which the heifers watch wondering whom all the herd will follow (12.718 ff.).

3.10 Camilla

When we first meet Camilla (see also 7.803–17 note), she is bringing up the rear of the catalogue, after Turnus (7.803 ff.), the final image of Book VII. She is an object of special fascination to the crowd – from the outset she is someone who draws our gaze, a collection of marvellous surfaces who herself is attracted by glitter (11.772 ff.): neither Virgil nor any of his critics ever seeks Camilla's private voice (11.664–724 note); she has an aura about her of the inhuman, or superhuman. (She is a falcon dismembering its catch without landing, 11.721 ff.) The peculiar prominence she is given is variously explained – she is a beautiful pendant to the catalogue;[110] the marginal exotic who diverts attention from and reveals the weakness in Turnus;[111] a counterpart to Penthesilea in position (last to be introduced), role (late defender of a besieged city) and destiny (female hero who will die in action), as Aeneas sees the Amazon depicted on the walls of Juno's temple (1.490 ff.);[112] a symptom of, from the Roman point of view, unnaturalness and therefore ultimate defeat for the Italians.[113] A mundane narrative reason is that in Book XI she provides the contrasting battle scene between that of Book X's Mezentius, who starts the catalogue (7.648), and that of Book XII's Turnus, who all but concludes it (7.783). Turnus and Mezentius from our first meeting with them both occupy our attention up to their final duels with Aeneas;[114] Camilla, however, having made her memorable entrance in Book VII, flouting the conventional domain of Roman women before it existed (see *Introduction* – 6.3.1 Women at Rome), vanishes until Turnus mentions her to the assembly (11.432). Then she bursts again onto the scene at the head of her troop and provides Book XI's heroic opposition to the Trojans while Turnus and Aeneas are elsewhere.

But this does not remotely account for her strangeness: as Book XI proceeds, after we have heard about her from Diana (11.535 ff.), she is made a more and more complicated set of opposites, dryad ('godlike' at 11.657) then Volscian citizen; woman votary/huntress of Diana then heroic warrior; simple rustic then princess with a taste for oriental accessories. We never learn why she allowed herself to be drawn into the war or how she became the Volscian commander (11.584 f., 11.499 note), where she acquired her retinue (11.655 ff.) or how she deploys her well-disciplined troops (11.500 f.). Her journey is from vulnerable girl rescued on one spear (11.552) to a virago-virgin ravished and made maternal by another (11.803–4 note, Arruns' javelin that sucks the blood at her breast); in between she is wholly at home in a man's world, counselling Turnus (11.502 ff.) and taking command in the cavalry battle in which she embarks on a blood-curdling *aristeia* (11.664 ff.), complete with taunts (11.686 ff.), that gains momentum until Arruns is her undoing – Arruns and her own 'woman's love of booty' (11.782), through which she reverts from a warrior intent on victory (7.805 ff.) to spoil-seeking huntress (11.780; see 9.176–8 note). She who came from Diana returns to Diana (11.593 f.).

On the battlefield her prowess overcomes all doubters. She addresses Turnus as an equal and expects him to treat her as one – he does,[115] calling her 'glory of Italy' (*decus Italiae*, 11.508, because she instantiates many aspects of the primitive hardiness and virtue that Roman nostalgia ascribed to their Italic ancestors, 9.603 ff., despite her purple and gold, 7.814 ff.) and pre-empting Arruns' word for her, 'disgrace' (*dedecus*). She is sensitive (11.687 ff.) to the sort of contempt for her woman's weapons to which Tarchon gives vent (11.732 ff.[116]) and that she receives from the son of Aunus (11.705 ff.) – having uttered it to her face he does not live long to regret it. As a woman of action she joins Penthesilea, Dido and Cleopatra in the pages of the *Aeneid* – 'she seems to embody Virgil's literary version of the Roman practice of visually presenting defeated peoples and nations through female personifications'.[117] After her death she remains an inspiration to her compatriots (11.892).

Transgressive as she is, Camilla by her ambush and death might be viewed as reinforcing the Roman stereotype of womanliness that she has rejected (**the distaff and wool-basket of Minerva** / *Minerva's spools and baskets filled with wool*, 7.805 – see *Introduction* – 6.3.2 Women in the *Aeneid*).[118] After all, her effectiveness in battle is betrayed when, as a woman, she is attracted to Chloreus' ornaments and her last words can be taken as urging Turnus to abandon his ambush (11.826 f.), which fatally he does: so she should have stuck to her knitting, a message terribly delivered by the feminising spear of Arruns. But if Virgil's aim were really to reinforce a stereotype of women he has gone a very long way about doing so. And on further consideration the phrase 'woman's love of booty' comes apart (11.782 note) – what really matters is the general 'love of booty', also displayed by men, which exposes her to Arruns' stealth. As for her last words, they are first and foremost those of a soldier urging the defence of the city – if they are strategically flawed (and they do not automatically mean, 'Abandon the ambush') the flaw is not a feminine one; they might not even have reached Turnus, who reacts not to them but to the situation Acca describes (11.898 ff.). In open combat, Camilla is undefeated (unlike Mezentius and Turnus); yet she never ceases to be womanly – as a huntress, Etruscan mothers wanted her as their daughter-in-law (11.581 f.), despite her determined chastity (11.582 ff.); as a warrior, she is continually referred to as 'maiden' (*virgo*).[119] Virgil seems to be confronting us with a thought-experiment, presenting in Turnus and Tarchon two possible reactions to it and leaving us to make up our Roman or non-Roman minds whether Camilla is aberrant or the conventions she defies arbitrary. It is typical of Virgil to provide evidence for either view.

CHAPTER 4
THE GODS AND FATE

4.1 Greek versus Roman gods[1]

Before the fourth century BCE, the Romans had mapped deities of Italy onto the main deities of Greece.[2] By the time poetry was being written in Latin, the mapping was complete.[3] Thus 'Saturn' took on the mythology of the Greek 'Cronus', father of Zeus (Jupiter) and Hera (Juno), presiding over the Golden Age.[4] Such syncretism was not confined to the Romans – Hannibal in honouring Juno Lacinia[5] was linking her with Tanit (1.13), and with good reason: such a celestial amalgamation was prudent religion and shrewd diplomacy. The following ready reckoner is for the twelve gods of Mount Olympus:

Greek	Roman	Domain
Zeus	Jupiter	King of the gods; weather, justice, hospitality
Hera	Juno	Queen of the gods; marriage and childbirth
Poseidon	Neptune	Sea; horses
Demeter	Ceres	Corn; agriculture
Athena	Minerva / Athena	Wisdom; handicrafts; war
Apollo	Apollo	Sun; prophecy; arts; archery; medicine; plague
Artemis (sister of Apollo)	Diana	Moon; hunting; chastity; archery; childbirth
Ares	Mars	Agriculture (the Italic Mars only); war
Aphrodite	Venus	Love; beauty
Hephaestus	Vulcan	Fire; blacksmithing; volcanoes
Hermes	Mercury	Messenger of the gods; guide of the dead; trade; thievery; eloquence
Hestia	Vesta	Hearth; family
OR (in the twelve Olympians the late-comer Dionysus sometimes replaces Hestia)		
Dionysus / Bacchus	Bacchus	Wine; ecstasy; theatre

The table shows how these were gods of this world, not outside it – they themselves were created beings associated with specific areas of human life; they 'resided' on a mountain. They were also adopted by cities or families, such as Jupiter by Rome, and Venus by the Julian *gens*: the Olympian gods were heavily politicized.

Virgil, like all his epic predecessors, inherited the Olympians as part of the epic apparatus from Homer, in whom they are worshipped by Greeks and Trojans alike (a poetic fiction that made the Trojans comprehensible – contrast Cleopatra's menagerie of Egyptian gods, 8.698). In addition to the Olympians, the *Aeneid* is populated by minor Roman gods, especially those of the hearth and home (4.5.5) and gives prominence to one goddess who never shed her exotic origins, Cybele (4.5.6).

Family is as important on Olympus as on earth; the relationships are confusing because of Jupiter's insatiable appetite for incest (with sister, aunt, cousin and great-granddaughter) – all the Olympians are either his siblings or his offspring:

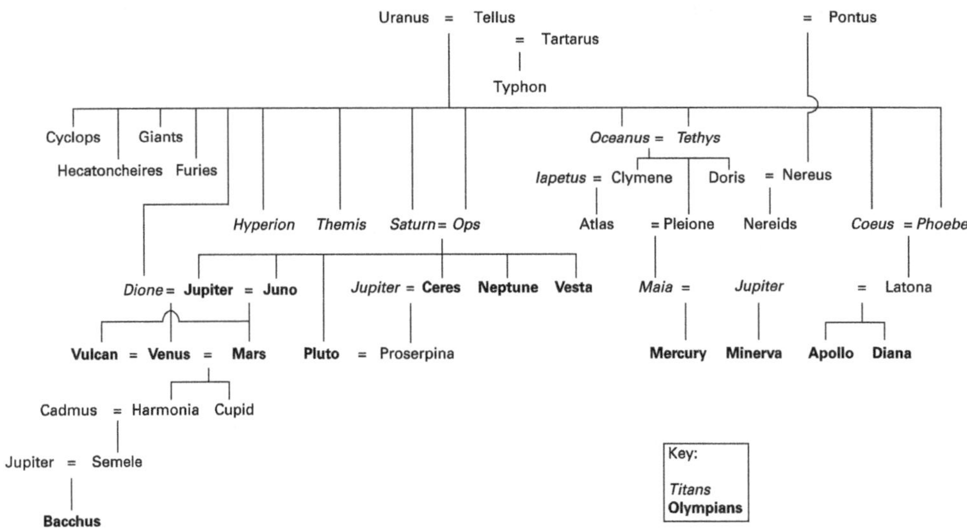

4.2 Olympian gods in Homer[6]

Neither Greek nor Roman mythology had an 'Authorized Version', a Bible or Koran to which devotees could refer for truths about the gods. Instead poets were the sources and they were free to embroider or reinvent: artistic conviction replaced theology. Pindar wrote,[7] 'Grace of song, which makes for mortals all soothing joys,... often makes believed what is not to be believed.' Preeminent in their influence were Homer and Hesiod,[8] because they were so early and so comprehensive in their coverage of divine affairs – they were the systematizers.[9] Thus in Homer the 'blessed' (*makares*) gods, in contrast with 'wretched' (*deiloi*) mortals, are unfamiliar with physical pain[10] and never know death; they enliven their humdrum eternity through rows,[11] betrayals[12] and feasting[13] and are only rendered serious when they engage with human affairs (invited or not).[14]

There was, nevertheless, opposition to this frivolous anthropomorphic amorality; it relied on an intuitive notion of what gods should be like. The philosopher Xenophanes (sixth century BCE) wrote:[15]

Homer and Hesiod attributed to the gods everything which in mankind is a disgrace and reproach: stealing, committing adultery and deceiving one another.

Xenophanes imagines a supreme deity who does not pop up here or there but, 'without toil brandishes everything in the scope of his mind' and 'always remains in the same place, not moving at all'.[16] This was a different way of looking at the gods from that of the poets, a philosopher's way; and, although framed as a corrective, it laid the ground for poetry to operate under separate rules.

Two main lines of defence evolved for Homer's and Hesiod's treatment of myth:[17] **allegorization**, where the gods and their behaviour stand for something else (such as Ares for folly, or the battle of the gods for the contest between elemental qualities in nature – hot and cold, light and heavy); or **rationalization**, where mythical beings, including the gods, become exaggerations of real beings (so Cerberus, with his poisonous bite, was in fact a snake). These defences would develop into more extreme forms of reductionism – explaining what the gods represent through their (supposed) etymology,[18] or postulating a historical incident to underlie a whole story.[19] The modern urge to factor out divine intervention as a shaft of human thought or emotion, or the force of human temperament, is heir to these approaches.[20]

For Plato's Socrates, however, when it came to formulating an educational programme for guardians of a city, these defences were famously not enough:[21]

'"No, by heaven," said he, "I do not myself think that <such stories> are fit to be told." "Neither must we admit at all," said I, "that gods war with gods and plot against one another and contend—for it is not true either . . .

'". . . the battles of the gods in Homer's verse are things that we must not admit into our city either wrought in allegory or without allegory. For the young are not able to distinguish what is and what is not allegory, but whatever opinions are taken into the mind at that age are wont to prove indelible and unalterable."'

(Trans. Storey)

In reaction to such immoderate censorship, Aristotle took a different stance. It followed from his definition of poetry's aim, to achieve a catharsis of pity and fear by the portrayal (*mimesis*) of action:[22] what is 'correct' in poetic terms is what makes the impact the poet wishes – 'correctness is not the same thing in ethics and poetry, nor in any other art and poetry'.[23] He continues, in his pared-down way:[24]

If it is neither true nor as it ought to be, one might reply that this is what people say; e.g. stories about the gods: it may be that talking like that is neither an idealization nor the truth, and perhaps Xenophanes was right; but at any rate, that is what people say.

(Trans. Heath)

In other words, if people in general 'talk like that' (i.e. in the myths that they circulate) they will understand a poet talking in the same vein (and possibly, though Aristotle does not say so, innovating beyond what is circulated). Ancient commentaries, the scholia, on Homer survive in manuscript margins and sometimes take the Aristotelian line, more often that of the allegorist or rationalist.

So, when a Homeric god impels a mortal to act in a particular way, who is responsible for what follows? The reductive answer would be 'the human', the Aristotelian answer 'the god' – but in truth we, ancient or modern, are expected to hover, or alternate, between the two. Diomedes says of Achilles sulking, 'He'll fight again when his heart tells him to, and when the god moves him.'[25] This simultaneous allocation of responsibility has been called 'double determination' (or 'over-determination');[26] it is what Lyne in the *Aeneid* describes as the god 'working with' existing human tendencies,[27] though we also witness the gods sometimes working against human tendencies, without removing ownership of the action.[28] Through such double determination Homer conveys with economy and paradoxical realism a character's internal conflict. Thus, when the disguised Aphrodite tells Helen to go to Paris, Helen stands up to her and she, revealing herself, intimidates Helen into obedience: thereby we know that, when Helen actually goes to Paris, it is under a form of compulsion; thereby, too, Helen's concurrent revulsion from and desire for Paris are made concrete.[29] We have two complete views of her action; in circumstances where we might speak mysteriously of 'diminished responsibility' (we can differ on how far it is diminished), a god has plugged the diminution. All the while, as Aristotle would remind us, the poet is not concerned with ethics but with emotional vividness.

4.3 Olympian gods in the *Aeneid*[30]

Roman religion, unlike Greek, as well as inheriting the mythology of Homer and Hesiod, contained a strain of what we would regard as animism and sympathetic magic (Evander at 8.347 ff., see 4.5.5).[31] It was also an affair of state. When the Epicurean speaker in Cicero's *On the Nature of the Gods* affirms,[32] 'we ought to combat <fables culled from the ancient traditions of the Greeks>, so that religion may not be undermined', he means by 'religion' the panoply of state ceremonies through which a healthy relationship with the gods was maintained (see *Introduction* – 6.4.1 State religion). This was about ritual, not stories; its observance was a manifestation of *pietas*.

So for Virgil his Homeric inheritance and the nature of religious worship at Rome were at variance. All the same, both he and his readers were used to taking epic poetry on its own terms, in which the gods had personalities, motivations and back history (put amply on display in the Proem to Book I). More than that, Virgil and at least his more erudite readers[33] were aware of scholiasts' commentaries[34] and of the critical traditions on which they relied.[35] Nisus is the voice of reductionism in the poem (9.184 f.): **'Is it the gods who put this ardour into our minds, or does every man's irresistible desire become his god?'** / *'do the gods light this fire in our hearts or does each man's mad desire become his god?'* If Nisus' second alternative is sufficient explanation of supposed divinity, the narrative loses any divine dimension – or at least Homer's. But Virgil, though he shows no god spurring Nisus on, in other situations regularly opts for Nisus' first alternative:[36] for his purposes, the gods are real and they intervene in human affairs. Above all, look at Juno: if she does no more than embody obstructive chaos in human affairs, the poem falls limp: obstructive chaos does not bear grudges. Like Aeneas at Troy (2.622 f.), however, we are given a glimpse of a very determined deity in operation: she, the root cause of so much disruption, even provides the structure of the poem (4.5.2).

Virgil's gods, then, are still Homer's gods. Virgil, however, shows more respect to divine dignity than Homer – the limits of scandal are set by Venus seducing her own husband (Book VIII), and sparring is verbal (between Juno and Venus, privately in Book IV, or publicly in Book X). Virgil refers to Jupiter's misdemeanours (Electra and Ganymede at 1.28; Ganymede again at 5.252; a Garymantian nymph raped at 4.198, Juturna likewise at 12.141) but moves swiftly on.

Fate in Homer is also more clearly 'the will of Zeus'[37] than it is 'the will of Jupiter' in the *Aeneid* (see 4.4):

1. Virgil places the gods in a triangular relationship with humanity and Fate (see 4.4): only Jupiter and possibly Apollo have complete knowledge of Fate – other gods are prophetic[38] (so Faunus, 7.81 ff.), as are the dead in the underworld (so Anchises in Book VI) or when returning to visit mortals (so Hector, 2.294 f.), but their knowledge is partial; other gods again are ignorant of it (so Venus consulting Jupiter in Books I and X). Fate does not govern the future of the gods themselves, but when it comes to terrestrial affairs is non-negotiable.

2. Virgil makes Fate determine the poem's goal (the foundation of Rome) and sets another of the gods, Juno, against it. In this he was influenced by his epic forebears, Naevius and Ennius (see *Introduction* – 3.2.2 Aeneas between the *Iliad* and the *Aeneid*: The Aeneas legend, as well as by Poseidon in the *Odyssey* (see 1.1–7 note). The mighty tug-of-war Virgil sets up is his own; by it he divides the gods, who either serve Juno in obstructing Fate, or Jupiter (and Venus) by nudging it on its way. Against the background of this struggle, the *Aeneid*'s divine perspective, shorn if it can be of its involvement in human affairs, is strangely parochial – Neptune concerned about unforecast storms (1.124) and Vulcan the manager of a busy production line (8.439 ff.).

Virgil describes divine intervention more impressionistically than Homer. Compared to Aphrodite's visit to Helen (4.2), the visit of Cupid to Dido (1.715 ff. – see 1.695–722 note) or Allecto's to Amata (7.349 ff. – see 7.341–72 note) are confusing interactions of the physical and the psychological, but confusing in a way that profoundly fits the inner turmoil they generate. Even Virgil's pellucid description of Mercury delivering Jupiter's message to Aeneas (4.238 ff.), is complicated by the later visitation (4.556 ff.), if it is a visitation at all. It could be a dream, the figure in it an impersonation of Mercury; just for a moment it casts doubt on the definiteness of the previous apparition. So we, the audience, are also troubled by the gods, even though to us they are manifested in action more clearly than to anyone in the poem – except, on one isolated occasion, to Aeneas (at Troy, 2.622 f.). Virgil must intend this; nowhere does he admit to vagueness in his own knowledge of the divine machinery, even if he sometimes leaves us uncertain how that machinery is working:[39] when he prays to the Muse to tell him Juno's grievances (1.8 ff.), the Muse immediately and comprehensively obliges (1.12 ff.).

Thus Virgil's Olympians are as pungent as Homer's but more alien (see 4.5 on the individual gods). For all their involvement with human affairs, they are cool towards the objects of their interest, riddle in what they reveal to them and bring them neither justice nor consolation. There is something amiss when the sole god who not only shows pity for a mortal unrelated to him/her but also acts on it is Juno (for Dido, 4.697 ff.; for Turnus, 10.611 ff.) – the gods pity passively at 10.758 ff.; Diana appreciates Camilla's devotion and mourns her end (11.593) but does nothing to prolong her life (11.587 ff.). Certainly, Venus claims to have wept for Aeneas

(8.380), whom she helps – but he is her son; Juturna pours forth tears for Turnus (12.154), whom she helps – but he is her brother. There is no equivalent to Homer's Athena delighting at Odysseus' wiliness.[40]

4.4 Fate

The word *Fatum* in Latin basically means 'what is stated':[41] it derives from the word *for*, meaning 'I say' (1.261–2 note) – also the origin of *Fama* ('rumour', 'reputation'); these are the stable and the unstable extremes of utterance (combined at 8.731) – and *Fatum* can be unclear where *Fama* can be misleading. *Fatum* can mean as little as 'death' (**Perhaps you may want to know how Priam died.** / *Perhaps you wonder how Priam met his end.* (2.504));[42] or it can mean the preordained future, at least for mankind.[43] In the latter, more philosophical, sense it is akin (but not identical) to the Stoic belief in a divine mind exercising ultimate control, such as was denied by Epicureans, who believed that the chance movements of atoms were the root of causation (see *Introduction* – 5.5 Stoicism, Epicureanism and the *Aeneid*).

The *Aeneid* does not analyse fate. Nevertheless, as the poem proceeds Virgil's 'Fate' becomes defined in terms of 'what leads to Rome's future'.[44] It shares history's fixity[45] and can plausibly be construed as history's continuation beyond the present[46] – with the important provisos that it is not exhaustive: it does not state everything that will happen,[47] and may skimp on the how or when. Vulcan says fate would have allowed Troy to last another ten years (8.938 f.); Jupiter postpones Turnus' day of reckoning (10.624 f.). So human decision-making and divine interference matter, not only because through them Fate will be fulfilled[48] – Fate of itself 'does' nothing[49] – but also because they can operate in its many gaps (see 10.113 note). Juno accepts what she cannot change (Aeneas coming to Italy and marrying Lavinia) but sets about delaying this outcome and doing whatever damage she can to it, hollowing it of any content (7.315 ff. – see also 7.293–4 note). Prophecy, if humans interpret it correctly, reveals the outlines of Fate but also gives a margin for manoeuvre within them.

Thus the *Aeneid* presents a narrative in which fortune (*fortuna*[50]), 'how things turn out' is made up of (1) *fatum*, 'what is stated'; (2) what is not yet stated as *fatum* but still might be (if, for example, Cybele asks Jupiter – 9.94 ff.); and (3) what *fatum* does not cover at all.[51] The past can be divided up similarly into (1) history that is recorded; (2) history still to be recorded, or to be amended; and (3) history that is irrecoverable: at the start of his journey through the underworld (Book VI), Aeneas encounters Palinurus, Dido and Deiphobus who, from among the crowd of nameless souls, come to complete and correct his ideas of the recent past.[52] It is a warning to watch out for the detail Anchises omits when he sets out Rome's future.

What of Jupiter? Does Jupiter will something because it is fated (i.e. predetermined by whatever *Fatum* describes) or is something fated because Jupiter wills it?[53] This makes a difference because Jupiter, unlike Fate, was accessible through prayer and sacrifice – or filial wheedling. For Venus, Jupiter decides Fate (1.241 note) and Jupiter addresses her consolingly as if he did, saying of the Romans, **'On them I impose no limits of time or place. I have given them an empire that will know no end.'** / *'On them I set no limits, space or time. I have granted them power, empire without end.'* (1.278 f.); later Helenus would have it that Jupiter allocates individual Fate (3.375 f.); and when negotiating with Juno, Jupiter acts without Fate constraining him (12.830 ff.); Fate here is what Jupiter has spoken and cannot afterwards unspeak. But then Vulcan speaks of Jupiter and Fate as independent – 'neither the all-powerful Father nor Fate' (8.398) – and Jupiter himself talks of Fate as outside himself (1.257 f., though he adds that he has not **changed his mind**, 1.260; cf. 10.471 f., 10.622 ff.); at one point he slyly pretends to leave Fate to 'find its own way' (10.113); and he puts the fates of Turnus and Aeneas in the scales to see, or show, whose will win out (12.725). One commentator concludes,[54] 'Juppiter [*sic*] does not create the decrees of fate … but they are identical with his will.' It seems fairer to say that Jupiter's relationship with Fate is not meant to be consistent throughout the poem; it bends to fit the circumstances.

Whatever that relationship, Jupiter's prophecy to Venus depicts progress, progress not only to Rome but onwards to Augustus (1.261 ff.). Fate and Rome justify each other (see *Introduction – 1 Historical Background*). Ultimately, however, what classifies as Fate in the poem is set by the poet, in turn influenced by his literary precursors;[55] he is therefore not so much concerned with its justification as in the cost to his characters of its fulfilment. Aeneas in distress declares, **'It is not by my own will that I search for Italy.'** / *'I set sail for Italy – all against my will.'* (4.361); Turnus, not remarkable for his insight into Fate (9.136–8 note)[56] comes as close as he can to realizing it has doomed him when he asks, **'What stroke of Fortune could grant me safety now?'** / *'What new twist of Fortune can save me now?'* (12.637). Juno's plots may have made the casualty list far longer, but Fate itself knows no mercy, even towards the innocent.[57]

Thus Fate becomes one of the poles of narrative tension, the other being Juno's wrath. We know from the Proem the poem's direction of travel even before Jupiter expounds it to Venus: the *Aeneid* will be a long exercise in retardation. What we cannot know are the vicissitudes of the characters on the way, or what will mark the resolution of the contest between Fate and Juno, especially given Jupiter's habitual disengagement. As Venus asks reproachfully on behalf of the Trojans (1.241), **'O great king, what end do you set to their labours?'** / *'What end, great king, do you set to their ordeals?'*

4.5 Gods in particular

4.5.1 Jupiter

At his first appearance (1.223) and again at his last (12.853) Jupiter is looking down from the upper air (*aether* – **height of heaven** / **high heaven**). This is his domain, the layer above Juno's *aer* (see 4.5.2); he is supreme in vision and power. When Venus has accosted him crossly, he looks on her with the benevolence that **clears** [literally 'makes serene'] **the sky and dispels storms** / *… calms tempests* (1.255; cf. 10.101 ff.). From this we might expect a ruler of the gods who keeps his house in order.

We have, by this first appearance, already met some of Jupiter's family: the wife implacably opposed to Aeneas and the daughter (not by Juno), Aeneas' mother. As the divine face of Fate (an allegory for 'history') and future tribal god of Rome, the 'father of gods and men' is already committed to one side – even though impartiality might have been required from the god of justice.[58] Compromised by his domestic quandary, Jupiter is for all his power[59] primarily reactive, accommodating both goddesses as far as he can and leaving Fate to its own devices – until, that is, it becomes bogged down in Juno's quagmires. Aeneas mentions Jupiter in dispatches during Book II, as presiding over Troy's destruction (Zeus' promise to Hera in the *Iliad* – 2.617–18 note) but then answering Anchises' prayer at the family's departure (2.689 ff.) and making way for Lavinia through the loss of Creusa (2.779). Juno's storm, which either he has not noticed or has done nothing to avert, moves Venus to complain that he has gone back on his promises (1.237); he confirms to her the destiny of Rome (1.257 ff.) and sends Mercury to Carthage to smooth the Trojans' path (1.297 ff.). After ensuring the Trojans' safe arrival in Carthage, he takes his eyes off the situation; wife and daughter scheme (4.90 ff.). It takes Iarbas to alert him (4.219 f.); off goes Mercury again, this time to shock Aeneas into resuming his voyage (4.223 ff.). In Sicily, Jupiter steps in once more to arrest the damage Juno's fire is causing to the fleet (5.693 ff.) – it must have sunk in by this time that she is the source of the trouble (12.804 f.). In Italy, his help to the Trojans is intermittent – he arranges the omen of eating tables (7.110, 7.142) and, when Ascanius targets Numanus Remulus, answers his prayer (9.630 f.). Now, however, the Trojans are in a perilous predicament, Aeneas far off and the mission of Nisus and Euryalus scotched: only when Turnus, invigorated by Juno (9.764) has burst into the Trojan camp does Jupiter finally dispatch Iris to call her to order (9.803 f.). The council of the gods (10.1 ff.), which Jupiter summons immediately, might seem his opportunity to halt a war that he claims he had forbidden (10.8). Rather it exemplifies Jupiter's evasive diplomacy: he brokers no deal between the goddesses, instead pretending to leave matters to Fate (10.113) – which he does not (see 10.1–117 note). Juno, who has been more circumspect since Jupiter's assembly (at last he is now watching[60]), has at the prospect of peace reverted to her usual subterfuge and recruited Juturna (12.142 ff.); Juturna in obedience stages a fake portent, debasing the language of communication between gods and men, through Jupiter's eagle (12.247 ff.). No reaction from Jupiter, not even when the truce, to which both sides have sworn in his name (12.178, 12.200), is ruptured. The poet himself upbraids Jupiter (12.503 f.) for apparently allowing a war that obstructs Fate. Aeneas and Turnus are at last deciding matters between themselves when Jupiter grasps the nettle he has avoided for so long (12.791 ff.). His settlement with Juno, permitting the Trojans in victory to be swallowed up by the Italians, delights her (12.841; see 12.791–842 note). At this point he might simply call off Juturna and allow the duel to play itself out to its fated conclusion. Instead he sends a Fury (or near relative) to displace her and befuddle Turnus (12.843 ff., 12.843–86 note). He is not stealing Juno's tactics; we learn he sends the Fury regularly (12.851 f.) – Virgil calls him 'the savage king' (12.849). He is, after all, Juno's brother as well as husband.

In all of this he shows a complete lack of emotion – no anger, no grief, only an indulgent smile, with one of the poem's great symmetries, to daughter (1.254) and to wife (12.829).[61] This is not the Zeus of the *Iliad*, watching vigilantly from Mt Ida, stringing Hera up with anvils tied to her feet or dispensing good and evil to men from his two jars.[62] Although he is the poem's most perfect Stoic (sexual liaisons apart – 4.198 note), and counsels Hercules against giving in to feeling (10.466 ff.), he is the very opposite of the divine mind in which the Stoics believed: not aloof, not a reference point for justice,[63] but enmeshed in celestial and domestic politics while administrating Fate (his own wishes) on earth with exasperating sluggishness.

4.5.2 Juno

Juno, like Jupiter, has local allegiances (to Samos and to Carthage, as the latter's goddess Tanit, 1.15 f.); but she has also, unlike Jupiter, very particular personal grievances (against him and against Paris, 1.25–33). Her element is the lower air (*aer*, also in Greek – cf. 'Hera'),[64] also associated with clouds.[65] Virgil uses this location distinct from Jupiter's to symbolize, when she leaves it (12.842), the eventual (transient) rapprochement between the two (12.792 note).

Unlike Jupiter,[66] she is also prepared to descend and act on earth without an intermediary (at the head of a crowd breaking open Janus' temple, 7.620 ff.; making a dummy Aeneas, 10.633 ff.). For the most part the poem observes their separation, and Juno operates invisible to, or at least unnoticed by, her spouse (but see 9.802–5 note).

Thus she is able, as long as Jupiter is quiescent, to take the initiative – and taking the initiative is what she always does, except at the assembly of the gods (10.62 ff.).[67] Her initiatives provoke responses from Venus and Jupiter, the former protecting her family and the latter trying to ensure that Fate does not become merely an empty letter. These responses in turn invite further action from Juno.

	Juno	Venus	Jupiter
Book I	Rouses storm to wreck Trojan fleet; remains an ominous presence when Dido and Aeneas meet at her temple	Pleads to Jupiter to intervene; reassured herself, goes to her son to tell him of Dido and of his fleet's rescue; causes Dido to fall in love with Aeneas	Reassures Venus and sends Mercury to ease the Trojan's passage to Carthage
Book IV	Proposes to Venus that Dido and Aeneas should be married and that she (Juno) and Venus should share dominion over them; finally sends Iris to end Dido's suffering	Accepts Juno's proposal knowing it falls foul of Fate	Hears Iarbas' prayer and sends Mercury to dislodge Aeneas and the Trojans and send them on their way
Book V	Sends Iris to stir up the Trojan women	Calls on Neptune to ensure the Trojans' safe crossing from Sicily to Italy	Extinguishes by a heavy downpour the blaze at the ships
Book VII	Sends Allecto to corrupt Amata and Turnus and to stir up war		
Book VIII		Provides Aeneas with weapons	
Book IX	Inspires Turnus in his attack on the Trojan camp		Orders Juno to back off and allow Turnus to be repelled
Book X	Casts war in Italy as an extension of the Trojan war and Aeneas as the belligerent Asks Jupiter if she can remove Turnus from the fight; when given permission, makes a decoy Aeneas from cloud	Attacks Juno for persecuting the Trojans and Jupiter for allowing it	Calls assembly at which proclaims official non-interference Allows Juno to give Turnus a short extension
Book XII	Persuades Juturna to help her brother Turnus (implying that she can break the truce)	Heals Aeneas' arrow-wound; returns his spear to him	Agrees a settlement with Juno; dispatches the **Dira** / *Fury* to remove Juturna and bemuse Turnus

The importance of Juno's interventions in Books I and XII is underlined by the corresponding mirror-interventions of Jupiter in in Book I (1.263 f.), his promise to Venus that Aeneas will be victorious and lay the foundations of a city, and Book XII, his settlement with Juno and the Fury's mission (12.834 ff., 12.853 ff.). The importance of her intervention in Book VII is brought out by the second invocation to the Muse (particularly 7.40), as her Book I intervention was prepared for in the invocation that all but opens the poem (1.8 ff.). She thereby sets up its entire framework. Within it, she builds a crescendo: her meddling in Books I–V is quickly counteracted, but that of Book VII takes all the remaining books to undo. More than contributing structure to the narrative, she is the underlying cause of what happens in it (1.1–7 note – Fate, of itself, causes nothing): new order must, apparently, be generated through violent disorder. In pique she views her stratagems as competing with Fate (**'A curse on that detested race of Phrygians and on their destiny, so opposed to our own!'** / **'*That cursed race I loathe – their Phrygian fate that clashes with my own!'* 7.293 f. – and 7.293–4 note). Her schemes, however, actually play into its hands – the marriage of Dido and Aeneas lights the long fuse to the destruction of Carthage; the Trojan women left behind on Sicily found Segesta, which rejected Carthage in favour of Rome during the First Punic War;[68] her settlement with Jupiter may obliterate the name of Troy, but allows the continuance of the blood line that will revive that name again, in such works as the *Aeneid*.

Juno's outstanding trait is wrath, pernicious and unremitting. In the *Iliad*, Hera is primarily treacherous – plotting to bind Zeus, seducing him as a diversionary ploy, lying to him.[69] The *Aeneid*'s Juno in her vengeful rage resembles more closely the Poseidon of the *Odyssey* (1.1–7 note) or the *Iliad*'s Achilles; yet both of these relinquish their anger, even if in Achilles' case he has to be careful not to flare up again.[70] Juno, it can be argued (12.791–842 note), relinquishes only part of hers – enough for Jupiter to broker a deal. In her occasional *furor*, Juno is also remarkable because it does not cloud her judgement (2.613, 10.62; compare Hercules, 4.5.4 further; on *furor*, see 1.1–7 note, **because of the fierce and unrelenting anger of Juno**): she is always frighteningly effective. As well as wrathful, she is vain (e.g. 1.48 f., on her need for worship) and callous (e.g. 4.101 ff., sacrificing Dido), but arguably no more so than any other god.[71] And, of a sudden, Juno can show a capacity for pity (4.3); as a victim of Jupiter's faithlessness (1.28) she, disconcertingly, acquires more human depth than any of the other gods.

4.5.3 Venus

Venus is goddess (of erotic love) and mother of Aeneas, not to mention of the whole Roman race;[72] as immortal daughter of Jupiter and grandmother of Ascanius she is the second of four generations in the poem, its greatest champion of a family survival that only makes sense among mortals. She is reminiscent of the *Iliad*'s Thetis, immortal mother of the mortal Achilles, but completely unlike her: Thetis is weighed down by the tragedy of her forced marriage to Peleus and the doom of her son;[73] Venus, though she cries when it suits her (1.228, 1.227–8 note), remains Homer's smiling (often translated 'laughter-loving') goddess,[74] who has indeed the last laugh: her son will live, and see his descendants thrive; she never rues her affair with Anchises, even though it too was forced upon her.[75]

Virgil relishes Venus' paradox (as both goddess and mother of a mortal)[76] and exploits it to give Venus' exchanges with her father and her son, and with the other gods, their peculiar piquancy. The pattern for Venus is to behave among the gods as mother stopping at nothing to champion her human posterity and towards her son Aeneas as unapproachable goddess (with one brief exception). Thus when she addresses Jupiter in Book I, she speaks of 'my Aeneas' (1.231) and identifies with the Trojans – **'As for us, your own children'** / *'We, your own children'* (1.251): Jupiter is the *pater familias*, through whom all family decisions must pass (see *Introduction* – 6.2.1 *Familia*). Immediately after this, Venus appears to Aeneas – but as a young huntress, whom he takes for Diana or a nymph, 1.329); she tells him Dido's background as a double love story, that of Dido for Sychaeus and of Pygmalion for gold (1.338 ff.); but she tells him only what it fits her disguise to know (so nothing of overarching Fate); and when she vanishes, she reveals her divine identity in the flash of her neck and the scent of her hair (1.432 ff.).[77] Aeneas' agonized protest, that she has cheated him so often even of the touch of her hand and sound of her own voice (1.408 f.), is belied in Book II, when he recounts how she appeared in her own person and took his right arm before showing him the other gods as wreckers and guiding him safely back to his house (2.589 ff.). But there she is still goddess, not mother, even as she calls him 'child'. In Book I, we next see her in the heavens with her son Cupid, pleading with him (and misrepresenting the situation) to help his brother Aeneas (1.664 ff.) – while on earth her work continues to be that of divine obfuscation, as Cupid substitutes for her grandson (Ascanius), deceiving Aeneas and rendering Dido infatuated (1.712 ff.). This manipulation continues in Book IV, when Juno, who does not know what Venus knows, tries to exploit her desire to make Aeneas secure in Carthage (4.93 ff.); and in Book V, where she pleads with Neptune on behalf of the 'ashes and bones' of Troy (5.787), which he unhesitatingly understands to mean 'Aeneas' (5.804). In Book VIII, she applies her erotic powers to Vulcan so that he will make armour for Aeneas; and in Book X, before the assembly of the gods: she identifies once more with the Trojans (10.42) and, as a measure of her outrage at their treatment, offers Aeneas himself in sacrifice for the survival of Ascanius (10.46 ff.) – safe in the knowledge that Jupiter would not, and could not, accept.

The memorable exception to her aloofness towards Aeneas comes when Venus, delivering as goddess (8.608 ff.) the weapons she has commissioned, fleetingly embraces her son (8.615). It is over in a moment, because such a great gift admits of no distractions.

Venus' self-demarcation makes her an enigma. She undoubtedly watches over Aeneas, not merely her own image:[78] in Book XII, as well as descending invisibly to heal his arrow wound (12.411 ff.) she implants the idea of attacking Latinus' city to precipitate the final duel (12.554). Aeneas knows that she cares, and declares to her (as the huntress) that he has been following her guidance (1.382 – as in Book II, 2.620; or as he will at 5.24, the return to Eryx – 5.21–5 note). All the same, Aeneas' complaint that she has shown him no affection carries weight, the greater for Venus' chilling gambit before the divine assembly. Other than that one hug, she remains for Aeneas untouchable and untouched: just after Aeneas has complained as much, she retires to Paphos in the best of spirits, to steep herself in incense and fresh garlands (1.415 ff.).

4.5.4 Hercules

Hercules (in Greek 'Heracles') like Aeneas straddles the divide between mortal and immortal, though never as vulnerable; in the poem we meet him on both sides of it, as hero in Book VIII and god in Book X. Or rather he occupies, says Silk,[79] 'the no-man's-land that is also no-god's-land'; he is the epitome of brawn (hence his club) and brain (hence his bow); his versatility is also a literary phenomenon, since he is found in comedy and tragedy as well as epic.

The worship of Hercules was popular in Rome from the early Republic – Livy, telling the story of Hercules and Cacus (see 8.184–279 note), says[80] that Romulus retained the Greek rituals in honour of Hercules that had been established by Evander. The presence of Hercules' head on some Republican Roman coins, in the style of Greek examplars, corroborates this.[81] Livy adds,[82] 'This, out of all foreign rites, was the only one which Romulus adopted, as though he felt that an immortality won through courage, of which this was the memorial, would one day be his own reward.' In Virgil's day, the cult of Hercules attracted tithes from wealthy citizens,[83] revenues that seem to have been spent on a regular public feast such as Aeneas witnesses. Although there is no evidence other than the date of the triple triumph and his inclusion in the Salian hymn (8.280–305 note) that Augustus affected a Herculean image (unlike Pompey and Mark Antony[84]), in the *Aeneid*,[85] both he[86] and Aeneas[87] are associated with the hero, for his endurance and his subjugation of savagery but also because of his eventual deification (see also 8.275 note).[88] Horace praises[89] the man of tenacity and righteousness:

> By these merits Pollux and far-wandering Hercules reached the citadels of heaven.
> Augustus will recline in their company and sip nectar with shining lips.

For the Greeks, Heracles' immortality was simply his next step.[90] For the Romans, he merited it by public service – Stoic activity rather than Epicurean passivity. As Cicero put it:[91] 'For what better disposition is there among mankind than that of those who believe they were born to help, protect and preserve their fellows? Hercules has departed among the gods. He would never have gone there if he had not, while he was among men, prepared such a way for himself.' Paradoxically, Hercules is also the archetypal solitary: 'The man who is unable to share in the benefits of political association, or has no need to share in them because he is already self-sufficient, is no part of the *polis*, and must therefore be either a beast or a god.'[92] It is possible to view Hercules' most explosive violence as removing him from the human, impelling him towards the divine.[93] Aeneas is not stateless as Hercules was, but when he runs amok in Book X and is compared to the hundred-hander Aegaeon challenging Jupiter himself (10.565 ff., 10.565–70 note) he puts himself in a league beyond Turnus or Mezentius.

As Juno's victim,[94] Hercules has something else in common with Aeneas.[95] In Hercules' case, the offence was to be Jupiter's offspring from yet another liaison. The Hercules of Euripides' play of that name is driven mad by Iris at Juno's command after he has completed his labours, so that he kills his wife and children.[96] (In other versions, Hercules is driven mad before his labours, which he undertakes to expiate the murders he commits[97] – Virgil (8.292 f.) seems to follow that plot line.) The *Aeneid* shows a Hercules of strong human emotion, non-Stoic in the *furor* which erupts in him against Cacus (ll. 219, 228) and non-Olympian in the tears he sheds for Pallas (10.465). These will be matched when Aeneas weeps at Pallas' side (11.29) and then in *furor* slays Turnus (12.945) – except that, whereas Hercules comes round from his divinely-inflicted madness, the *Aeneid* leaves its final *furor* hanging.

4.5.5 Gods local, domestic and minor

Olympus is both a mountain in Thessaly and ubiquity, synonymous with 'heaven': from it Jupiter can see anything, if he chooses to look (e.g. 11.725 f.). Other Olympians rove more widely – Juno loves Carthage and Samos (4.5.2) and catches sight of Aeneas' fleet on the shores of Italy when 'returning' from Argos via Cape Pachynus in Sicily (7.286 ff.). In general the Olympian gods represent universals; they may be connected to places but not monopolized by them. Thus Roman Jupiter is Greek Zeus and Egyptian Ammon (Amun).

Nevertheless, Virgil hints that religious awe began, as it were, from the other end, from a vague sense of divine aura in a particular location: the hill that would become the Capitol, even covered in scrub and woodland, inspires fear in the country people; Evander remarks, '**This grove … is the home of some god, we know not which.**' / '*This grove … is a god's home, whatever god he is.*' (8.351 f.).[98] Thus Aeneas twice prays to the anonymous 'spirit of the place' (5.95, 7.136): no god could be nearer or more approachable, and less intertwined with Olympian intrigue[99]. This 'spirit' is one of a category of 'local gods' – a useful category even if it proves leaky: Tiberinus is firmly god of the river Tiber (8.31 ff.); Picus and Faunus (7.45–80 note) are progenitors of Latinus, but are not tied to Latium (outside the *Aeneid*, Faunus acquires horns and followers, like a Greek satyr,[100] and is often identified with the Greek Pan[101]); the nymph[102] Carmentis, despite her Latin name, is mother of Arcadian Evander (8.333–6 note); of Pallanteum's early rulers (8.357), Janus (7.177–82 note) has no Greek equivalent but Saturn is Greek Cronus and reigned in Latium only after he had been banished from heaven (8.319 f.). The nymph Juturna (10.439 note) is from Ardea, being Turnus' sister, but is a goddess of lakes and rivers further afield (12.139 ff.). Despite this fluidity, there is a strong feeling in the *Aeneid* that Virgil is attaching the Trojans and their Penates to the gods of Italy. Faunus (7.98 ff.), Tiberinus (8.35 ff.) and Carmentis (8.340 f.) all further Aeneas' cause by predicting his settlement and his descendants' future greatness. Even Juturna, his opponent, will give her name to a pool in the Roman Forum (the *lacus Juturnae*). In the Georgics,[103] Virgil praises country life over urban stress in terms of its gods:

> But fortunate too is the man who is friends with the country gods –
> Pan and old Silvanus and the sisterhood of nymphs.

(Trans. Day Lewis)

The most local of all gods were those associated with home: as well as the *pater familias'* protecting spirit (*genius*)[104] and its own miniature Vesta, the house would have (like Evander's, 8.543) its Lar (strictly a god of boundaries, tied to a specific place[105]) and its Penates (1.1–7 end of note; protectors of the pantry, and portable[106]). They were peculiarly Roman, the divine aspect of the everyday. They were worshipped at mealtimes (5.62, 7.121)[107] and greeted when leaving and returning home;[108] they guarded the household.[109] Both the Lar and the Penates had a public equivalent;[110] in the case of the Penates, they belonged to the city. Thus when Anchises on Aeneas' shoulders carries the Penates (2.717 ff.), they are at once civic and domestic: Aeneas' family represents Troy.

Closely tied to the family, but to a tomb[111] rather than the house, are the spirits of the dead. 'Consider dead kinsfolk as gods,' says Cicero;[112] and their spirits were venerated, at least within the calendar of Roman festivals,[113] where they were buried (see *Introduction* 6.4.3 Personal religion). Misenus (6.234 f.), Palinurus (6.381) and Caieta (7.3 f.) all give their names to the sites of their graves: they are the first Trojans to take ownership of Italy.

Minor deities without local associations also populate the *Aeneid*,[114] often given their own particular functions – Cupid does his mother's behest in love just as Opis does Diana's in archery and Aeolus (storms), Iris (messages) and the Furies (discord and destruction) do Juno's or Jupiter's; the Tritons and Nereids attend on Neptune (5.823 ff.); the muse, acolyte of Apollo,[115] is invoked by the poet (1.8, 7.37, 7.64; cf. 9.77, 9.525, 10.163) to provide otherwise inaccessible information (e.g. on Juno's psychology, or on the panorama of Latium). These are not rococo ornaments but characterize their summoners: Cupid is as frivolous as his mother (1.689, 1.696, cf. 1.314 ff.); Juno hides behind her envoys (so that when Jupiter sends Iris, Juno's message-runner disguised as a rainbow, to Juno it is partly to signal that her games are up – 9.802–5 note); Jupiter, king of the gods, uses not a minor deity but another Olympian, Mercury, to deliver his behests, or a Fury as his agent of destruction – in the latter case, just like Juno (12.843–86 note); Opis expresses the sentiments her mistress Diana does not, but we imagine Diana feels (11.839 ff.). Virgil's relationship with his Muse(s) is unlike any other between summoner and summoned: the poem's opening line, especially when set against the invocations that begin the *Iliad* and the *Odyssey*, seems to assert the poet's creative independence (**I sing**); but when he acknowledges that without the Muses he is confined to the realm of *Fama* (**Our ears can barely catch the faintest whisper of the story.** / *all we catch is the distant ring of fame* – 7.646), he admits that his authority comes from beyond himself.

Where minor deities are not summoned by their superiors, they add their own note of superhuman sympathy (Aurora is no mere synonym for dawn (1.306, 4.584–5, 5.104–5 notes); or animate the abstract (Bellona brings her particularly brutal intensity to the battle of the gods at Actium (**cracking her bloody whip** / *lash*, 8.703); the gods of the underworld enrich the darkness of their realm (4.510 f., 6.264 ff., 6.274 ff.). In Roman society, minor gods endowed nooks and crannies of everyday life with a numinous aspect – Fabulinus presided over children learning to talk, Mellona over bees.

4.5.6 Imported gods

Thanks to polytheism's absorbency, settlers or merchants in Rome could worship gods from their own lands, at least privately;[116] Cybele,[117] from Phrygia, was different, because the Romans themselves introduced her to the city in response to a crisis[118] and then an oracle; they assimilated her as the 'Great Mother' (2.788 note). It is worth comparing her treatment to the stop-go reception of Isis. Since the end of the second or beginning of the first century BCE, Isis had been worshipped on the Capitol.[119] In 53 BCE, the senate ordered the removal of any temples to Isis and Serapis, including private ones, from the city boundary[120] and the shrine to Isis on the Capitol was destroyed five years later – but the triumvirs ordered a temple to both gods to be constructed in 43 BCE, outside the boundary,[121] on the Campus Martius. In the aftermath of Actium, 28 BCE, Augustus banned Egyptian rites that had crept back inside the city, while protecting any temples that had survived there;[122] Agrippa extended the ban to a mile beyond the boundary in 21 BCE.[123] We can watch Augustus and his predecessors fending off the worship of Isis without completely suppressing it. For Virgil, Egyptian deities are **monstrous** / *monster* **gods** (8.698).

So one might have expected the worship of Cybele, whose core mysteries (as portrayed for instance by Catullus[124] – 2.788 note) were both secret and violent, to be more deserving of containment. But Cybele served Rome well: Hannibal left Italy the year after she reached Rome's Temple of Victory in 204 BCE and he was defeated in Africa the year after that. An annual six-day festival had been established in honour of her arrival,[125] the Megalesia, (from the 4th of April); a temple to her on the Palatine was dedicated in 191 BCE. Since then she had been taken to the hearts of the patrician class, which used the festival, its raucous procession, circus games and theatre entertainments, as an opportunity for mutual entertaining on a lavish scale (their expenditure had to be curtailed in 161 BCE[126]). And Cybele continued to foster Rome's winning ways: in 189 BCE her priests greeted the consul Gnaeus Manlius Vulso as he crossed the river Sangarius in Phrygia with promises of victory;[127] and in 103 BCE, another priest, Battaces, came to Rome to proclaim that she would triumph over the Teutones and Cimbri.[128] She appeared regularly on coins of the first century BCE, usually in her chariot drawn by lions[129] (as emulated by Antony – see 2.788 footnote). Augustus favoured Cybele, whose temple next door to his house on the Palatine he restored after a fire[130] in 3 CE, but whether his favour anticipated or followed the *Aeneid* it is impossible to say. In any case, she became part of his iconography[131] and of his wife Livia's.[132] Despite all this, caution remained: while Cicero could describe the Megalesian games as 'pure, solemn and reverent',[133] the procession was unRoman. Dionysius of Halicarnassus writes:[134]

> Notwithstanding the influx into Rome of innumerable nations which are under every necessity of worshipping their ancestral gods according to the customs of their respective countries, yet the city has never officially adopted any of those foreign practices, as has been the experience of many cities in the past; but, even though she has, in pursuance of oracles, introduced certain rites from abroad, she celebrates them in accordance with her own traditions, after banishing all fabulous clap-trap. The rites of the Idaean goddess [Cybele] are a case in point; for the praetors perform sacrifices and celebrate games in her honour every year according to the Roman customs, but the priest and priestess of the goddess are Phrygians, and it is they who carry her image in procession through the city, begging alms in her name according to their custom, and wearing figures upon their breasts and striking their timbrels while their followers play tunes upon their flutes in honour of the Mother of the Gods. But by a law and decree of the senate no native Roman walks in procession through the city arrayed in a parti-coloured robe, begging alms or escorted by flute-players, or worships the god with the Phrygian ceremonies. So cautious are they about admitting any foreign religious customs and so great is their aversion to all pompous display that is wanting in decorum.
>
> (Earnest Cary, Loeb 1937)

It appears Virgil was the first to associate Cybele with the story of Aeneas. In the poem, she is less a symbol of victory than a divine parallel to Aeneas: an immigrant to Italy who would make Rome her place of settlement – Anchises even compares Rome to her (6.784 ff.). Her interventions are few but memorable – she **keeps** / ***detains*** Creusa in Troy (2.788), with protection implied (though Creusa may be sparing her husband worse news); and in parley with her son Jupiter she asks for her Idaean pine trees that the Trojans made into ships to be spared Turnus' incendiaries (9.82 ff.) – a wish he rather officiously grants (9.94 ff.). So Phrygian Cybele looks after her own, respecting her local ties, and Aeneas is wise to pray to her after the omen of the tables (7.139 f.) and, more portentously, after he has met the sea-nymphs into which she changed his fleet (10.251 ff.).

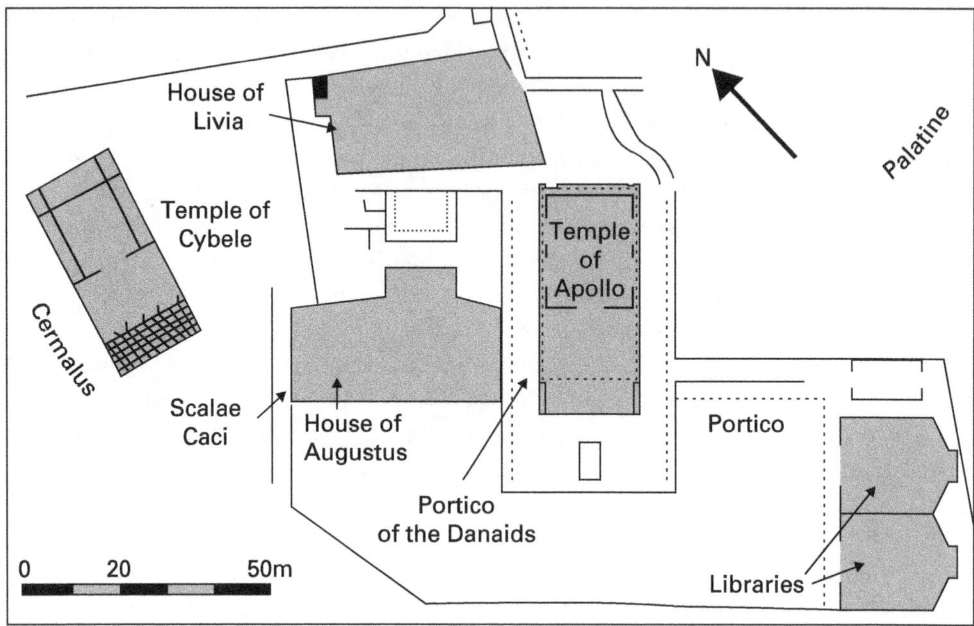

Plan of the Augustan buildings on the south-west corner of the Palatine, after F. Coarelli's *Guida Archaeologica di Roma* (Verona: A. Mondadori, 1974).

4.6 Gigantomachy

Hercules also takes a central role in the mythological battle between the Olympian gods and the giants, a recurrent image in the *Aeneid* for the struggle between order and chaos.[135] The background to this is as follows:

The first children of Gaia (Earth, = Tellus in Latin) and Uranus (Heaven) were the Titans, of whom the youngest was Cronus (= Saturn). Gaia's second brood were the three Cyclopes, the next the three Hekatoncheirs (hundred-handers). Uranus imprisoned all his children within Gaia (i.e. underground). Growing more and more uncomfortable, Gaia incited Cronus to rescue his Titan brothers and sisters; she gave him a sickle of flint with which he reached out at Uranus as he lay upon her, lopping off his genitals and casting them into the sea. The blood from the wound dripped onto Gaia, and from these drops she conceived the Giants[136] (as well as the Furies)[137] – humanoid to the waist but serpentine below, and not divine.[138] Cronus became ruler of the Titans, married his fellow-Titan Rhea and with her had several children, including Hera, Poseidon and Hades; these he devoured, to escape a palace coup like his own. Last born was Zeus, whom Rhea hid.[139] The adult Zeus returned from hiding, induced Cronus to vomit up his siblings, released the Cyclopes and Hekatoncheirs from their captivity under the earth and with their help fought a ten-year war with Cronus and his fellow Titans – the Titanomachy. The Cyclopes equipped Zeus with his thunderbolt. The victorious Olympian gods shut up the Titans in Tartarus and set the Hekatoncheirs over them as guards.[140]

Gaia was annoyed at the imprisonment of her Titan offspring. She therefore incited her other offspring, the Giants, to take up arms – specifically, rocks and flaming oak trees – against the children of Cronus (and Zeus' further progeny, Apollo, Artemis, Athena, Hephaestus, Dionysus and Hermes). The Olympians had received an oracle that the Giants could only be slain by a mortal; so they recruited Hercules. In the Gigantomachy[141] that ensued, he finished off with his arrows the Giants whom the gods had incapacitated. Gaia's last throw of the dice was to couple with Tartarus itself, producing Typhon (also 'Typhoeus', 8.298, 9.716) – another hybrid monster 'of such prodigious bulk that he out-topped all the mountains, and his head often brushed the stars'.[142] After initial defeat, Zeus finally imprisoned this creature under Etna.[143]

Lucretius inverts[144] the theodicy implicit in the Gigantomachy and makes mankind glorious giants, toppling through materialist reasoning the sky-gods of traditional religion (see *Introduction* – 8.4.6 Lucretius). Horace drew an elaborate parallel between Augustus' supremacy and Jupiter's subjugation of Titans and Giants.[145] Virgil, even though at one point (10.565 ff., 10.565–70 note) he makes Aeneas fight like a Hekatoncheir *against* Jupiter, returns to the original values, where the Giants represent lawlessness – but also makes his gods wrangle with or manipulate each other, unless on a shared mission of destruction (2.608 ff.).

4.7 Orphism and Pythagoreanism

4.7.1 Orphism[146]

While ostensibly the Olympian gods were safe-guarders of morality on earth, Iarbas was not alone in finding their oversight deficient (4.206 ff., admittedly an outburst of self-pity). Mystery religions, of which Orphism can be counted one,[147] were much more personal than public ceremonies, in Roman as in Greek culture; they offered the hope of personal salvation through particular behaviour and ritual practice. Orphism acknowledged the Olympians but rewrote their genesis so that it could concentrate on one in particular: Dionysus.

Orphism was not a sect; rather it was a set of beliefs and practices grounded in writings attributed to the legendary Orpheus,[148] Virgil's bard (6.645), whose descent into the underworld is retold in the *Georgics* (Introduction – 2.4 *Georgics*). It is set apart from other mystery religions by its textual underpinning. What has survived, however, are scant remains of these cosmogonies and theogonies,[149] plus a corpus of hymns from the second century CE (or later) and an Orphic Argonautica[150] probably from the fourth century CE.[151] (For a fragmentary example of the Orphic genre of 'descents to the underworld', see 6.548–627 note.) Information about Orphism comes from outsiders and over a long period; thus what the Neoplatonist Proclus says of the Orphics in the fourth century CE might well not apply to the Orphic initiates of Euripides' time.[152]

The core myth of Orphism was the birth and death of Zagreus, the first incarnation of Dionysus.[153] Unfortunately, it is nowhere set forth entire and has been pieced together, amid controversy:[154] Dionysus was born of Zeus and Persephone, but the Titans tore him apart, boiled and roasted him;[155] Athena saved his heart.[156] Zeus meanwhile smote the Titans with his thunderbolt. From their ashes mankind was born, a compound of Titan and Dionysus (because the Titans had eaten him);[157] the Titanic component of mankind is its 'original sin';[158] the

Dionysiac component is what enables salvation.[159] With or without this mythological underpinning, Orphics (it is claimed) believed that mankind left to itself is reincarnated continuously (quite possibly as another animal, with or without the implication of punishment);[160] on the other hand, if someone is initiated into the Dionysian mysteries[161] and abides by the rules of the initiates,[162] he/she can escape this cycle and live for all time alongside Orpheus.[163]

In truth, this composite picture of Orphism stretches the evidence, however enticingly. Adeimantus in Plato's Republic[164] gently guys the pretensions of Orphic rites to be redemptive but without mentioning reincarnation:

And they produce a host of books written by Musaeus and Orpheus ... according to which they perform their ritual, and persuade not only individuals, but whole cities, that expiations and atonements for sin may be made by sacrifices and amusements which fill a vacant hour, and are equally at the service of the living and the dead; the latter sort they call mysteries, and they redeem us from the pains of hell, but if we neglect them no one knows what awaits us.

(Trans. Jowett)

Socrates in Plato's Meno[165] mentions Pindar on reincarnation as a way to moral improvement but with no mention of Orphism:

Some of them were priests and priestesses, who had studied how they might be able to give a reason of their profession: there have been poets also, who spoke of these things by inspiration, like Pindar ... they say that the soul of man is immortal, and at one time has an end, which is termed dying, and at another time is born again, but is never destroyed. And the moral is, that a man ought to live always in perfect holiness. 'For in the ninth year Persephone sends the souls of those from whom she has received the penalty of ancient crime back again from beneath into the light of the sun above, and these are they who become noble kings and mighty men and great in wisdom and are called saintly heroes in after ages.'

(Trans. Jowett)

For what Virgil writes on reincarnation in Book VI, Plato is a sufficient wellspring (6.548–627 note; *Introduction* – 5.1 Plato and the Academy (first half of the fourth century BCE)), whether Plato himself drew on the Orphics, the Pythagoreans (4.7.2) or both; but the presence of Orpheus (6.645) and his regular associate Musaeus (6.667 and note[166]) in Elysium, and the fact that Musaeus guides Virgil and the Sibyl (over a **ridge** and onto an **easy path**) to Anchises (6.676), indicates that Virgil wanted to evoke Orphic beliefs for this stage of Aeneas' journey. In the *Aeneid*'s underworld, Jupiter and Juno hold no sway; the future is formed by a mysterious process of metempsychosis interacting with Fate.

4.7.2 Pythagoreanism

Although a philosophy and way of life,[167] the metaphysical component of Pythagorean thinking has much in common with a mystery religion; the relationship between Orphism and

Pythagoreanism is vigorously debated. The shadowy but charismatic figure of Pythagoras (*c.* 570–490 BCE),[168] who seems to have written nothing himself, quickly attracted doctrinal accretions and nominal followers ('so-called Pythagoreans', says Aristotle[169]) until the Neopythagoreans of the first century BCE mixed a grand amalgam of their own, incorporating Platonic thinking.

Three 'lives' of Pythagoras are extant but all date from the third century CE, by which time it had become difficult to salvage fact from hagiography. One of these, however, by Porphyry, when he credits earlier sources does offer a glimpse behind the incense screen:[170]

> What he told his audiences cannot be said with certainty, for he enjoined silence upon his hearers. But the following is a matter of general information. He taught that the soul was immortal and that after death it transmigrated into other animated bodies. After certain specified periods, the same events occur again; that nothing was entirely new; that all animated beings were kin, and should be considered as belonging to one great family. Pythagoras was the first one to introduce these teachings into Greece.[171]

The notion of transmigration would have been novel to Greeks accustomed to Homer's view of Hades, where souls were ghosts trapped for ever and needed blood to speak.[172] Too novel for some, the philosopher Xenophanes, Pythagoras' contemporary, reacted with ridicule:[173]

> Once they say that he (Pythagoras) was passing by when a dog was being beaten and spoke this word: 'Stop! don't beat it! For it is the soul of a friend that I recognised when I heard its voice'.

From these extracts we might gather that for the Pythagoreans reincarnation had no moral aspect; this was left (possibly) to the Orphics to supply. Anchises, unlike Plato, does not connect the soul's next incarnation with its previous life (6.748–51 note, **are called out by God**); in this he is Pythagorean.

CHAPTER 5
PHILOSOPHICAL BACKGROUND

Although Virgil might have been taught by an Epicurean (*Introduction* – 2 Virgil's Life and Works), the *Aeneid* is no philosophical treatise, nor does Virgil have a specific philosophical agenda (see, for example, *Introduction* – 3.2.5 Aeneas in the *Aeneid*: A Stoic hero?; and 3.4.1 Dido as an Epicurean). In the *Aeneid*'s, and quite probably Virgil's, view of the world, philosophy is subordinate to religion.[1] Nevertheless, not only could Virgil not avoid reflecting or reacting to the thought of his time, but also he deliberately refers to certain ideas or forms of expression from philosophical texts, not to build a system of his own but to enhance the effect he is after[2] Book VI (see 'Literary sources') is the best example of such *bricolage*[3]. Even a brief acquaintance with the philosophical origins of the eclectic mix reduces its strangeness and helps us to gauge to what extent Virgil might in passing imply a critique of his philosophical source material.[4]

5.1 Plato and the Academy (first half of the fourth century BCE)

That Virgil read at least some Plato is evident from his description of reincarnation (see 6.548–627 note). The inconsistency of the relevant passages in Plato would have liberated Virgil from any doctrinal dependence on him – and reincarnation in the *Aeneid* is indeed not Plato's depiction of the significance of individual choice but a map of Rome's destiny.[5]

Apart from reincarnation, most of Plato's wide-ranging concerns are far from the world of the *Aeneid*. Socrates' emphasis on education in his ideal state, however, would have resonated with Virgil, if he had read that part of the Republic – Virgil would himself have experienced Homer, especially the *Iliad*, as a school text[6] and so could foresee the *Aeneid* on the syllabus.[7] Socrates asserts the importance of stories, both true and false, to the formation of the ideal state's guardian class (376e–377a), in particular to manage their spiritedness (375b) – but rejects tales that are unedifying, even if they might be true, such as Hesiod's account of Uranus and Cronos (377c–e) and much found in Homer (379d).[8] The tragedians are subjected to the same censorship (380a), also because pity for others might encourage pity for oneself (606a–c); so, too, are frightening accounts of the underworld (386b). It is key that God is seen only as the source of good (380c) and that human examples are improving ones (607a). Virgil defies all these prohibitions but does not ignore the *Aeneid*'s didactic role:[9] above all Anchises' words to Aeneas (6.851 ff.) enjoin Rome to rule and to impose its own peace (neglecting the arts and sciences), while Aeneas' to Ascanius (12.435 ff.) exhort him, and by implication all Romans, to courage and perseverance – on the lines of Aeneas or Hector, not of Socrates' philosopher-soldier (376b–c). Anchises and Aeneas come across as more extreme in their Spartan focus than Socrates. In which there is a certain irony, for like Socrates, Anchises demotes art from within the setting of a great literary work.

Plato founded the Academy at Athens in the 390s BCE; Aristotle taught there before eventually establishing himself at the Lyceum in 334 BCE. The Academy after Plato[10] became a stronghold of academic scepticism, which maintained that, though there is a truth to be known, knowledge of that truth is beyond the reach of humans[11] – rather as Aeneas struggles in vain to comprehend his destiny, and must correct his suppositions about the past (see *Introduction* – 4.4 Fate), while seeming to inherit a suspicion of speech as a vehicle for truth (*Introduction* – 7.6 Speeches).

5.2 Aristotle and the Peripatetics (from the late fourth century BCE)

Although the philosophy of Aristotle and his successors (the Peripatetics) at the Lyceum, like that of the Academy, was much debated at Rome in Virgil's time (see 5.6 below), there is little trace of Aristotelian philosophy in the content of the *Aeneid*. That said, it has become a commonplace to use his Poetics as a tool in its formal analysis (see *Introduction* – 3.1 Characterization in the *Aeneid*; 3.4 Dido; 7.2 The hero). Heinze further applied precepts from the Poetics to the poem as a whole.[12] He takes as the unifying 'action'[13] of the poem the settlement of the Trojans and the transportation of the Penates to Latium (Aeneas' goal in the Proem, 1.5 f.); he then justifies Virgil not ending with the foundation of the city of Lavinium on dramatic grounds: it is implied by the death of Turnus and would be an anticlimax after it. Heinze also views the construction of the overall plot in Aristotelian terms, as having a beginning, middle and end, diversified by episodes,[14] while avoiding episodes that are 'neither necessary nor probable'.[15] So far, so good – but Heinze's conclusion, 'it is clear that Virgil was attempting to follow Aristotle's rules', goes too far. Even so, Aristotle's observations on epic[16] have a bearing on the *Aeneid*: he remarks that epic has the advantage over tragedy, that the former can represent what is happening in two different places at one time, (as in Books VIII and IX of the *Aeneid*, with ample Homeric precedent);[17] in looking at how the sought-after astonishment can be created, he judges 'the irrational (which is the most important source of astonishment) is more feasible in epic because one is not looking at the agent' – some way towards an extenuation of the metamorphosis of the ships in Book IX (9.117 ff.). On one point he might have taken issue with Virgil: 'The poet in person should say as little as possible.'[18]

5.3 Epicureanism: History

In first-century BCE Rome, the two most prominent philosophical schools were Epicureanism and Stoicism. Each provided a comprehensive system that embraced physics, metaphysics, cosmology, epistemology, language and ethics – they offered guidance on how to live. And each had further specialities of its own – such as evolutionary theory for the Epicureans and logic for the Stoics. Stoicism was a reaction against Epicureanism;[19] the exponents of either philosophy could therefore acquire an evangelical zeal[20], as did Lucretius for Epicureanism, 5.3.1; on the (later) Stoic side, Seneca viewed Epicureanism as 'an alien camp, into which I venture not as a deserter but as a scout';[21] Epictetus was less moderate (Diogenes Laertius says that he 'calls Epicurus a preacher of effeminacy and showers abuse on him'[22]); Marcus Aurelius, in his Meditations, quotes Epicurus on ethics approvingly.[23] A Roman might advertise Epicurean allegiance, or have an allegiance imputed by others: Horace says[24] to Albius, a potential visitor:

> When you want a laugh, you will find me in fine fettle, fat and sleek, a hog from Epicurus' herd.

Cicero, in lampooning M. Porcius Cato ('the Younger') half compliments him:[25]

All these <Stoic> opinions that most acute man, Marcus Cato … has embraced; … not for the sake of arguing about them as is the case with most men, but of living by them.

There were, naturally, all degrees of devotion or antipathy. (Cicero distanced himself from either school; if anything he was an academic sceptic – see 5.1 and 5.6.) Virgil very possibly was taught by one Epicurean, Siro, and associated with another, Philodemus (see *Introduction* – 2. Virgil's Life and Works), though the *Aeneid* can be seen as a riposte against Epicurean beliefs (see 5.3.1 Lucretius, 5.5 Stoicism, Epicureanism and the *Aeneid*).

Epicureanism is named after its founder, Epicurus (341–270 BCE), who came from Samos to Athens when he was eighteen. After a period of study in Colophon (on the coast of Turkey), he returned to Athens and set up 'the garden', a school of his own. He died at Athens more than thirty years later, popular and respected.[26] Of his writings, the thirty-seven books of On Nature and an outpouring of other works[27] are mostly lost;[28] three letters are preserved by Diogenes Laertius,[29] who claims they provide an epitome of Epicurus' whole system: 'To Herodotus', on physics; 'To Pythocles', on astronomy and meteorology (this letter is sometimes said to be by a pupil); and 'To Menoeceus', on ethics. Diogenes also catalogues sayings of the philosopher. Epicurus' disciple Lucretius and Cicero both mediated his thinking to a Roman audience; they are, to judge from comparisons with the letters, faithful reproducers of his teachings.

5.3.1 *Lucretius*[30]

Lucretius' poem in six books, *On the Nature of Things*,[31] possibly unfinished, as well as expounding Epicurean physics and their consequences, is a paean to Epicurus and the blessing of his philosophy, above all how the physical theory leads to a mind at peace and freed from fear of death.[32] It is of key importance to the *Aeneid*: first poetic, in that it accommodates scientific explanation, natural description and impassioned argument to Latin hexameters with power and beauty and a distinctive ring that influenced Virgil from the Eclogues on; second philosophical, since Virgil invokes Lucretian ideas mostly – but not exclusively – to contradict them.[33] 'The *Aeneid* is a positively anti-Lucretian work', asserted Heinze.[34]

Lucretius' language was a particularly rich mine because he adopted epic themes, though with the intention of subverting them. Thus Lucretius evokes storm and flood magnificently,[35] not to manifest Aeolus at work but to demonstrate the power of nature operating on atoms; once this real reason is appreciated, gods and their worship become redundant.[36] Virgil listens intently to Lucretius' words[37] but rehabilitates the god Aeolus (1.52–63 note), as well as portraying Neptune as he restores calm: where Lucretius' aim is to make the Homeric pantheon no longer an object of human dread, Virgil's is to reaffirm it and *pietas* towards it (*Introduction* – 4.3 Olympian gods in the *Aeneid*; 4.6 Gigantomachy). But Virgil draws on Lucretius precisely because the earlier poet's descriptions endow even minute details of nature with cosmic grandeur. For Lucretius, not only storms but everything was made up of, or explicable in terms of, atoms; thus in a simile each side of the 'equals sign' illustrates the atomic behaviour of the other: the motes of dust in a sunbeam provide a model for the atoms in a solid object or in the immensity of the void, and are themselves made up of atoms.[38] Since he does not adopt Lucretius' scientific system, Virgil strives for the same sense of scale through historical span, the reintroduction of the gods and the hyperbole natural to epic – and, through the interconnectedness of things within his similes (men compared to ants, Neptune to a political orator, troops as waves or ears of corn[39] – see *Introduction – 7.5 Similes*), conveys something of nature's 'grand design' as a Stoic would have seen it (5.5 Stoicism, Epicureanism and the *Aeneid*).

Hardie would go further,[40] making the case for the *Aeneid* as similarly therapeutic to *On the Nature of Things*:

> For the *Aeneid* may be read as the history of the construction of a universal order which will in future allow man to live the good life … The precondition for this universal order in Virgil is the permeation of the universe by the benevolent forces of a good providence, mirrored on the human level by the physical expansion of Roman power to fill land and sea. The theme of both Lucretius and Virgil is the description of a universe and of the way in which man should live in that universe.

But does the *Aeneid* provide convincing evidence of the 'benevolent forces of a good providence'? The Fate that, as Hardie says, decrees the foundation of Rome entails the destruction of Carthage (10.11 ff.); this is a nationalist interpretation of 'benevolence'. And even if that is accepted, would Aeneas at the end of the poem, isolated on the field of battle having slain his foe in a fit of rage, consider himself in the hands of a 'good providence'?

5.4 Stoicism: History

Stoicism, another school of philosophy that came into being during the Hellenistic period, was so-called because its debates took place in the *stoa poikile*, a painted colonnade on the north side of the Agora (Forum) in Athens. This already highlights a difference between its public engagement and the more withdrawn Epicureans in their teacher's 'Garden'. Although its foundation is credited to Zeno of Citium (344–262 BCE),[41] it was never tied to one individual and was given new directions and emphasis as it evolved. This evolution is often divided into three (arbitrary) phases based on the writings of Stoicism's major exponents:

- Early Stoa (third century BCE): Zeno, Cleanthes and Chrysippus proposed different physics from the Epicureans and different ethics (see 5.5): instead of pleasure and pain being the moral drivers, they followed the Cynics[42] in making virtue and discipline the foundations of well-being (*eudaimonia*; see 5.5). None of their writings survive other than as fragmentary quotations and doxographies, even though Chrysippus was especially prolific.

- Middle Stoa (first century BCE): Panaetius, the last head of the Stoic school at Athens, simplified Zeno's physics and made Stoic teachings in general more accessible; he also introduced them to Rome. His work 'On Duties' became the model for Cicero's treatise of the same title. Posidonius, a polymath who incorporated Platonic and Aristotelian thought into his own, travelled widely and was known to Pompey and Cicero. Cicero is our primary source for the writings of both Panaetius and Posidonius, none of which are extant. On Augustus and the Stoics, see *Introduction – 3.2.5 Aeneas in the Aeneid: A Stoic hero?*

- Late Stoa (first–second century BCE): The essays and letters of the first century senator from Cordoba, Seneca, also playwright and tutor of Nero, at last give us a detailed account of Stoic moral thinking; these are followed in the second century by the Discourses and Handbook of the Phrygian[43] ex-slave and Stoic teacher Epictetus, and the Meditations of the emperor Marcus Aurelius. Both of them likewise focus on morality, not underpinning it with science. These three diverse authors extend the teachings of the Middle Stoa in their own personal directions.

5.5 Stoicism, Epicureanism and the *Aeneid*

The following table boils down the Epicurean and Stoic (up to the Middle Stoa) systems and examines their relevance to the *Aeneid*:

	Epicureanism[44]	Stoicism[45]
1. Cosmology	The universe comprises infinite atoms moving through infinite void over eternity. Out of these atoms an infinity of universes (*cosmoi*) can form and be dissolved, some like this one and others unlike it.[46]	The universe is a living thing, in which inert matter is animated by God, an intelligent designing fire or breath (*pneuma*)[47] that structures matter in accordance with Its plan.[48] The universe is locked into a cycle of endless recurrence, beginning and ending in conflagration (*ekpyrōsis*).[49]
	Anchises' description of the earth, moon and stars as a great body animated by spirit (6.724 ff.) is thoroughly Stoic – except that any notion of that body's destruction and recreation is absent.	
2. Physics	Atoms left to themselves are in a constant motion downwards – but collisions have always occurred that throw them into one another's path. Objects are aggregates of colliding atoms.[50] Lucretius adds that atoms can, for no apparent reason, swerve lightly and so collide;[51] the world is thus at the mercy of 'pilot fortune'.[52] Soul is fine material dispersed through the substrate of the body.[53]	Only bodies can act on bodies;[54] out of the initial fire come the four elements (considered bodies), in order: fire then air (together = *pneuma*) act on the other two elements, water and earth, to make all things, inanimate or animate.[55] *Pneuma* gives rise to the nature of plants, the movement of animals and reason/ decision in man.[56]
	This scientific substratum barely intrudes on the *Aeneid* except perhaps in the archery competition of Book V when, again in Stoic fashion, the dove seems to be escaping into thin air **leaving her life among the stars of heaven /…** *in the stars* (5.515 f.) and Acestes' arrow becomes celestial fire (5.525 f.; see 5.517–18 note).	
3. Perception	When we see a body, what we see is a film of atoms emanating from it.[57]	When we perceive something, we receive a cognitive impression of it, to which we must assent if we are to treat it as true.[58]

	Epicureanism[44]	Stoicism[45]
	Although Virgil never encumbers his descriptions with philosophical mechanics, he does present a variety of misleading perceptions – and the assent or dissent given to them reveals much about the perceiving character. So, Pyrgo refuses to take Iris' impersonation of Beroe at face value (5.646 ff.) and Palinurus spurns the blandishments of Sleep (5.848 ff.); Turnus, on the other hand, swallows the dummy Aeneas without hesitation (10.647 ff.) and Aeneas himself is very suggestible – in Book IV, although Mercury's second admonition is delivered by what seems to be a phantom look-alike (4.556 ff.), Aeneas is as immediately transfixed as he had been by the god himself (4.279 ff.). It is different again when Allecto confronts Amata and Turnus in Book VII. Dissent is not an option: the physical invasion of the impressions made by Allecto turns Epicurean theory into nightmare. Does Amata even see Allecto (7.346 ff.)? Turnus does, and – it is his most considered action in the poem – deflects the fake Calybe, only to be irresistibly assailed (7.435 ff.). So, Virgil could be said to doff his cap to both schools.	
4. Gods	The gods exist, as otherwise we would have no notion of them[59] – but common beliefs about the gods are in error.[60] Nevertheless, honouring the gods offers a glimmer of hope.[61] In what mode the gods exist is unclear in Epicurus[62] – Lucretius states that their image is a figment of man's minds;[63] they dwell in contentment detached from the world.[64]	God is intelligence, Fate, Zeus;[65] he is a body but not material[66] (see 1 above). Instead It is *pneuma*, and as such immanent in all creation. It is also intelligent, the rational design behind everything.
	The occasional voice of (Epicurean) scepticism notwithstanding,[67] Virgil retains the Homeric Olympians. Lucan would, less than a century after Virgil, compose an epic in whose action the gods take no part (Pharsalia), but in it the protagonists (Caesar and Pompey) acquire an almost godlike aspect: epic craves divine agents.	
5. Fate/free will	The idea of fate is incompatible with common sense.[68] Free will is reintroduced to the determinist world of atomic motion by the swerve (2 above), though how it should translate into intentional action, rather than random movement, is unclear.[69] Prediction of the future is impossible.[70]	Fate is to be identified with an infinite lattice of causes and effects[71] – as follows from the divine design of 3 above.[72] To escape from a crystalline determinism, Chrysippus distinguished between the auxiliary cause (fate) and the primary cause (agent).[73] (See also 7.373–405 note, on Chrysippus' roller and spinning top.) Prediction of the future is nevertheless possible,[74] even if pointless.[75]
	The *Aeneid* makes Fate paramount, contrary to Epicurus' teachings. On the other hand, the Fate of the *Aeneid* is conveniently looser than that of Stoicism, even after the latter's qualification by primary versus auxiliary causes. Also the relationship between Fate and the supreme deity is left unclear. (See *Introduction* – 4.4 Fate.) A consequence of the looser Fate is that only some things can be prophesied. Also it does not pose a contradiction with free will: you can, if aware of Fate, choose to act against it, only you will regret it.	

	Epicureanism[44]	Stoicism[45]
6. Ethics	For beings made of atoms, the physical sensations of pleasure and pain are the ultimate guide to what is good or bad. Happiness is maximizing (enlightened) pleasure and minimizing pain: this should result in peace of mind (*ataraxia*). You cannot be happy without prudence, honour and justice; with them you cannot be unhappy.[76] But attaining peace of mind requires practising these precepts day and night.[77]	Virtue, of which a detailed taxonomy is headed by prudence, temperance, justice and courage,[78] is the only good; things often counted as goods that are not always so (e.g. money), are considered 'indifferents'. Practising virtue is what permits happiness.[79] Attaining virtue is a matter of life-long practice (*askesis*), and of prudence (i.e. right judgement, e.g. in assenting to cognitive impressions, 3 above; or restraining harmful emotions, 7 below; or recognizing fate and following it – 5.21–5 note) and of fortitude (i.e. maintaining that judgement[80]). The Stoic sage is one who has advanced far in this:[81] his choices are 'in accordance with nature',[82] i.e. the divine design.

Venus' protest, '**Is this our reward for piety and obedience?**'/ '*Is this our reward for reverence?*' (1.253), expresses the poem's frustration at the apparently broken link between virtue and happiness. At the final duel, *pietas* skewers Aeneas on the horns of a dilemma – to respect Turnus' father or Pallas' (12.933 ff.)? His decision to kill Turnus is not made from prudence (see *Introduction* – 3.2.5. Aeneas in the *Aeneid*: A Stoic hero?). It is as if Virgil is rejecting any facile entailment of rewards for good behaviour. At the same time he does not suggest abandoning *pietas* – the models for that, Salmoneus (6.585 ff.) and Mezentius (10.853 ff.), are given their just deserts; nor does he opt for Epicurean pleasures instead, since Dido's experiment in following her desire also brings disaster (see *Introduction* – 3.4.1 Dido as an Epicurean).

Even if Aeneas is not portrayed as a sage (Epicurean or Stoic) in the making, it is perhaps possible to view Rome corporately as gradually attaining Stoic wisdom – Roman history, in Book VI and Book VIII, is the *askesis* leading to Stoic mastery, embodied in the chaining of *Furor* (1.294 ff.) and barbarians paying homage to Augustus (8.714 ff.).

	Epicureanism	Stoicism
7. Emotions	Emotions are assessed for how they conduce to pleasure or pain.[83] Desires are categorized into natural – necessary / natural -unnecessary / groundless.[84] Anger can be natural or empty – the latter is either based on error (including empty desire) or the result of an irascible disposition.[85]	There are four classes of disruptive emotion:[86] (1) immoderate delight and (2) distress (over present circumstances); (3) immoderate desire[87] and (4) fears (for the future). Set against these are three positive classes of emotion, (A) proportionate joy (present – this equates to the two negative classes (1) and (2)); (B) volition (versus (3)); and (C) caution (future, versus (4)). All emotion requires assent[88] – 3 above.

	Epicureanism[44]	Stoicism[45]
	As befits a story propelled by wrath (Juno's), the mastery of emotion is conspicuously absent from the poem – Aeneas' attempt to check the tempers that have flared at the broken truce is arrested mid-sentence (12.313 ff.). Epic cannot, of course, be about peace of mind, but it seems to be a working principle of the *Aeneid* that, 'Reason is … the slave of the passions':[89] it may be highly desirable to discipline the emotions, as both Epicureanism and Stoicism assert, but is it humanly possible? Aeneas' Stoic (and possibly Epicurean) renunciation of Dido in Book IV required divine intervention to make it happen; the Stoic counsel of Nautes (5.704 ff.) had to be reinforced by Anchises.	
8. Politics v. friendship	The history of society's development is of great interest,[90] but political engagement is unwise (disturbing to peace of mind);[91] friendships, on the other hand, are key to happiness.[92]	The wise man will engage in politics, to restrain vice and promote virtue.[93] Friendship is to be desired for its own sake.[94]
	A poem about the foundation of Rome, especially one that treats the foundation as an ongoing process continuing to the poet's own day, does not just promote political engagement but itself exemplifies it. By contrast, it is curiously sparse in its depiction of friendship – Nisus and Euryalus are lovers (9.182); however faithful Achates (1.188 note), he is not an equal; Lausus and Pallas, though equals, are enemies (10.434 ff.).[95] Aeneas' main support is Anchises: family eclipses friendship.	

Though an erstwhile Epicurean (see *Introduction* – 2 Virgil's Life and Works), Virgil seems to approach more nearly to Stoicism. An Epicurean narrative might have made the happiness of the hero the goal of the poem; in the *Aeneid*, individual happiness is subordinated to the health and prosperity of the commonwealth. This is as true of Helenus and Andromache as of Aeneas and future Romans.

5.6 Cicero's philosophical writings[96]

Although best known as a statesman and orator, Cicero (106–43 BCE) was a student of philosophy all his life[97] and during two periods of it[98] wrote philosophical works[99] – he remarked about the second:[100]

> I was languishing in idle retirement, and the state of public affairs was such that an autocratic form of government had become inevitable. In these circumstances, in the first place I thought that to expound philosophy to my fellow-countrymen was actually my duty in the interests of the commonwealth, since in my judgement it would greatly contribute to the honour and glory of the state to have thoughts so important and so lofty enshrined in Latin literature also.

His ambition was no less than to compile a philosophical encyclopaedia.[101] In his own beliefs he inclined to the academic sceptics (5.1 above), at least in method[102] – he wanted his readers to assess all available views before favouring any one of them;[103] he usually espoused dialogue form (as Plato and Aristotle[104] before him) to give each rival in turn its airing and expose it to criticism. There are relatively few quick-fire exchanges as in Plato – most of the time a speaker explains at length before his ideas are examined. Two works (*On the Nature of the Gods* and *On Ends*) are tripartite – the first part puts forward and argues the Epicurean point of view, the second the Stoic and the third debates both or adds that of the New Academy. Cicero draws on other schools as well, not least Aristotle and the Peripatetics.[105]

Cicero's earlier philosophy was political (*Republic, Laws*). In his later phase, he ranged widely – religion (*On the Nature of the Gods, On Divination*); ethics (*On Ends, On Duties, Stoic Paradoxes*); emotion (*Tusculan Disputations*); determinism (*On Fate*); epistemology (*On Academic Scepticism* – in Latin *Academica*); and *On Friendship, On Consolation* (now lost) and *On Old Age*. Cicero has been accused of simply reproducing Greek ideas in Latin without adding his own original twist, though that was already an achievement not to be underestimated. For the reader of the *Aeneid*, the debate on his personal contribution can be left on one side, since Cicero's importance lies in representing the philosophical currents of Virgil's time and in providing the nearest we have to a Latin conceptual glossary (e.g. of *furor*, 1.1–7 note). The recollection of Scipio's Dream, from Cicero's *On the Republic* (6.703–23 note), proves Virgil had at least some acquaintance with Cicero's philosophical writing.

CHAPTER 6
SOCIETY

All the societies presented in the *Aeneid* are in some sense incomplete: Troy has been demolished and its reconstituted version at Buthrotum is a pathetic wraith (3.349 ff.); Dido's Carthage, though on a monumental scale, remains a work in progress (4.86 ff.); Latinus' city and Evander's Pallanteum are rustic and ripe for urban development; the towns mentioned in Book VII's catalogue are no more than names. So the *Aeneid*'s reflection on Roman society is communicated by contrast as much as by example.

6.1 Romanness[1]

A sense of identity, whether personal or local, waxes and wanes, more felt than pinned down by definitions. But after sixty years of on-and-off civil war in the first century BCE, initially between Rome and the rest of Italy and then between members of the upper echelon at Rome itself, Romans must have wondered what, if anything, their city stood for. The *Aeneid*, as the story of Rome's foundation, revisits the 'why' and 'how' of its origins (both are included in *aetiology*); it tries to establish a continuity, genuine or artificial, that can identify some, or much, of what is essentially 'Roman'. It does this piecemeal, through the mouths of its characters as much as through the narrative itself, and by contrast with other races or its own ancestors, leaving many questions unanswered (e.g. what was, and what became of, Trojanness?).[2] Here are some constituents of the identity it constructs:[3]

- Genealogy (see also 6.2) – 'father Aeneas' stands at the head of Julian dynasty but also in a paternal relationship to all Romans.[4] His men are also seen as progenitors of Roman *gentes*, not necessarily the most illustrious or spotless ones – the point is their visible posterity (5.116–23 note). In the underworld, those awaiting rebirth are already organized by clan – Tarquinii (6.817), Decii and Drusi (6.824), Gracchi and Scipiones (6.842 f.), Fabii (6.845); again, the family name can evoke black sheep as well as white (see 6.656–853 note).

- Place – Evander's Pallanteum is an eery prefiguration of the Rome known to Virgil's audience – the narrator deliberately uses the later names (Tarpeian seat, Capitol – 8.347; Carinae – 8.361). Such prefiguration is not confined to Pallanteum: Picus' palace, inherited by Latinus, is a primitive version of the Temple of Jupiter Optimus Maximus (7.170–91 note). Elsewhere Virgil delicately reminds us that anonymous places will acquire, or be acquired by, Roman names (12.134) and that they can fall back into obscurity again (Anchises' towns that by Virgil's time were backwaters, 6.776): continuity does not entail perdurability.

- Traditions and religious rituals (see further 6.4 below) – These might be inaugurated by Aeneas (the *Parentalia*, 5.45 ff., and *Lusus Troiae*, 5.596 ff.), imposed on him (Helenus' instructions to cover his head during sacrifice, 3.404–9 note) or taken over from others – such as the Latin custom of opening the gates of Mars' temple at the outbreak of war (7.601 ff.) or Evander's celebration of Hercules, perpetuated by Romulus (8.102–25 note). Thus as well as expressing a natural *pietas*, they also represent Rome's ability to absorb traditions from outside.

- Civic institutions – Of all the halts on the Trojans' voyage, the one that provides them with the nearest to a blueprint for Rome is, arrestingly, Dido's Carthage; Virgil has copied it from Rome to be a pattern for Rome (Aeneas takes note – 1.437). As well as theatre, senate-house (1.426 ff.) and monumental temple (1.446 ff.), Dido allocates the guests at her banquet to couches while slaves deploy napery (1.697 ff.) and lamps glimmer from the coffered ceiling (1.726). We hear of nothing so Roman in the Troy of Book II; Picus' palace trebles as parliament, temple and banqueting house (7.174 f.) – which is not Roman at all. Jupiter populates the urban scene when he anticipates Romans as **'the race that wears the toga'** / **'*the race arrayed in togas*'** (1.282), a transformation from the Trojans mocked elsewhere in the poem for their love of hats, long sleeves, colour and perfume (by Iarbas, 4.216 f.; by Numanus Remulus, 9.613 ff.; by Turnus, 12.99 f.).

- Native Italianness – Jupiter's settlement (12.833 ff.) allows the Italians to keep their names, customs and language; the Trojans will **submerge** / **subside.** Jupiter will add the **ritual . . . and . . . modes** / **rites and forms of worship** – he does not specify whether he adds Trojan to Italian, the reverse, or entirely new ones; but we know Cybele will coexist with Faunus. Evander's words when Aeneas enters his house (8.364 f.), on having the courage to despise wealth, moulding himself to become a god and not spurning rusticity, could apply to this process of racial absorption. The pride of the catalogue of Italy in Book VII makes new sense: these are the ancestors of Virgil's Romans (whom Virgil deliberately makes strange, with hints of a foreignness already assimilated[5]). It also explains why the poem is silent on Trojanness, other than its disparagement by Iarbas, Numanus Remulus and Turnus; the splendour of Priam's palace and all it represented lie prostrate (2.554 ff.); Aeneas brought with him only the men of his family, the Penates and a few keepsakes (e.g. Anchises' wine cup, 5.535 f.). All races beyond the Trojans are, from the perspective of these indigenous Italians, which is also adopted on Aeneas' shield, exotic or threatening – Antony with his eastern fleet (8.685), or the embassies who offer their submission to Augustus (8.722 ff.).

- Openness to foreigners (paradoxically) – the other side of Jupiter's settlement is that the Italians must receive the Trojans, as Latinus foresaw and Tarchon (as an Etruscan) welcomed: only a non-Italian could marry Lavinia (7.96 ff.) or command the Etruscans (8.502 ff.). The definition of 'non-Italian' is 'one who arrives from abroad' – origins are here irrelevant,[6] since Aeneas' ancestor Dardanus from Corythus, according to the Aurunci quoted by Latinus (7.205 ff.[7]), would theoretically make him Italian; and Turnus' claim to descent from early kings of Argos, according to Amata (8.371 f.), would turn him into a Greek and thus a foreigner. There is ample precedent within the poem for successful immigration: by the Pelasgians in Latium (8.602) or the Arcadians at Pallanteum;[8] Evander says there were multiple arrivals (8.328 f.). And, though the poem never states it, what will enable the transformation of rural Italians into sophisticated Romans is precisely that acceptance of urban, city-founding Trojans.

Rome after the Social Wars had already expanded its citizenship (see *Introduction* – 1.6 The late Republic (from 133 BCE onwards))[9] and would continue to do so;[10] *imperium* ('command' 'empire') would mean not just ruling others but also giving them the opportunity to rule.[11]

- Values – Aeneas' *pietas*, exemplified by his faithful conveyance of the Penates, is something he wants to bequeath along with them (12.192); it is the overriding characteristic that Jupiter singles out as Roman (12.839 f., admittedly to a Juno pining for honours). Aeneas' speech to Ascanius, designed to be overheard by the bystanders, opens with other virtues: **'From me, my son, you can learn courage and hard toil.'** / *'Learn courage from me, my son, true hardship too.'* (12.435 f.). Yet there is a dislocation between stay-at-home endurance, a Romanness in continuity of family (6.2 below), place and (religious) custom, and the Romanness of expansion inherent in *imperium* ('rule', 'empire'), as in the three great visions:[12] Jupiter has granted it 'without limit of time or space' (1.278 f.);[13] Anchises predicts that Augustus will extend it to the four points of the compass (6.794 ff.), euphemistically portraying its 'art' as **to impose a settled pattern upon peace** / *to put your stamp on the works and ways of peace* (6.852) (the other arts have been bleakly swept aside);[14] and Vulcan depicts Augustus, once Anchises' prediction has come true, accepting homage from his far-flung dependencies (8.720 ff.). The optimism of these projections is not without qualification;[15] nevertheless, it can be argued[16] that Aeneas' defeat of Turnus is on a Gigantomachic trajectory connecting Hercules' victory over Cacus to Augustus' over Antony and Cleopatra and stretching on and on till Rome and the world are coextensive – as Ovid wrote,[17]

> Land with a defined boundary is given to other peoples;
> The city of Rome and the immensity[18] of the world are the same.

At the limit, as in Ovid's paradox, the nation that contains all other nations needs no identity beyond its own supremacy – Anchises likens its worldwide *imperium* and Olympian spirit to Cybele the Berecyntian mother, processing through the cities of Phrygia (6.781 ff.); up till that point, however, Rome would still have boundaries and differentiate itself from the peoples beyond them, both by what it is and by what it is not.

6.2 Family

The word 'family' in current English covers both 'extended family' (those of the same blood and related by marriage) and 'nuclear family' (those under the same roof). There are no exact equivalents in Latin – the two main words for 'family', *familia* and *gens*, 'small-scale' and 'large-scale', respectively, both cover a spectrum of meanings only partly overlapping the English phrases.[19] Their core concepts, examined below, are vital in the *Aeneid*, and for opposite reasons.

6.2.1 Familia

The *familia* in the legal sense was a unit comprising the male relatives and their children, under the authority of the senior man, the *pater familias* (head of the household, owner of any property – a woman in the latter position would also be a legal *pater familias*).[20] He also acted as religious leader in the home.[21] The male relatives (*agnati*) did not have to reside under the same roof – the normal word for a 'household', including women and slaves, was not *familia* but *domus*. As for wives, they did not change their names on marriage[22] and usually remained under the authority of their father's family; they could own property independently of their husbands. Adopted males, on the other hand, did change their names and came under the aegis of their new *pater familias*.[23] Paternal authority – which applied to all fathers, not just the *pater familias* – could be stern: the right of life and death over a son;[24] while, under Augustus' Julian law of 17 BCE, a father was entitled to execute on the spot his daughter and her adulterer if caught in his house.[25] But all these legalities seem stiffly formal beside the more natural warmth in Cicero's delineation of moral ties (not once does he use the word *familia*):

> Now, if a contrast and comparison were to be made to find out where most of our moral obligation is due, country would come first, and parents; for their services have laid us under the heaviest obligation; next come children and the whole household (*domus*), who look to us alone for support and can have no other protection; finally, our kinsmen, those with whom we live on good terms and with whom, for the most part, we share our fate.

> (Trans. Miller, adapted)

The father was primarily a guardian – senators were known as '(conscript) fathers' and Cicero, having quelled the Catilinarian conspiracy in 63 BCE, was hailed unofficially as 'Father of his country' (*pater patriae*);[26] Caesar was officially commemorated by this title on a statue.[27] When, in 2 BCE, Augustus allowed himself to be awarded the title 'Father of his country' by – as he himself insists – 'the senate, equestrian order and whole people of Rome',[28] he was paving the way for the transfer of power within his family.

Sons in the *Aeneid* are, as Seneca would have it, 'the perpetuation of family (*familia*) and household (*domus*)';[29] **'last comfort of my old age'** / *'the only balm of my old age'*, says Euryalus' mother (9.481 f.); **'A father should not survive his son'** / *'I defeated Fate, a father doomed to outlive his son'*, says Evander (11.160 f.). This sounds a very different note from the decadence that Horace bemoans,[30] but is in keeping with the encouragement Augustus' laws gave to marriage and childbearing, in part to replace citizen losses during the Civil Wars.[31] Giving birth was fraught with danger for mother and baby and a child, especially a son, a cause for celebration (Augustus only had one child, his daughter Julia). Catullus compares the preciousness of his love for Lesbia to the preciousness of the grandson born late to a man's only daughter (Augustus was luckier – Julia had five children by Agrippa).

The deference shown to 'father Anchises' in the *Aeneid* (especially Book III – 3.1–12 note), guardian not just of his family but of the whole Trojan company, can be set against this background. And distraught as he may be, without Creusa Aeneas has at least salvaged the *familia* and its male lineage. But *familia* – here the women are very much included – although it is an escape from the poem's prevailing loneliness is above all the locus of grief and bereavement. This is much more than a political point about recent conflict; Augustus' loss of Marcellus and the associated sadness (6.883 ff.) levels the godlike figure of elsewhere in the poem with any other of its agonized parents – Euryalus' mother, Evander. It is a sombre feature of the poem that, of its parent–child relationships the only ones to survive are Aeneas–Ascanius and Latinus–Lavinia (though Aeneas is promised another son, Silvius, at 6.763–6.760–6 note). The only marriage to survive the poem is that of Helenus and Andromache, a childless dichotomy of prophetic husband and nostalgic wife.[32]

6.2.2 Gens

Gens is often rendered 'clan' – its members are of the same freeborn (male) bloodline and carry its name (e.g. the Decii and Drusi, 6.824; the Fabii, 6.845[33]) traced back to a single ancestor: of the captains in the boat race, Mnestheus is the originator of the Memmi, Cloanthus of the Cluentii (5.116 ff.). Its legal importance can be seen in the laws of inheritance,[34] under which the estate of a man who died without male relatives in his *familia* passed to the male relatives in his *gens*. In contrast to *familia*, the *Aeneid* associates *gens* with continuity – but not with affection; that would exceed the tact needed to trace the Julian link from Ascanius to Augustus (1.267–71) without enmeshing them both in the partisanship surrounding Julius Caesar.

6.3 Women: At Rome and in the *Aeneid*

6.3.1 Women at Rome[35]

The voices of women in ancient Rome, as in ancient Greece, if heard at all, are almost always ventriloquized by men – like Dido's speeches, penned by Virgil. What we pick up from the void tends to raise more questions than it answers; the male view gives us vivid characters as if glimpsed through a grating – and they are of the senatorial class, not the lower orders, let alone slaves.

The conventional model for late Republican womanhood is exemplified in the longest personal inscription to survive from ancient Rome, transcribed from a husband's funeral eulogy for his wife of towards the end of the first century BCE. Her name has been lost, but she is regularly referred to as 'Turia', for no better reason than that her deeds tally with those of a Turia who rescued her husband from the proscriptions after Caesar's death, mentioned by Valerius Maximus.[36] The grateful eulogist asks:[37]

> Why should I mention your domestic virtues: your loyalty [cf. 1.344–5 note], obedience, affability, reasonableness, industry in working wool [cf. 8.407–53 note], religion without superstition, sobriety of attire, modesty of appearance? Why dwell on your love for your relatives [*pietas*], your devotion to your family [*familia*]? ... and you have innumerable other merits in common with all married women who care for their good name [*fama*].

> (Trans. Wistrand)

Such a paragon was capable of nuances – Cornelia, in 129 BCE, came under suspicion of (improbably) suffocating her son-in-law Scipio Aemilianus to prevent him from rescinding the legislation of her son Tiberius Gracchus;[38] this did her reputation no lasting harm, and later a statue was erected in her honour, whose base carried the inscription, 'Cornelia, mother of the Gracchi'.[39] She, however, is no preparation for the new breed of upper-class woman that in the late Republic was emerging from the shadows, apparently freed of the constraints of male supervision,[40] and willing to take advantage of the relative freedom of Roman wives – Sempronia, possibly a member of the family of the Gracchi, married to the senator Decimus Brutus, is portrayed[41] by Sallust as an aging but accomplished beauty impelled by her debts to join the Catilinarian conspiracy (63 BCE):

> She was> . . . a woman who had committed many crimes with the spirit of a man. In birth and looks, in her husband and her children, she was extremely fortunate; she was skilled in Greek and Roman literature; she could sing, play, and dance, with greater elegance than became a woman of virtue, and possessed many other accomplishments that tend to excite the passions. But nothing was ever less valued by her than honour or chastity. Whether she was more prodigal of her money or her reputation, it would have been difficult to decide. Her desires were so ardent that she oftener made advances to the other sex than waited for solicitation. . . . But her abilities were by no means despicable; she could compose verses, jest, and join in conversation either modest, tender, or licentious. In a word, she was distinguished by much refinement of wit, and much grace of expression.
>
> (Trans. Watson, adapted)

Sallust, who might have seen her, was obviously fascinated and not alone in being so (hence the need for Augustus' moral legislation, 6.2.1[42]) – but the asymmetrical, masculine morality[43] that allowed patrician men their 'fun'[44] but patrician women nothing of the kind, except the small affection that a usually political or dynastic marriage would offer,[45] was bound to cast women like Sempronia as *femmes fatales*.[46] Cicero makes[47] the vilification of Clodia, the probable recipient of Catullus' Lesbia poems,[48] into riotous entertainment, to salvage his client Caelius:

> I am not saying anything now against that woman: but if there were a woman totally unlike her, who made herself common to everybody; who had always someone or other openly avowed as her lover; to whose gardens, to whose house, to whose baths the lusts of every one had free access as of their own right; a woman who even kept young men, and made up for the parsimony of their fathers by her liberality; if she lived, being a widow, with freedom, being a lascivious woman, with wantonness, being a rich woman, extravagantly, and being a lustful woman, after the fashion of prostitutes; am I to think anyone an adulterer who might happen to salute her with a little too much freedom?
>
> (Trans. Yonge)

One occasion where we do hear a woman's voice is in the verse of Sulpicia, a young member of Tibullus' literary circle.[49] Set against the devaluation of feminine love, her simple avowal, which would be conventional for a man, rings like a protest:[50]

> At last the love I've waited for has come.
> (No shame to say so: more to cover up).
>
> (Trans. Mahoney)

Involvement in politics was frowned on as trespassing on men's territory – Cornelia was commemorated for producing her sons, not their policies. Antony's wife Fulvia was a remarkable instance of full-blooded political engagement – Plutarch says of her,[51] 'She was a woman who took no thought for spinning or housekeeping, nor would she deign to bear sway over a man of private station, but she wished to rule a ruler and command a commander.' She had been married to the mobster Clodius, and caused a riot over his dead body by exhibiting its wounds;[52] after she married Antony she made full use of her influence to stir up trouble against Octavian while Antony was abroad.[53] Her demonization is illustrated by the tall tale[54] of how she treated the corpse of Cicero, who had committed full-scale verbal assault on Antony in his Philippics: when his head was brought to Antony, she spat on it, set it on her knees, pulled out its tongue and transfixed it with her hairpins, jesting at its expense. We are a very long way from Turia, but also from a measured appreciation of the myriad ways in which women might not have conformed to her matronal stereotype.

6.3.2 *Women in the* Aeneid

The *Aeneid*'s female figures, which include the goddesses, take as their point of departure epic (e.g. Andromache), tragedy (e.g. Dido) and mythology (e.g. Camilla); they are not social commentary (see also *Introduction* – 3.1 Characterization in the *Aeneid*). Nevertheless, they often seem to have half an eye on their context in Virgil's Rome (or the masculine view of it): Dido is a counterpoint to Cleopatra, seductive and dangerous to Rome's destiny, a Sempronia making advances unsolicited; Juno is spiteful and manipulative, a Fulvia on the immortal plane, and working against her husband to boot; Venus perhaps a Cornelia; Creusa, although we never see her at the loom, a Trojan Turia, the embodiment of home (she is juxtaposed with *domus* at 2.562 f. and 2.651 f.). But this can be taken too far: it would be a travesty of the poem to claim that it simply reinforces a Roman male typology[55] of the opposite sex. If anything the poem casts doubt on such a typology. To take just Dido: her need to protect her kingdom is real enough (1.563 f., 4.47 f., 4.325 f.) but that is not the main motivation for her liaison with Aeneas (for Cleopatra, first with Julius Caesar and then with Antony, it looks otherwise) nor does she lightly abandon moral scruple (as Sempronia).

Camilla offers another case study. Livy writing shortly after Virgil, describes how in the aftermath of the Second Punic War (195 BCE), the tribunes were proposing to repeal the Oppian Law, a piece of sumptuary legislation from the days of rationing, which restricted what women could own and wear. In the face of mass protests by women against it, Cato the Elder had spoken in favour of its retention. Here[56] are the words Livy puts in the mouth of the consul, L. Valerius Flaccus, arguing for what we might be tempted (wrongly) to call the 'womens' rights' (which won the day):

No offices, no priesthoods, no triumphs, no decorations, no gifts, no spoils of war can come to them; elegance of appearance, adornment, apparel – these are the woman's badges of honour; in these they rejoice and take delight; these our ancestors called the woman's world.

(Trans. Sage)

Thus when Camilla, the Volscian warrior maiden of Book XI is undone by her love of bright colours and gold (11.768 ff., and, damningly, line 782: **burning with all a woman's passion for spoil and plunder** / *afire with a woman's lust for loot and plunder* – see note*)* it might be said she is merely proving, after all, that she would have been better off keeping house and wearing her finery on an occasional foray outdoors[57]. And when the spear pierces her breast and drinks her blood, like milk (Virgil does not spell this out) she is being wrenched back into the role of wife and mother under the sway of men (11.794–835, 11.803–4 notes; *Introduction* – 3.10 Camilla). But is this the right interpretation? If the sense of 11.782 is that Camilla is fatally attracted to spoils that, unlike most armour on the battlefield, would appeal to her as a woman, then the line is less about the nature of women than about the rarity of such spoil; and if the description of her wound expresses Arruns' lasciviousness, then it implies nothing about male domination – unless men find themselves relishing it as they read. Above all if it did imply male domination, Virgil would be putting the genie of Camilla, explored over 150 lines up to her death in Book XI alone and including her *aristeia*, peremptorily back in its bottle. It is, rather, Arruns who is forgotten in the dust of the plain (11.865 f.).

Even if they cannot be reduced to types, the *Aeneid*'s women invite generalizations. Mercury's caustic dismissal (**Women are unstable creatures, always changing** / *Woman's a thing that's always changing, shifting like the wind*, 4.569 f.) is supposed to drive Aeneas from Dido (though Dido is constant – 4.554 note) – but while his dictum might apply, for example, to the women rising up in Book V and then succumbing to shame (5.678), or to Amata roused by Allecto, it does not to Creusa or Andromache.[58] The patriarchal contention that 'women make trouble and men restore order'[59] is vulnerable to the same exceptions, and it seems to be stretching a point to say that 'Camilla causes trouble' (except to the enemy; she does not actually tell Turnus to abandon his ambush – 11.823–7 note.) If the passivity of Lavinia has a point, it is to demonstrate that trouble is caused over her rather than by her. Does even Dido in Book IV cause 'trouble' that Aeneas, or any other man, within the compass of the poem puts right? Keith finesses the proposition into 'the representational strategy that aligns women with war aligns 'the man' with peace':[60] she cites a succession of queens – Juno, Helen, Dido, Amata, Cleopatra – and Juno's ministers, Allecto, Isis, Juturna; set against them are Jupiter and Latinus, with minor contributions from Galaesus (7.535 f.), the spiteful Drances (11.336 ff.) and Anchises' exhortation (of 6.852), **'to impose a settled pattern upon peace'** / *'to put your stamp on the works and ways of peace'*. The evidence is irrefutable but takes no account of the women's provocations – Juno and Dido have been scorned by men (1.26 ff., 4.373 ff.); Amata is recruited by Juno, along with Juno's other instruments. Cleopatra, although she steals the limelight from Antony at the Actium of Aeneas' shield (8.696 ff.), is said to 'follow' him as his 'Egyptian wife' (8.688). Something has gone wrong in all these cases with the man's role as guardian; Keith recalls, as well as Octavian's propaganda against Cleopatra, 'the unprecedented visibility of upper-class Roman women in the political upheavals of the decade after Caesar's assassination'.[61] Let it be said, in fairness to the poet, that the visions of other wars either in Anchises' gathering of souls or on the shield do not make women responsible (especially 6.828 ff.); and Mezentius makes war without any feminine prompting whatsoever.

The view of women as bringers of war is superficially hard to reconcile with another generalization, that women in the *Aeneid* are systematically marginalized: they have a habit of vanishing, dying or being spirited away.[62] This, though it cannot apply to the goddesses (except perhaps to Juturna, 12.885 f.), can apply to mortals, both in bulk (the women left in Sicily) and as individuals (Euryalus' mother); and their exclusion generates their outbursts of emotion (the long voyage imposed on them, 5.615 ff.; the grief that was not and cannot be assuaged by any speech with Euryalus, 9.483 ff.). Again, 'women tend to be repeaters, "mindful" . . . of the past and blind or violently resistant to the future'.[63] The 'tend to' hints at exceptions – does the description apply to the Sibyl, or Venus?

There is, however, much more to scholarship on women in the *Aeneid* than generalizations. Keith explores in depth the sexualized descriptions of lingering death reserved for Dido and Camilla (4.672–92 note). Not only, from a man's perspective, is 'the death . . . of a beautiful woman . . . the most poetical topic in the world',[64] but also these particular deaths remove an obstruction to the foundation of Rome.[65] It could be added, however, that Virgil has not left the male and the Roman gaze with the monopoly – the sisters, Dido's Anna (4.672 ff.) and Camilla's Acca (11.820 f.), are reminders both of a female gaze and of family grief; they are the nearest Dido and Camilla have to a guardian (Dido's is dead; Camilla never wanted one). Keith further points out[66] how chauvinism could be inculcated by educators and compounded by commentators – so Quintilian, on the recitation of Homer and Virgil in schools, gives directions for a boy:[67] 'his reading must be manly, combining dignity and charm'; Servius, on **what a woman is capable of when driven to madness** (*furor*) / *the lengths a woman driven mad can go* (5.6), discusses instead 'the familiar madness of women'.[68] If Quintilian and Servius speak for a prevailing culture, Roman men were unlikely to be alert to any sympathy Virgil shows for his female characters – but our own assessments of how women are portrayed in the *Aeneid* can be no more 'value-free' than theirs. Among today's scholars a split has opened, which Giusti and Rimell, in their forward to a collection of papers on the feminine in Virgil, summarize as follows:[69]

> Taken together, the papers act out the central dichotomy in feminist criticism . . ., in that they tend either to diagnose misogyny, the exploitation of women, and oppressive gender norms, or make moves to recover female voices, characters, ways of being in the world that are downgraded *qua* female/feminine, often in sympathy with what is construed as the text's own disruptive or destabilizing potential.

6.4 Religion

There is no Latin word that has the same breadth as 'religion'; *religio* could be unpacked as 'a sense of reverence and duty towards the gods manifested in ceremonial'.[70] It lacks any ethical component: Cicero asks[71] who would go to diviners to settle what is right or wrong; 'that is the domain of philosophers'. There were no religious doctrines, only a proliferation of myths; these were the domain of the poets.[72] For the everyday Roman, religion was an affair of state, that is, of communal festivals and civic rituals,[73] and of personal observances.

6.4.1 State religion

The question, 'Did the Romans believe in their gods?', for all its beguiling simplicity, comes apart in the answering: the phrase 'believe in' can mean different things to different believers (or sceptics), or in different societies;[74] it follows that evidence for belief will not be easy to agree on – even professions of it cannot be taken at face value; and the Roman élite certainly embraced a variety of opinions on what was meant by 'god' (as Cicero's religious dialogues indicate, in which the speakers are split between Epicurean, Stoic and Academic Sceptic).

Cicero can stand as a specimen of educated flexibility on the subject. On the existence of the gods, he remarks,[75] 'Most thinkers have affirmed that the gods exist, and this is the most probable view and the one to which we are all led by nature's guidance.' Thereafter, however, his investigation is wide open – he continues, 'But Protagoras declared himself uncertain, and Diagoras of Melos and Theodorus of Cyrene held that there are no gods at all.' He invites[76] his fellow-citizens:

> . . . to attend in court, try the case, and deliver their verdict as to what opinions we are to hold about religion, piety and holiness, about ritual, about honour and loyalty to oaths, about temples, shrines and solemn sacrifices, and about the very auspices over which I myself preside [Cicero had been elected to the college of augurs in 53 BCE] for all of these matters ultimately depend upon this question of the nature of the immortal gods.
>
> (Trans. Loeb)

This might be taken as willingness to question the very foundations of Roman religion. Not so: when debunking divination in any form, Cicero – an augur – declares:[77]

> Soothsaying, . . . according to my deliberate judgement, should be cultivated from reasons of political expediency and in order that we may have a state religion.
>
> (Trans. Loeb)

In other words, state religion is a given; more, it is the basis of Rome's success (as Jupiter might imply from 1.279 and 12.839):[78]

> It is in and by means of piety (*pietas* – 1.8–11 note) and religion (*religio*), and this especial wisdom of perceiving that all things are governed and managed by the divine power of the immortal gods, that we have been and are superior to all other countries and nations.
>
> (Trans. Yonge)

Cicero mentions the components of state religion above ('rituals . . . oaths . . . temples, shrines and . . . sacrifices') but does not explain, because he does not need to, how integral they were to political life: as well as the conduct of religious festivals that constituted the majority of any Roman's holidays, within 'state religion' fell the taking of auspices and their interpretation before any important public activity, such as elections or going to war;[79] thanksgiving after success (such as a triumph); and expiation after a disaster (such as an earthquake or a military defeat). The celebrants in these rituals might be the city magistrates (consul, praetor, aedile) or (and sometimes protocol required it) a priest or an augur (the only priestesses were those of Ceres and the Vestals). These were elected to a college[80] and their office was for life, unlike the magistracies, which lasted only for a year. Priests and augurs could therefore wield long-term influence – Julius Caesar's first post of note was as *flamen Dialis* (he was 16 at the time) and he was elected *pontifex maximus* in 63 BCE.[81] Members of the priestly colleges were drawn from the same senatorial ranks as those that filled the magistracies, required no religious credentials let alone training (they learned the arcana on the job) and could hold other offices at the same time. If religion was political, politics were also religious: tenure in one sphere eased the way to appointment in the other, and according to Cicero improved the performance of duties in both.[82]

Augustus, aware of the personal opportunity offered by religious hierarchies and the social benefit of festivals to both people and patron, revived several of each that had fallen into abeyance during the civil wars – of priesthoods, the *flamen Dialis*, the Arval brethren, Fetial priesthood and Titian brotherhood;[83] and, of festivals, the Lupercalia (8.663–5 note), Secular Games and Compitalia.[84] By the end of his life he could boast that he was a member of every priestly college,[85] when it was very rare to be member of more than one. As to becoming *pontifex maximus* like his adoptive father, he claimed he refused encouragement to displace the incumbent, Lepidus, and that he only allowed himself to be elected on Lepidus' death in 12 BCE.[86] Then there was the senate's decree, no doubt also with tactful prompting, that Augustus' name be inserted in the Salian hymn (8.280–305 note). Above all the Ara Pacis (3.404–9, 8.84–5 notes) embodies in stone the importance that Augustus laid on religious institutions for promoting his own image.

Which returns us to the *Aeneid*. Virgil's scrupulous attention to the matters of religious ritual[87] reflects the insistence within his own society on perfect execution (see 6.4.2). That execution also comments on the *pietas* and professionalism of the executant – the correct performance of religious tasks lends Aeneas credibility as a leader.[88] In this Aeneas really does develop – and, arguably, decline. Initially, at Troy, the instructions he receives from Hector in a dream to flee Troy with the Penates (2.293 ff.), soon entrusted to him by Panthus (2.320 f.), go unheeded; it is Anchises, as *pater familias*, who prays, interprets the omens (2.684 ff.) and takes the Penates in hand (2.717). Aeneas' first sacrifice, at his hasty settlement in Thrace, is thwarted when he incurs pollution from tugging insistently at the bloody branches on Polydorus' tomb (3.27 ff.). Thereafter Anchises resumes the religious reins, interpreting Apollo (wrongly – 3.103 ff.) and Aeneas' vision of the Penates (rightly – 3.182 ff.), praying to avert Celaeno's curse (3.265) and for an easy landing in Italy (3.528 f.), explaining the portent of the four white horses (3.539 ff.) and, finally, (at least by implication) leading the prayer to Minerva and sacrifice to Juno (3.543 ff.). As far as Drepanum (the end of Book III), Aeneas' only other religious contribution has been to nail a shield to the door of Apollo's temple at Leucas (3.286 f.). At Carthage in Books I and IV, Aeneas is a secular commander – when the Trojans land, they make no sacrifice (1.177 ff. – calling their damp corn 'Ceres' fruit' does not count), not even when they have venison in plenty (1.210 ff.); thereafter the gods visit Aeneas unasked (Venus, Mercury) and only when he severs the moorings does he offer up a prayer (4.576 ff.). It seems to be his duty to the dead, first and foremost his father, that makes of Aeneas a religious leader: in commemorating Anchises' death (5.45 ff.) and conducting a successful sacrifice (5.72 ff.), he dons the mantle of *pater familias*. For the burial of Misenus, Aeneas joins with his men in the tree-felling (6.183 f.) and oversees the cleansing of the pollution that prevents him from visiting the underworld (6.149 ff.).

From Book VII on, Aeneas grows in religious stature. He accepts the omen of Ascanius' words about table-eating (itself a religious act) and turns them into an occasion of full-blown prayer and sacrifice (7.135 ff.), recognized by Jupiter himself (7.141 ff.). In Book VIII, after

Tiberinus has appeared to him he takes up the river water in his hands and prays (7.68 ff.); immediately afterwards, he finds the white sow and piglets that Tiberinus had promised and makes of them the foundation sacrifice for Alba Longa (8.81 ff.). After the battles of Book X he sets up a trophy to Mars (11.7 f.) and his respect for the dead resumes when he agrees burial rites with the Latin envoys (11.118 f.). Finally his appearance in front of the armies in Book XII, with a priest alongside him, to take an oath of peace with king Latinus (12.166 ff.), should make a fitting climax to this religious progress: by this point, Aeneas has offered sacrifice; interpreted omens; proclaimed a festival; consulted the Sibyl; and sworn to a truce – the domains of five different colleges of priests.[89] But his sacerdotal role has already been compromised: in Book X, his feelings for one particular death, that of Pallas, have driven him in a fit of merciless killing to 'sacrifice' the priest Haemonides (11.541), as they will drive him eventually to 'sacrifice' Turnus (12.949). And when the truce lies in tatters, the two chieftains Latinus and Aeneas suffer the indignity in the first case of scrambling for cover with his gods (12.285 f.) and, in the second, of being struck down by an arrow as he pleads for restraint (12.318 f.). We are left to imagine how the two of them might restore their religious authority; we have seen how important it was to Augustus to bolster his.

6.4.2 Ritual of sacrifice

The attention to ritual detail in sacrifices stands out for its effect on the narrative, which halts to accommodate it and thus gives space to the participants' emotions. The most extreme example of this is the ratification of the truce in Book XII, described over 55 lines (12.161 ff.). There would have been a visceral drama to such an occasion, from the dignity of the procession[90] and prayers to the animal fear and stench of slaughter, but there was also much at stake if the tightly defined ceremonial was flawed by any error (*vitium*) – that would mean repeating it from scratch.[91] A sacrifice correctly made placed the god under a virtual obligation[92] (as Iarbas stresses to Jupiter at 4.217 f. and Juno more or less acknowledges, 1.48 f. – gods need homage); so if the prayer that went with the sacrifice was not answered in some fashion, the explanation must be a flaw in the execution of one or the other. Pliny the Elder illustrates[93] the care that was taken:

> In fact the sacrifice of victims without a prayer is supposed to be of no effect; without it too the gods are not thought to be properly consulted. Moreover, there is one form of words for getting favourable omens, another for averting evil, and yet another for a commendation. We see also that our chief magistrates have adopted fixed formulas for their prayers; that to prevent a word's being omitted or out of place a reader dictates beforehand the prayer from a script; that another attendant is appointed as a guard to keep watch, and yet another is put in charge to maintain a strict silence; that a piper plays so that nothing but the prayer is heard. Remarkable instances of both kinds of interference are on record: cases when the noise of actual ill omens has ruined the prayer, or when a mistake has been made in the prayer itself.
>
> (Trans. Loeb)

Worship in the *Aeneid* is much more spontaneous than this. And the solemnities of the truce are negated not by some barely detectable offense against rubric but through Juturna's fake portent then, crucially, Tolumnius' acceptance of it (12.244 ff.). Even so, there are definite components to sacrificial ritual, never slavishly listed by Virgil but most completely observed in this run-up to the truce (12.169 ff., 12.213 ff.):

- Washing – ignored in the *Aeneid*, except when Dido sends instructions to her sister to purify herself before coming for a sacrifice (4.635); and a hint of it when Turnus prays in response to Iris' visitation (9.22 ff.); covering the head is not mentioned in the description of the truce, but is a feature of sacrifices, after Helenus' directions (3.405 ff. – thus 3.543 ff., 5.72 ff.; the rule does not apply to non-celebrants; at funerals women's hair is untied, 3.65);

- Scattering of salted meal (cf. 4.517);

- Pouring of libations, of milk and/or wine on the ground (5.77 f. – Dido does this between the victim's horns, 4.61, as does the priest at 6.243); blood was for funerals (3.67);

- Prayer, usually following a certain structure (1.64 note – though for the truce it takes the form of an oath calling the gods to witness, not a request), optionally with hands raised heavenward (Aeneas prefers a drawn sword at 12.175);

- Slaughter of the victims – these had to be both appropriate to the god (2.201 note, 3.118–20 note) and perfect specimens; the topknot of the victim might be cut off and sacrificed first (6.245 f.);

- Burning of entrails on the altars – the remaining carcase was customarily roasted and consumed by those attending the sacrifice (as implied at 8.284 f.).

The carefulness of sacrificial ritual, in all contexts,[94] makes the summary brevity of its perversion – in one word, as when Aeneas 'sacrifices' the priest Haemonides (10.538–41 note) – particularly arresting. In Book XII the counterpoise to the protracted ceremonial of the truce at its opening is the 'sacrifice' of Turnus, at 12.949.

6.4.3 Personal religion

Roman religion was more than an affair of state; as well as petitioning Olympian deities on his or her own account, an individual would have had a personal relationship with favoured minor gods, with the gods of home and the immediate vicinity and with ancestral spirits (*Introduction* – 4.5.5 Gods local, domestic and minor). He or she could also participate in mysteries, consult soothsayers and astrologers – or turn to magic.

Put crudely, Aeneas here represents the good example, Dido the bad, or at least the desperate. Aeneas cherishes the Penates, not only carrying them from Troy but also bringing them to meals or sacrifices (5.62, 7.121); they appear to him in a vision, promising to him prosperity in return for the protection he has given them (3.156 ff.). When he arrives in Italy, Aeneas invokes, among other powers, the **rivers not yet known** / *rivers still unknown* (7.137); later, when he is panicking at the Italian muster, Tiberinus responds with guidance and aid (8.31 ff.). Before Aeneas visits the underworld (whose eschatology, in Book VI, is far from traditionally Roman), he visits his father's ashes on the anniversary of his death, offering prayer and sacrifice (5.42 ff.). Ovid states that this act established the festivals of Parentalia and Feralia (5.42–103 note), when families would make an annual excursion to the tomb of close family members and carry out a modest ritual. As Ovid describes it:[95]

And the grave must be honoured. Appease your fathers'
Spirits, and bring little gifts to the tombs you built.
Their shades ask little, piety they prefer to costly
Offerings: no greedy deities haunt the depths of the Styx.
A tile wreathed round with garlands offered is enough,
A scattering of meal, and a few grains of salt,
And bread soaked in wine, and loose violets:
Set them on a potsherd left in the middle of the path.
Not that I forbid larger gifts, though these please the shades:
Add prayers and proper words to the fixed fires.

(Trans. Kline, adapted)

Aeneas is also scrupulous towards other dead – Polydorus in Book III and Misenus in Book VI.

Dido, by contrast, petitions the gods to help her without success (4.56 ff.) – mostly because she is already the gods' victim and so in no state to benefit from her sacrifices, but also because she conducts them with more hunger than diligence over protocol. She tended a shrine to Sychaeus with greatest respect (4.457 ff.); but after she had by implication agreed with Anna that the dead would not mind her new love (4.34) and – we assume – slackened her attentiveness, she thought she heard his voice calling to her from it (4.460 f.). Finally she turns to magic, or the pretence of it, as a ruse to disguise her preparations for suicide (4.477; 4.474–503 note). Magic was viewed by Romans with distrust, not so much because it was ineffective as because they feared its ill effects, and its frequent malevolence.[96] Ovid discourages the use of love philters as they harm the mind and induce madness: 'abstain from all wickedness; to be loved, be lovable.'[97] Horace tells[98] of two witches who think otherwise and bury a boy up to his neck so that, once he has starved to death, they can brew the marrow of his bones and his shrivelled liver into a love potion. In comparison Dido was a mere dabbler.

6.4.4 Portents, divination and prophecy

Appearances of gods to mortals belong in poetry. The three methods by which Romans believed that the gods communicated with them were:

- portents (events in the natural world that somehow drew attention to themselves – often by disrupting the natural order); 'prodigies' had often a more restricted sense, of portents that indicated the favour of the gods had been forfeited;

- divination (augury = reading the behaviour of birds; haruspicy =reading entrails; astrology; interpretation of dreams and visions[99]); and

- prophecy (from an oracle or as set down in the Sibylline books, 3.443–52 note), consulted only at moments of particular doubt or crisis.

These might be combined; in particular the senate might check with the *haruspices*[100] whether a portent counted as a prodigy and, if it did, might ask the *quindecimviri* to consult the Sibylline books on what to do about it. Thus in 217 BCE, the year of the disastrous defeat of the Romans by Hannibal at Lake Trasimene, the campaigning season began with a welter of portents that included javelins bursting on fire, shields sweating blood and the sun battling the moon;

the senate decreed vague expiation and supplication rituals, but the priests[101] consulting the Sibylline books gave detailed instructions on how to make offerings to Jupiter, Juno and Minerva.[102] Disaster was not averted, however, because (so the senate were persuaded) the commander in the field disdained omens and auspices before giving battle.[103] Such obsession with signs was not restricted to times of crisis; Cicero wrote,[104] 'after the expulsion of the kings, no public business was ever transacted at home or abroad without the auspices first being taken.'

The *Aeneid*, especially the first half, abounds in omens (sought or unsought – 2.689–91 note) and prophecy, of every kind except astrology.[105] A brief survey of omens highlights the difficulties, sometimes in noticing them and always in evaluating or interpreting them. Except for dreams, they do not speak; what they convey is only as precise as their correspondence to features of reality (as Venus explains her swans, 1.393 ff.). Hence they are often complemented by a prophecy in their wake (notably in Book III, but also 7.81 ff.) – rarely they confirm one (so the white sow, 8.81 ff.). Furthermore, omens are not clearly demarcated from events that take on a portentous quality – for instance, Dido's and Aeneas' meeting in the cave is attended by lightening (4.167).

Book I	The omens begin with Venus' swans (1.393 ff.), from which she, augur-like, gives Aeneas the encouraging news about his remaining twelve ships – she draws a veil over the drowned Orontes.
Book II	The Trojans themselves construe the snakes devouring Laocoon as a sign that they need to take the horse into their city (2.232 f.) – we never find out how the monsters were dispatched. Hector then appears to Aeneas in a dream, but Aeneas ignores him (2.270 ff.), as the Trojans ignore the hesitation of horse at the gates (2.242 ff.) – an omen only in retrospect. Anchises needs to confirm that Ascanius' flaming hair is indeed a positive sign – Jupiter answers his request with thunder and a shooting star (2.679 ff.).
Book III	Omens are part of the book's formal skeleton (see Book 3 – Structure) – they provide correctives to the errors in the Trojans' choices of settlement (Polydorus' corpse (3.41 ff.); the plague on Crete (3.137 ff.), the Harpy raid (3.225 ff.)) until, in the final example, the four white horses of both war and peace (3.537 ff.) give them only equivocal information about Italy.
Book IV	Dido's haruspicy (4.63 f.) is the sole ceremony of divination in the poem (Anchises and Aeneas prefer oracles); its results, whatever they are, are irrelevant against the force of her love. Her nightmares (4.465 ff.) do not point to any action she can take. Aeneas, on the other hand, has a dream of Mercury (4.556 ff.) that insistently reinforces the god's earlier commands.
Book V	The snake that emerges from Anchises' tomb, given the snakes that killed Laocoon, troubles Aeneas until it proves itself harmless (5.84 ff.). Aeneas accepts the omen as favourable – a decisive moment for snake imagery as well as for Aeneas. In the final contest of the games, he welcomes Acestes' flaming arrow (5.522 ff.). Divine favour is manifested again when Jupiter, in response to Aeneas' prayer, extinguishes the ships (5.685 ff.).
Book VI	Two doves guide Aeneas (6.190 ff.) to the golden bough – itself an omen when it yields to his tug but also key, granting right of passage (6.140 f.).
Book VII	The swarm of bees (= invaders) and Lavinia's incandescent hair (= war over her) perturb Latinus, who consults Faunus (7.59 ff.). The omen of the table-eating, by contrast, comforts the Trojans, proving they have reached the end of their voyage; Jupiter corroborates their interpretation with thunder and a radiant cloud (7.141 f.).

Book VIII	The white sow, forecast by Helenus (3.389 ff.), endorses the Trojans' arrival at the site of their city (8.81 ff.). In front of Evander, the intimidating apparition of Aeneas' weapons is an opportunity for Aeneas to proclaim his destiny, and the defeat of the Latins (8.524 ff.). On the shield, Augustus' greatness is symbolized by the twin jets of flame from his temples and the comet above (8.680 f.).
Book IX	Turnus dismisses the wonder of the Trojan fleet converted into nymphs, saying Jupiter has removed the Trojan means of flight (9.128 f.); despite this disregard, his side almost captures the enemy camp. Jupiter answers Ascanius' prayer with thunder (9.631 ff.).
Book X	Aeneas, coming to the rescue, becomes Vulcan's Augustus as his helmet and shield take fire; he resembles a comet (10.270 f.)
Book XI	–
Book XII	Juturna stages a fake portent, of an eagle swooping down on a swan and being forced by the other birds to release its prey (12.244 ff.) – this, the mirror image of Venus' portent in Book I, causes the Italians to break the truce and triggers the final conflict of the war.

Omens can be indispensable guides or, if deceptive or wrongly interpreted, lethal. They are instruments of Fate. *Pietas* seems to be a partial guard against their potential treachery (so Aeneas in Book V sacrifices after the omen of the snake, and in Book VII after the omen of table-eating), but it did nothing for the Trojans as they ignored the signals at Troy (2.244 f.). Cicero voices[106] the sceptic's view:

> Why need I give instances – and, in fact, I could give countless ones – where the prophecies of soothsayers either were without result or the issue was directly the reverse of the prophecy? Ye gods, how many times were they mistaken in the late civil war! What oracular messages the soothsayers sent from Rome to our Pompeian party then in Greece!

> (Trans. Loeb)

But this view is not the poem's: in the *Aeneid* omens grab our attention and reconfigure our expectations because they might in some way be true.

Prophecies in the *Aeneid* are, like omens, not straightforward, for two reasons: first, that Aeneas seems so impervious to them (Book III – Inconsistencies in Book III note); second, and more fundamentally, because being so often uttered to encourage the hearer, they edit out bad news and/or in phraseology can be misleading.

Jupiter, 1.257 ff.	This prophecy, addressed to Venus to reassure her of Aeneas' prospects, is a table of contents for the rest of the poem and then (very partially) for Roman history, down to Augustus. Jupiter makes short work of the fighting in Italy and implies that the Trojans will impose their customs on the losers (1.264 – contradicted in his agreement with Juno, 12.834 f.). He also implies that the rulers of Lavinium and Alba Longa will be descended from Ascanius (1.272 ff. – not so at 6.760 ff.), omits to say how long Juno will take to let go her wrath (1.279 ff.) and concocts a reconciliation between Romulus and Remus (whom Romulus or his henchmen murdered) as lawgivers (1.292 f.).

Creusa, 2.776 ff.	In a vision she foretells to Aeneas that, after a long voyage, he will reach the land of Hesperia (or 'a western land'), where the Tiber flows. Aeneas soon afterwards claims he does not know where he is heading (3.7) – oddly, because he has retailed Creusa's prophecy in his narrative to Dido; he remembers again in conversation with Helenus (3.495 ff.). Creusa makes no mention of the struggle Aeneas will face in Hesperia before he can secure prosperity, a kingdom and a royal bride (2.783).
Apollo, 3.94 ff.	The god assures Aeneas that his dominion will be universal (3.97) – this is stronger even than Jupiter (1.278 f.). He foretells that the land to receive the sons of Dardanus will be the one that bore their ultimate ancestor (3.94 ff.) – a hint that Anchises misses, when he perversely decides Teucer is meant instead of Dardanus (3.104 ff.).
Penates, 3.154 ff.	The Penates are the first to define 'Hesperia' as Italy for Aeneas (3.165) and they promise his descendants a glorious future (3.158); but they too mention nothing of the war to be fought or of the losses Aeneas must face along the way.
Celaeno, 3.247 ff.	The Harpy takes her cue from Apollo himself in predicting that Aeneas will only found a city when hunger has compelled the Trojans to eat their own tables (3.255 ff.). This is the only wholly negative prophecy in the poem (Dido's curse, 4.612 ff., is prophetic but not a prophecy as such); it will turn out, as Helenus foretells (3.394 f.), a damp squib (7.112 ff.); its only point is to discourage Aeneas.
Helenus, 3.374 ff.	The seer, asked how Aeneas might reach Italy and face the ordeals ahead of him, prefaces his prophecy with the qualification that he is revealing only what Fate allows him to know and Juno allows him to say. He proceeds to give Aeneas invaluable information, such as the omen of the white sow marking the site for his city, that events will bear out – as Anchises recognizes (3.559). He can be forgiven for not predicting Juno's interruptions to Aeneas' fated course, the storm off Sicily that opens the poem and the ship-burning on Sicily of Book V; he does urge sacrifices to win her over. It is also pardonable, if strange, that he omits all mention of the Cyclops. What Aeneas really regrets is Helenus' failure to foretell the death of Anchises (3.712) – though this would have been hard to bear at any time; Helenus also promises that the Sibyl will guide him on what to do in Italy though it is Anchises who does this (6.888 ff.)
Mercury, 4.275 f.	Mercury paraphrases Jupiter (4.234) to promise Ascanius the kingdom of Italy and the land of Rome – a reduction on Jupiter's unlimited dominion of 1.278, but still enough to constitute a stern rebuke to Aeneas, who by lingering in Carthage denies these to his son.
Anchises, 5.730 f.	Aeneas' father lets him know that he must defeat a tough people in Latium.
Sibyl, 6.83 ff.	The prophetess is unsparing in listing the bloodshed – another Trojan War, another conflict over a foreign bride – that the Trojans face. She discloses Juno's enmity and exaggerates the difficulty Aeneas will have in finding allies. But she ends on a note of paradoxical hope – aid will come from a Greek city (confirmed by Tiberinus, 8.51 ff.).
Apollo, 6.343 ff.	Aeneas recalls in bafflement that the otherwise reliable Apollo had prophesied Palinurus' safe arrival on Italian shores. In fact, Palinurus had arrived there unharmed, but was promptly done to death by the local tribesfolk.

Anchises, 6.756 ff.	The gallery of future Roman heroes, intended to impress Aeneas with both the glory and longevity of Rome, is not unequivocal – how equivocal is controversial (6.756–853 note). Anchises also tells Aeneas that he will live long (6.764), in contradiction to Jupiter (1.265). But at the end of their encounter, Anchises gives Aeneas vital information on what he will have to accomplish in Italy and kindles in him a passionate acceptance of his destiny (6.888 ff.).
Faunus, 7.96 ff.	Consulted by Latinus, his father Faunus warns him not to find a home-grown son-in-law but to expect a foreigner, whose descendants will rule from furthest east to furthest west – a reprise of Apollo's and Jupiter's global perspective for Rome.
Juno, 7.315 ff.	A statement of intention more than a prophecy, Juno's declaration of a new Trojan War in Italy, destructive to the new marriage, is not fully achieved because she is brought to terms in Book XII.
Tiberinus, 8.36 ff.	The river god confirms that Aeneas will find the site for his city where the white sow lies (so Helenus before, 3.389 ff.), gives the city its name and predicts Ascanius' rule. He instructs Aeneas to seek help from Arcadian Evander at Pallanteum (the Greek city predicted by the Sibyl) and to sacrifice to Juno – Aeneas makes the victim in her honour the very white sow foretold. But his assertion that the anger of the gods has ended (8.40 f.) is simply wrong – Juno's wrath is rampant.
Carmentis, 8.340	This nymph, to whom in Pallanteum an altar and gate had been dedicated, was the first to predict the future greatness of Aeneas and stature of Pallanteum.
Vulcan, 8.631 ff.	On the shield for Aeneas, Vulcan has depicted the complete line of Ascanius' descendants and its wars 'in sequence' – incomprehensible to Aeneas but resonant to the Roman audience. On the choice of scenes perused by Aeneas, see 8.628–728 note. Ignorant of what the shield displays, which includes precarious moments for Rome, Aeneas is cheered by it (8.730).
Iris, 9.6 ff.	Iris visits Turnus to spur him to attack the Trojan camp. Although more a summary of the opportunity presented to Turnus by Aeneas' absence than a prophecy, her argument has a similar tendentiousness – the opportunity that comes with Aeneas' absence is undeniable, but the extent of his search for allies exaggerated.
Apollo, 9.640 ff.	In an aside to Ascanius (heard by him or not), Apollo predicts he will be the father of gods and that all wars will subside under his descendants – a less colourful echo of Jupiter's Book I prophecy to Venus on the chaining of *Furor*.
Jupiter, 10.11 ff.	A brief prediction of the Punic Wars.
Cymodocea, 10.228 ff.	This nymph, coming from Aeneas' beleaguered camp, both reports its precarious resistance to Aeneas and promises the day will see mounds of Rutulian dead – without mentioning the Trojan losses, above all of Pallas, needed to achieve them. (Her words are in fact ambiguous – see note.)
Diana, 11.587 ff.	Diana orders Opis to take vengeange on whoever kills Camilla; Fate has specified that Camilla will die, but Diana does not know how.
Jupiter, 12.830	Jupiter's settlement with Juno sees to it that the Trojans submerge their cultural identity in that of the Latins (while retaining the royal blood line). The loss of Trojan customs is at variance with what Jupiter had undertaken to Venus (1.264).

From the list above, what quickly becomes clear is the importance of context – who is consulting whom, and why or, if the deity is not consulted, what need it meets by appearing; and any agenda the prophesying god, goddess or person might have. Moreover, Aeneas receives, as well as detailed practical and partly factual guidance, prophecies destined more for the audience of the poem than for him (in the underworld and on the shield); the most that such prophecies can induce in Aeneas is a vague optimism. Is this optimism deluded, as has been argued, in view of the pain and cost that the prophecies conceal?[107] But prophecies, like omens, are a tool of Fate and must accord with its rules: the petitioner wants an answer that is correct, clear and complete within the remit of the question;[108] that answer, however, even if it must be in some sense correct,[109] cannot be so clear and complete that it might allow the petitioner to tamper with, or retract from, Fate's outcome. And even if the (strictly) partial revelation of Fate acts as a narrative spoiler, we can guarantee that its revelation will not be the whole story. Jupiter's rhetorical question to Cybele (9.96 f.) captures the predicament for the consultor of oracles: **'Is Aeneas to face all his doubts and dangers and never know uncertainty?'** / ***'Should Aeneas go through scathing dangers all unscathed?'*** (Fagles' translation is less close to the Latin). The cumulative effect of prophecy on Aeneas is to motivate him – much as state religion was intended to motivate the people – paradoxically by its very lack of small print. And when the *Aeneid* itself prophesies Rome's greatness after Augustus (7.41 note), it does so conscious of the losses such future greatness is bound to incur.

6.4.5 Deification

Hercules (*Introduction* – 4.5.4, see especially the parallels with Aeneas and Augustus) sets the precedent for immortality earned through great deeds; he is described by Homer and Hesiod[110] after they have been accomplished ensconced on Mt Olympus with Hebe (Youth) for his wife. Rulers given divine honours were a feature of Egypt; the 'god-kings' of Persia acquired their divinity through the defeat of a pharaoh, Psammetichus III; Alexander the Great, when he conquered the Persian empire, was in turn expected to behave like a Persian monarch, though he seems hard-headedly to have exploited the divinity that went with the role for political ends.[111] His magnetic example told on Julius Caesar, for whom no *grandeur* was *folie*; his insistence on the family connection to Venus (*Introduction* – 3.2.2 Aeneas between the *Iliad* and the *Aeneid*: The Aeneas legend), and his greed for homage, angled for superhuman status.[112] After his assassination, Octavian celebrated funeral games (2.692–704 note) in his honour. In 42 BCE, the senate declared Caesar a god.[113] Accounts of the death of Romulus, Rome's founder and only previous deified ruler, linked him to Caesar through the suggestion that Romulus also had been killed by conspiring senators.[114] Henceforward Octavian would regularly refer to himself as *divi filius*, 'son of a god'.[115] It was not long after this that Tityrus (*Introduction* – 2.3 *Eclogues* (or *Bucolics*)), in Virgil's first *Eclogue*,[116] breaks off from making music under his beech to explain to the departing, dispossessed Meliboeus, 'A god [i.e. Augustus] created these carefree times for us'; he goes on to vow unflagging offerings at this god's altar.

Augustus, however, stopped shy of claiming divinity for himself: the name, which Octavian assumed in 27 BCE (*Introduction* – 1.7 Augustus in the *Aeneid*), means 'well-augured' and so has religious connotations but tactful ones. He allowed himself to be thanked along with the gods after the Parthian settlement in 20 BCE,[117] and did not oppose precincts being consecrated to him outside Italy.[118] The effigy of his *genius* was placed in the shrines at Rome's crossroads, along with the Lares (*Introduction* – 4.5.5 Gods local, domestic and minor). And poets continued to claim divinity on his behalf: Horace's farmer looks forward[119] to toasting Augustus' return from Gaul (in 13 BCE) with his own wine, and welcoming him as a god to the table:

> You, you he importunes with prayer after prayer
> and wine poured in libation from a dish, your godhead he combines
> with the Lares over the main course.

Ovid in the *Fasti*[120] (published in 8 CE) describes Augustus' Palatine house, next door to Apollo's temple and incorporating a shrine to Vesta (see plan in *Introduction* – 4.5.6 Imported gods):

> Phoebus holds one part; a second has been made over to Vesta;
> what they leave he himself occupies, the third of them ...
> ... a single house contains three eternal gods.

On his death in 14 CE, Augustus was officially deified.[121] His wife Livia was eventually conceded divine honours by the emperor Claudius, the first woman to receive them.[122]

The *Aeneid*, while adopting Augustus' self-awarded title of 'son of a god' (6.792), goes further when shunting him into divine company as a second Saturn (6.788–94 note) and when paralleling Augustus with Aeneas himself (8.678–81; 10.260–86 notes) – Aeneas' immortality is guaranteed by no less than Jupiter (1.259 f.). This comes across today as repellent, if at the time fashionable, adulation, but can also be seen as challenging Augustus to continue earning his divine promotion by his own equivalent of Herculean labours. The piety of the Roman people (12.839) would expect Augustus to exert himself on their behalf (1.253 note).

6.5 Battles[123]

Inevitably, Virgil's scenes of combat take the Iliad as their paradigm. Of the *Iliad*, approximately a third is taken up with them;[124] of the *Aeneid*, rather less: surprisingly little of Book II describes actual fighting and of the last four books the fighting is relieved by substantial interludes.[125] Virgil has a greater variety than Homer of techniques and equipment:[126]

- **Siege warfare**: this is described by Aeneas at Troy (2.440 ff.) and by the narrator at the Trojan camp (9.168 ff.) and at Latinus' city (12.672 ff.). It incorporates Roman techniques, tortoises in attack and towers in defence.[127] Scaling city walls is mentioned only once in the Iliad,[128] and the city in question in not Troy: Greeks and Trojans engage each other on the plain outside the city and the siege that succeeds is that of the Greek camp: Apollo fills in the ditch for the Trojans and kicks down the palisade as a child would a sandcastle.[129]

- **Cavalry and horses**: There are no cavalry engagements in the Iliad; horses are not ridden but yoked to two-man chariots; these chariots are used primarily[130] as taxis to and from the front. In the *Aeneid*, a cavalry battle, between the Arcadians and Etruscans[131] and the Italian forces under Camilla, provides a panoramic if somewhat improbable set piece (11.598 ff.);[132] Camilla fights from horseback until challenged not to (11.705 ff.) and can be assumed to remount afterwards. Turnus careers round the battlefield in his chariot dealing death (10.440, 12.477 ff.) – he rides (9.47 ff.), but only for speedy conveyance; the Trojans do not have chariots at all.

- **Armour**: Virgil has iron for swords and spearpoints, bronze for defensive protection (it remained in use for this purpose alongside iron into Roman times). In Homer, all weaponry is bronze. Shields in Virgil are never, as Ajax's, from neck to ankles,[133] but either round (*clipeus*) or oblong (*scutum*), and the latter never in single combat (apart from 10.505 note) – they are only found in bulk, as when Evander burns a pile of them at 8.562. Homer says little about cuirasses and Virgil follows contemporary practice – the design of scales or platelets of bronze (or iron) wired together – e.g. at 9.707, 11.487 – seems to have been a first century BCE invention. On spears, unusually, Virgil is a simplifier – he does not distinguish between the pike (which Ajax wields to such effect in defending the ships[134]) and the throwing spear (which Homeric warriors carried in pairs[135]), even though Roman soldiers also had separate types (*hasta* and *pilum*).

The *Iliad* and the *Aeneid* above all share their focus on encounters of individual warriors – there were massed troops (e.g. 12.662 f.) but these, their manoeuvres and the tactics of their deployment over the terrain, are not the poet's concern:[136] Homer and Virgil want to name victor and victim. Even archers aim at a specific opponent; the anonymity Aeneas' assailant preserves (at 12.320 ff.) is remarked on as exceptional reticence.[137] Duels are shaped by convention: combatants throw their spears before closing with their swords (12.710 ff.); throwing a rock instead fares as badly as might be expected in the *Aeneid* (10.381 ff., 12.896 ff.), though one wounded Aeneas in the Iliad.[138] Variety is injected into the otherwise repetitive killing through verbal taunts and ripostes, the advance of the adversaries towards each other, potted biographical information (especially of family, dabbing in touches of humanity), attire, the passage of the spear (and whom it actually hits, if anyone), the meeting of armour (spear and sword on shield, helmet and breastplate), the sometimes grisly wounds dealt (almost always fatal[139] – the battlefield is not choked with the injured or their extrication), the fate of the corpse, the handling of spoils – and occasional similes. Virgil, like Homer, sometimes addresses one of the combatants directly, making the narrative suddenly personal (a device called 'apostrophe'; e.g. 10.508, Pallas[140]).

The moments of greatest heroic glory, whether in the Iliad or the *Aeneid*, are the *aristeiai*, cadenzas of carnage when one warrior dominates the action. In the Iliad, the three main examples belong to Diomedes, Agamemnon and Achilles[141] – the latter progresses via a hallucinatory confrontation with the river Scamander to his defeat of Hector in single combat. Other *aristeiai* on a smaller scale give a framework to the ensemble fighting – notably of Idomeneus and Patroclus.[142] In the *Aeneid*, each of the last four books contains an *aristeia*, or – in Books X and XII – more than one:

Where in the text	Hero	Tally
9.672-777	Turnus	18
10.310-44	Aeneas	7
(345-52)	(Clausus – Italian)	7
362-425	Pallas	8
(411-24)	(Halaesus – Italian)	5
426-30	Lausus	1
10.510-605	Aeneas	11
10.689-746	Mezentius	7
11.664-724	Camilla	12
12.324-82	Turnus	13
12.500-547	Aeneas PLUS	7
	Turnus	6+

There is nothing in the *Aeneid* that rivals the extent of Achilles' destructiveness, but the nested format of Aeneas' *aristeia* in Book X builds from routine efficiency when he enters battle to blazing frenzy after the death of Pallas. On the other hand the double *aristeia* that he shares with Turnus in Book XII, where the narrative artfully juxtaposes them although they are widely separated on the battlefield, balances them evenly before they come together for the dénouement.

There is one difference of principle between the battle descriptions of the Iliad and those of the *Aeneid*. In the Iliad, the ebb and flow are clearly marked:

- The static phase (*stadiē*), when both sides are evenly matched – killings alternate, Greek on Trojan, Trojan on Greek. This is how battle is joined in Book 4.[143] It is easy to follow who is on which side either because one of the combatants is a familiar name or because we are given an obvious clue, such as family or place of origin.

- The turning point, usually a decisive intervention, sometimes heralded by a simile – so Diomedes is inspired by Athena at the start of Book 5 and his armour shines like Sirius.[144]

- The rout (*phobos*), when the casualties are all on one side – sometimes in pairs, as the fugitives take to their chariots. Here Homer does not need to clarify which side the participants are on. So, it is when Diomedes enters the heart of the battle and heartens his colleagues.[145] Homer sometimes lingers over the slain, as here, sometimes lists them like (named) flies.[146] 'Minor figures die; they do not kill.'[147]

The *Aeneid* does not abide by these conventions. There is only one, very brief, instance of a sequence of killings by alternate sides (12.289-310 – Messapus (Italian), Corynaeus (Trojan), and Alsus (Italian)); a splurge of names at 10.747 ff. turns out, on careful inspection, to be a flurry of Latin wins, concluded by a Trojan one to halt them. Elsewhere a complex exchange of missiles (9.569 ff.) shows Virgil anxious not to be too schematic – victories (Trojan / Italian) in quick succession run T I I T 7I (all Turnus) T I – the last being Mezentius' with a sling shot; again, the Italians might be said to have ended on top, except that Ascanius then shoots Numanus Remulus. There is only one example of different members of one side (as opposed to a single hero in an *aristeia*) gaining the upper hand in a series of kills (12.458 ff., when Aeneas returns to the fray after medical treatment). And as for turning points, these are obscure: the cavalry battle has a life all its own (11.618 ff.).

In short, Virgil is much more attracted to the fog of war than Homer; names can intensify as much as disperse it. Heinze, assuming that Virgil's historical material contained relatively few major figures and that out of respect for it he could not invent too many Camillas, summarizes[148] Virgil's approach as follows:

> He would concentrate the interest on the smallest possible number of characters, and by careful use of Roman and national material, make the battle scenes as graphic as possible and emphasize the overall human interest or psychological aspect of the events.

This might explain the paradox that the *Aeneid*'s battle scenes are at one and the same time grittily physical and strangely disembodied.

CHAPTER 7
LITERARY ASPECTS

This chapter looks at several literary features of the poem to which it is worth drawing the attention of a reader in translation – except for allusion, which needs a chapter of its own (see *Introduction* – 8.1 Intratextuality: Self-allusion; and 8.2 Intertextuality, narrow sense: External allusion) and literary theory, because it belongs more fittingly in the chapter on Reception and Interpretation (see *Introduction* – 9.6 Literary theory).

7.1 Structure[1]

7.1.1 *The poem as a whole*

To see how ideas on the structure of the *Aeneid* have developed, we can start from Heinze in 1902:[2] 'The fact that the action consists of two major parts, equal in content . . . had to be reflected in the form. This is done by dividing the material into two groups of six books, which are then further divided into pairs.' These pairs were later characterized as alternating epic and tragic;[3] this will not quite do, as Books VI and VIII do not end tragically, unlike II, IV, X and XII; and in the latter two books the tragedy is Aeneas' triumph. A more satisfactory formulation is that the even-numbered books deal with the hero, his mission and his Fate while the odd-numbered ones set these in a broader context; but the more cautious the analysis, the weaker it appears.

As to the halves, there is certainly a clear demarcation brought about by the invocations to the Muse (1.8 ff. and 7.37 ff.) and Juno's major interventions, in the storm (Book I) and Allecto's mission (Book VII). The contrast between them was related to the *Odyssey* and *Iliad* by early commentators,[4] and they are often still described respectively as 'Odyssean' and 'Iliadic', for example by Otis:[5] the journeys of Aeneas take place, like those of Odysseus in the *Odyssey*, in the first half of the epic, while the Iliadic battles on the plain between city and ships take place in the second. Again, qualifications must be made – the *Odyssey*, as Otis recognizes, offers a complete model for the *Aeneid* in that its second half is set in the destination country and ends with a battle (the fighting in the *Aeneid* does not start till Book IX), a battle that moreover provides a form of closure;[6] and there are intrusions[7] from the *Iliad* (such as the funeral games of Book 23) into the first half of the *Aeneid* (Book V).

Not content with a division into two halves, scholars have related the two halves to each other, but in different ways. Most straightforwardly, Duckworth has worked out[8] correspondences between the books of each half in order (I–VII, II–VIII, III–IX . . .) – the following table abbreviates his:

I	• Arrival in Carthage	VII	• Arrival in Italy
	• Dido offers friendship		• Latinus offers friendship
	• Juno's storm		• Juno's war

II	• Troy destroyed by the Greeks	VIII	• Rome is born on a Greek site
	• Ascanius' hair seems to burn		• Augustus on the shield emits flames
	• Aeneas shoulders his father		• Aeneas shoulders his shield/destiny
III	• Aeneas yields place to Anchises	IX	• Aeneas absent, Ascanius the focus
	• Episode – Helenus/Andromache		• Episode – Nisus and Euryalus
	• Escape from danger (Cyclops, Scylla/Charybdis)		• Escape from Turnus' invasion of the camp
IV	• Juno and Venus agree	X	• Juno and Venus at loggerheads
	• 'Fault' of Dido leads to her suicide		• 'Fault' of Turnus leads to his death
	• Death of Dido, without Aeneas		• Death of Mezentius, without Lausus
V	• Lessening of tension – games	XI	• Lessening of tension – truce
	• Tension bursts out – ships torched		• Truce broken, fighting resumes
	• Death of Palinurus		• Death of Camilla
VI	• Retardations climax in Aeneas meeting Anchises	XII	• Retardations climax in Aeneas meeting Turnus
	• Anchises reveals Rome's future		• Jupiter and Juno agree the nature of Rome's people
	• Death of Marcellus made present		• Death of Turnus

Some correspondences succeed better than others (1–VII, II–VIII appear strongest). There is an alternative: Otis detects a pattern that reflects the Eclogues (*Introduction – 2.2 Virgilian Appendix*; see also 7.1.3 Ring form):

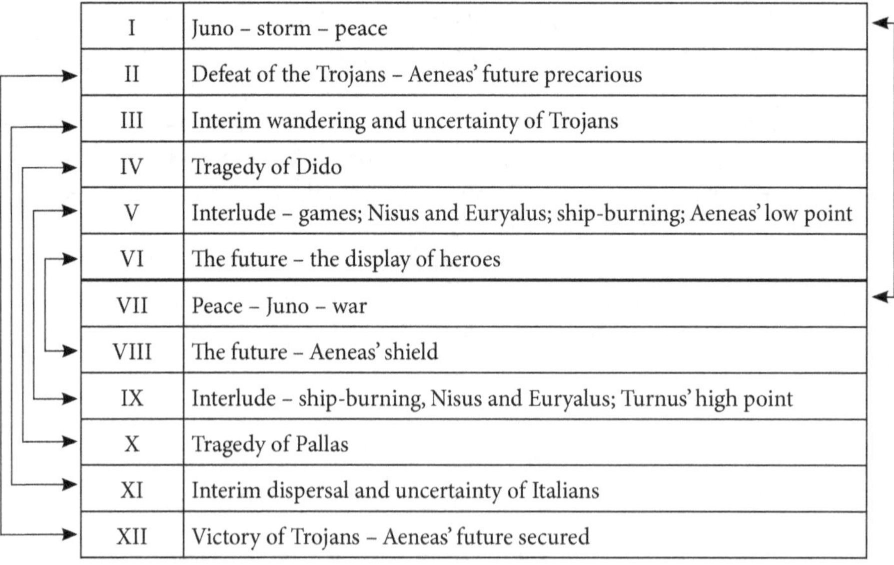

I	Juno – storm – peace
II	Defeat of the Trojans – Aeneas' future precarious
III	Interim wandering and uncertainty of Trojans
IV	Tragedy of Dido
V	Interlude – games; Nisus and Euryalus; ship-burning; Aeneas' low point
VI	The future – the display of heroes
VII	Peace – Juno – war
VIII	The future – Aeneas' shield
IX	Interlude – ship-burning, Nisus and Euryalus; Turnus' high point
X	Tragedy of Pallas
XI	Interim dispersal and uncertainty of Italians
XII	Victory of Trojans – Aeneas' future secured

Otis supplements this with a parallel between the two quintets of books in each half (that is, other than I and VII): Aeneas is the main figure in the even-numbered books, while Anchises dominates III and V, Turnus IX and XI. In VI, Aeneas and Anchises share the attention, as Aeneas and Turnus do in XII. If I and VII are bolted on to the rule for odd-numbered books, this parallel becomes less persuasive (Anchises does not appear in I, Turnus relatively briefly in VII). And for Otis, unlike most others, VII and not VI becomes the heart of the poem.

There are those who advocate the *Aeneid*'s division into thirds as well. Pöschl, for one, describes[9] the three quartets of books as an alternation of dark–light–dark, and Duckworth emphasizes[10] the difference in character of the four middle books, not least due to their wholesale importations from Homer.[11] So we have another possible analysis:

I		Dido in action
II	CARTHAGE – Love and Tragedy of Dido	Loss of Troy and Creusa
III		
IV		Death of Dido
V	LATIUM – Arrival and preparation for battle; the destiny of Rome	Burial of Anchises and the past
VI		The future of Rome – individuals
VII		
VIII		The future of Rome – city and war
IX	LATIUM – Battle and Tragedy of Turnus	Turnus in action
X		Aeneas' victory over Mezentius
XI		
XII		Aeneas' victory and death of Turnus

This organizing principle gives pride of place to the even-numbered books and does not try to integrate III, VII and XI. Nor does it attempt to correlate the books across the quartets, though such correlations can be made (as under the system of two hexads).

Are these various proposals somehow compatible? Duckworth believes,[12] 'the tripartite division is not a substitute for the twofold arrangement but is superimposed upon it'. This would allow each system to complement the other; each system stresses features of the individual books differently. It seems implausible, however, that Otis' nested correspondences should coexist with Duckworth's mirroring halves – at some point the poem would cease to be a work of art and becomes a work of geometry, with too many axes of symmetry.

Which leads to the more fundamental question, how the design matters. For the author, the structure dictates the patterning of the text; for the listener or reader the process is reversed, as the structure arises from the text once read or heard. An audience must pick it up while listening, without the benefit of a manuscript to pore over; an author cannot rely on it to make an impact in itself. Structure, therefore, however it may enhance or clarify meaning and have an aesthetic of its own, cannot itself be the main vehicle of meaning.[13] Insofar as it enhances or clarifies meaning, Otis' view that the second half of the *Aeneid* constitutes the fulfilment of the first half is *prima facie* contradicted by the tripartite view's sandwich of hopeful destiny by tragedy.[14] Those who retain both views, without modifying Otis' of the second half, must take Virgil's ending as ambivalent.

7.1.2 Within individual books

Although the breakdown of the constituent episodes within books of the *Aeneid* is usually evident give or take a few lines, the way those episodes are grouped into sections, if at all, is much more open to debate. One commentator's tabulations of a book's contents will differ from another's. Duckworth has indefatigably deduced a general rule – division into three[15] – that can be applied to all the books without strain, except (as he ruefully notes) Book V. But to illustrate the problem, what are the three parts in Book I? Duckworth divides it into, (1) Juno and the storm (1.1–222), (2) Venus episodes (1.223–417) and (3) Trojans in Carthage (1.418–756). This is 'structure by category' – Juno, Venus, Trojans. Otis (as followed in Book I – Structure) prefers 'structure by symmetry' – the first part is made up of the mirror image of Juno undermining Jupiter and Venus approaching him to restore order – three pairs of sections that are nested inside each other (ring form – 7.1.3), with a coda of Jupiter taking action (1.1–304). (In this commentary's tables of structure for each book, arrows tentatively suggest links between episodes.) On this construction the book's second part would be Venus' encounter with Aeneas followed by Aeneas' arrival at Juno's temple, another juxtaposition of Juno and Venus (1.305–493). The third part would be Aeneas' encounter with Dido (1.494–756), the book ending with the human actors, having begun with the divine ones. The reader (what listener could discern this, other than in broadest outline?) will opt for the dissection he or she finds most persuasive: Otis' view makes clearer the gradations of knowledge about the future, from Jupiter (all-knowing) through Juno and Venus (knowing some but not all) to Aeneas (knowing little) and Dido (knowing nothing).

The very openness to debate makes too assertive a formalism turn into a bed of Procrustes. Besides, a theory of the structure may contribute greatly to our appreciation of Virgil's artistry but will not alter our reaction to the text; this is the case even when the structuring principle seems clear, as in the number of lines allocated to sections within speeches. Perhaps for this reason, after its heyday in the 1950s and 1960s, structural analysis seems to have fallen from fashion.

7.1.3 Ring form

A characteristic particularly of Homeric speeches, where the end returns to the beginning; it can take a Dutch doll (ABC...(C′)B′ A′) format.[16] Homer also uses it on a larger scale (indeed, overarching the entire *Iliad*, since the wrath of Achilles at the outset is stilled in the final book). Virgil uses it more to define structure than as a rhetorical method of closure: it can highlight the contrast between the ring's start and end (as in Otis' analysis of Book I's first section, above); or it can highlight the central point – Book III, although a journey, can be viewed as ring form with a light touch, starting and ending with a death (Polydorus <> Anchises), moving inwards with two prophecies (Apollo's <> Scylla and Charybdis, as foretold by Helenus) and further in with two portents (the plague <> the white horses). The central section, in Greece, is the core of the book, from Celaeno's prophecy to Helenus': it is where Aeneas begins to find his sense of direction. On the grander scale, the *Aeneid* could be said to use ring form in the relationship between its books (so Otis, 7.1.1); and, like the *Iliad*, the *Aeneid* begins and ends with wrath (*ira*), even if of different protagonists – Juno (1.11) and Aeneas (12.946).

7.2 The hero

The concept of 'the hero' has developed over time. In the *Iliad*, a hero is a warrior[17] whose aim, as Hector puts it, is 'to take my place in the front line and try to win glory for my father and myself'.[18] This glory is the source of an undying name – Hector soon afterwards imagines a visitor to a burial mound: '"This is the monument of some great warrior of an earlier day who was killed in action by glorious Hector." That is what he will say, and my fame will never die.'[19] It is such 'eternal glory' that Achilles chooses over a long life in the land of his fathers.[20]

In the *Odyssey*, although Odysseus is a great warrior (as the final show-down in his palace proves), his epithets stress other qualities – 'much enduring', 'of many wiles';[21] he shares nevertheless Hector's and Achilles' awareness of their reputations, as when he introduces himself to Alcinous,[22] 'I am Odysseus son of Laertes, known among men for craftiness of all kinds, and my fame has reached the heavens.' This is the introduction that Aeneas echoes to Dido (1.378–80 note), but making *pietas* his particular mark of distinction. With *pietas* comes a significant shift in values, from self-promotion or self-preservation to a sense of duty towards others (on *pietas*, see 1.8–11 note; on Aeneas as different, see 1.1–7 note.). But *pietas*, too, brings renown.[23]

This is a long way from our concept of the hero as the subject and prime mover in a story[24] or as its moral example.[25] The Greek word *hērōs*, and like it the Latin *heros*, have no literary connotations; they denote either warriors, or else 'individuals, normally held to be descended from gods, whose tombs received quasi-divine honors'.[26] Neither word, nor any other in either language, could convey the meaning of 'hero' in the phrase 'she is the hero of the poem'. Why, then, the name 'Aeneid'? The idea that a single protagonist[27] might unify a story is alien to Virgil as to Homer in the *Odyssey*. Aristotle, speaking of plot whether in tragedy or epic, says:[28]

> A plot is not (as some think) unified because it is concerned with a single person. An indeterminately large number of things happen to any one person, not all of which constitute a unity; likewise a single individual performs many actions, and they do not make up a single action … When <Homer> composed the *Odyssey*, he did not include everything which happened to Odysseus … instead he constructed the *Odyssey* about a single action of the kind we are discussing [i.e. his return home].

> (Trans. Heath)

What unifies the *Aeneid* is the project Aeneas must undertake (see *Introduction* – 5.2 Aristotle and the Peripatetics (from the late fourth century BCE)). DServius' comment[29] on the opening of Book I strikes a similar note, however drily. The beginning of an epic, he says, will consist of the announcement of the subject, the invocation of the Muse and the start of the narrative. In the *Aeneid*'s case, 'Virgil takes up his announcement of the subject in four ways: from the leader ("I sing of arms and the man," 1.1); from the journey ("who first from the shores of Troy," 1.1); from the war ("he suffered also much in war," 1.5); and from the establishment of the race ("whence comes the Latin race", 1.6). Thus Aeneas serves the fourfold subject of the poem but is not himself the subject. In fact the notion of the single character subject, the hero given equal billing with what he does, evolved fully only in the Renaissance. It was first enunciated in English by Dryden, when he wrote[30] that the proper subject for a tragedy or epic poem was 'the great action of some illustrious hero'.

It is easy to assume that Aeneas is just such an 'illustrious hero', thereby going subtly further than the literary man, quoted[31] by Socrates in Plato's dialogue *Hippias Minor*, who held that 'the *Odyssey* was composed with reference to Odysseus and the *Iliad* with reference to Achilles'. The danger with this view of Aeneas is that he becomes loaded with the expectations on a modern hero (such as self-determination or the ultimate triumph of virtue) and then turns out a disappointment. Virgil does not use Aeneas to edify in the manner of Livy, who wrote in the preface to his history:[32]

> The subjects to which I would ask each of my readers to devote his earnest attention are these – the life and morals of the community; the men and the qualities by which through domestic policy and foreign war dominion was won and extended. Then as the standard of morality gradually lowers, let him follow the decay of the national character ...

The *Aeneid* is no exercise in nostalgia – the great achievements it celebrates are attended by moral failure (as in Anchises' gallery of Roman 'heroes').

7.3 Narratology[33]

Narratology,[34] or the theory of narrative, is not new – much of what Aristotle has to say about plot in the Poetics, for example, falls within it. The real blooming of narratological system, however, had to wait till the 1960s and 1970s: it was an offspring of Structuralism[35] (see *Introduction* – 9.6.4 Structuralism) but has surpassed its parent in the use to which it has been put in the analysis of classical texts. Nevertheless, a full-blown narratological commentary on the poem, of the kind that already exists on the *Odyssey*,[36] had yet to be produced. What follows here is an introduction to some of the concepts of narratology as they might be applied to the *Aeneid*, and already are in parts of this and other commentaries.

7.3.1 Narrators and narratees

Narratology first of all is keen to distinguish between narrator and author. The narrator's voice, even when in the first person, is as much the creation of the author as any of his characters.[37] This cautions against at a gallop identifying Virgil with the narrator of the *Aeneid*, even when he steps out of the third person to address his characters[38] (as to Nisus and Euryalus at 9.449 ff. – and Virgil, as if to remind us of the artifice, has the narrator quote Euryalus when speaking to him: 9.446–9 note). This narrator is imagined in relation to his Muse(s) (e.g. 1.8) and has his competitors – Juno hears from elsewhere about the destined sack of Carthage (1.20). He sings (1.1 but not at 7.41), a word applied to prophets as well as poets.[39] Still more the 'narrator as creation of the author' warns against deducing a biography of Virgil from his poetry (see *Introduction* – 2 Virgil's Life and Works).

Narratology also distinguishes between the narrator and other narrators inserted in the narrative, each with his or her own contrasting identity. So in Book II, Virgil, the primary narrator on whom we rely absolutely, makes Aeneas secondary narrator, ostensibly frank and open (see Book II – Description)– while Aeneas' inserted, and thus Virgil's tertiary, narrator, Sinon, is utterly deceitful: Aeneas gains credibility as Sinon loses it. And it is vital for Aeneas and for the progress of the plot that Aeneas, talking to Dido, should come across as the polar opposite of a Ulysses with his tricks (2.44).[40] Analogously, Virgil himself gains credibility when he distances himself from the word on the streets, from what 'is said' – as when he reports the popular attribution of Etna's fires to the buried Enceladus (3.578 ff.). He is aware that his own authority can be impugned and bolsters it by his appeals to the Muses (*Introduction* – 4.5.5 Gods local, domestic and minor).

Narratees, the recipients of the narrative, are not homogenous: do women members of the audience react to Dido's story in the same way as men? Are they intended to react differently? A tale-within-a-tale creates secondary and, with Sinon, tertiary narratees in addition to the primary narratees (us, or the Roman audience), for each of whom the narrative fulfils a different function. So Sinon's fiction impresses the Trojans (tertiary narratees), appals Dido (secondary narratee) and confirms to the Roman audience (primary narratees) what many of them always thought about the Greeks. Aeneas' flashback[41] is for Dido an invitation to love, but for the Roman audience a flash-forward to the foundation of Troy's successor, Rome. Narratology offers a framework for such analysis.

7.3.2 Focalization

Narratology defines three strata to a narrative:

- Underpinning everything is the *text*, the words on the page or in the head of the bard;
- Through this a narrator tells a *story*, with actors, plot and narrative artifice;
- From this the narratees (re)construct a *fabula*, or story-for-them, in which events are ordered, actors turned into characters, emotional colouring applied. In the absence of other guidance, the narratee forms their own view of (focalizes) events. But there is often other guidance.

In its strongest form, such guidance is an intrusion from the narrator – **'This day was the beginning of her death, the cause of all her sufferings.'** / ***'This was the first day of her death, the first of grief, the cause of it all.'*** (4.169 f.) This is rare. More commonly, the narrator will say how a character feels, or the character can say it for him or herself; the narrator can also signal the emotion indirectly – Aeneas' acute disquiet at the mobilization of the Latins is fixed by a simile at the start of Book VIII (8.18 ff.). Most often the narrator lends a quality to the scene, often through adjectives, that evokes what the actors in it remark or experience: the description of Charon (6.298 ff.) is loaded with detail, some of it neutral ('thick grey beard'), some attitudinal ('unkempt') and some out-and-out emotional ('terrible'); it is barely noticeable that the narrator is looking through Aeneas' (probably not the Sibyl's) eyes. Very occasionally the viewpoint of character and narrator combine – so, when Aeneas is surveying the nascent Carthage: **'Aeneas was amazed at the size of it where recently there had been nothing but shepherd's huts'** / ***'Aeneas marvels at its mass – once a cluster of huts'*** (1.421 and note) –

Aeneas is unlikely to have known what was there before and could never have used the word the narrator uses for 'huts', which DServius says derived from the Carthaginian.

It is when the splashes of emotional colour could belong to either the narrator or one (or more than one) of the actors that focalization becomes more ambiguous and suggestive. The first time Dido is called 'unhappy' (1.712), this must be the narrator's judgement – she is quite the reverse, full of the excitement of attraction. At 4.68, she is burning with uncontrolled passion, perhaps too much to notice anything like unhappiness. At 4.529, sleepless and beset by nightmares, she is deeply unhappy – and at 4.596 she avows it herself. When the narrator describes the sympathetic spectators watching Turnus approach the altar and Turnus' youthful cheeks and pallor (12.220 f.), it seems clear that this is what they see, not what the narrator sees – what became of Turnus the one-man army at the end of Book IX? Or is this the narrator after all, and Turnus actually playing to the gallery? So the answer to the question 'Who sees?', as distinct from 'Who speaks?',[42] is a choice for the narratee to make, and that choice matters. In Book X (10.565–70 and note), when Aeneas is compared to the hundred-hander Aegaeon, the narrator leaves it open whether this is his own perspective or that of the daunted Italians facing Aeneas – it is tempting to suppose both because the narrator can hardly on his own account declare Aeneas a monster, but the Italians have no leisure to make a four-line allusion to the recesses of mythology. The simile could even be an example of the hypothetical focalizer – 'you might have taken him for Aegaeon ...'. 'Virgilian narrative admits (often, even) a multiple, and elusive, point of view.'[43] To leave the focalizer ('Who sees?') indeterminate here seems a more tenable approach than to switch the focalizer away from the primary narrator ('Who speaks?) as a way of excusing him from an unpalatable sentiment.[44]

Servius observes focalization and makes up a muddled rule for it.[45] Heinze noticed that Virgil used focalization (though Heinze did not use the term) systematically, not intermittently, as in Homer – 'the feelings of the protagonists are intended to be suggested to us by the narrative, without being expressly mentioned ... he has put himself into the heart of his characters and speaks from inside them'.[46] The idea was developed by Otis in his chapter 'The Subjective Style' (a phrase which has caught on) – 'Virgil is constantly conscious of himself inside his characters; he thinks through them and for them.'[47] For Otis, this has consequences for characterization (see *Introduction* – 3.1 Characterization in the *Aeneid*). But, *pace* Otis, when Virgil's narrator has his characters focalize their experiences ('embedded focalization'), that is not the same thing as himself focalizing their experiences for them – the characters retain their autonomy, as far as invented characters can.[48] If anything, their autonomy is enhanced, especially if the character's perspective is different from the narrator's: when Euryalus is told by Nisus to stop laying about him (9.355 f.), he seems to obey – **They left behind them many pieces of men's armour wrought in solid silver, and mixing bowls besides, and lovely rugs. . . /** *And they leave behind a haul of soldiers' armor struck in solid silver, mixing bowls in the bargain, gorgeous rugs.* The feeling here belongs to Nisus' regretful glance back; and Euryalus proceeds to take some consolation loot, which proves fatal. Virgil's attitude to this is expressed elsewhere, when he bemoans Turnus' lack of restraint (10.501 f.); so it is not Virgil who admires the armour, mixing bowls and rugs – as narrator he has momentarily stepped back.

Focalization in the *Aeneid* is the property of narrators; you rarely see one character focalizing the feelings of another, standing in his or her shoes.[49] Evander understands Pallas' longing for glory (11.154 f.); Juno calls Venus' infection of Dido with love for Aeneas a 'fine victory' (4.93) and Jupiter, with similarly sarcastic inverted commas, opines to Juno that the Trojans are succeeding not through their own efforts but through Venus' (10.608 ff.). The most conspicuous display of sympathy is when Anna puts into words one side – only one side – of the argument going on in Dido's head (4.31 ff.). But these insights are partial, or malign, or after the event. Nobody in the *Aeneid* (not even Anna) could be said to persuade anyone else to change their minds by appreciating their point of view, though some try;[50] the nearest to it is the poem's closing scene, when Aeneas stops just short of being persuaded. This accentuates the loneliness of the *Aeneid*'s characters – above all of Aeneas, for whom such mutual understanding seems so often just out of reach, and who, as narrator in Books II and III, shows himself well able to display it (see *Introduction* – 3.2.3 Aeneas in the *Aeneid*: Filling in the blanks).

7.3.3 Visual narration

The term 'focalization' has taken over from older words such as 'perspective', or 'point of view'. These have one advantage, however, in that they capture the spatial component of focalization – if the focalizer is within the text, the focalization takes place from an identifiable somewhere. So Aeneas' men scurrying to prepare the fleet are compared to ants – not just for their industry but also because Dido is surveying them from the heights of her city walls (4.402 ff.).

The third-person ('external') narrator is free to shift spatial viewpoint, something Virgil does as naturally as a film-maker. At the death of Camilla (11.799), he tracks the spear from Arruns' hand, as it passes the Volscians and draws their attention, on to Camilla who is oblivious to it, finally to halt with it as it strikes home and dwell on its lethal effect. Quinn describes[51] the technique: 'The camera starts at some distance from a scene and moves progressively closer to it, securing not only greater detail, but an illusion of participation in the action.' As Quinn implies, the technique is a good way of following a character's onward motion, for instance when Aeneas passes through the throng of untimely dead to his encounter with Dido (6.426 ff.) – it matters little whether the focalizer is the narrator or Aeneas. The ensuing close-up slows the pace of the narrative (7.3.4), which resumes as soon as the narrator changes vantage-point, usually by zooming out again; Dido dashes away into the shadows of the wood (6.472) and, when Camilla expires (11.834 ff.), a clamour reaches the heavens as the Trojans with their allies charge *en masse*. Visual narration, ubiquitous in the *Aeneid*, is a device that Virgil exploits with unflagging ingenuity.

7.3.4 Time

Narratology pays close attention to the manipulation of time. The chronology of the *Iliad* is forty-five days; of the *Odyssey*, twenty years (though the action of the poem takes place in some forty days of the last year); of the *Aeneid*, over 1,000 years (the judgement of Paris to Augustus, with the action of the poem taking place over a year and a bit[52]). In fact the *Aeneid* is two stories and two *fabulae*, each with its own temporal perspective: the first story-*fabula* is that of Aeneas and his men; the second that of Rome:

1. For <u>Aeneas and his men</u>, the past is contained in:
   - flashbacks (in narratological jargon *analepsis*), such as Venus' on Dido (1.340 ff.); Aeneas' on Troy (in Books II and III); Palinurus' and Deiphobus' on themselves

in Book VI (6.347ff., 6.513 ff.); Diana's on Camilla (11.535 ff.), though no Trojan hears it;

- *ekphraseis*, of Troy on Juno's temple (1.456 ff.), of Ganymede on a cloak (5.252) and of the minotaur on Apollo's temple (6.20 ff.).

Their prospects within the poem and just after it ends take the form of:

- flash forward (in narratological jargon *prolepsis*), as in the Proem to Book I (1.1 ff.);
- prophecy (also *prolepsis*) such as Helenus' mixture of instruction and prediction, 3.381 ff.; the Sibyl to Aeneas, 6.83 ff.

2. For <u>Rome</u>, the past is contained in:

- the primary narrator's preamble (1.12 ff., 7.45 ff.); Evander's account of Cacus and Mezentius (8.190 ff., 8.481 ff.);
- archaeology, of Latinus' palace (7.170 ff.) and Pallanteum (8.337 ff.);
- the catalogue of Italic (7.647 ff.) and Etruscan peoples (10.166 ff.).

For its future beyond the poem:

- flash forward, in the array of great Romans (6.760 ff.), Evander's tour of the city (8.337 ff.) or the *ekphrasis* of the shield (8.626 ff.);
- prophecy from Jupiter (1.258 ff.), Apollo (3.94 ff.);
- Jupiter's settlement with Juno (12.830 ff.).

In the first story-*fabula*, of Aeneas and the Trojans, where they are narratees they can construct a *fabula*. The second story-*fabula*, of Rome, is destined for the Roman audience – Aeneas, where he is the narratee, cannot make head or tale of the information (except the story of Cacus).

In neither of the stories from which the narratees construct their *fabulae* are they given anything approaching a chronology. For the Rome 'story', it takes previous knowledge of Roman history to put in order the people and events mentioned in the various *prolepseis*. For the story-*fabula* of Aeneas and his men, only in the second half of the *Aeneid* (as in the second half of the *Odyssey*, or the *Iliad* throughout) does the narrator conscientiously mark the passage of days (Book VIII onwards – see 9.1–24 and 11.133 notes). Thus in Book IV, three dawns are mentioned (4.7, 4.129, 4.585) but they are not successive and are there to initiate a new phase in the drama. As for years, an unaccountably large number – seven – are taken up by the voyage to Sicily but that number then sticks (see Book III – Inconsistencies). Error or not, it illustrates the impressionistic feel to time's passing in the first half of the poem (especially the intense action of Book II contrasted with the telescoped voyages of Book III); but then Book I, plunging *medias res*into the storm at sea, has alerted us not to expect annalistic history.

Differences between the time taken in the 'story' (i.e. the number of lines in the text) and the time taken in the narratee's *fabula* are thus built into the design of the *Aeneid*. Such differences are everywhere, also, in the narration itself. It is conventional to distinguish between 'scenes', to whose narration poetic space is allocated according to duration and importance, and 'transitions', which are condensed. But within scenes, too, time is elastic – it is hard to conceive how Ascanius could have forborne to fire his arrow at Numanus Remulus until the end of the latter's speech (9.595 ff.).[53] Conversely in transitions, there are examples where story and *fabula* are almost in step: Aeneas and the remains of his fleet make for the shores of Libya (1.157 ff.); in a short digression the narrator describes the sheltered bay they are entering; and ten lines on, the next we hear of them, the ships have taken advantage of that digression to enter and are now floating by the shore. Narrative pace (in the terminology 'rhythm') can be manipulated to capture a subjective experience of time: when Rumour claims that Dido and Aeneas are spending the whole winter in licentiousness (4.193 f.), their months pass as quickly for us as for them, stamped with a single image (by the salacious gossipers); when Aeneas hurls his spear at Turnus (12.919 ff.) Turnus watches it flying as if through viscous fluid, the instant of its arrival delayed by a simile and individual pieces of armour (see also 7.3.3 above).

Akin to narrative pace is narrative direction. If we, the audience, know where the narrative is heading but it turns off the route or becomes obstructed, then we have a case of retardation. This can be momentary – Dido hesitates before she comes out to join the hunt (4.133 ff.); the three lines preserve narrative rhythm (i.e. the hesitation is described in 'real time') but create a retardation that is eloquent of something not right that we cannot identify. Retardation is more often, however, on a larger scale; Juno's ploys are all retardations of Fate – in fact the *Aeneid* is a giant retardation, since we know the poem's direction from 1.5: we are fascinated by Juno's manoeuvres at the same time as being frustrated, for ourselves as well as for Aeneas.

7.3.5 Place and space

Descriptions of place offer the narrator possibilities analogous to the handling of time, and others besides. They can allow a pause inviting the audience's contemplation of a wider scene, where the details chosen reflect the atmosphere – such is the geographical *ekphrasis* (1.52–63 note) that covers the interval while Aeneas marks the turning point for the boat race (5.124 ff.); the narrator contrasts the waves that thrash the rock in winter with the fair-weather seagulls now basking on it above a looking-glass sea. At the other extreme, place becomes a blur in the action – such is the background to Aeneas chasing Turnus, where the geography of the simile bleeds into the narrative (12.749–57 and note) and the circuits woven by pursued and pursuer become abstract shapes (12.763 f.). Like time, place can be focalized through a character (see also 7.3.3) – the description of the entry to Hades is in the third person but we realize that Aeneas is experiencing its horror when he draws his sword (6.268 ff.). Just as the immensity of time is evoked by the *prolepseis* that stretch into the future; so the immensity of space is reached after in descriptions such as that of the storm in Book I, with its 'constant pull in the direction of the universal and hyperbolic'[54] – the sea gapes to its sands below and rises as high as a mountain, even to the stars (1.102 ff.). This cosmic scale is rarely forgotten: shouts also rise to the stars, or at least the heavens,[55] a turn of phrase familiar from the *Iliad*[56] but more pertinent in the *Aeneid*, where the gods shape much of the plot (at 11.832 ff., Diana seems roused by the upward clamour following Camilla's death). But place has human specificity in a way that time does not – the catalogues of Book VII and X, the list of nations doing homage to Augustus (8.722 ff.), conjure up lands in the remote past or remote distance through their inhabitants; these peoples, however far-flung, have homes that Aeneas and his Trojans still lack. For them Italy, or 'Hesperia', is at the same time *terra incognita* and much more than a destination. Loyalty to place enters even in the short topographical digressions of the final duel – the olive stump that grips Aeneas' spear (12.766 ff), the boundary stone lying on the plain (12.896 ff.), not only interrupt the narrative but also look away from it, to the local god jealous of his respect, and to squabbling landowners. Looking-away like this reaches its most developed form in the *ekphrasis* of an artefact – 7.4 – where the object described glimpses one or more other worlds, temporal, geographical or both, and *tableaux vivants* within them.

7.4 *Ekphrasis*

There are two types of *ekphrasis* in the *Aeneid*: geographical, where the narrator takes a moment to describe the backdrop, usually beginning with, 'There is (an island, a mountain, a river …)' – 7.3.5; and the extended description of an artefact (now the more common use of the term). 'Extended' does not have to mean more than a few lines – the cloak (5.250 ff.) and Anchises' mixing bowl (5.536 ff.) (both prizes at the games), or Turnus' helmet (7.785 ff.) and Pallas' baldric (10.495 ff.), all have the requisite property of turning the attention of characters within the poem to an artefact and to the craftsman's workmanship. (The *Aeneid* places works of art in a dramatic setting – with someone looking at and reacting to them – unlike some of Virgil's models,[57] where the work of art is described as in a museum catalogue.) That implies six possible focalizers (in the table below bold indicates the principal one), not necessarily all named in the three major *ekphraseis*:

	Temple of Juno at Carthage (1.441 ff.)	Doors of Temple of Apollo at Cumae (6.20 ff.)	Shield of Aeneas (8.630 ff.)
Maker	Several and anonymous	**Daedalus, overwhelmed by grief at the loss of Icarus**	Vulcan, whose choice of scenes is said to represent 'Ascanius' lineage and the battles they fight, in order'
Maker's patron	Dido and the Carthaginians	?	Venus, who makes no comment
Observer	**Aeneas, who interprets the scenes favourably**	Aeneas, who like Daedalus does not finish; he might or might not find hope in the escape from the labyrinth	Aeneas, who understands nothing
Observer's audience	Achates	Sibyl – an interrupter, not an audience	Venus (though Aeneas says nothing to her that Virgil records)
Narrator	Virgil, who follows Aeneas' gaze	Virgil, who aids in the focalization (of the missing Icarus scene)	**Virgil, who identifies the scenes**
Narrator's audience	Roman audience, us … – remembering Homer and the Epic Cycle	Roman audience, us … – troubled by what is omitted	Roman audience, us … – who are left unaided to work out what thematic connection there might be

In addition to the different points of view, there is sometimes play with the relationship of the materials to the subject. On the Temple of Juno, the scenes from the Trojan War might be painted or in stone relief but the medium is not as important as Aeneas' astonishment that he can recognize the events (including ones where he was not present) and the individuals involved – even himself (as Augustus, listening to the poem, will later hear of himself embossed on the shield). The doors of the Temple of Apollo are presumably bronze, but Daedalus was planning to depict Icarus, tumbling out of the sun, in gold (6.32). It is on the shield that the miraculous vividness, even animation, of the action is most consistently brought back to the metals that constitute it (8.626–728 note).

The reflective pause in the narrative that a long *ekphrasis* makes is justified by the dramatic significance of what follows (Dido's entry, the descent into the underworld, the start of battle in earnest); but the *ekphraseis* themselves are also some of the most self-conscious compositions in the poem – Virgil applies a distinct focalization to each. It is a metapoetic invitation to watch ourselves looking at the poem and to realize the limitations of our perspective – Aeneas, the observer in all three *ekphraseis*, sees what he wants to see in the first, does not finish the second and is mystified by the third. Putnam sees more in them than that, developing the thesis that each *ekphrasis* is a microcosm of the whole poem.[58]

7.5 Similes

One of the *Aeneid*'s most conspicuous inheritances (see *Introduction* – 8.2 Intertextuality, narrow sense: External allusion) from Homer, and from Apollonius of Rhodes, is its peppering of similes – short (e.g. of Turnus, 'like a huge tiger among helpless cattle', 9.730), or longer, often rounded off in ring form with an '... even so ...' to balance the 'just as ...' at the start (e.g. the first simile in the poem, 'As when a riot ... so did all the crashing...', 1.148 ff.). In the *Iliad*,[59] there are over 300 similes, occupying some 7 per cent of the poem, on almost eighty subjects (natural phenomena, animals wild or domestic, human activities; all familiar to the audience); they can become carried away with their own detail, working their way round to the point of comparison[60] or changing it midstream;[61] when of animals or natural phenomena, they often add a human onlooker.[62] They tend to exalt a point of high emotion or pathos, and can be piled up to do so;[63] in battle scenes they yank the violence momentarily back to peaceful activities:[64]

> Helenus struck Menelaus' chest with his arrow on a plate of his body-armour, but it ricocheted off. As black beans or chickpeas on a broad threshing floor leap from a flat shovel with the whistling wind and the winnower's force behind them, so the painful arrow ricocheted off Menelaus' body armour ...
>
> (Trans. Rieu – Jones)

The *Aeneid*'s similes, some 163 in total of which 38 are short,[65] offer parallels to many of these Homeric characteristics (see previous footnotes), while retaining their independence: thus in subject matter, roughly a third of the longer similes take as their point of comparison something not in Homer at all – occasionally something distinctly Roman, such as a collapsing pier at Baiae (9.710 ff.) or a missile from a siege engine (11.616). More distinctive is the care with which Virgil manages his comparisons. West has produced an analysis that underscores their suggestiveness and economy – taking 'O' for the object being compared and 'S' for what it is compared to in the simile:[66]

- The descriptions of both O and S feature the point of comparison ('bilateral correspondence')

- Either O or S only features a point of comparison that can be applied to the other ('unilateral correspondence')

- S features a point of comparison that applies to the real world beyond O ('irrational correspondence')

Correspondences between O and S can be multiple.

To take an example from the simile likening Amata, inoculated with Allecto's serpent, to a child's top (7.376 ff.):[67]

> She's now a force of fury herself unleashed through the city's
> Vastness, whirling about like a whip-lashed top such as children,
> Rapt in their play, will propel in a great circle all round empty
> Courtyards. When lashed into motion it travels in segments of curving
> Arcs; and the uncomprehending young throng stands in a stupor
> Over it, gazing in awe at the fast-spinning figure of boxwood
> Energized by their blows.
>   And Amata's propelled in no slower
> Course through the centres of cities, amid some ferocious peoples.
>
>   (Trans. Ahl)

Here bilateral correspondence is clear between the 'vastness of the city' and the 'great circle' that the top describes; 'lashed', of the top, and 'propelled', of Amata, are the same verb in Latin; 'whirling about', in Latin of the top, is related to the verb for **she flew** / *darts* (into the forests). And there are unilateral correspondences, too – the top is not said to be travelling fast, but Amata's 'no slower' tells us, if we had not pictured it already, that it is rocketing round the empty courtyards. But why are those courtyards 'empty' and why are the peoples 'ferocious'? One explanation might be that these touches anticipate the **desolate haunts** / *deserted lairs* of **wild beasts** (7.404) where Amata fetches up: an irrational correspondence. By the same token, **the lash of Bacchus** / *that whips her Maenads* (7.405) is not part of regular Dionysiac worship, but a throwback to the boys thrashing the top. Why does the simile incorporate so much detail on those boys, 'rapt in their play', who hardly resemble Allecto? Perhaps to comment on the frivolous and uncomprehending gods, fascinated by the world of mortals and by their own power to interfere in it. Of course, the reader, weary of the search for correspondences, might simply see the simile as taking on a life of its own.

Linked similes pose a further challenge to the ingenious interpreter[68]. There is no such artifice in Homer: here Virgil is innovating. Take the case of Dido, compared to Diana in Book I (1.498–502 and note); as if in antiphony, Aeneas is compared to Diana's brother Apollo in Book IV (4.143–50 and note). In both cases, this is focalization: how Dido strikes Aeneas and how

Aeneas strikes Dido. Does this mean no more than the symmetry of mutual attraction? Or does the narrator imply compatibility between them? Or, given the intervening simile of Dido as a hunted doe (4.143–50 and note) and the gods' exploitation of Dido to protect or ensnare Aeneas, are we to view the Apollo simile as a signal of power transferred from Dido to Aeneas? These are not mutually exclusive alternatives. And the Apollo simile even if focalized by Dido, is not wholly positive: the Dionysiac references it also contains look ironically forward, to when Dido will be raving like a Maenad (4.301 ff.), possessed by her passion for Aeneas. A rather different example of linked similes comes in the last quarter of the poem, where Turnus' animal imagery (9.47–76 note) takes him from predator to quarry and – possibly – modifies our sympathies for him. Linked similes are the exception; most similes sit complete within their immediate context.[69] Thus, although the impact of storm similes[70] may be increased by the reverberation of Book I's mighty tempest, symbolic of divine disruption, and the impact of fire similes[71] by the inferno of Book II, symbolic of human destruction, they do not appear thematically linked.

7.6 Speeches

The importance of oratory in education and society for both Greece and Rome does not need repeating; the literary importance of speeches is evident in Homer, in whose *Iliad* some 45 per cent of the text is made up of direct speech, uttered by eighty-eight speakers, while in the *Odyssey* 68 per cent is direct speech (counting Odysseus' narrative to Alcinous as a whole), uttered by 66 speakers.[72] Crude indicator as it may be of any difference,[73] the *Aeneid* comprises 37 per cent direct speech (or 47 per cent if Aeneas' narrative is counted as a whole), uttered by ninety speakers:[74] its speeches are made on similar occasions to those in Homer,[75] and the longest speech in the poem after Aeneas' account of his ordeals to Dido, Turnus' at 11.378-443, can vie for length with almost any in the *Iliad*.[76] The main reason for the smaller proportion than in Homer lies in Virgilian economy of presentation:[77] 'Virgil avoids everything which does not directly contribute to the artistic effect or tell the reader anything new, and which would only be included for the sake of completeness.' This results in shorter conversations (see *Introduction* – 3.1 Characterization in the *Aeneid*) but also no redundancy; Homer will have a messenger be told his message and then regurgitate it unchanged, but not Virgil. For the *Aeneid*, speech should contribute to the action even as it impedes it: thus Numanus Remulus (7.3.4) provokes Ascanius into adulthood. Then again, Virgil's characters resist the Homeric temptation to turn speech into narrative,[78] however inclined to digress – Evander, though modelled on Nestor, only once indulges in random reminiscence, for seven lines (8.561-7), about his exploits at Praeneste; Nestor will happily lose himself for 82 lines, (on his victory over the Eleans[79]). Evander's other tales, Cacus (8.190 ff.), meeting Anchises (8.159 ff.), Saturn (8.319 ff.) and Mezentius (8.483 ff.) arise naturally from the context, although they also tell us much about Evander. One other Homeric touch, the soliloquy where a character debates what to do next, addressing his 'temper' (*thūmos*),[80] is not adopted by Virgil except for Juno, in her speeches at 1.37 ff. and 7.293 ff, and once by Dido (4.534 ff.).; apparent soliloquys by other characters are more like spontaneous outbursts wanting to be heard, such as a prayer (e.g. Aeneas at 6.187 ff.) or lamentation (e.g. Anna at 4.675).

The rhetoric of Virgil's speeches was quarried for examples by Quintilian[81] and Macrobius' 'book club' could produce a numbingly sterile rhetorical analysis of, for instance,[82] the indignation in Juno's speech at 7.293 ff. The admiration is evident: one speaker later asserts that, 'Virgil alone is found to have fused together eloquence of every type.'[83] The ancient commentators did not confine rhetoric's influence to the speeches; Tiberius Claudius Donatus, a contemporary of Macrobius' from the start of the fifth century CE, viewed the whole poem as a eulogy and, in part, defence of Aeneas.[84] This now seems massively misguided. Since the toolboxes of poetry and rhetoric shared so many instruments, it is more plausible to say that the speeches are infused with poetic sensibility; they do not stand out from the rest of the narrative as in a radically different register. Nevertheless two features of the speeches seem quintessentially rhetorical. Firstly, however extreme the emotion, they never descend into incoherence or disorder: Dido's apoplectic anger is conveyed by content lucidly expressed (4.305 ff., 4.365 ff.); only Aeneas, recalling the loss of Creusa, loses the thread of his sentence (2.738 ff. – though it does not come over in translation). Second, as Highet puts it,[85] 'It would be feasible to maintain that, in every important speech of the *Aeneid* which is intended to persuade, there is at least one lie.' This can be debated for Aeneas' speech to Dido in Book IV (4.337–9 note; in it he seems to fear the treachery of language itself, as he does in the *Iliad*[86]); but is hard to refute for Aeneas' speech to Evander (8.126–51 note). Falsehood as a speaker's means to a desirable end was not frowned on – Cicero, recalls Quintilian,[87] boasted that 'he threw dust in the eyes of the jury in the case of Cluentius'. Servius makes it a matter simply of not being caught:[88] 'In public speaking, it is legitimate for us to tell lies when nobody can refute them.' Even Virgil's picture of an orator calming the mob through the force of his **goodness and services to the state** / ***devotion and public service*** (1.148 ff.) makes no claim for his veracity. This is where Virgil's poem differs fundamentally from a speech: oratory, even oratory within the *Aeneid*, is occasional, whereas the *Aeneid* as a poem is built to last (9.446 ff., 10.791 ff.).

7.7 Diction[89]

Though a translation cannot replicate the linguistic qualities of the original, a good translation might convey something of its feel, like a texture through thin gloves. Virgil, unlike Homer, was not using a dialect that automatically identified itself as 'epic' (in Homer's case, a blend of Mycenaean, Ionic and Aeolic that nobody would ever have spoken). Metre (7.8) was a clue to genre, but hexameters could also be used for verse epistles or conversation pieces (as by Horace). The type of content, especially when presented according to Homeric conventions (invocations to the Muse, epithets, similes, hyperbole), certainly define a work as epic, but that still leaves out what language to use. Ennius, Latin epic's most illustrious exponent and the national poet some 150 years before Virgil, (see *Introduction* – 8.4.5 Early Roman epic and drama), added gravity to his Annals by archaism and a rough finish; Virgil, though 'deeply devoted to the antique',[90] and more than ready to add colour from Ennius,[91] could not repeat this expedient wholesale without pastiche – he needed a different palette. A tantalizing glimpse of how the *Aeneid* came across comes from Suetonius / Donatus' *Life of Virgil*, where the author talks of Virgil's detractors:[92] 'M. Vipsanius <Agrippa>[93] called Virgil a puppet of Maecenas, inventor of a new kind of affected style, neither inflated nor jejune but composed of ordinary words and therefore unobtrusive.' Analysis[94] of Virgil's vocabulary in the *Aeneid* does confirm that he is more sparing with archaisms, technical vocabulary and compounds or coinages than his immediate predecessors, Lucretius, Catullus (in his *Epyllion*[95]) and Cicero (in his poetry). At the other pole of linguistic usage, the commentator James Henry,[96] writing of the Latin word for 'huge' (*ingens*) in the *Aeneid*, lets off steam: '*Ingens* is our author's maid of all work – cook, slut, and butler at once … it is *ingens* here, *ingens* there, everywhere *ingens*.' But Virgil's language, with its intense literary awareness (not just of Ennius – see *Introduction* – 8.2 Intertextuality, narrow sense: External allusion), is more than versified demotic. So how does Virgil's language incur Agrippa's slur, 'a new kind of affected style'?

The notion of poetry from everyday vocabulary was itself far from new – Aristotle remarks,[97] 'A poet can beguile us successfully by picking and combining words from the language of daily life. This is what Euripides does, and he was the first to indicate the way.' The words in themselves are not enough, however; their aura comes from elsewhere. Horace speaks[98] of 'making a familiar word fresh by clever collocation', and this is how we, to whom the words are much less familiar, might suspect that Virgil generates a frisson. Some examples stand out, such as when Dido longs for a 'mini Aeneas' (4.328), or Messapus lays Aulestes low with the shout used over a defeated gladiator, 'He's had it!' (12.296 – 12.289–97 note). Such colloquialisms are, however, at the extreme. When it comes to the pabulum of speech, as Wilkinson asks, 'How are we to recapture the sense of novelty that may have excited a Roman?' And indeed, when Macrobius lists[99] cases where Virgil has purportedly invented a 'new usage', those from the *Aeneid* are striking not for the new-minted glint at which Horace excelled,[100] but for a mildly metaphorical glow.[101] Even given different sensitivities to metaphor, this seems inadequate to explain Agrippa's remark.

If Horace's 'clever collocation' is taken as 'clever use of context' (which, admittedly, goes beyond how the Latin is normally taken), we have a wider net: when Ascanius exclaims, 'Hey, are we actually eating our tables?' (7.116), his quip follows five ponderous circumlocutions for 'bread'. This is exceptional because it seems so overdone – but another instance, cited in Macrobius[102] for being 'as it were plucked and shorn and indistinguishable from everyday speech', is '**your body will lie naked** / *your naked corpse will lie* **on an unknown shore**' (5.871). This line follows an emotional apostrophe to Palinurus, who trusted too much to a clear sky and a calm sea, and its words are as cold and spare as the scene it describes. So Virgil's boldness, enough to impress Agrippa (adversely), might lie in his abandonment of the props of epic (the conventions mentioned above) at crucial moments for directness, 'in harmony with the Augustan idea that the poet had a right and a duty to address the citizens at large'.[103] This is one effect after which the translator has no need to strive.[104]

The accessibility Augustus was after is also achieved by the largely uncomplicated sentence structure that is habitual in the *Aeneid*: paratactic (using clauses in parallel, joined by 'and', 'or') rather than hypotactic (nesting clauses within one another with conjunctions like 'when', 'who', 'because' – something to which Lucretius, in constructing his arguments, is far more prone).[105] This makes for easy assimilation but not always clarity – what is the relationship between the parallel clauses? Do they reinforce one another or strike a contrast? (The translator will often sit on the fence.) Clarity can be a casualty also of concision – or ambiguity deliberately created through it.[106] Thus at 10.501, the poet exclaims (literally), 'unknowing mind of men of fate', which could be construed generally, 'mens' mind unknowing of fate' (as both West and Fagles do – **The mind of man has no knowledge of what Fate holds in store** / *How blind mens' minds to their fate*); or alternatively, 'mind unknowing of the fate of men', talking specifically of Turnus, i.e. 'you who are ignorant of your own and others' fates'. Here the exasperated translator chooses for the reader where, in Latin, the reader chooses for him or herself, or chooses not to choose. As the Victorian commentator, Conington, put it,[107] Virgil had 'a peculiar habit of hinting at two or three modes of expression while actually employing one'.

7.8 Metre

A preliminary note on word stress versus syllable length (some prefer 'weight'). English metres work by word stress:

'Unléss my nérves were bráss or hámmer'd stéel'

(Shakespeare, Sonnet 120 line 4)

Emotion upsets the regular rhythm of the iambi (di-dum):

'Hów have mine éyes óut of their sphéres been fítted'

(Ibid., line 7)

Latin metres work by syllable quantity – roughly speaking, a 'long' vowel ('ūnique', as compared to 'ŭp'), or any vowel followed by two consonants,[108] is considered 'long' (or 'heavy'); otherwise the vowel, and its syllable, is 'short' (or 'light').

The *Aeneid* is composed in the metre of epic (Homer, Apollonius, Lucan, Statius), dactylic hexameter – six 'feet' (or 'metra', singular 'metron'), for two thirds of which the poet has the option of either a dactyl (long-short-short) or a spondee (long-long):

$$- \smile\smile \mid - \smile\smile \mid - \smile\smile \mid - \smile\smile \mid - \smile\smile \mid - \smile \mid$$

This can be mimicked in English (as by Richard Stanyhurst, 4.327–30 note; *Introduction –* 10.2 *Aeneid* in English translation), and the results retain the distinctive reining-in at the end of the line.[109] Walter Savage Landor, in his poem 'English Hexameters', written in English hexameters, concluded:

Múch as old| méters de-|líght me, tis| ónly where| fírst they were| núrtured,
Ín their own| clíme, their own| spéech; than| pámper them| hére, I would| ráther
Tíe up my| Pégasus| tíght to the| scánty-fed| ráck of a| sónnet.

As can be seen, the English stress falls on the first syllable of each foot. Since Latin words are positioned in the line according to the length of their syllables, their stresses can fall elsewhere, in practice on the second syllable of the foot; the congruence or conflict between the 'first beat of the bar', from the tread of the metre, and the word accent, not necessarily coinciding, create a unique music, impossible to replicate in English.[110] Virgil's manipulation of this, like the effects he achieves from the sound and positioning of words,[111] is unsurpassed in Latin literature; it must elude translators, even if they employ hexameters themselves.[112] And the music can only be realized in recitation – it does not work on the page. The primary experience of the *Aeneid* is aural, without explanatory notes: Augustus, if the Life is to be trusted, asked for a recitation from the poet himself.[113]

CHAPTER 8
READING THE *AENEID*

The *Aeneid* was composed to be listened to (*Introduction* – 7.8 Metre). It is perfectly reasonable, therefore, for a modern to read it, in a congenial translation (see *Introduction* – 10 Translating the *Aeneid* (into English)), as a well-spun yarn, occasionally brambled-over by mythological, historical, geographical or ethnographic references. This would, however, conceal something other than those references that would have made a Roman audience, or at least the better-read among them, prick up their ears: a wealth of literary allusions. Virgil's learning, antiquarian or literary, quickly became the subject of commentaries (see *Introduction* – 9.1 The first 150 years after Virgil; and 9.2 The second to the fifth centuries: Servius and Macrobius). This hunt for his literary sources (often referred to as *Quellenforschung*) has continued, with waxing or waning enthusiasm, to this day. It began in an arid and – for a culture that set so much store on good imitation[1] – peculiarly hostile fashion. Donatus, in his *Life of Virgil*, records:[2]

> Herennius collected only his defects, Perellius Faustus only what he had 'stolen.' But Quintus Octavius Avitus' eight volumes of Correspondences include both the lines that are derivative and their sources. In a book which he wrote as a response to Virgil's detractors, Asconius Pedianus[3] set forth a few of their objections especially those concerning his plot and the fact that he took most [of his material] from Homer; but he says that [Virgil] was wont to defend this very crime thus: 'Why is it that they, too, do not attempt the same "thefts"? Indeed, they will perceive that it is easier to steal the club of Hercules than a line from Homer.'

> (Trans. Wilson-Okamura)

None of this suggests that even Virgil's advocates were sensitive to the influence of Alexandrian erudition (8.4.3, 8.4.6) or much more importantly, to the degree that Virgil made the 'stolen' material his own, let alone the (possible) reasons for his adaptation. It took a very long time for the latter to be appreciated; Servius and Macrobius (see *Introduction* – 9.2 The second to fifth centuries: Servius and Macrobius) are spotters rather than exegetes:[4]

> But if it's granted that writers of prose and poetry ought to engage in this sharing and exchange of material, who would blame Virgil if he borrowed some things from older writers to increase his refinement? We even owe him a debt of gratitude on this account, since ... he saw to it that we not entirely forget those ancient authors whom – as current opinion shows – we have begun to consider not merely negligible but actually risible.

Macrobius' speaker goes on to say that Virgil makes the 'borrowing' (a kinder word than 'theft') more effective than it was in its original context but does not explain what he means by that. Heinze, talking of whole scenes 1,500 years later, is careful to be more precise:[5]

Virgil often takes a scene from elsewhere and develops it in his own manner – he develops it, so to speak, backwards or forwards, by giving it either a motivation or consequences that differ from those which it had in his source.

Heinze explains how allusion is much more than emulation (or quotation) and illustrates how it happens at several levels. In fact the whole poem is an allusion (to the epics that went before); episodes, similes, individual phrases or even single words can allude; allusions reverberate with the source context (whether inside the *Aeneid* and Virgil's own works, 8.1; or outside them, 8.2) to point up similarities or differences, or to add an implication.[6] They could be said to construct meaning, and often to add ambiguity – but only insofar as the member of the Roman audience picks them up[7], or today's reader has taken the trouble to pursue the reference behind them. The occurrence of allusions in the *Aeneid* is frequent enough to bed the poem in its literary past. They matter because through them Virgil establishes himself as heir to and domesticator of that literary heritage,[8] eastern and western Greek as well as Roman, rather as Aeneas brings together Trojans, Arcadians and, eventually, native Italians into Rome. And through the allusions Virgil can mobilize the sensibilities of other genres, such as tragedy (Dido) or love lyric (Nisus and Euryalus, Lavinia), to enrich the emotional range of epic. The same is true, but to a lesser degree, of self-allusion.

8.1 Intratextuality: Self-allusion

Self-allusion is inevitable for any author because it will happen unconsciously. In Homer, however, Virgil had a precedent for self-allusion of a very particular and conscious kind: the *Iliad* and the *Odyssey* were composed orally,[9] that is to say the bard would recite from memory and improvise changes and additions as he went along. Since doing this in hexameter (*Introduction* 7.8 Metre) is very challenging, the bard had a repertoire of stock phrases or sentences – formulae ('spacious Sicyon', 'the wine-dark sea', 'swift ship'[10]) – and of type scenes (arming, welcoming a guest) that he could incorporate; he would also allow one character to quote another verbatim over long stretches (*Introduction* – 7.6 Speeches).[11] When the poems were written down, such repetitions (which constitute roughly one fifth of all Homer) were retained; they add to the incantatory quality of the verse and Homer's genius is such that they can take on colour from their context. For Homer, therefore, working within this tradition is inevitably 'allusive', whether he adopts his material lock stock and barrel from another bard, or creates it himself from modular components; in fact it hardly makes sense to speak of 'allusion' at all, even though, when material from the *Iliad* is recycled in the *Odyssey*, or characters or events from the earlier poem are mentioned in the later, the new context refreshes the old.

Composing a literary epic, Virgil was not under the constraints of the Homeric bard. He therefore avoids exact repetition (the longest instance is four lines on Italy, spoken by Ilioneus to Dido and by the Penates to Aeneas 1.530-3 = 3.163-6 – as though Aeneas had reported on the Penates to his men, and Ilioneus on him). When Mercury delivers Jupiter's message (4.228 ff.) to Aeneas (4.265 ff.) he uses his own words, not Jupiter's. Virgil is sparing with epithets (another means for the Homeric bard to buy time for himself – Homeric phrases are rare in the *Aeneid* ('Messapus, tamer of horses', 7.691 – the same is said of Picus, 7.189, and Lausus, 7.651; 'Mezentius, scorner of the gods', 7.648), and the single adjectives 'unhappy Dido', 'faithful

Achates', '*pius* Aeneas' are melded with the situations where they occur so as hardly to sound like epithets at all. Although Virgil usually introduces and closes speeches with standard verbs of utterance, although when he marks the coming of dawn or night he does so with Homeric ceremony, although he has set pieces for recurrent scenes (as in the voyaging of Book III), nevertheless he does not resort to formulae. So where Virgil does reuse a phrase, line or idea, it is worth asking why. Here are possible rationales:

- Structural – **looking at his daughter with a smile** / *smiling down on her* (Jupiter to Venus, 1.254) is in Latin *olli subridens*, which also occurs at 12.829 (**smiled and replied** / *Smiling down*, Jupiter to Juno). Jupiter at the end of the poem agrees the immediate future of Rome, a future he had prophesied to Venus at the beginning of the poem. (See 1.254 note.) In Book I, he is preceded by the *furor* of the storm; in Book XII he is followed by the *furor* of Turnus' death. The allusion imparts irony to symmetry.

- Associative – the flame shooting up from Aeneas' helmet (10.270 f.) as he comes to the rescue of the cornered Trojan camp recalls the twin flames radiating from Augustus' temples as he is rowed into battle in the depictions of Aeneas' shield (8.680 f.). Aeneas and Augustus in their command of armies acquire superhuman stature. Amata in her despair and death (12.593–611 note), and Camilla in her final agonies (11.794–835 note), both recall Dido, whose ghost thereby looms larger.

- Thematic – the fire and snake motifs in Book II (2.199–227 note) are built up, in the first case, from single words (2.40, 2.256, 2.304 f. when the fire takes hold) and, in the second, from the startling scene of Laocoon, ambushed by two sea-serpents (2.203 ff.), which alerts the audience to snake-related vocabulary (2.269, 2.550–3 note) and generates two similes (2.379 ff., 2.471 ff.) feeding off the earlier horror.

The repetition of a line or part of a line assimilates one set of circumstances, or one character, to another – and this might or might not be by design. Thus the Latin *olli subridens* (above) is also used of Turnus (9.740) when he responds to Pandarus' taunt and then cleaves his head in half. This is far from Jupiter politicking with his daughter or wife but shows a similarly serene confidence (and perhaps does not reflect well on Jupiter). Another example: the phrase 'voice stuck in throat' ('my voice … / 'his voice …) occurs four times, as human meets superhuman: when Creusa's ghost appears to Aeneas, when Polydorus reprimands Aeneas, when Mercury does the same and lastly when a **Dira** / *Fury* is hounding Turnus to his death (see 4.279–82 note); on the first three occasions Aeneas cannot speak, but on the last it is Turnus who cannot. Is this intended to draw attention to the different treatment Aeneas and Turnus receive from the powers above and below?

It would be impossible for a translator to capture every self-allusion; some are more scrupulous in their attention to the shared Latin than others (so, with *olli subridens*, Fagles tries harder than West). The consolation is that it also takes an attentive reader in Latin to notice them; even inhumanly vigilant digital search tools struggle when what is recollected is an idea rather than specific words.

Self-allusion, as well as within the *Aeneid*, can be to other works in Virgil's own corpus. This might seem more akin to external allusion (8.2) but in fact retains the functions outlined above (other, of course, than structural): that is, associative, or thematic, or recalling an atmosphere or mood from an earlier poem. Thus Creusa's vanishing in Book II is associated with that of

Eurydice in the fourth Georgic (2.705–44 note); the theme of the Golden Age, explored by Evander at 8.319 ff., is broached in the fourth Eclogue and developed further in the first Georgic (8.306–36 note). Silvia's care of her stag at 7.483 ff. paints an idyll out of the Eclogues, one, like the world of the Eclogues, to be shattered by war (7.483–92 note). The similes Aeneas uses to bring alive the destruction of Troy (2.304 ff. – at the end comes the shepherd high on a rock who listens uncomprehending) hark back to the Georgics' descriptions of countryside ravaged by storm or fire (2.298–317 note and footnote) – Aeneas is like the farmer struggling against adverse nature. The bull to which Turnus is compared at 12.103–6 (see note) evokes another in the Georgics, ousted from the stall after losing the fight over the heifers; it embarks on a protracted training regime before returning to avenge its defeat: Turnus' resolve could not be better embodied.

8.2 Intertextuality, narrow sense: External allusion[12]

Allusion in the *Aeneid* to other works of literature is often referred to as 'intertextuality'.[13] This is a different use of the term to that, or those, in literary theory (see *Introduction* – 9.6.5 Intertextuality: Wider sense) – and not consistent with it, in that here intertextuality is a matter for the reader to arbitrate whereas in literary theory it is something the reader cannot help. The way, or ways, in which external allusion takes place in the *Aeneid* depends to some extent on the author alluded to (8.4) – but a general rule is that every external allusion, unlike every self-allusion, carries with it an invitation to look at how Virgil has departed from his model. He sets out an allusive manifesto at the very start of the poem – the Proem to Book I conjures up the openings of both the *Iliad* and the *Odyssey* (1.1–7 note); the audience's immediate reaction is to sink back into the familiar embrace of war and travel and only on reflection, or on returning to the older poems, to notice that there are novelties here too, which turn out to be among the *Aeneid*'s key preoccupations: the merging of myth with history, the hero who suffers for a mission far greater than himself, the interplay of Fate and the gods.

This property of allusion to release an undercurrent to the text is one seized upon by proponents of 'further voices' – voices, that is, discrepant from the apparent tone. Thus when Aeneas tells Ascanius (12.435 f.), **'From me, my son, you can learn courage and hard toil. Others will teach you about Fortune.'** / *'Learn courage from me, my son, true hardship too. Learn good luck from others.'*, he is reminiscent of Hector talking about his son in the *Iliad* (the helmet is prominent in both scenes), but his words allude more directly to the *furor*-ridden Ajax in Sophocles' tragedy – see 12.411–44 note. R. Lyne combines this with the mention of Aeneas as 'leader from Rhoeteum', Ajax's burial place (12.466), to deduce that Virgil is linking Aeneas at this point to the tragic Ajax:[14]

> While . . . the epic voice presents us . . . with Aeneas the selfless Roman hero returning to battle to secure victory, peace and the common good of Italians and Trojans alike, a further voice naggingly insinuates a quite different message: that there is something of an Ajax in Aeneas, a hero honour-obsessed and doomed.

If this is so, Virgil is an undercover critic; but the argument chooses to take the allusion in a particular way: in the dock, Virgil could wriggle out of a charge of subversion, for example by saying that its real purpose was to juxtapose Ascanius with Ajax's son Eurysaces, soon to be bereaved, and so to makes these words of Aeneas resonant of farewell; and as for 'Rhoetean', that adjective is used elsewhere without any connotations of Ajax (3.108, 5.646, 6.505). Lyne, of course, multiplies his examples of such 'further voices', and each must be taken on its own merits.

What this example also illustrates is the two-tier nature of much allusion: as Cairns puts it,[15] Virgil often 'looks through' another author to an earlier, mostly Homeric point of origin (so, in this example, to Homer via Sophocles). In the unflattering terminology, the earlier text is said to be 'contaminated with' the later. Macrobius was aware of the phenomenon, though he assumed Virgil was only alluding to the later text.[16] This, in view of Virgil's intimate knowledge of Homer, is not credible; but also, it deprives the allusion of its ambivalence – are we meant to be reminded of the maddened Ajax or of both him and Hector?[17] The difficulty in gauging the poet's intention behind any allusion at all is brought home by Aeneas' reference, in the agony of his underworld encounter with Dido, to a *jeu d'esprit* of Catullus – on a lock of hair shorn from the Egyptian Queen Berenice (6.458–60 note and footnote). The allusion must be deliberate (the words tally) but the incongruity is breathtaking – as if Virgil wants to remind us that his caring narrator is also a figment.

External allusion is not merely literary – mythology, geography and history, too, are 'texts' to which Virgil makes reference, a reference that can be loaded. To take mythology: the death of the bugler Misenus is accounted for by his rash challenge to the gods while blowing into a conch shell, as a result of which he was dashed on the rocks by Triton[18] (6.171 ff.); Virgil adds **if the tale is to be believed** / *if we can believe the story* (though the **tale** / *story* is most probably his own invention), but it is too late, for we have already been put in mind of divine jealousy. Turning to geography: the Latin towns Anchises lists to Aeneas at 6.773-6 are 'nameless earth now, one day to be names'; by Virgil's time they had reverted to obscurity, so whereas Aeneas hears 'names to be conjured with', Virgil's contemporaries (and we) might hear, 'names – and nothing more'. And finally, history: Anchises' commentary on the souls passing to be incarnated as great Romans, all of them strangers to Aeneas, can sometimes sound revisionist, at least to our ears – the Brutus who deposed Tarquin 'the proud' is himself called 'proud' (6.817), with **a limitless desire for glory** / *boundless lust for praise* (6.823 – see 6.817–23 note); how might it have sounded to Virgil's audience, still recovering from Caesar's assassination and the civil wars that followed?

8.3 Allusion and subjectivity

Allusions can be open to more than one interpretation; the reader chooses. In fact, the reader's discretion enters much earlier – in identifying what is to count as an 'allusion' at all. Are there verbal or thematic resemblances that can be disregarded as mere coincidence? This same question has already been encountered with internal allusion (8.1). Making a judgement is a matter both of familiarity with the texts involved and of personal conviction. Camps represents one school of thought:[19]

> While some of the echoes and repetitions in the *Aeneid* can be seen to reflect an intention, and thus to give the value of 'allusions' to the passages where they occur, it is equally evident that many such echoes, whether of motif or diction, occur without any intention

behind them; the poet uses a phrase or an idea that comes to his mind from past literature or legend or from another passage in his own poem simply because it is apt to the requirements of his present context …

The word 'apt' begs the question why it should be. Lyne is more thorough-going:[20]

> Source texts are *part* of the new text, constantly and in detail, continually inviting the process of comparing and contrasting … The situation is what we might call one of designed intertextuality. To read the *Aeneid* is to be constantly aware of other texts in and behind the new creation.

For Lyne, talking here about external allusion, the author's intention is not what matters (although he claims more than an inkling of what such an intention might be). Certainly it is easier for Camps to speak of a clear 'intention' than it is in practice to discern or define it. But the Lyne position runs into the difficulty that anything might be considered an allusion, that nothing is off-limits; hence he confines his principle to Homer and Apollonius, with some leaks round the edges, and points out how the reader can be sensitized to allusions – 'explicit appearances by Diomedes signal Diomedes allusions'. The reader will want to draw a line somewhere (though see also *Introduction* – 9.6.5 Intertextuality: Wider sense), most probably by whether he or she is persuaded that an 'allusion' adds something to its context. And this is not decided objectively.

This raises the larger question of subjective association: what am I to do if Amata reminds me of Lady Macbeth, or of my aunt? Camps observes:[21]

> Nor … are we to shun as irrelevant associations evoked in a reading of the *Aeneid* which cannot possibly have been present consciously or sub-consciously to the poet because they could not be within the range of his direct experience, the meaning given to a phrase by the reader's own experience or by its recorded influence on the lives of other men, the symbolic value added to an episode by the symbolic role of something similar in later literature. To reject these as irrelevant because fortuitous would be to reject a distinctive virtue of Virgil's poetry.

Whether or not this applies to all poetry, it follows that the range of possible reactions to the *Aeneid* was broad from the first and only broadens with time – the *Aeneid* is not an equation with a limited number of solutions. It also follows that what validates a reader's reaction to the poem is not identifying more and more allusions and their supposed purpose but relating the text as a whole to the reader's (and other readers') experience; in this some allusions will resonate more than others. So while search engines and artificial intelligence can locate and suggest linguistic parallels, perhaps soon thematic or conceptual ones, they cannot legislate on their interpretation.[22]

8.4 Epic and other literary antecedents[23]

The literary tradition to which Virgil alludes is as cumulative as an archaeological site, one through whose layers you may pass without disturbing them. His range is wide, even if more discriminating – and methodical – than Macrobius makes out:[24] 'He did not harvest fruit from one vine, but turned to his purposes whatever he found anywhere worthy of imitation.' It is tantalizing to try imagining what Virgil had access to, and how;[25] and scholars are increasingly aware that he used ancient scholarship on texts, their scholia, as well as the texts themselves.[26]

8.4.1 Homer, the epic cycle, the Homeric hymns and Hesiod

The two poems attributed to Homer, each in twenty-four books, the *Iliad* and the *Odyssey*, were written down, it is estimated, in the late eighth or early seventh century BCE and constitute the starting point not just for epic but for all classical literature. The *Iliad*, on the wrath of Achilles and its consequences for the Greek army besieging Troy, is largely of war and its toll on both men and women, but ends with the quenching of Achilles' wrath in the grief of Priam; the *Odyssey*, on the return of Odysseus to his home in Ithaca, contrasts the voyages of Telemachus, his son, and of Odysseus himself, surviving fantastic ordeals at a relentless pace, with the slow plot of Odysseus reclaiming his family and household from the Ithacan nobility. According to G. Knauer, the first scholar systematically to catalogue all Homeric references in Virgil, 'he in fact incorporated the whole *Iliad* and the whole *Odyssey* into the *Aeneid*.'[27] This turns out, by Knauer's own admission, to be an exaggeration,[28] but his mapping of the books of both *Iliad* and *Odyssey* onto those of the *Aeneid* shows that Virgil was astonishingly comprehensive. Knauer's 'incorporated' needs unpacking. There are many and complex affinities of structure (Knauer's mapping often changes the Homeric order; see also *Introduction* – 7.1 Structure) The poem as a whole); there are conflations or expansions of character (Dido conflates Arete, Alcinous, Circe and Calypso, not to mention the non-Homeric Medea; Palinurus, Caieta and Misenus are expansions from Elpenor); there are echoes of situation (so the Trojans rejoicing as they leave Sicily, only to be storm-tossed and driven to Carthage, equate to Odysseus cheerily leaving Ogygia and drifting, after his raft has been smashed, to Phaeacia – 1.81–123 note); there are close renditions of the Greek in Latin (e.g. 11.794–8) and less close, too, that indicate divergence as well as imitation (e.g. in a simile – e.g. 10.260–86 note). The commentary indicates how thoroughly the *Aeneid* is spliced into both the *Iliad* and the *Odyssey*.

Evolving alongside and after the *Iliad*, as an oral prequel and several sequels to it, are the shorter poems that constitute the so-called Epic Cycle. These have not survived except for some 150 lines and a summary by Proclus (the fifth century CE Neoplatonist, an earlier grammarian of the same name or neither), preserved in a manuscript of the *Iliad* from the tenth century CE. Proclus itemizes:

- the *Cypria*, narrating the judgement of Paris and events of the first nine years of the Trojan War up to the *Iliad*;

- the *Aethiopis*, telling of the arrival of Penthesilea and Memnon, their deaths at the hands of Achilles and Achilles' death in turn;

- the *Little Iliad*, in which the arms of Achilles are awarded to Odysseus and the Trojan horse is built;

- the *Iliou Persis* ('Sack of Troy'), which speaks for itself;

- the *Nostoi* ('Returns'), covering the voyages home and events that greeted the Greek heroes on arrival, culminating in the cases of Agamemnon and Menelaus;

- the *Telegony*, recounting Odysseus' further voyage after his return from Troy, to Thesprotia and back, and his death at the hands of Telegonus, his illegitimate son by Circe.

Aristotle criticizes[29] the poets of the Epic Cycle for not unifying their plots about a single action:

> <They> write about a single person, a single period of time, or a single action of many parts – e.g. the poet of the *Cypria* and the *Little Iliad*. This means that only one tragedy can be made out of the *Iliad* or the *Odyssey*, or at most two, but many out of the *Cypria* and the *Little Iliad* (more than eight) . . .
>
> (Trans. Heath)

The *Aeneid* draws on these, or their reworkings by later authors, for its non-Iliadic material, such as the story of the sack of Troy in Book II and for some scenes on Juno's temple.

Further offshoots of Homeric epic are the so-called *Homeric Hymns*, a collection of thirty-three poems written in hexameter and Homeric dialect in honour of various gods and goddesses, dating from between the end of the seventh century to possibly Hellenistic times. They vary in length from a few to 580 lines; the shortest are no more than starting points for the rhapsode's performance. It is highly likely, given the interest excited by the origins of the Julian dynasty (*Introduction* – 3.2.2 Aeneas between the *Iliad* and the *Aeneid*: The Aeneas legend, that Virgil would have gained access to the *Homeric Hymn to Aphrodite* (1.326–34 note), and others with it.

The first epic poet to emerge from anonymity is Hesiod, who wants us to form a picture (however fictitious) of his father and his troubled relationship with his brother,[30] to lend urgency to his advice on good husbandry. This advice, in his *Works and Days*, is a major inspiration for the Georgics (*Introduction* – 2.3 *Eclogues* (or *Bucolics*)); his other major surviving poem, the *Theogony*, provides names and topography for Virgil's underworld, or for sea-nymphs and Cyclops.[31] The poem *Shield of Heracles* is no longer thought to be by Hesiod but is another point of reference for Aeneas' shield in Book VIII.

This upwelling of early written epic did not dry up, but its stream of narrative that told of men and gods, was partly diverted in the fifth century BCE into choral lyric (8.4.2) and into drama (8.4.3). The first, in the form of epinician odes, i.e. to commemorate sporting victories at the great festivals, came out of the wish, or need, of the victors to aggrandize their achievement – the divine being added to the human; the second, at least tragedy, is said by Aristotle[32] to have developed from dithyrambic processions, that is to say the ecstatic worship of Dionysus – the human being added to the divine. Epics continued to be composed – Herodotus' cousin or uncle, Panyassis of Halicarnassus (executed in 454 BCE), produced a *Heracleia* in fourteen books – but, as Herodotus was to show, when myth yielded to systematic investigation of causes, the natural medium for historical narrative became prose.[33] Epic had to be given a new lease of life, by Apollonius of Rhodes (8.4.4).

8.4.2 Early lyric: Pindar

The greatest of choral lyric poets, Pindar, wrote richly allusive odes to honour his patrons,[34] in complex metres and using a mythology surprisingly independent of Homer's. The portion of

Anchises' speech in Book VI where he compares Augustus' reign to Saturn's (6.789) is Pindaric in its combination of praise and myth, but the prophetic tone is very different to that of straightforward encomium. The clearest mark of Pindar on the poem is the description of Etna in Book III, where Virgil opts for a scene of explosive violence rather than Pindar's calmer lava flows and night-time cannonade of rocks (3.570–7 note). In general there is relatively little interaction between the *Aeneid* and Pindar's *Odes*; much closer to them is the Proem to *Georgics* Book 3 (3.13 ff.).[35]

8.4.3 Attic tragedy

Greek tragedy flowered and faded in the fifth century BCE. It drew largely on epic (Homer, the epic cycle and other epic poems) for many of its characters and plots (see Aristotle in 8.4.1) but it used them to explore contemporary issues and their emotional impact. Its three great exponents whose tragedies have survived (Aeschylus, Sophocles and Euripides, in chronological order – though Sophocles and Euripides largely overlapped), like Homer, exploit divine intervention but not to deflect attention from the human drama.[36]

Macrobius declared,[37] 'Virgil had a vast familiarity with the writers of Greek tragedy'; Martial calls[38] him, 'Virgil in buskins.' Hardie[39] observes, 'Tragic intertexts are particularly dense in Books II, IV and VII (see Literary sources for these books; also Book IX), but they are to be found throughout the poem.'[40] Nevertheless, Martial means more than that Virgil can quote the texts. So, in what way is the *Aeneid* 'tragic'? To answer this by restricting the word to 'pessimistic' or 'anti-Augustan', hardly does justice to the genre; likewise to make 'tragic' virtually synonymous with 'private' and 'epic' with 'public' (as in Aeneas' 'private' and 'public' aspects), however appealing to a modern concern with the individual, leaves out tragedy's concern for society and society's claims on rulers and citizens. The epic hero, too, could find his private obsession causing serious public consequences – look no further than Achilles.

Commentators turn to theories of tragedy which, although they always fit some plays better than others, are a place to start:

- For Aristotle's applied to Dido, see *Introduction* – 3.4; a similar treatment can be made for Turnus. For Aristotle's thought applied more generally, see *Introduction* – 5.2 Aristotle and the Peripatetics (from the late fourth century BCE).

- Hegel's view of tragedy was of humanity caught in a collision of rival goods.[41] It highlights the potency of contradictions that, as Conte puts it,[42] 'can coexist without one right prevailing over the other; or at least there is in the wrong a residue of right which cannot be cancelled out'. Turnus, for instance, up against Fate and poisoned by Allecto, sacrifices peace and the possibility of an accord with Aeneas to his hope of Lavinia (supported by Amata and possibly Lavinia herself) and the expulsion of interlopers who (he believes) threaten his liberty. Conte continues, 'For Virgil . . . destabilizing the meaning of his text by fuelling it with internal contradictions is a genuine strategy of composition, a strategy by which the 'ambiguous' manner of Greek tragedy infects the language of epic.' (See further *Introduction* – 9.5 The twentieth and twenty-first centuries: Re-evaluation.)

- A structuralist (see *Introduction* – 9.6.4 Structuralism) view of tragedy,[43] of more recent vintage, would examine the genre's fascination with the liminal and transgressive. In Athens, not long a democracy, this arose from the changing roles within household and city and the developing relationships between individual and community. In the *Aeneid*, written not long after the battle of Actium had spelt the end of Republican government and the birth of autocracy, the boundaries that are crossed – or not – include those between power and powerlessness (Latinus, Turnus and Amata); the world of men and the world of women (Dido and Camilla); youth and manhood (Pallas and Lausus); foreign and local (Aeneas); civilised and uncivilized values (Mezentius).

There is no need, however, to subscribe to any theory of tragedy (Martial almost certainly did not) to have a strong sense of the tragic in the *Aeneid*, especially if you accept Vernant's dictum, 'Tragedy turns reality into a problem';[44] one resolved only through suffering or death. The sheer number of doomed youths in the poem is an agonized reflection of the price Rome had paid to resolve a crisis that lasted thirteen years after the death of Caesar. And for those who would regard Aeneas himself as tragic, he is so because he is hollowed out by the very destiny he must fulfil. One of the more unexpected hallmarks of tragedy in the *Aeneid* is its multiplicity of viewpoints, each of which, like the voices of the different characters in a drama, has its own autonomy. They contrast with tragedy, however, in that their conflict is not only with each other but also with a Fate that stands aloof and inexorable, that communicates only so that it cannot be forestalled and that, unlike a god in a tragic play, never accounts for itself on stage.[45]

8.4.4 *Alexandrian poetry and epic: Callimachus, Theocritus, Apollonius of Rhodes, Lycophron*

The next major impetus for literary innovation came from within the libraries of the Hellenistic age. The *diadochi*, successors to Alexander the Great who carved up his empire, often created repositories of literature and learning to bring together their own Greek heritage and the culture of the near east, attracting scholars and thereby lending prestige to their cities. Of these, the most important, because part of the Museum, literally 'Temple of the Muses' and a kind of university, was in Alexandria:[46] it benefitted from the ambitions of its builder, Ptolemy II Philadelphus (pharaoh from 284–246 BCE), and from inexhaustible supplies of papyrus. Its librarians were scholar-poets for whom erudition came with the job: **Callimachus** compiled a bibliographical guide to all branches of Greek literature in his *Pinakes*, of some 120 books – the first catalogue. They were also arbiters of literary taste, and even of ideology. Callimachus opens[47] his longest poem, the *Aetia* (Origins) with a retort to his critics:

> For, when I first placed a tablet on my knees, Lycian Apollo said to me: '. . . poet, feed the victim to be as fat as possible but, my friend, keep the Muse slender. This too I bid you: tread a path which carriages do not trample; do not drive your chariot upon the common tracks of others, nor along a wide road, but on unworn paths, though your course be more narrow. For we sing among those who love the shrill voice of the cicala and not the noise of the <din of> asses'. Let others bray just like the long-eared brute, but let me be the dainty, the winged one.
>
> (Trans. Loeb)

Although the Aetia (which only survives in fragments) was long (it is estimated to have run to over 4,000 lines), it was a miscellany of short mythological poems assembled into a careful structure; it was also not in hexameters, the metre of epic, but alternating hexameters and pentameters. Most characteristic of the poem is the way the poet constantly asserts his presence. Recounting the marriage of Cydippe,[48] he tells how she slept her prenuptial sleep with a boy and is about to digress onto a story of Hera when he interrupts himself: 'Dog, dog, stop, shameless soul, or you'll sing what in holiness you shouldn't!' After an extended and allusive prophecy from Apollo, he dwells only briefly on the delight of her husband Acontius and their progeny before concluding with a lengthy digression telling Acontius, as if the latter were interested, his source for the story. If this is epic, then it is revisionary epic: artifice on show takes determined precedence over narrative urgency. It is mostly consistent with Callimachus' other works – six hymns to various gods in the genre rather than the style of the Homeric hymns[49] (see Book III, VIII – Literary sources; 7.435–6 note); satirical iambi and epigrams (see 7.378–83 note). And then, as if against all his principles, there is a mini-epic, or *epyllion*, the *Hecale*, which tells how Theseus was entertained by an impoverished old woman with whom he formed a friendship (see Book VIII – Literary sources), reminiscent of Odysseus in the house of the swineherd Eumaeus; but Callimachus has an ulterior motive, to explain how Theseus established a cult to his humble hostess. It is another, extended, *aetion*. The influence of Callimachus' doctrine or example was patchy, both in space and time – full-blown epics were still written after him, and in large number – but it did reach Rome (8.4.7) where, two centuries on, it spurred something of a poetic revolution.

The influence that Callimachus had on Virgil is apparent less in echoes of individual works and ideas than in what might be called the conduct of poetry.[50] Like the Aetia the *Aeneid* is fascinated by origins, whether of Juno's anger (1.8–11 note), of the Lusus Troiae (5.545–603 note), of the name of Cape Palinurus (6.381) or of Rome's reverence for Hercules (8.185 ff.). Its antiquarian and literary learning are not flaunted in the same way as Callimachus flaunts his,[51] but are of fundamental importance to its composition – the detail of the catalogues owes as much to the Alexandrian elevation of the catalogue to an independent literary form (Callimachus might have considered his *Pinakes* in that light) as to Homer. Virgil, like Callimachus, composes an *epyllion* in the story of Nisus and Euryalus. Changes of tone, too, that shake the listener out of the bath of epic sublimity are very much in the manner of Callimachus – not just the metamorphosis of the ships into nymphs (9.107 ff.) but also the incident of table-eating (7.107 ff.) or the tableau of Silvia's stag (7.483 ff.). And yet the *Aeneid* embodies epic on the scale that Callimachus and, earlier in his career, Virgil, referencing Callimachus, had disavowed (see *Introduction* – 2.3 *Eclogues* (or *Bucolics*)). The partial defiance of Callimachean values in favour of the epic tradition, or, more likely, the discovery of a new way to apply them to it,[52] was down to **Apollonius of Rhodes** and his *Argonautica*; its impact on the *Aeneid* has long been acknowledged,[53] but the full extent of that impact has only been appreciated relatively recently.[54]

Apollonius, if we can go by the meagre information on his life,[55] was a pupil of Callimachus and became head of the Library at Alexandria and, in that position, royal tutor. His *Argonautica*, in four books, tells of the voyage of the Argo from Pagasae to Colchis and back, to fetch the golden fleece. The story on which it is based is found not in Homer but in Pindar.[56] The following synopsis will serve to suggest parallels with (and differences from) the *Aeneid*:

- **Book 1**: Jason is sent on his mission by King Pelias of Iolchus; the boat; the crew are described in a catalogue that includes Heracles and the Dioscuri; Jason bids farewell to his mother; Jason is elected captain (at Heracles' request); he succumbs to depression; the troublemaker Idas accuses him of cowardice and a row ensues among the crew, soothed by the song of Orpheus; they cast-off from Pagasae, Iolchus' harbour.

When they arrive at Lemnos, an island without men, queen Hypsipyle and her parliament decide to keep the Argonauts with them; when Heracles rebukes them for staying too long, they resume their voyage.

The next stop is among the Doliones; Heracles destroys the neighbouring six-armed giants but confusion between the Argonauts and Doliones leads to many deaths among the latter as well; the Argonauts are delayed because of unfavourable winds but finally depart.

On landing at the mouth of the river Cius; Heracles' young companion, Hylas is abducted by a water nymph; while Heracles and Polyphemus search for Hylas, the rest re-embark without them; Glaucus, a sea deity, assures them that the loss of the three was the work of the gods.

- **Book 2**: When they reach the territory of the Bebrycians, king Amycus challenges the Argonauts to a boxing match; Polydeuces (one of the Dioscuri) wins by a lethal punch and the Argonauts repulse the consequent attack by the Bebrycians.

  Crossing to the opposite side of the Propontis they meet with the prophetic king Pheneus, punished by Zeus for indiscretion with visitations from the Harpies; Zetes and Calais, Argonauts and sons of the north wind, expel the Harpies; Pheneus prophesies their journey, explaining how to reach Colchis and to thread the Clashing Rocks.

  The Argonauts pass through the Clashing Rocks; landing on the island of Thynias, in the Black Sea; they construct an altar to Apollo, whom they have seen passing overhead; advancing to the mouth of the river Acheron, they are received amicably by Lycus, king of the [pi]Mariandynians and enemy of the Bebrycian Amycus; the seer Idmon and helmsman Tiphys meet their deaths and are given funerals.

  More landfalls – at the tomb of Sthenelus, former comrade of Heracles, and at Sinope, where they pick up three more comrades of Heracles; at the port of the Amazons (Thermodon), which they leave before the warrior-maidens can muster; and at the island of Ares, defended by birds (which they scare off); they encounter and take on board the four ship-wrecked sons of Phrixus (who had brought the golden ram to Colchis), grandsons of Aeëtes, king of Colchis.

  They near Colchis and sight the eagle that gnaws Prometheus' liver, then moor in a backwater of the river Phasis.

- **Book 3**: Hera and Athena confer on how to further Jason's expedition; they strike a pact to induce Medea, Aeëtes' daughter, to fall in love with Jason; Hera suggests requesting Aphrodite's aid; Aphrodite, troubled by Eros' insubordination, bribes him with a toy meteor.

  Jason and the Argonauts arrive at the palace of Aeëtes, with Phrixus' sons; Medea and her sister, Chalciope, greet them; during the general welcome in the courtyard, Eros fires his shot at Medea, with instant effect; Aeëtes refuses, when told of Jason's mission, to hand over the golden fleece, then feigns a compromise: the golden fleece will be

Jason's if he ploughs the plain of Ares with the fire-breathing oxen, sows four acres with dragon's teeth and kills the armed men who will spring up; Jason reluctantly agrees.

Medea is in anguish for Jason; she manipulates Chalciope into siding with her in helping Jason; Medea remains agonized, torn between suicide and going through with her plan to help; but in the end she selects from her medicine chest an ointment to protect and fortify Jason.

At a secret tryst with him, he pleads with Medea to help him; Medea insists, as she produces the salve, that he never forget her; Jason promises to take her back with him and marry her; Medea returns home, without accepting; Jason returns to his ships, where only Idas fails to rejoice.

On the day of the trial. Spectators gather, including the Argonauts, now moored in full view; Jason subdues the oxen, sows the dragon's teeth and – thanks to a trick taught him by Medea – defeats the 'sown men' who spring up; Aeëtes is dumbfounded.

- **Book 4**: Medea hesitates between suicide and flight – her treason is known to her father; Medea escapes to the Argonauts' camp and the sons of Phrixus; she warns of her father's hostile intentions; Jason pledges to marry Medea; they steal the golden fleece from its guardian serpent, lulled to sleep by Medea.

  The Argonauts are pursued by two fleets of Aeetes, one sailing down the Propontis, the other, under Medea's half-brother Apsyrtus, following the Argo up the river Ister (Danube); the Argo is pinned down on the Brygean Islands (in the Adriatic); Jason makes an agreement to keep the fleece but submit Medea's fate to arbitration; Medea objects; she sets a trap instead for Apsyrtus, baited with the promise to return the golden fleece; Jason murders and dismembers Apsyrtus; Apsyrtus' fleet disbands, and its crew settle on the coast rather than face Aeëtes' wrath.

  Zeus condemns the Argonauts not to return to Iolchus until Circe has purged the couple's guilt; the Argo voyages up the Eridanus (Po) and down the Rhodanus (Rhone) to the sea, south along the west coast of Italy and across to Aea, the island of Circe (Medea's aunt); Circe has already performed the sacrifices that expiate Jason's and Medea's crime, but receives them coolly; Hera sends Thetis to ease the Argonauts' passage south; the Argonauts, having evaded the Sirens (drowned out by Orpheus) and the Wandering Rocks, arrive in Phaeacia (Drepane, Corfu).

  Aeëtes' second fleet appears in the offing there; Phaeacia's king Alcinous, spurred on by his wife Arete, resolves not to surrender Medea to them if she is married; Arete tells Jason and Medea to marry, and fast; Jason and Medea do so, on the golden fleece in a cave; Alcinous rebuffs the Colchian fleet, which also disbands, rather than face Aeëtes' wrath.

  The Argonauts' efforts to reach home are blown off course to the Syrtes, off Libya; there the despairing Argonauts are visited by the nymphs of the shore; after Peleus has interpreted their instructions, they lug the Argo across the desert to the Hesperides, where by chance Heracles has just been stealing apples; Mopsus and Canthus die; the marine deity Triton indicates a route to the sea and gives them a clod of earth (that will become the island of Thera, from which Greek colonists would settle Libya); they make their last halts on the journey at Anaphe, where the Argonauts perform modest rites in honour of Apollo, and Aegina, where the heroes turn water-carrying into a race with amphorae, now an annual event; and so to port in Pagasae.

Jason, like Aeneas, undertakes a voyage forced upon him; like Aeneas, he is flawed (Jason is for most readers a weak leader and a warrior whose feats of arms are achieved through Medea's drugs rather than his own prowess; like Aeneas, he needs modern advocates[57]); the episodic nature of the poem resembles a through-composed *Aeneid* Book III). It is also plain how much the *Argonautica*, a prolonged *nostos* (= return journey) full of incident, owes to the *Odyssey*, though the end of its Book 3 echoes the *Iliad* as well. Apollonius is Callimachean in his willingness to spotlight his own control of the poem – he draws attention to material he is excluding,[58] or reacts to his own narrative – 'Is it true, then, Father Zeus, that people are not killed only by disease or wounds, but can be struck down by a distant enemy? *The thought appals me.*'[59] In this he goes further than Virgil, though Virgil too interjects at moments of high emotion (e.g. 10.791 ff.). Apollonius' depiction of Hera, Athena, Aphrodite as women discussing a troublesome child, Eros, has all the playfulness of Callimachus and nothing of the intensity of Virgil's gods, even at their most irresponsible – still, the interaction between Virgil's Venus and Cupid in Book I and Hera and Venus in Book IV derive from it.[60] The proportion of direct speech in the *Argonautica* is approximately 29 per cent (compared to 37 per cent in the *Aeneid*; *Introduction* – 7.6 Speeches) from 46 speakers (90 in the *Aeneid*, but over twelve books);[61] characters are sparely sketched in, with the exception of Medea, whose portrait is given a psychological depth unprecedented in epic (she stands out even more than Dido). Apollonius, like Callimachus before him, avoids Homer's direct repetition of phrases or lines (8.1); and, again like Callimachus, is profuse in allusion, internal and external. When Virgil references Apollonius, whether in simile, character or episode, alluding to an alluder, he incorporates rather than imitates his model. Homer's recombinant constituents are equally visible in both poets, but Virgil exploits the aura previously cast on those constituents by Apollonius – the diagram below shows a divine curse being fulfilled in all three poems:[62]

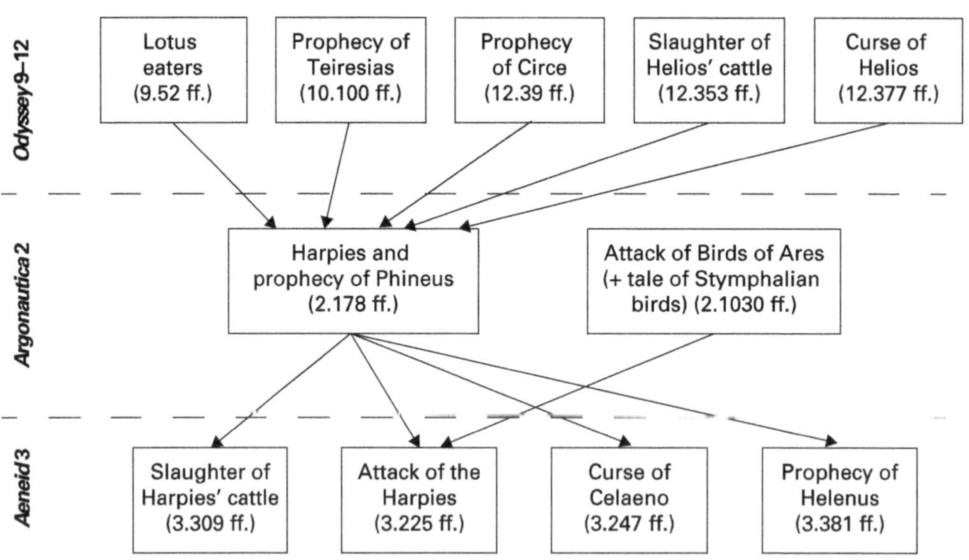

The consequences for Odysseus' expedition are that all except Odysseus lose their lives, while in the *Argonautica* the threat is seen off by a fast chase and some bird-scaring, and then in the *Aeneid* Ascanius' joke renders the threat altogether trivial (7.116).

The fantastical atmosphere of the *Argonautica* can distract from its political relevance. Like Virgil, Apollonius is keen to bridge the gap between the mythological past and his own day, in the manner of Callimachus' *Aetia*[63] (and not at all of Homer). The visit of the Argonauts to Libya and the reference to Thera in Book IV is a reminder of the Greek colony in North Africa, Cyrene (founded by Theraeans *c.* 631 BCE,[64] and the main city of the Roman province of Cyrenaica). Thus, Nelis states[65] (though with caution because Apollonius does not make much of this), 'In the hands of Apollonius, the story of the Argonauts becomes a myth of foundation, the ultimate *ktisis*, an explanation and a history of the Greek cultural presence in North Africa.' Alexandria, a generation old at the time of Apollonius, was in quest of its origins no less than Augustan Rome.

Callimachus' disciple **Theocritus**, a Sicilian who might have spent time at Alexandria. found an 'unworn path' of his own by inventing pastoral poetry; his collection of 30 so-called idylls includes two mini-epics (*epyllia*), the longest (25, on the young Heracles) stretching to 281 lines, three hymns and three poems set in town, but the rest are concerned largely with the imagined lives of shepherds; these poems provided the model for Virgil's *Eclogues* (*Introduction* – 2.3). Two of them, 13 and 22, treat episodes also recounted in Apollonius – the kidnap of Hylas and the boxing match between Amycus and Polydeuces.[66] The differences between Theocritus and Apollonius are marked: in *Idyll* 13, gone is the heroic Heracles and instead we have Heracles the agonized lover; in *Idyll* 22, instead of Apollonius' onrush of similes and final crunching blow, we have a proper match commentary. This is not so much a correction of Apollonius,[67] as another angle on two gods – Heracles as love-sick, Polydeuces as professional sportsman. Virgil's Hercules in Book VIII (8.184–279 note) and Entellus in the bout of Book V (5.362–86 note) are something else again.

The poem *Alexandra*, attributed to **Lycophron**,[68] illustrates the fine line between allusiveness and obscurantism. It consists of 1,474 iambic trimeters (the metre of tragedy) and is cast as a prophecy of Cassandra (also called 'Alexandra'), on the fates awaiting both Greeks and Trojans after the fall of Troy; it is a miniature 'history-in-advance' of the colonization of the Mediterranean as the heroes disperse, including Aeneas' Italian adventure. It is an important source for the Aeneas legend post-Troy (*Introduction* – 3.2.2 Aeneas between the *Iliad* and the *Aeneid*: The Aeneas legend) – although some[69] speculate that the 'Roman' passages[70] might be later interpolations. Here is Lycophron on Aeneas (of course not named as such):

There he shall find full of eatables a table which is afterwards devoured by his attendants and shall be reminded of an ancient prophecy. And he shall found in places of the Boreigonoi a settled land beyond the Latins and Daunians – even thirty towers, when he has numbered the offspring of the dark sow, which he shall carry in his ship from the hills of Ida and places of Dardanus, which shall rear such number of young at birth. And in one city he shall set up an image of that sow and her suckling young, figuring them in bronze.

The omen of eating tables (7.116) and of the white sow (8.82 f.) are glanced at (with some discrepancies from Virgil's account), as are the statues of the sow at Lavinium (3.389–93 note);

if Lycophron is to be comprehensible at all, the words he puts in Cassandra's mouth must allude to more detailed accounts elsewhere, such as those on which Virgil drew.

8.4.5 Early Roman epic and drama

Latin literature began to take shape in the third century BCE, a little later than the flowering of the Alexandrian library and, initially, independently of it. Roman authors were able to emulate Greek epic and Greek drama in one fell swoop: Livius Andronicus (the name, the first identification of a poet in Latin, would indicate he was a Greek freedman), wrote both tragedies and comedies,[71] and translated the *Odyssey* (Odusia) into the old Italic metre of saturnians; and then Q. Naevius, as well as plays, composed Rome's first epic of its own, also in saturnians, on the historical theme of the Punic War (see Book IV – Literary sources).

They were followed by the most influential epic poet (and tragedian) in Latin before Virgil, Q. **Ennius**, in the first half of the second century BCE. He wrote in his *Annals* a history of Rome from the sack of Troy down to his own day, in fifteen books later expanded to eighteen, of which approximately 620 lines survive. Since we do not know the contexts of these individual fragments, we cannot judge exactly how Virgil exploited them. But Ennius tells us what he thinks of his predecessors. Cicero quotes[72] Ennius in answer to his own question, what had become of the ancient poetry of his countrymen . . .:

'Such as the Fauns and rustic Bards composed,
When none the rocks of poetry had crossed . . .
Nor wished to form his style by rules of art,
Before this venturous man . . .'
Old Ennius here speaks of himself.

(Trans. Jones)

Cicero agrees with Ennius about Livius, whose *Odyssey* he compares to 'one of the rough and unfinished statues of Daedalus' and whose drama he considers 'barely worth a second reading'. About Naevius, however, he is kinder:[73] 'The Punic War of that antiquated poet . . . affords me as exquisite a pleasure as the finest statue that was ever formed by Myron.' He acknowledges Ennius' greater polish, but also ticks him off – 'You borrowed much from Naevius, and if you deny it then it was theft.' But Ennius' self-promotion had an agenda. He was selling an innovation, in that he had modelled his epic on Homer, from the hexameters he used to the apparatus of gods, speeches, *aristeiai* and *ekphraseis* and, at the linguistic level, renditions of Homeric Greek in Latin. In his prologue to the *Annals* (now lost), he even claimed that, in a dream, Homer had told him that he was his (Homer's) reincarnation.[74] It is tempting to detect here an awareness of Callimachus:[75] the proem to the Aetia, having espoused brevity, went on to record a dream of the Muses on Mount Helicon instructing the poet about origins.[76] Ennius would then be alluding to Callimachus only to oppose him, as he embarks a mighty history of Rome. His success was such that he became a school text.[77]

In the *Aeneid*, Virgil, without resorting to dreams of reincarnation, is evidently donning Ennius' Homeric mantle. We cannot tell quite what Ennius made out of the Aeneas legend in the relatively small portion of his poem that was concerned with the myths of Rome's early history (three books up to the reign of Tarquinius Superbus), but we know he has Venus appearing to all the Trojans[78] and that he compresses the chronology by making Aeneas the grandfather of Romulus (as Naevius does – *Introduction* – 3.2.2 Aeneas between the *Iliad* and the *Aeneid*: The Aeneas legend) – in neither of which did Virgil follow him. With that proviso at the level of plot, the numerous verbal borrowings[79] are testimony to Virgil's intimate knowledge of the *Annals*; in fact the danger is that their partial sample should disproportionately influence our view of Ennius.[80] Enough citations occur outside the *Aeneid*, however, for us to gather that in the *Annals* epic grandeur cohabitated with the prosaic, archaic and quaint – Ovid pronounced on the poem, 'Nothing is hairier than it.'[81] When Horace complains that mere age is enough to take a poet beyond criticism, for that reason (and not, it is implied, poetic merit), he says,[82] 'Ennius, the "wise" and "brave", "a second Homer", as the critics call him, is apparently unconcerned how his claims and Pythagorean dreams turn out'. The satirist Lucilius (mid to late second century BCE), says Horace again,[83] makes Ennius his butt for verses 'inadequate to the gravity of their subject'. Yet for Horace Ennius could produce lines that, however you tinkered with them, would still show the 'limbs of a dismembered poet'.[84]

For all his failure to meet Horace's exacting standards, Ennius gave an impetus to historical Roman epic that lasted into the next century; its composition became something of an accomplishment for the *literati* – the orator Q. Hortensius Hortalus, like Ennius the author of *Annals*, was mocked[85] by Catullus for knocking off '500,000 lines in a year'. Cicero, who produced three historical epics of his own, *Marius*, *On His Consulship* and *My Times*, wrote to his brother Quintus,[86] on active service with Caesar in Gaul urging him to join in the fun:

> You, however, I can see, have a splendid subject for description, topography, natural features of things and places, manners, races, battles, your commander himself – what themes for your pen! I will gladly, as you request, assist you in the points you mention, and will send you the verses you ask for, that is, 'An owl to Athens'.[87] But come on, now – I think you are keeping me in the dark. Tell me, my dear brother, what Caesar thinks of my verses. For he wrote before to tell me he had read my first book. Of the first part, he said that he had never read anything better even in Greek: the rest, up to a particular passage, somewhat 'careless' – that is his word.
>
> (Trans. Shuckburgh, adapted)

Two decades before Virgil began the *Aeneid*, Varro of Atax, who had written a historical epic *War on the Seine* (*Bellum Sequanicum*),[88] translated Apollonius' *Argonautica* into Latin – Ovid considered it immortal,[89] though it has perished. It is likely that Virgil used it side by side with Apollonius' original (see 1.249 note). But the most remarkable cross-current to historical epic came from a different quarter altogether: the philosophical, scientific and moralizing work of Lucretius.

8.4.6 Lucretius

(See also *Introduction* – 5.3.1.) Some Greek philosophers such as Empedocles,[90] and scientists such as Aratus,[91] had written on their subjects in hexameters. Lucretius, in his didactic poem on the principles of Epicureanism, dating from the first half of the first century BCE (the poet died *c.* 55 BCE), chose to follow their example. He was not, therefore, writing an epic.

Nevertheless, his opening with an invocation to Venus (as to the Muses in Homer and the *Aeneid*), the almost narrative drive of the argument he puts forward, the influence of Ennius on his language, his visual analogies for invisible processes – similes adapted to be scientific illustrations,[92] give his verse the gait and sweep of epic. And although it has no plot, it has a direction, as a brief summary can show:

- **Book 1**: After the proem to Venus, the poet announces his purpose to show how Epicurus and his philosophy have triumphed over religion and its wicked consequences. He begins from the principles that nothing comes from nothing, and that something cannot become nothing. From this it follows that everything is made up of imperishable atoms moving in a void. He explores the nature of atoms and the infinity of the universe, attacking rival theories as he does so.

- **Book 2**: After a picture of the man who has attained wisdom contemplating the folly of the world's feverish pursuits, the poet returns to the composition of matter and how atoms explain the physical properties of things by their types and combinations; how sensation is possible for a creature made of insensate atoms. On the dissolution of an object, its atoms combine elsewhere into something different. This world is therefore one of many worlds, coming into being and decaying.

- **Book 3**: Eulogy on Epicurus, who freed men from fear, and vision of the gods in blissful detachment. The poet contemplates the harm done by the fear of death. He explains how the mind and the soul (animating spirit) are corporeal – the first is located in the breast, the second dispersed throughout the body; both are subject to birth and death. He goes through the arguments against immortality, and concludes that there is nothing to be afraid of in death, which brings eternal rest.

- **Book 4**: On the senses – first of all sight, which is the perception of a film of atoms emanating from an object; analogous accounts are given of hearing, taste and smell. The poet considers how the mind processes images and how these images contribute to the will and to movement, and to dreams. This leads to reflection on sex (a pleasure) and love (a morbid delusion).

- **Book 5**: A second paean to Epicurus, more worthy to be called 'divine' for his benefactions than Ceres or Hercules, since he purged the mind of its vices. The poet moves on to speak of the earth, sea and sky – themselves doomed to die and neither animate nor divine: the gods inhabit other realms entirely; the world is too harsh to be their handiwork. Continuous flux affects not just the world but also the sun, moon and stars; nothing is eternal except atoms, the void and universe as a whole. The poet traces the order in which things came into being – from random associations and dissociations of atoms earth separated from sun and stars, then on earth land from sea, air and fire. He continues on to stellar motion, night, day, the phases of the moon and eclipses of the sun; then speaks of the evolution of life on earth, from plants to animals and birds, with those unfit for survival dying out, and progresses to early man, his primitive state and gradual advance to civilization – language, fire, monarchy, (erroneous) belief in gods, use of iron, warfare, weaving, agriculture, music and poetry.

- **Book 6**: A final homage to Epicurus, the remover of fear. The poet rationalizes meteorological and geological terrors, digressing onto curiosities that interest rather than intimidate him. So he takes in thunder and lightning; waterspouts and whirlwinds; clouds, rain and rainbows; earthquakes and volcanic eruptions; the rise of the Nile in summer; toxic lakes; springs; and magnets. The poet's depiction of the plague at Athens brings the work to a grim close that jars with his ostensible aim, to bring peace of mind to his readers.

Lucretius' poem does have a hero, in the form of Epicurus – and men who emulate him. It charts man's making (from basic atoms to a living, intelligent, sensate organism, to a social being who looks out on and analyses the world around him or her); and at the same time it persuades the reader of the comprehensiveness of Epicurus' theory (which paradoxically brings peace of mind by detaching man's intellectual appreciation of nature from the nature in which man accepts his part). There is an analogy here with the formation of Aeneas as a Roman in the *Aeneid* – Aeneas assembles, in his own mind and for the audience, the components of Romanness until, by the end of the poem, his Roman audience, and we too, are on the threshold of the first instantiation of it at Lavinium. And as we listen, we are both initiated into and detached from the Romanness that the poem defines: it is this that enables us to look with a critical eye at the Rome that over centuries was its realization.

On the other hand, the *Aeneid* is fundamentally 'anti-Lucretian' (*Introduction* – 5.3.1 Lucretius, on the philosophical discrepancy). Virgil undoes Lucretius' 'theoclasm' (further than 'iconoclasm'; Lucretius wanted forcefully to break the hold of the gods themselves, not merely remove their images). Virgil not only reinstates the gods in the world, baneful as they can at times be, but also restores the mystery of natural phenomena (see 12.921–3 note). Nowhere are the two poets' antagonistic aims more visible than in the contrast between *pius* Aeneas and Lucretius' vaunted Epicurus:[93]

> He was not cowed by fables of the gods
> Or thunderbolts or heaven's threatening roar . . .
> . . . his lively intellect prevailed
> And forth he marched, advancing onwards far
> Beyond the flaming ramparts of the world,
> And voyaged in mind throughout infinity,
> Whence he victorious back in triumph brings
> Report of what can be and what cannot
> And in what manner each thing has a power
> That's limited, and deep-set boundary stone.
> Wherefore religion in its turn is cast
> Beneath the feet of men and trampled down,
> And us his victory has made peers of heaven.

(Trans. Melville)

This is a far cry from Aeneas, whose last act in the poem is preceded by hesitancy (12.940).

8.4.7 *Latin lyric and love poetry before Virgil*

With Ennius, it might have seemed that the influence of the Alexandrians, and of Callimachus in particular, had been set aside, even buried. That it was not is at least in part[94] down to one man, the poet Parthenius of Nicaea, who was brought to Rome as a captive *c.* 73 BCE by a certain Cinna and freed 'because of his teaching'.[95] According to Macrobius,[96] he tutored Virgil in Greek; according to Aulus Gellius,[97] he was one of the poets from whose work Virgil borrowed with discernment. Unfortunately, of his elegies and *epyllia*, we have nothing; what has survived is a set of thirty-six lesser-known love stories from mostly Alexandrian sources dedicated to Cornelius Gallus which,[98] as Parthenius says in his preface,[99] 'I have put . . . together and set . . . out in the shortest possible form . . .: you will thus have at hand a storehouse from which to draw material, as may seem best to you, for either epic or elegiac verse.' Such are the sparks of an Alexandrian revival.

Parthenius' captor Cinna leads us on to Catullus: for if he was not C. Helvius Cinna, the poet, he may well have been a relation; and C. Helvius wrote an epic, 'Zmyrna', on the heroine Smyrna's incestuous love for her father, her metamorphosis into a tree and the subsequent birth of Adonis from her trunk.[100] The poem is praised by Catullus,[101] who admires its brevity following a long gestation:

> My Cinna's Zmyrna finally has been published, the ninth harvest and ninth winter after it was begun ... Zmyrna will be sent to the curving waves of innermost Satrachus,[102] hoary ages will roll out Zmyrna long hence. But Volusius' Annals[103] will die at Padua itself,[104] and will often furnish loose wrappings for mackerel. May the short works of my comrade remain in my heart; as for the people, let them rejoice in bloated Antimachus (8.4.1 above and footnote 32).

So Cinna's Zmyrna was an *epyllion* rather than an epic; and the allusive style of Catullus' tribute hints at its learned style. The Alexandrian revival becomes more populous.

C. Valerius Catullus, whom we feel we know far better from his poetry than from any of the scant biographical information we can piece together,[105] apparently did not need Parthenius to become a torchbearer for Callimachus – at least he never namechecks Parthenius in his surviving work. His poetic creed, which he seems to have shared with fellow poets such as Calvus,[106] together known as the 'new poets' (or neoterics),[107] was in elegant craftsmanship on a small scale, pretending to be private, for the consumption of friends; politicians are objects of scorn.[108] His dedication[109] of a volume of his work to Cornelius Nepos describes it self-deprecatingly as 'charming', 'my trifles' – which, nevertheless, he asks the Muse to endow with more than a century's life. He could, in his love poems to or against Lesbia, concentrate explosive emotion into the narrow space; but he could also adopt a Callimachean playful tone – his poem 66 translates a (mostly) lost portion of the Aetia on the origin of a constellation from a lock of hair (6.458–60 footnote). His own most Callimachean creation is poem 64, of 408 lines, an epithalamium (= celebratory wedding ode[110]) for Peleus and Thetis – or rather an *epyllion* on the voyage of the Argo, then on the wedding of Peleus and Thetis and, at its heart, the embroidered quilt on the marriage couch: this depicts the story of Theseus and Ariadne from their meeting to Ariadne's abandonment, the death of Theseus' father Aegeus and her rescue by Bacchus. The *ekphrasis* from the beginning is a 'tale within a tale' rather than a static tapestry; the artifice is constant – at one point the narrator, refusing to lie low, addresses the needlework Theseus and Ariadne in quick succession.[111] The poem returns from the *ekphrasis* to the wedding itself, catalogues the guests and looks forward to the marriage's offspring, Achilles, and to Polyxena sacrificed on his tomb. This complex structure obviously fascinated

Virgil, above all the link between the abandoned Ariadne and Dido in Book IV,[112] but there are other more nebulous parallels with the *Aeneid*: to a voyage, to a wedding (Dido and Aeneas, Aeneas and Lavinia), to the death of a father, to the loss of a son and to human sacrifice. These are details of Catullus' poem that the *Aeneid* magnifies into themes. Particular poems of Catullus other than 64 seem to exert a magnetic pull on the *Aeneid* – his bitter farewell to Lesbia (11 – see 9.176–449 note), a wedding song (62 – 11.59–99 note), his mourning address to his dead brother (101–3.325 note). Here the resonances exploit the intense emotion concentrated in the shorter poems.

So Virgil's Alexandrian spirit (8.4.4) has a double provenance, from his own reading of the Alexandrian poets but also from his immediate precursors in lyric and *epyllion*. But Virgil – unlike Propertius at the start of his last book of elegies – does not pose as a 'Roman Callimachus'.[113] He had no literary axe to grind, unlike the 'parroters of Euphorion' who, according to Cicero, look down on Ennius.[114] On the contrary, by their catholicity the *Aeneid*'s allusions retain their ability to surprise; they are able to bend the epic genre without ever breaking out of it. They also represent Virgil's ambition: the *Aeneid*, by encompassing so much previous poetry, was to surpass the literary scope of the epics already entrenched in the national psyche – Homer, Apollonius or Ennius.

CHAPTER 9
RECEPTION

The word 'interpretation' has been displaced by 'reception', perhaps because 'interpretation' suggests the undisciplined proliferation of personal responses (*Introduction* – 8.3 Allusion and subjectivity) whereas 'reception', with its connotation of a consensus, better captures the way that particular understandings or uses of the *Aeneid* have prevailed at different times and in different places – as will quickly become apparent from what follows. The topic of the *Aeneid*'s reception is vast and growing;[1] in our own time it is being enriched, and perhaps made more baffling, by the application to it of modern (i.e. twentieth century) literary theory (see 9.6). The vital contribution of translation is discussed in the next chapter. A thorough-going account of reception should also include the visual arts and music; but that lies beyond the scope of this short survey.[2]

9.1 The first 150 years after Virgil

The *Aeneid*'s reception began even before it was written, so eagerly was it anticipated (see *Introduction* – 2.1 Life). Virgil's reputation was unsurpassed among his contemporaries – the historian Velleius Paterculus called him the 'prince of poets';[3] Ovid announced with pride,[4] 'It's acknowledged that I've done as much for elegy as Virgil for epic.' And the *Aeneid* on publication in 17 BCE became an instant patriotic classic.[5] Tacitus' speaker Maternus compares the public success of orators to that of poets:[6]

> We have the testimony of the letters of Augustus, the testimony too of the people themselves, who, on hearing in the theatre some of Virgil's verses, rose in a body and did homage to the poet, who happened to be present as a spectator, just as to Augustus himself.
>
> (Trans. Church and Broadrib)

It was not long before the *Aeneid* became a school text – a freedman of Cicero's friend and correspondent Atticus, one Q. Caecilius Epirota, was said[7] to be the first teacher to practise the reading of Virgil (and other contemporary poets). Quintilian speaks[8] of Virgil's use, along with Homer, for learning how to recite with expression but also for moral instruction:[9]

> It is therefore an admirable practice which now prevails, to begin by reading Homer and Vergil, although the intelligence needs to be further developed for the full appreciation of their merits: but there is plenty of time for that since the boy will read them more than once. In the meantime let his mind be lifted by the sublimity of heroic verse, inspired by the greatness of its theme and imbued with the loftiest sentiments.

Quintilian's slightly later contemporary Juvenal pictures the poorly paid schoolteacher in the dark before dawn leading his pupils in the stench of their oil-lamps, 'while your Horace grows wholly discoloured, and soot sticks to your blackened Virgil'.[10] Being a set text was 'the obvious reason for the swift diffusion of … the *Aeneid* throughout the empire';[11] it also generated even early on the need for commentary, from Greek translations of the Latin in the margin, or illustrations of linguistic usage,[12] to explanation and criticism of the poet.[13] For older students, the situations in the *Aeneid* – such as the confrontation of Venus and Juno in Book X[14] – could offer exercises in debate and declamation. The fate of the *Aeneid*, to be read in the classroom, largely excerpted, along with the perdurable wish to make it a moral handbook, has dogged its appreciation to this day.

Dramatizations further popularized the *Aeneid*'s story – even the *Eclogues*, for all their brevity, were staged;[15] Dido was an ideal subject for pantomime;[16] Nero planned himself to dance 'Virgil's Turnus'.[17] Augustine later preached[18] to his congregation that more of them would know of Aeneas' descent to the underworld from the theatre than from books. The prevalence of the *Aeneid* among graffiti at Pompeii (including the barracks, ironmonger's and brothel)[19] and in mosaics and works of art attests to its common currency; in Petronius' *Satyricon*,[20] a slave quotes a line of Virgil and then mixes it with other bawdy verse. The interest in the poet himself naturally grew, as is evident from the legends that encrusted his life story – Suetonius wrote a 'Life of Virgil' in *Lives of the Poets* late in the first century CE (*Introduction* – 2 Virgil's Life and Works), which we do not have but, given the author's taste for anecdote, would have embellished any facts at his disposal; by the time it became the basis of Aelius Donatus' *Life of Virgil*, those facts had undergone two centuries of further accretion.

There was an inevitable backlash to the *Aeneid*'s instant canonical status: 'the *Aeneid* has never wanted for detractors', says Suetonius / Donatus in his *Life*,[21] and mentions Carvilius' '*Aeneid*omastix' (= '*Aeneid*-scourge')[22] before turning to particular areas that roused objection – Vipsanius on style (*Introduction* – 7.7 Diction), both Perellius Faustus and Octavius Avitus on Virgil's 'thefts' (*Introduction* – 8 Reading the *Aeneid*) and Asconius Pedianus on plot as well. The parodists' back-handed mockery was almost a compliment: Seneca's lame Claudius progresses towards deification 'with unequal steps',[23] like Ascanius following Aeneas out of Troy (2.724).

At the same time as cheap editions became available for educational use, luxury copies were being made for men women of letters and (or) high rank. Virgil was recited at dinner parties[24] and discussed on the couches (for example, by the society hostess who pits him against Homer and exculpates Dido),[25] or quoted in conversation.[26] The poets who came after Virgil in the first century CE reacted variously to his gravitational field:

- **Ovid** as an elegist (see above) saw himself as a Callimachean.[27] But like Callimachus, who in his Aetia squared a long poem with miniaturist principles by making it highly episodic (*Introduction* – 8.4.4 Alexandrian poetry and epic: Callimachus, Theocritus, Apollonius of Rhodes, Lycophron), in his *Metamorphoses* he strung together innumerable tales of 'change' into fourteen books (two more than the *Aeneid*), tracing, as the epic-style invocation of the Proem states) the world from its origins to the present – the greatest change of all over the most ambitious timescale until Milton. The poem (epic in metre and much else, but light of touch) therefore subsumes (in Books 13 and 14) the story of Aeneas, retold with a mixture of homage to the *Aeneid* and gentle parody of it: the journey to the underworld is condensed into four lines,[28] and the wearisome footslog back with the Sibyl is whiled away by her recounting Apollo's advances and how her rejecting them made her a spinster-crone.[29] Above all, the premise of unceasing mutability in the *Metamorphoses* stands in ideological opposition to any permanent Augustan settlement. Ovid's inventive mischief is also apparent in his letter of abandonment from Dido to Aeneas, in which she fears she might actually be bearing Aeneas' child (not just wanting to, as at 4.328), so that Aeneas will be guilty of two deaths;[30] and in the *Fasti*:[31] he narrates the sequel to Anna's story in Book IV of the *Aeneid*, giving her an Aeneas-like adventure. She flees Carthage after Dido's death and Iarbas' invasion, wanders in exile until by chance she reaches Latium; Aeneas welcomes her ('To you we are grateful for much, and we are not without our debts to Dido'[32] – Ovid makes him more grudging than Virgil does) and entrusts her to Lavinia, who suspects a previous liaison between Anna and Aeneas; warned by the blood-stained Dido's ghost, Anna jumps out of a window and takes refuge with the river god Numicius, becoming the nymph Anna Perenna.

- **Lucan**, who completed the ten books of his *Pharsalia* ('Civil War') before Nero forced him to commit suicide at the age of 25,[33] opens his historical epic by looking forward to Nero's apotheosis (as Virgil had to Augustus', in the *Georgics*[34]). But the poem is a protracted inversion of the *Aeneid's* foundation legend, telling instead how Rome through internecine strife had laid waste to itself;[35] in Book 9,[36] Caesar pays a visit to Troy and looks on the scrubland into which its ruins have decayed – ruins for which, in Rome's case, Caesar, Aeneas' remote descendant, is responsible. In other respects, too, Lucan was an innovator within the epic genre. He has no central figure or, in the modern sense, 'hero'. The gods play no part in the action; apotheosis is thus a way of removing Nero from interfering with Rome. The peace Lucan prophesies on Nero's death in fact became another civil war, the year of four emperors (68/69 CE); but it would be too much to attribute prescient irony to the poet.

- **Silius Italicus**, who survived Nero's reign, probably in retirement wrote the seventeen books of his sprawling 'Punic Wars' (*Punica*, the longest poem in classical Latin). He was Virgil's disciple to the point of idolatry – Pliny the Younger writes[37] that he celebrated Virgil's birthday more sedulously than his own and visited Virgil's tomb (in Naples), as if it were a temple. His account of the struggle with Carthage is a sequel both to its mention in the *Aeneid* (10.12) and to their treatment by Ennius. Silius imitates the *Aeneid* in divine involvement (Rome versus Carthage as a Gigantomachy), episodes (he opens with Juno's continued wrath), characters (Hannibal as Turnus; Scipio as Aeneas) and style; but he casts the wars as rousing the Romans from decadence, not as a staging post to an Augustan golden age.[38]

- **Valerius Flaccus**, also after the time of Nero, reworked Apollonius of Rhodes into his own *Argonautica* (eight books) – 'but if his primary source is Apollonius his primary model is Virgil'.[39] His style is individual, an individuality that some have attributed to rebellion against his model, but others account for by the subject matter.[40]

- **Statius**, who wrote his *Thebaid* (on the Seven against Thebes; twelve books) and unfinished *Achilleid* (a life of Achilles; two books) late in the first century CE, declares his deference towards Virgil – in his envoi to the Thebaid, he tells his poem, 'Live on, I pray, but do not try to compete with the divine *Aeneid*'.[41] In Dante,[42] Statius (apocryphally) claims that Virgil made him a poet before the fourth Eclogue made him a Christian. Of course the deference does not have to be taken at face value; Statius'

Thebaid does seem to compete with the *Aeneid* in its unbridled *furor*, unleashed by the Fury Tisiphone (2.336–6 note, 6.555) and culminating, at its penultimate book, in the mutually fatal duel of the two brothers Polyneices and Eteocles. When, in the final book, Theseus pursues and kills Creon (in the manner of Aeneas and Turnus), peace is not so much restored as war exhausted.

The degree to which these successors to Virgil are thought to be extrapolating from the *Aeneid* or setting themselves up against him (Lucan has been called an 'anti-Virgil'[43]) must depend on how far the *Aeneid* is judged to contain the germs of its own opposition. For the later poets, Silius and Statius, Virgil's direct influence was also mediated through Ovid and Lucan (and Seneca, in his tragedies). So while the challenge to respond to the *Aeneid* did not diminish, it became harder and harder to do so in an individual way. Perhaps this is why there is a notable paucity of (extant) epic in Latin from the second century onwards.

9.2 The second to fifth centuries: Servius and Macrobius

Christianity, whose acceptance around the Roman world was made more possible by its enlightened tolerance of Roman literary heritage, was especially kind to Virgil.[44] Thanks to the fourth Eclogue (*Introduction* – 2.3 *Eclogues* (or *Bucolics*)), he fitted the notion of the 'naturally Christian soul',[45] pagan only by an accident of chronology. Thus, whether the prevailing environment was Christian or pagan, he could not lose. Jerome (born in the 340s CE) repudiated classical authors but quoted Virgil;[46] Augustine (born 354 CE) like Jerome from boyhood steeped in Virgil,[47] pronounced him 'the great poet, best and most renowned of all';[48] after Julian the Apostate's brief attempt to reinstate paganism (361–3 CE), there came, under the Roman families of the Symmachi and Nicomachi, a flowering of Virgilian scholarship. Our first surviving manuscripts of Virgil date from this period, the end of the fourth century; and this (383–4 CE) is the dramatic date of a peculiar work, the Saturnalia of Macrobius (Ambrosius Theodosius), in fact written some decades later, but featuring Aurelius Symmachus and a Nicomachus among others, in a party that meets at the house of Vettius Agorius Praetextatus for dinner each of the seven nights of the festival of Saturnalia (17–23 December).[49] We have only the first two nights'-worth of conversation in the seven surviving books, and even these are not complete; but of what we have (on topics ranging from the calendar and jokes to the price of fish, digestion and other matters of physiology) the bulk, that is four books, concerns Virgil – Virgil the expert on astrology, augury and philosophy (the speakers are all pagans), Virgil the rhetorician, Virgil the pilferer from every available text, and Virgil conversely their conservator – the case for his defence.

Virgil's advocate in this informal trial is a young man called Servius. The real Maurus Servius Honoratus was probably dead by the time Macrobius was writing; he was a grammarian and the author of a commentary on all Virgil's major works, the earliest that has come down to us complete,[50] as well as a treatise *On a Hundred Metres* (actually about scansion). Macrobius chooses him for the role not to portray his character but simply because Servius, in his commentary, manifests a similar preoccupation with Virgil's recording of religious ritual and literary sources. That commentary[51] follows the format of Homeric commentaries before it and of commentaries ever since: a snippet of a line is quoted (the 'lemma') and then a crux, of grammar or interpretation, discussed and background information (historical, mythological, geographical) given. Servius likes to list different options, which can range from the sensible to the flagrantly speculative. Because of the narrow focus of a note, on issues which require larger treatment his judgement can be frustratingly broad-brush (as famously on Book IV: 'Apollonius introduced Medea in love to the third book of his *Argonautica*; from there this whole book is derived'). And though he can display insight (see, for example *Introduction* – 7.3.2 Focalization) he remains conformist in his view of the poem:[52]

> Virgil's intention is to imitate Homer and to praise Augustus by means of his ancestors.

A century before, Aelius Donatus had written:[53]

> Last of all he began the *Aeneid*, a varied and complicated theme, a sort of equivalent of both Homer's poems; also in it he was concerned with characters and events which were both Latin and Greek, while in it (and this was his special interest) there would be contained the origin of the city of Rome and of Augustus.

And Macrobius' contemporary, Tiberius Claudius Donatus (no relation to Aelius) prefaces his commentary on the *Aeneid* (see *Introduction* – 7.6 Speeches) with the words:[54]

> He had to depict Aeneas as a worthy first ancestor of Augustus, in whose honour the poem was written.

Commentaries inexorably became an integral part of Virgil's reception, and have a reception of their own – in the Renaissance, Variorum editions[55] of Virgil were printed in which 'a page typically displays a few lines of Virgil surrounded by a sea of commentary'.[56] Servius for seven centuries enjoyed primacy among his fellows, even though other commentaries were steadily being produced.[57] This primacy was consolidated at some time between the sixth and eighth centuries when an unknown (possibly Irish) compiler inserted into the copy of Servius he was making a wealth of other material, source also unknown. The new version is called either *Servius Auctus* (= 'Servius Augmented') or *Servius Danielis* (because first published in the edition of Pierre Daniel, 1600) – in these commentary notes it is referred to as *DServius*. By the twelfth century, it was felt that Servius needed updating: Hilarius of Lyons revised the commentary, omitting some of Servius' quotations and grammatical expositions while adding historical and rhetorical explanation of his own, including bridges across into Biblical chronology.[58] To Bernardus Silvestris is attributed a wholly new, allegorical commentary on the first six books of the *Aeneid* (on the lines of Fulgentius below), of about the same period. Early in the fourteenth century, one Zono de' Magnalis of Montepulciano compiled an ample commentary on the whole of Virgil. The Florentine scholar of Dante Cristoforo Landino produced another allegorical interpretation, also of the first six books, in dialogue form[59] in the second half of the fifteenth century. But with the rise of Renaissance humanism and the rediscovery of classical texts, Servius reasserted his claim for attention. It was Servius that Petrarch, more than a hundred years before Landino, had used to accompany his reading of Virgil.[60] Many manuscripts of Servius survive from the fifteenth century. And the first printed Servius, of 1470, came out only a year after the first printed Virgil.

The respect for Virgil in his early commentators erects him into a sage with the scope of, but more elegance than, an encyclopaedia – Macrobius' opening speaker on Virgil talks of his 'profound learning in a single word', (1.2.7), or his 'knowledge as profound as his talent is beguiling' (1.2.10); Servius heads his Book VI commentary with, 'All of Virgil is replete with knowledge.' This is in part nostalgia during the declining decades of the western empire for the (pagan) heyday of Augustan Rome. But Servius was aware the future of his commentary lay with Christian readers – this might explain his allegorical interpretation of the gods, as when he comments on 1.47, where Jupiter's incestuous marriage with Juno would raise Christian eyebrows, as follows:

> **both sister and wife**: the natural philosophers take Jupiter to be understood as the upper air, this is fire, but Juno as the lower air, and, since these elements are equal in thinness, they called them siblings. But since Juno, that is the lower air, was subject to fire, that is Jupiter, logically the name of husband has been given to the element on top.

(Trans. Fowler)

The inclination to allegorize the *Aeneid* was taken much further in late antiquity and the Renaissance. The Christian Fulgentius (sixth century) in his 'Exposition of the Content of Virgil according to the Moral Philosophers', maps stages of personal development onto the books – from birth (I), to childhood (II and III), love (IV), return to parents (V), wisdom (VI) and then to confrontation with vices (VII–XII). It is the precursor of viewing Aeneas as a Stoic hero (see *Introduction* – 3.2.5 Aeneas in the *Aeneid*: A Stoic hero?).[61]

Into the gap in Roman epic composition after the first century CE step Christian authors of epics on biblical subjects; the *Aeneid*, after all, with its tale of a 'promised land' and prophesied 'redeemer', has points of contact with the Old and New Testaments. The earliest example we have, by Juvencus (early fourth century), *The Four Books of the Gospels*, dresses the life of Christ in Virgilian garb – not merely Latin hexameters, but also allusions to Virgilian verses and episodes. The pagan tradition was revived belatedly by Claudian, who at the turn of the fifth century wrote panegyrics of the emperors Theodosius and Honorius (he himself was a courtier of Honorius) and of the general and regent Stilicho. His matter and manner are Virgilian enough for him to incorporate familiar motifs such as Allecto stirring up trouble via an assembly of the (underworld) gods,[62] the return of the Golden Age, symbolized by a child, under Theodosius,[63] and the winds of Aeolus, now turned to Honorius' advantage;[64] he sets the example for Virgilian panegyrics in the Renaissance and afterwards. But if epics were lacking, a new genre sprang up that demanded intimate familiarity with Virgil's text, both from the author in its composition and (almost as intimate) from the reader in its appreciation. This was the cento (from Greek *kentron*, a 'piece of patchwork'), in which units of half lines, whole lines and lines-and-a-half were culled from different poems of one or more authors and stitched together into a new piece on an entirely different topic. The earliest attested example from Virgil is a 'Medea' by Hosidius Geta, of the early third century;[65] a more incongruous transformation is the 'Nuptial Cento' of Ausonius (in the fourth century), which tracks the stages of a wedding up to its explicit finale, 'The Deflowering', composed largely out of snatches of battle and to a lesser extent of underworld descriptions.[66] The cento form was also appropriated by Christian authors, eager to bring Virgil into the fold: the first such example is by a woman of the mid-fourth century, Faltonia Betitia Proba, 'who uses Virgilian language to retell Old and New Testament episodes from the Creation to the Crucifixion.'[67] Sacred and erotic centos enjoyed something of a revival in the Renaissance, and even in the late seventeenth century two encomiastic centos were compiled on the Hapsburg emperors Rudolf I and Rudolf II.

9.3 The Middle Ages and Renaissance: Survival

After the fall of Rome, Virgil continued to be copied in the scriptoria of monasteries without interruption and his works remained accessible to those with sufficient interest and determination. Thus, it is said that Alcuin,[68] the teacher from York who was invited to be Charlemagne's tutor, as a boy was fonder of Virgil than the psalms (compare Augustine, 9.2). After Charlemagne was crowned Holy Roman Emperor in Rome on Christmas Day, 800 CE, Alcuin delivered a panegyric that compared the new monarch to King David but also echoed Anchises' words to Aeneas at 6.853: 'Raise up the defeated and now put down the proud, so that peace and holy piety may reign everywhere'[69] – the word 'holy' Christianizes the *pietas* of the *Aeneid*. The Holy Roman Empire, as an explicit refoundation of its Roman predecessor, found in the *Aeneid* its own affirmation; the poet of an epic in Latin, 'Charles the Great and Pope Leo', of which only the third of four books survives, compares Charlemagne to Aeneas and calls him *augustus*, while Aachen, his court, becomes a second Rome. The 'second Rome' features also in the court poet Moduin's 'Eclogue', which hails it as reborn in gold; the Golden Age that Anchises predicts Augustus will bring back (6.792 ff.) is here not one of rustic simplicity, as the first Golden Age had been, but of conquest. Either way, the survival of the *Aeneid* as a foundational text was more or less guaranteed within the libraries of the Carolingian and Ottonian Renaissance.

Meanwhile epic was being composed outside the *Aeneid*'s sphere of influence, *Beowulf* in England (eighth century), or the *Edda* in Iceland (ninth century onwards) among the nearer at land. Something of Homer, too, but independent of him, was stirring in the formulaically composed *chansons de geste*, such as the Song of Roland, in France (twelfth century onwards). More than something of Virgil stirred in the *roman d'Énéas* (*Aeneas Romance*, also twelfth century), which recounts the story of Dido and Aeneas but extends it, via many tribulations, to the marriage between Lavinia and Aeneas, who has become a paradigm of chivalry and courtly love.[70] Other folk traditions could assume the guise of Virgilian literary epic: the poem *Waltharius*, by a monk of St. Gall in the tenth century, took popular songs about the exploits of Walter of Aquitaine and converted them into hexameters with many Virgilian borrowings. The fresh spirit of adventure in the genre is captured by the opening of the earliest poem on the Cid, the eleventh-century *epyllion*, *Song of the Campeador*, written in Latin but a rollicking Sapphic metre:

> Deeds of war we can recite aplenty,
> Of Paris, Pyrrhus, not to mention Aeneas,
> That many poets, lavish in their praises,
> Wrote down together.

But what pleasure lies in pagan stories
Losing their lustre as they grow ever older?
Now let's sing of princely Roderigo's
Latest engagements.

For if I chose to list all the successes
Of such a victor, what could hold the detail?
A thousand books? No, not even if Homer
Sang to his utmost.

The ancient paragons were ever-present, but their yoke weighed less heavily, or differently. In the fourteenth century, Dante's admiration for Virgil is certainly literary:[71]

You are my master and my author, you –
the only one from whom my writing drew
the noble style for which I have been honored.

(Trans. Mandelbaum)

Much more than that, however, it is moral and spiritual. Virgil's shade guides Dante through Hell and Purgatory as far as Dante's beloved, Beatrice, then as a pagan can go no further. Dante's Statius had described[72] Virgil as one 'who goes by night and carries the lamp behind him—he is of no help to his own self but teaches those who follow'. On beholding Beatrice,[73] Dante turns to Virgil, as a child to its mother, to tell him, 'I recognise the signs of the old flame' (= 4.23, Dido to Anna) – but Virgil, 'gentlest father', has disappeared; Dante repeats his name three times, as the dying head of Orpheus repeats Eurydice's in the Georgics;[74] but, like Eurydice or Creusa, Virgil is gone. Still, Dante's quotation of those words of Dido to Anna shows that the parental Virgil is ever-present, internalized: Dante will bring his verses, even if not Virgil himself, into paradise. And in paradise will take place the conclusion to the *Divine Comedy*, by contrast to what Virgil in Dante calls[75] his 'high tragedy'.

The structure of the Divine Comedy could therefore be said to extend that of the *Aeneid*: it begins with a descent to the underworld, such as lies at the heart of the earlier poem, and progresses to a celestial, not a terrestrial, state. Dante was writing in exile from Florence, as the Italy of the early fourteenth century was engulfed in chaos, and through his ancestor Cacciaguida of five generations ago looks back, not forwards,[76] to the glory-days of his mother-city. But in matters of this world Dante is not correcting Virgil: if his sentiments can be taken to match those of Justinian in the Paradiso,[77] he, like the Virgil of Aeneas' shield, saw the Roman empire as guarantor of ultimate peace. Dante, however, sees no way back to stable security; Virgil's image of it is what is left to him. What Dante in turn leaves his epic successors is a reverence for his avowed master.

Meanwhile the tussle between Virgil as moral teacher and the taste for a happy ending had not been resolved by the *Aeneas Romance*. An attempt to provide definitive closure to the *Aeneid* came in Maffeo Vegio's fifteenth century Supplementum, an *Aeneid* Book XIII that tied up the ends left loose after Book XII (see Book XII Description). Again, this was not a correction but a redirection of the *Aeneid*; Virgil retained his immense authority, as both poet and *clair-voyant*, the Latin *vates* (see 7.41 note). It was probably during the Renaissance that the custom of consulting his verse at random for guidance in perplexity, as Augustine had consulted the Bible,[78] became established.[79] The so-called *sortes Vergilianae* had a long life – see 4.613–21 note; in 1783, Dr. Johnson's friend Mrs. Thrale, contemplating marriage with the Italian musician Gabriel Piozzi, opened an *Aeneid* and lit upon Turnus' words to Camilla, 'O glory of Italy . . .' (11.508). She took the plunge.[80]

9.4 The sixteenth to nineteenth centuries: Resurgence and eclipse

Dante's tribute to Virgil was unique; when other Christian poets, possibly prompted by the influx of new pagan literature from Constantinople (sacked in 1453) and its dissemination in printed form, produced a spate of Christian epics, they turned to Virgil rather as a template. Marko Marulić, a Croatian lawyer-poet, was unusual in taking the Old Testament as inspiration for his *Davidiad* (1517) – King David is the hero, a model for Christ (on the Aeneas – Augustus pattern). Jacopo Sannazaro's *The Virgin Birth* (1526) referenced the *Eclogues*; Marco Girolamo Vida's *Christiad* (1535) in narrating the crucifixion compares it to a duel between two young warriors in which one falls, to the consternation of his impotent companions, who rise up *en masse* – as the Rutulians do when Turnus is struck down (12.928). Christ evokes Turnus; his triumph is achieved not by force but through being vanquished.[81]

The mediaeval amalgam of romance and epic, in varying proportions, with an admixture of moral allegory, now achieved a stature of its own: in Ariosto's *Orlando Furioso* (1516–32, partly on the madness – *furor* – of Orlando, as he combats the Saracens), Torquato Tasso's *Gerusalemme Liberata* (1581, on the Crusades), both written for the d'Este ducal court at Ferrara; and Edmund Spenser's *The Faerie Queen* (1590–6), tales of Arthurian knights, dedicated to Elizabeth I. Ariosto and Spenser echo the *Aeneid* in certain scenes;[82] Tasso is the most Virgilian in manner as well – his proem and invocation to the muse strike an immediately familiar chord.[83] Both *Gerusalemme Liberata* and *Orlando Furioso* contain a momentous duel between Christian and pagan in which swords are broken or made useless, recalling the encounter between Turnus and Aeneas. Ariosto's ends the poem, *Aeneid*-like; but there is no moral ambivalence, since the vanquished Saracen Rodomonte is more of an unreformed Mezentius than a Turnus (he, like Mezentius, begins the fight on horseback): just as Ruggiero (ancestor of the d'Este family) is pausing and offering to spare him, he tries to stab Ruggiero in the loins. Tasso's combat, like Ariosto's, has the pagan Argante attempting to kill his opponent Tancredi while being tendered mercy;[84] but it does not end the poem. Instead, Tasso closes with the leader of the Christian army, Godfrey, sparing the wounded Altamoro:[85] Christian 'pity' over Roman *pietas*,[86] at the same time exemplifying knightly honour. Spenser, unpredictable in the way he followed Virgil,[87] further subdivides his allusion to the *Aeneid*'s final duel; he gives different aspects of it to different combats in the first three books, and makes reference to it even in one of the earliest bouts in the poem, when the as yet unchivalric Redcrosse Knight, just embarking on his adventures, corresponds to Aeneas.[88] Spenser is not just in dialogue with the *Aeneid*, Ariosto and Tasso,[89] but also with himself.

If Shakespeare's bow to the *Aeneid* in *The Tempest* (1610/11) amounts to a puzzle,[90] Milton, in *Paradise Lost* (1667) is monumentally revisionist. Lucan had the excuse of Nero's unpredictability for glorifying the monarch, but Milton, even after the Restoration, did not mask his avowed republicanism. Despite the poem's form, in twelve books, and its proem, invoking the Muse to recount the loss of Eden and the source of all man's woe, an aetiological programme as pervasive as the *Aeneid*'s, its goal is novel – to 'justify the ways of God to men'.[91] The *Aeneid* had already been recast for Christian purposes (Vida's *Christiad*, above, was only one of the more significant examples); and the *Aeneid*'s theme of colonization had already spawned a series of New World epics (9.4.1).[92] But Milton shocks by merging Aeneas and Juno into his Satan, at first languishing in 'floods and whirlwinds of tempestuous fire' and then voyaging across a 'vast vacuitie' in quest of 'honour and empire with revenge enlarged'.[93] By the two final books the identity of Aeneas has shifted onto Adam – it is Adam that the Archangel Michael takes up onto a hill and to him displays his posterity, including the Saviour: 'Then to the Heav'n of Heav'ns he shall ascend | With victory, triumphing through the aire | Over his foes and thine'.[94] Adam and Eve, however, taste nothing of such a victory; the close of the poem is their departure with slow steps in solitary exile from Eden; such was Aeneas' starting point in Book II.[95] Shifting of identity is what Virgil does between Turnus – Achilles and Turnus – Hector (not to mention Aeneas – Paris and Aeneas – Achilles; 6.88–90 note). Milton treats Virgil as Virgil treats Homer – and Milton's allusions to the Bible, to Homer and to Ariosto and Tasso (alluding in turn to Virgil) share the intertextual density of the *Aeneid* itself.[96] It would be a hard act to follow, but Klopstock's *Der Messias* (1748–73), a poem in German hexameters that is longer than the *Iliad*, achieved considerable success.

The *Aeneid*'s panegyric strain, on which the Carolingian poets had seized and that Milton had eschewed, was resurgent between the sixteenth and eighteenth centuries – under the Holy Roman Emperor of this new age, the Hapsburg Charles V, under the Tudors and Stuarts in England, and under French monarchs from Henri IV (1589–1610 – later the subject of Voltaire's lukewarm epic *La Henriade*) up to Louis XIV (1643–1715).[97] As early as 1496, Pope Alexander VI, angling for military support, had presented Henry VII with an illuminated manuscript of eulogies including – broadminded on the Pope's part – the Sibyl of Cumae foretelling that Henry VII would be a successor to Aeneas and representing him in a Parade of Heroes as a second Augustus. The Golden Age thereafter kept on returning to England. Elizabeth I is likened to Astraea, the virgin goddess who had fled earth after the race of Gold declined to Silver (8.306–36 note), in a play performed before the queen at Greenwich in 1588.[98] In his description of James I's triumphal entry into London of 1604, the dramatist Thomas Dekker quotes a speech claiming that James' four kingdoms 'kiss heaven, from which Astraea is descended hither'.[99] Seven arches punctuated the king's route into London, each inscribed with Virgilian phrases and the last bearing 'The reign of Saturn returns', from the *Eclogues*.[100] When Charles II in 1660 similarly entered the city through four arches, his return was celebrated by John Dryden in a poem, *Astraea Redux* (Astraea Come Home), headed by the same line from the *Eclogues*.[101] Of Queen Anne Alexander Pope wrote, 'Peace and plenty tell, a Stuart reigns',[102] in his panegyric *Windsor-Forest* (1713); the poem concludes with the binding of Discord (cf. 1.294 ff.) and Envy prey to her own snakes (as in the Tartarus of the *Georgics*, where Envy is relegated after Augustus' universal victories[103]).

Virgil's poetic supremacy was thus only sporadically challenged down almost to the end of the seventeenth century (e.g. Chapman, see further). The redoubtably named Julius Caesar Scaliger, a French scholar and polymath who wrote a highly influential treatise, the *Poetics* (of 1561), pronounced,[104] 'Virgil should be our example, our rule, the beginning and the end.' Commentaries continued to be produced, especially after the first printed edition – about 150 between it (1469) and 1599 alone[105] these included the commentary of Julius Pomponius Laetus, unpublished until pirated in 1490, which advanced from Servius and 'can be considered the first Virgilian commentary of the modern age'.[106] A further landmark was the three-volume complete Virgil by the Spanish Jesuit Juan Luis de la Cerda, whose two-volume *Aeneid* was published in 1612 and 1617, with the aims of explaining the text and of teaching students at the Colegio Imperial de Madrid how to compose verse.[107] It was widely disseminated; Milton consulted it. It is remarkable for the sensitivity of its interpretations, which have been rediscovered by modern commentators; its bibliography of scholarship consulted was immense; more impressive still was the vast erudition with which La Cerda, building on the work of his fellow scholars, identified the Greek and Latin texts to which Virgil makes allusion. Of these he says:[108]

> Virgil is very frequently accustomed to undertake the imitation of Greek authors in such a way as to add things which are lacking in the Greeks, to remove things which are redundant, and by his labour and industry to make more perfect and resplendent things in them which are imperfect or too little cultivated.

This is an advance on Macrobius, in the attention it draws to addition and subtraction (partly to enhance the relevance of Virgil's imitation to its new context; the notion of 'improvement' is more dubious). He also is subtler than Servius, when he separates Virgil from the more extreme patriotic tracts in the *Aeneid*. On making Anchises recommend that the arts be left to others while the Romans specialize in conquest and imposing peace, La Cerda's note (to 6.847–53) runs:

> There is no doubt whatever that Virgil does this to fawn upon Augustus, who was renowned in these arts, not because [he really thought that] other people outdid the Romans in those other arts.

The liveliness of his style is infectious – this is commentary as a creative act (see 12.919–52 note, ***clementia***). It was not till the end of the eighteenth century that Christian Gottlob Heyne's four-volume Virgil commentary displaced him as the standard,[109] and its emphasis on understanding the text against an ancient way of life marks less of a shift in method than did La Cerda 150 years before him. And not till James Henry in 1853 did a commentator burst onto the scene with greater effervescence (see *Introduction* – 10.2 *Aeneid* in English translation).

What, at the end of the seventeenth century, shook Virgil from his pinnacle in England[110] were the Glorious Revolution of 1688 and the Greek revival. To take each in turn: whereas Augustus restoring peace after the civil war in Rome mirrored the peaceful monarchy of Charles II that succeeded to the English Civil War and the Protectorate, the establishment of a constitutional monarchy in 1689 weakened the hold Augustus' settlement had on poets and returned their attention to the Republic that he had displaced. Dryden, in his translation of 1697 (see *Introduction* – 10.2 *Aeneid* in English translation) had a nuanced view, that Virgil's purpose was 'to infuse an awful respect into the people towards such a prince [Augustus]; by that Respect to confirm their Obedience to him; and by that Obedience to make them Happy'; even though 'I may safely affirm for our great author . . . that he was still of republican principles in heart.'[111] Such even-handedness did not last: by 1740 the anonymous author of a satirical poem *Plain Truth, or Downright Dunstable*, could damn Horace and Virgil – 'Were they not flattering, soothing tools? | Fit to praise tyrants, and dull fools.'[112]

Meanwhile, translators of Homer, as well as making him available to a public among whom knowledge of ancient Greek was much scanter than of Latin, were reawakening the old contest between the two epic poets, and to Virgil's disadvantage. George Chapman, whose *Iliad* and *Odyssey* so exhilarated Keats, in 1598 had sounded the notes that would be reiterated over the next three centuries:[113]

Homer's Poems were writ from a free furie, an absolute & full soule, Virgil's out of a courtly, laborious, and altogether imitatorie spirit: not a Simile hee hath but is Homers: not an inuention, person, or disposition, but is wholly or originally built upon Homericall foundations, and in many places hath the verie wordes Homer useth.

Even Dryden, who after translating all Virgil published in 1700 a translation of the first book of the *Iliad*, averred:[114]

I have found by Trial, Homer a more pleasing Task than Virgil, (though I say not the Translation will be less laborious.) For the Grecian is more according to my Genius, than the Latin Poet ... Virgil was of a quiet, sedate Temper; Homer was violent, impetuous, and full of Fire. The chief Talent of Virgil was Propriety of Thoughts, and Ornament of Words: Homer was rapid in his Thoughts, and took all the Liberties both of Numbers, and of Expressions, which his Language, and the Age in which he liv'd allow'd him: Homer's Invention was more copious, Virgil's more confin'd.

So, with the first stirrings of the Romantic movement, what was seen as Homer's wild inspiration came to be preferred to Virgil's attempted 'replication' of it. Edmund Burke, in his *A Philosophical Inquiry into the Origin of Our Ideas of the Sublime and the Beautiful* (1757) provided almost a blueprint for Wordworth and Coleridge thirty years later when he wrote:[115]

The passion caused by the great and sublime in nature, when those causes operate most powerfully, is astonishment; and astonishment is that state of the soul, in which all its motions are suspended, with some degree of horror. In this case the mind is so entirely filled with its object, that it cannot entertain any other, nor by consequence reason on that object which employs it. Hence arises the great power of the sublime, that far from being produced by them, it anticipates our reasonings, and hurries us on by an irresistible force.

This is the sublime as irresistibly experienced (i.e. the shock of Homer). By contrast, the ancient critic known as Longinus, in his treatise *On the Sublime*, spoke of the sublime as an effect, declaring that it resided in 'loftiness and excellence of language'[116] (a characteristic few would begrudge Virgil); he went on to quote the proto-Romantics of his day: '"The vigorous products of nature" (such is their view) "are weakened and in every respect debased, when robbed of their flesh and blood by frigid technicalities."' His reply to them is, 'The fact that there are some parts of literature which are in the power of natural genius alone, must be learnt from no other source than from art.' The 'genius' – 'art' antithesis is too extreme; there is much art in Homer and no little genius in Virgil, nor are the two inevitably in opposition: the poet and critic Joseph Warton remarked in his notes to Christopher Pitt's translation of Virgil of 1763:[117]

The art of Virgil is never so powerfully felt, as when he attempts to move the passions, especially the more tender one. The pathetic was the grand distinguishing characteristic of his genius and temper.

Nevertheless, the polarization stuck, and Warton's 'pathetic' made out badly against Chapman's 'free furie'. Byron was not merely the rebellious pupil when he wrote[118] of Mantua as the 'birthplace of that harmonious plagiary and miserable flatterer, whose cursed hexameters were drilled into me at Harrow'. The German Romantic August Schlegel, translator of another natural genius, Shakespeare, deprecated Virgil as a 'skilful worker in mosaic', whose merit lay in his grout and emery paper (i.e. his tiles came from elsewhere);[119] Hegel likewise saw no vigour in him[120] – 'Virgil seems to have copied Greek models completely, imitating them slavishly and lifelessly, and so they appear as plagiarisms more or less devoid of spirit.' Such dismissals sufficed largely[121] to bury Virgil in Germany until the end of the nineteenth century, and were influential in England (not least on Matthew Arnold[122]) and in France. This did not prevent serious scholarship: the first critical edition of the text by Ribbeck (1859–62) and commentaries on Virgil's works in Germany (Wagner, 1830–41), England and Ireland (Conington, 1858–71; Henry (1873–92) and Italy (Sabbadini, 1884–8).

It was in France, however, that Virgil's relegation was most conspicuously challenged, by the literary critic Charles-Augustin Sainte-Beuve.[123] In his *Study on Virgil* of 1857, originally a set of lectures, he divided poets into the primitive and the studious; Homer (whom he admitted to favouring) belonged to the first classification, Virgil (whom he called 'since he appeared, the poet of the whole of Latinity'[124]) to the second. Both groups had their originality and inspiration and took their place in a cultural tradition – even Homer had his antecedents. Expanding on Warton's 'pathetic', he drew attention to Virgil's *humanité*, *pitié*, *sensibilité* and *tendresse profonde*.[125] And this was the side of Virgil that Tennyson addressed[126] in 'To Virgil', commissioned by the Mantuans for the nineteenth centenary of Virgil's death in 1881:

> Thou that seëst Universal
> Nature moved by Universal Mind;
> Thou majestic in thy sadness
> at the doubtful doom of human kind ...

Tennyson was not just gratifying the Mantuans when he declares of Virgil, 'I that loved thee since my day began'; his *Idylls of the King*, to take just one example, were a creative adaptation of Virgilian themes and language – not epic in form, but a chamber of echoes. And when the academic John Churton Collins, in his book *Illustrations of Tennyson*, set about tracking down the poet's classical and other sources, describing him as 'essentially imitative', Tennyson defended Virgil as much as himself when in reply he described Collins as 'a louse on the locks of literature'.[127]

As well as those who imbibed Virgil's *tristesse*, there were other Victorians who gave prominence to the cross-weave of imperialist resolve that prevents the poem's mood from ever sagging. The Cambridge professor J. R Seeley, lecturing on 'Phases of Expansion' in 1883, acknowledged that the annals of empire were bloodstained but also contended:[128]

> In some pages of those annals there is a real elevation of thought and an intention at least of righteous dealing, which are not often met with in the history of colonization. Some of these founders remind us of Abraham and Aeneas.

This is empire as mission. In the same vein, the *pax Romana* could be viewed as a precursor to a *pax Britannica*; the historian James Bryce, writing in the early twentieth century, could maintain[129] that Virgil 'became the national poet of the Empire, in whom imperial patriotism found it highest expression'. In such a guise the *Aeneid* was fated to travel.

9.4.1 Diaspora: The Aeneid and Hispanic America

The European Age of Exploration coincided with the high-water mark of Virgilian influence. The voyage westwards of exiles seeking a new home; a land of pastoral innocence in which they meet natives both friendly and hostile; the outbreak of war; the foundation of a new settlement that will grow into a mighty city; these are the ingredients of the *Aeneid* that could be incorporated into narratives about the New World.[130] The earliest neo-Latin verse account of Columbus' voyage is to be found in Girolamo Fracastoro's didactic epic *Syphilis*, of 1530, on the origin of the toxic mercury cure for the disease – aetiology again. In it, when Columbus and his men reach Hispaniola, they shoot many of the multicoloured parrots that are flying around; one of these then perches on a crag and foretells that the incomers will not found cities or introduce Christianity until they have been plagued by syphilis;[131] the parrot is a reincarnation of Celaeno in Book III. The welcome that Columbus and his men then receive from the native king is modelled on that of Evander towards the Trojans in Book VIII. Fracastoro, unlike Virgil, looks at colonization as an ongoing process, not a *fait accompli*; he does not ignore the disruption brought by explorers and treats the natives with a sympathetic curiosity for the culture and religion he is conjuring up.

The ensuing New World epics (written by poets from the Old World) were more orthodox in their subjects, but varied widely in style. José de Anchieta, a Jesuit missionary in Brazil, wrote a neo-Latin hexameter epic *On the Deeds of Mem de Sà* (1563), Mem de Sà being a governor who fought against the French protestants, and whom Archieta portrays as ousting Satan from his territories. In 1569, the Spanish soldier Alonso de Ercilla published the first of the three parts of his historical epic *Arauncana* in Spanish, on the war against the Araucanian (Mapuche) Indians in southern Chile. (The other two parts were issued in 1578 and 1589.) It is a poem of conquest but also of heroic resistance, so it has something of Lucan the anti-imperialist as well as Virgil; it strives for factual accuracy, however embellished.[132] The Portuguese Camões wrote what became his country's national epic *The Lusiads* (1572 – the 'sons of the Lusus' are the Portuguese), on the explorer Vasco de Gama, complete with divine apparatus; the tenth and final canto is a vision of future Portuguese discoveries and dominions, and of the functioning of the Ptolemaic universe. The *Columbeis* (1585, 1589 – two out of a projected four books) by the Italian Giulio Cesare Stella tells the story of his fellow-Italian Columbus as a religious mission, opposed by Satan (in the manner of Juno). The availability of Latin texts in Latin America seems to have increased dramatically by the start of the eighteenth century;[133] so in 1724, the Mexico City scholar José Antonio de Villerías y Roelas produced a home-grown epic, *Guadelupe*, on the expulsion of Pluto / Satan from the Americas after the apparition of Our Lady of Guadelupe to a Mexican in 1531, and the subsequent institution of a cult to her. On earth Pluto's disgust at being thwarted verbally echoes Juno (1.37) while in heaven the Virgin Mary importunes God for a western empire much as Venus had Jupiter (1.229 ff.). Instead of an imported identity however, the Virgilian props now help erect an indigenous one.

9.4.2 *Diaspora: The* Aeneid *and North America*

In North America, the pattern was very different, one of reluctance.[134] The Boston Latin School was founded in 1635 and Latin (with Greek) was from the start a component of American education; the Pilgrim Fathers in their exile might seem nearer in spirit to Aeneas than Columbus on his voyage of exploration. Still, there was among the press-ganged Boston scholars little evidence of sympathy with the *Aeneid*. The link between New England and Hesperia was made – the Puritan Cotton Mather, product of the Boston Latin School, began his prose ecclesiastical history of New England, *Magnalia Christi Americana* ('The Glorious Deeds of Christ in America', 1702) with a resounding Virgilian proem: 'I write the wonder of the Christian religion, flying from the Depravations of Europe to the American Strand.' And the *Aeneid* was sometimes appreciated – the bookish president John Adams effused (note the horticultural imagery), 'The *Aeneid* is like a well-ordered garden, where it is impossible to find any Part unadorned, or to cast our Eyes upon a single Spot that does not produce some beautiful Plant or Flower.'[135] His son, John Quincy Adams, as a student translated all the *Eclogues* for pleasure and wrote that the *Georgics* were, 'the most perfect composition that ever issued from the mind of man'.[136] And the Great Seal of the United States, first used in 1782, carries three phrases quarried from Virgil (but not the *Aeneid*).[137]

Herein lay the problem: the *Aeneid*'s political ideology (particularly if ingested through Dryden's translation[138]) jarred with the beliefs of the settlers, its project of the foundation of a city with their agrarian lifestyle and Dido with Puritan morality. So the *Eclogues* and *Georgics* found favour where the *Aeneid* found little or none;[139] the most conspicuous attention paid to the *Aeneid* was in a travesty of Book IV, *Aeneas and Dido: Burlesqu'd from the Fourth Book of the* Aeneid *of Virgil*, by Rowland Rugeley, of 1774 (not long before the Great Seal).[140] With the swell of nationalism and the call for an American literature, two locals stepped up with epics designed to supersede, respectively, the *Iliad* and the *Aeneid*: Timothy Dwight's *The Conquest of Canaan* (1785), on the biblical hero Joshua, and Joel Barlow's *The Vision of Columbus* (1787), revised and expanded into the ten-book *Columbiad* (1807).[141] In his preface to the *Columbiad*, Barlow praises Homer the bard but sternly deprecates his ethical effects; he continues, 'Virgil wrote and felt like a subject, not like a citizen. The real design of his poem was to increase the veneration of the people for a master, whoever he might be, and to encourage like Homer the great system of military depredation.' Nonetheless, Barlow took lessons from his target – 'Not the least of the Virgilian qualities of the *Columbiad* is its ambition to sum up a long previous epic tradition.'[142]

In the mid-nineteenth century, a spirit of anti-classicism prevailed, and the Classics fell from grace in the curriculum. This provoked an anonymous translator in 1870 to publish, in a small Connecticut newspaper, the *Winsted Herald*, a 'Free and Independent Translation of the First and Fourth Books of the *Aeneid* of Virgil'. His avowed aim, as his preface stated, was:[143]

to rescue the Bard of Mantua from the oblivion to which this degenerate age seems bent upon consigning him; ... the *vade mecum* of all who ever pretended to any sort of scholarship down to a generation ago has been supplanted in our schools by such syllabub trash as *Parlez vous* and *Book Keepings*; has been kicked out to make room for 'Brewer's Familiar Science' and a whole brood of contemptible Ologies, that are no more a substitute for Virgil than burnt beans are for old Java.

As might be expected from this mischief, the translation itself is more Rugeley than Dryden,[144] though the intention to popularize the Latin is very genuine. The Latin itself, meanwhile, had become the province of academics, whose scholarly studies began appearing around the time of the centenary of Virgil's death, in 1881. They were the means, abetted in some measure by the poet of Winsted and more mainstream twentieth century American translations, whereby Virgil was restored to the syllabus – with, for instance, the Great Books movement of the English professor at Columbia, John Erskine, initiated in 1919.[145] Since its doldrums, American intellectuals have driven the reception of the *Aeneid* in a very distinctive direction (9.5).

9.4.3 Diaspora: The Aeneid in China

Countries can be multiplied as test cases;[146] let one more suffice, China,[147] which illustrates how Virgil can, eventually, bridge a cultural and linguistic gulf, on pontoons of individual initiative and benign accident. The Jesuit missionaries in the late sixteenth and early seventeenth centuries first brought ancient Greek and Roman classics to China but, although they translated part or all of several works[148] into Chinese and cited many more in their writings, did not include Virgil among them. Protestant missionaries of the nineteenth century (German and English), keen to promote at least awareness of western poetry, followed the philhellene preference of the time and advocated Homer over Virgil. After the establishment of the Chinese Republic in 1912, Chinese intellectuals began a quest for a heroic example that would suit the new nation: China lacked such models in its own poetic tradition, so it turned to Homer and Byron, another philhellene. Awareness of Rome, which was considered merely a cultural appendage to Greece, was at first restricted to James Baldwin's *Fifty Famous Stories Retold* (1896) and *Thirty More Famous Stories Retold* (1905), widespread in translation and as English texts in Chinese schools. Worse, the image of Rome was dominated by Gibbon's *Decline and Fall* and Mussolini's bellicose reinvention of the Roman past from the 1920s. This outlook on Rome did not spare the *Aeneid*: 'Being artificially composed, it was different from natural poetry, and thus could not be put on a par with Homer.'[149]

What changed this inhospitality was the bimillennium of Virgil's birth in 1930. It prompted translations into Chinese of *Aeneid* Book I and Eclogues 4 and 8, as well as articles and even a short book on Virgil. The translator in question, Fu Donghua, was strongly influenced by (and published a Chinese version of) an article by John Erskine, of Columbia, issued that year, 'Vergil, the Modern Poet'.[150] In it Erskine portrayed Virgil as critical of empire, questioning the cost of civilization and the value of progress to the lonely main characters in the *Aeneid* – in some respects an anticipation of the later 'Harvard' school (9.5). This coloured Fu's rendering, which he made using the English of John Conington's *Aeneid* (1866) but deviating from the more confident spirit of its time and place: 'Fu's translation tells a story of a kind-hearted hero who was to lead his soldiers, with the support of the supreme god, to utterly destroy the local Italians who would resist the conquest.'[151] The book on Virgil that appeared at the bimillennium, in complete contrast, was the work of Shi Zhecun, a translator, essayist and pioneer of the modern novel. He was influenced by Sainte-Beuve and by late Victorian English criticism, notably William Sellar's *Roman Poets of the Augustan Age* (first published 1878), which says that Virgil 'recalls the simpler virtues of the olden time, he represents the humanity of his own age, he anticipates something of the piety and purity of the future faith of the world'.[152] Thus, in

1930, China was presented with two very different Virgils, as luck would have it roughly on the two sides of the divide that would open in the west during the 1950s. But not many noticed.

For a long time after this the supply of Virgil to the Chinese remained a trickle: a translation of the *Eclogues* directly from the Latin, in rhyming couplets (like Dryden's), by Yang Xianyi came out in 1957, with its preface providing a Marxist wrapper for the verse ('the poet shares common feelings with the people').[153] Finally, in 1984, the veteran academic Yang Zhouhan produced a prose version of the *Aeneid*, with an introduction that was light on Marx and comprehensive in covering historical context, themes, structure and poetic characteristics. In the tumult of the fifty years since Virgil's bimillennium, he had had little access to contemporary western scholarship, so his references to it were eclectic and the view of the *Aeneid* his own: he compared its sense of melancholy and compassion to that in the great Chinese poet Du Fu, placed hope in a belief in the gods and took great trouble, when rendering *pius*, to capture its connotation of duty and devotion to an end greater than the individual. The China of the 1980s was on its way to becoming a major economic power; so Yang's translation coincided with his compatriots' new sense of their own destiny, wish to contribute to it and curiosity about China's place in the world – here was a demand for the *Aeneid* at last. This was confirmed when, in 1999, the Yilin Publishing House issued a series *World Heroic Epics*, claiming that epics as a genre represented 'the cultural codes and unique characteristics of a nation'; they included the *Aeneid*, the study of which has been intensifying in China ever since.

9.5 The twentieth and twenty-first centuries:[154] Re-evaluation

At the end of the nineteenth century, Virgil was ripe for rediscovery; in Germany this was achieved punctually in 1903, by two ground-breaking books that between them inaugurated modern criticism of the *Aeneid*:

- Richard Heinze's *Virgil's Epic Technique*, whose countless insights into many aspects of the poem, supported by vast erudition, have outlived its overarching theses that Aeneas is a Stoic hero (*Introduction* – 3.2.5 Aeneas in the *Aeneid*: A Stoic hero?) and that the aim of the *Aeneid* was to 'have a didactic, inspiring and elevating effect' on politics and patriotism.[155]

- Eduard Norden's commentary on Book VI, the first on a single book of the poem, another monument of sensitive scholarship that, even though its Augustan perspective is no longer fashionable, remains in print. The single-book commentaries that Norden inaugurated were rounded off as recently as 2012, with R. Tarrant's edition of Book XII.

But the First World War intervened before they could be properly digested abroad – Wilfred Owen's 'Arms and the Boy' casts a bitter eye back on the *Aeneid*'s opening words as on a poem that glorifies war, ignoring the youth laid waste that it mourns. Ezra Pound, compiling his short list in 1931, classified Virgil as a 'dilutor' rather than an 'inventor' or 'master' and gleefully announced,[156] 'I am chucking out Pindar, and Virgil, without compunction.' (So much for Erskine.) Despite such antipathy, come the bimillennium of Virgil's birth, the work of Heinze and Norden had begun to be absorbed in England; and then arrived another homage, *Vergil: Father of the West*, by Theodor Haecker, an Austrian Christian and committed anti-Fascist

(1931, translated 1934): 'The *Imperium Romanum* [Rule of Rome], which Vergil knew in all its natural grandeur and revealed in the splendour of beauty, is no hazy ideal; nor is it merely a true ideal, but a reality, deep though that reality may at times be buried.'[157] The Second World War might have been expected to disrupt such conviction; but it could also encourage tenacity to it – T. S. Eliot was strongly influenced by Haecker when he wrote two widely read essays, 'What is a Classic?' (1944, an address given to the Virgil Society) and 'Virgil and the Christian World' (1951).[158] In the former, Eliot holds up the *Aeneid*, the 'classic of all Europe', as the preeminent example of maturity (in civilization, language, mind and manners[159] – English literature has no such specimen of 'maturity' beyond Alexander Pope) before clinching his argument:[160]

> We need to remind ourselves that as Europe is a whole (and still, in its progressive mutilation and disfigurement, the organism out of which any greater world harmony must develop), so European literature is a whole, the several members of which cannot flourish, if the same bloodstream does not circulate throughout the whole body. The bloodstream of European literature is Latin and Greek . . .

This is a position more dogmatic than grounded in the poem – Eliot writes on an idea of the *Aeneid*. It is hard to understand in what sense he called Roman civilization at the time of the *Aeneid*'s composition 'mature', when it stood at a pivot between civil war and civil peace, between the Republic and the emperors and between pagan and Christian. Eliot's fellow-poets were provoked; Auden's 'Shield of Achilles' (published 1952, 8.626–728 note) and 'Secondary Epic' (published 1955, 6.756–853 note)[161] are both retorts; with slower reflexes, Robert Graves waited till 1961 before inveighing against 'The Virgil Cult'.[162]

All the same, a profoundly learned, eloquent advocacy of a similar position to Eliot's came in the German Viktor Pöschl's, *The Art of Vergil: Image and Symbol in the* Aeneid (1950). In it, he looked at the way the storm of violent chaos of Book I, roused for a second time in the guise of Allecto in Book VII, was finally quelled by Jupiter through Aeneas in Book XII – 'The struggle and final victory of order – this subduing of the demonic which is the basic theme of the poem – appears and reappears in many variations'. What is at stake for Pöschl 'concerns the foundations of Western civilization. We are seeking ties of communication to bind us together.'[163] This sense of mission does not blind him to the suffering or tragedies in the poem – of Dido and, for all his savagery, Turnus. Such a faith in the march of Rome towards Augustan dominion, which still does not deny the pain and sadness of the poem, continued in Germany[164] and in the Anglophone world was notably embodied in Brooks Otis' *Virgil: A Study in Civilised Poetry* of 1964:[165]

> Aeneas is, in effect, an Augustan type – a *divine man*, not necessarily copied after the Emperor himself but embodying the ruler-ideal, who . . . imposes upon a more primitive . . . society a defeat that is the means to unity, peace and civilization on the Augustan plan.

But – and it is a massive 'but' – during the 1950s, a split, possibly a reaction to the Second World War diametrically opposed to Eliot's, had already opened between certain Americans (later baptized the 'Harvard School'[166]) and the Europeans already mentioned. Their views surfaced in print during the early 1960s – Adam Parry, in his famously entitled, 'The Two Voices of Vergil's *Aeneid*,' says,[167] 'We hear two voices in the *Aeneid*, a public voice of triumph' and a private voice of regret. The private voice, the personal emotions of a man, is never allowed to motivate action.' Wendell Clausen calls not just Aeneas' progress but Rome's history 'a long Pyrrhic victory of the human spirit'.[168] Michael Putnam narrows his focus to the ending of the poem (see 12.919–52 note):[169] 'The progress of empire, as Virgil puts it before the reader, is attributed only to madness, vengeance and death. The slaying of Turnus is the ultimate, all-embracing tragedy of the *Aeneid*.' These three subversions of the Augustan ideal form a crescendo – Parry's is personal, Clausen's social but inward-looking and Putnam's outward-looking and universal; they are compatible but do not entail each other. All three make of Aeneas a central figure flawed and self-unknowing, as would be recognizable in a modern novel.

This view of a critical Virgil was also in tune with liberal individualism,[170] then and since – 'He's a worldly-wise republican after all.' Although it has been resisted,[171] it has been developed, or at least partially absorbed – for example, by William Johnson in *Darkness Visible* (1979), in which the author portrays the chicanery of the gods in Book XII as Juno's triumph;[172] at the same time, Johnson draws back from the Harvard School, preferring to oscillate between optimism and pessimism – the poem is 'polysematic', in that it operates on several levels at once: literal, symbolic, moral and metaphysical;[173] for example (but not Johnson's), the killing of Turnus symbolizes the restoration of order, is morally ambiguous and in metaphysical terms is ordained by Fate. Oliver Lyne in *Further Voices in Virgil's* Aeneid (1987) builds on Parry by suggesting that internal reference and external allusion regularly 'add to, comment upon, question and occasionally subvert the implications of the epic voice'.[174] Gian Biagio Conte, in an essay of 2007, argues that both the Harvard and European 'schools' miss the inherent dualism of the poem, indeed they each instantiate one side of it only: Virgil pegs up contradictions everywhere, in characters and situations, and leaves the tension between them to 'open up to welcome antagonistic claims and forces: the meaning of the discourse would be enriched by it and so inevitably would become complex'.[175] Hardie's quotation[176] of Walt Whitman is apposite:

> Do I contradict myself?
> Very well then I contradict myself.
> (I am large, I contain multitudes.)

These few instances of many different interpretative approaches taken illustrate how the *Aeneid* is increasingly seen as unresolved, and deliberately so.[177] The dynamic equilibrium between its opposites is the territory of modern literary critical theory; into this classicists after some hesitation have been making more forays (9.6).

9.5.1 Book and film

The *Aeneid*, unlike the *Iliad* and *Odyssey*, is poorly represented on film[178] – 'a couple of silent versions, now lost, on Dido and Lavinia, a 1962 sword-and-sandal movie *The Avenger* with Steve Reeves as Aeneas, a 1987 art film *Didone non è morta* directed by Lina Mangiacapre, an Italian television series based on the *Aeneid*. And there is *Battleship Galactica*, with its 'rather

Virgilian plotline of a leader guiding the remnants of a destroyed civilization towards a fated new home'.[179]

Certain poets of the twentieth century and beyond have drawn inspiration from the *Aeneid*: Robert Lowell, Allen Tate, Eavan Boland, Rosanna Warren and Louise Glück.[180] (On Heaney, see 10.2 *Aeneid* in English translation.) Nevertheless, 'contemporary poets' original responses to the *Aeneid* . . . have been scattered and occasional'.[181] Since Hermann Broch's *The Death of Virgil* (1945), where the *Aeneid* has been used as a jumping-off point for fiction, it is notably by women novelists. They, by 'creating and defining this new *aetas Vergiliana* ["Virgilian age"]',[182] have broken the patriarchal monopoly once and for all.

After the Great Seal had failed to include any phrase definitely from the *Aeneid*, the National September 11 Memorial, on the site of the World Trade Center, was inscribed with the words, 'No day shall erase you from the memory of time' (9.447, on Nisus and Euryalus[183]). Where Virgil had promised that his poem would keep alive the memory of the fallen, here they return the favour.

9.6 Literary theory

Harrison calls[184] the caution of Latinists in their relatively late consideration of modern hermeneutic studies, 'in many ways highly justified'. Schmitz makes a virtue of it:[185] 'It could be argued that this belatedness is an advantage rather than a drawback: while the turmoil of the last century has subsided and given way to a more dispassionate view, the fundamental questions that literary theory has raised remain with us'. The delay has at least given an opportunity for exegetes to help those lost in the idiolects of some of the luminaries of this criticism; nevertheless, simplification (what follows is extreme as well as selective) is bound to give an illusion of clear outlines where there are few (e.g. around the terminology). Theory cannot be completely swerved – Eagleton paraphrases[186] J. M. Keynes, who took anti-theorists to task, 'those economists who disliked theory, or claimed to get along better without it, were simply in the grip of an older theory'. Theory has a history, too; what follows is therefore roughly chronological, but aims above all to relate the various currents of thought to the *Aeneid*. More schools could be added: it is possible to imagine a Marxist or existentialist take on the poem.

9.6.1 New Criticism

In reaction to the soullessness of an industrial age, the literary movement known as 'New Criticism', which specialized in poetry,[187] made the poem into a self-contained object of reverence – it was to be analysed formally in terms only of its own text (with the minimum of explication for archaic words or concepts), that is, without reference to the author, the reader, the historical or social context. 'A typical New Critical account of a poem offers a stringent investigation of its 'various "tensions", "paradoxes" and "ambivalences", showing how these are resolved and integrated by a solid structure'.[188] This at first sight seems impractical for an ancient literary work in which so much, even the basic meaning of words, requires explication in terms of other contemporary writing; and it removes intertextuality, except where it re-enters unconsciously in the mind of the reader. The approach does, however, encourage the reader to grant the *Aeneid* the potential to establish a world of its own with meaning of its own, for the detection of which the intratext holds all the requisite clues. Certainly, the intratext holds many clues (*Introduction* – 8.1 Intratextuality: Self-allusion), but only the reader who can also identify allusions outside the text can assess whether those internal clues exhaust its meaning.

9.6.2 *Hermeneutics*[189]

Hermeneutics (= 'science of interpretation') attempted originally to bring a clear method to biblical exegesis.[190] At first the model was comparatively simple: a phrase or sentence within the text was understood in context; it might fit the context as already understood, or clash with it; if it clashed, the understanding of what had gone before might need revising (or there is an insoluble contradiction, indicating that the text needs amending); the new understanding of the context is then applied to the next passage and so on. This iterative model is captured in the so-called 'hermeneutic circle'.[191]

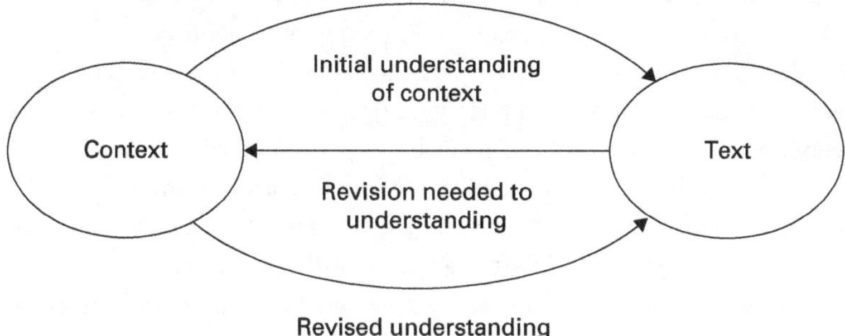

The same model can be applied to the understanding of a phrase or sentence (or episode, or indeed a whole work) within its cultural setting – Virgil's use of *furor* can only be understood by comparing it to its use in other authors; Aeneas' attention to ritual detail must be made sense of within Roman religious practice; further, since Virgil is part of that cultural setting, we might amend our understanding of *furor,* or of ritual detail, from the evidence of the *Aeneid.* That is not all. We, as engaged readers provide a 'context' of our own, with ancient Rome and the *Aeneid* as its text: we start from an understanding of both that we have absorbed from within our own culture (itself influenced by Rome and the *Aeneid* – this is 'tradition'). But, as we read, we modify that initial understanding. So you might start off with the idea that the *Aeneid* is a Roman *Iliad,* move on to take it as a panegyric for Augustus. then view it as a criticism of the Augustan project (as far as it could have been). One term for this progressive readjustment is the 'fusion of horizons' – each revision brings you nearer to the text until your 'own "horizon" of historical meanings and assumptions "fuses" with the "horizon" within which the work is placed. At such a moment <you> enter the alien world of the artefact, but at the same time gather it into <your> own realm, reaching a more complete understanding of <yourself>.'[192] This is not the same thing as identifying the author's intentions, which might not have been consistent or fully worked out; but it allows the artefact to have its effect on something like its own terms.

There is a problem here: since the initial understanding and subsequent readjustments are subjective, what is to stop you from misconceiving the text from the outset, or revising your understanding in the wrong direction, or imagining a (false) fusion of horizons? There are two answers to this: first, any misconception is taking place within the 'tradition', so that as you attend further to the text you are likely to correct it; and second, you are part of a community of readers, all of whom can justify their 'horizon' to others from the 'text': the game you are playing has rules and it makes sense to speak of better and worse players. These answers go some way but not all the way to removing the problem – the 'tradition' might not exist (as for Virgil in China) or have been interrupted or distorted; then the game might become a free-for-all. What, too, if the work of literature itself sets out to elicit a diversity of responses and we have a choice of horizons to fuse with (as, arguably, in the *Aeneid*)? Hermeneutics' method of progressing, a dialogue with the text, would remain indispensable but its goal, a 'fusion of horizons', fugitive or illusory.

9.6.3 *Reader response and reception theory*[193]

Reception theory (a type of reader response theory) steps back from this 'fusion of horizons' to focus instead on the reader. It therefore does not address the communal reception discussed in Chapter 8. It arose in part as a reaction to the Romantic promotion of the creative genius and aimed to give the artistic consumer his or her due; the performer of, and listener to, a piece of music have roles as vital to its impact as the composer. One phrase has become almost its slogan: 'Meaning is always realised at the point of reception.'[194] Much hangs on how the word 'meaning' is unpacked;[195] substituting 'communication' or 'interpretation' for it in the original proposition makes it banal; taking it as 'what the author intends' is clearly untrue. The French philosopher Ricoeur declared[196] with disarming simplicity that the interpretation of texts follows the structure of any human communication, namely someone saying something about something to someone else. Neither speaker nor addressee reads the mind of the other; 'meaning' is an encounter somewhere in the middle. But precisely because this is not the same as a 'fusion of horizons', it opens the door to as many interpretations as there are readers – again, arbitration can only be through criteria within the text itself or through the arguments of other better informed and so more persuasive interpreters of the work. This describes but does not resolve the predicament of the *Aeneid*.

9.6.4 *Structuralism*

A radically different way of constructing meaning in texts, one that distances the reader and aims to introduce scientific rigour to the process, is structuralism.[197] Part of its attraction is its applicability across different disciplines (anthropology, sociology, psychoanalysis). Its strangeness is best approached through its origins, in linguistics, and in particular the thinking of Ferdinand de Saussure: for Saussure, all it took for an individual word (signifier) to be able to be associated with a concept (signified) was for it to sound distinct from other words (a few homophones can be allowed). 'Red' does not have to be 'red'; we could attach 'sef' to the same concept. What enables an utterance containing it to make sense are then the rules that govern the concatenation of signifiers. To take an analogy: when getting dressed, we put on a combination of socks (two, matching), a shirt, trousers/skirt (not more than one, colours not clashing), and so on; merely putting on a sock (cf. using a word in isolation) does not count as 'getting dressed' (making sense).[198] An analogous 'structural' view can be taken of a work of literature within a given genre: what makes the *Aeneid* an epic at all is that it uses certain themes, features or patterns in ways that characterize the epic 'system'.[199] The relationships between these components will determine how the *Aeneid* means something (in the same way as, trivially, the structural difference between 'hunter flees alligator' and 'alligator flees hunter' generates a different meaning). Note, however, that the structuralist analysis will not tell us what the *Aeneid* means – only the role of structure in that meaning; nonsense, too, can be perfectly structured according to rules.[200] As Eagleton puts it,[201] 'Having characterized the underlying rule systems of a literary text, all the structuralists could do was sit back and wonder what to do next.'

This should not prove structuralism irrelevant to the *Aeneid*; after all, one of its offspring, narratology[202] has provided a useful toolkit for dissecting and appreciating narrative (see *Introduction* – 7.3 Narratology). Rather, as regards the *Aeneid*, it is unfinished business: a structuralist analysis of the genre of epic[203] might also yield insights into how its components combine to achieve, or at least reinforce,[204] meaning in the text.

9.6.5 Intertextuality: Wider sense[205]

Structuralism was not the only way of rendering both author and reader immaterial. Intertextuality, when previously met (*Introduction* – 8.2 Intertextuality, narrow sense: External allusion) was synonymous with external allusion or reference. When coined, however, the word meant something very different: following from Mikhail Bakhtin's notion that a novel was a collection of different voices (or views of the world) in dialogue with each other and with the reader, Julia Kristeva came up with the idea that we ourselves, as authors or readers, are the sum of what we have heard and read and define ourselves by what we say and write – a text is a 'mosaic of quotations',[206] and in producing them we prove ourselves the products of the texts (in the widest possible sense of the word) that we have consumed. Thus there is nothing but a wash and backwash of (un)conscious allusion, which communication in every form keeps in constant motion and for which we, as authors or readers, are the medium. Such an extreme philosophy had to be domesticated before it could be applied to the literary criticism of a particular work – hence its narrowing to the 'intertextuality' of identifiable external allusion. Literary theory reclaimed some of the original territory of the doctrine with declarations such as, 'the poem carries meaning only by referring from text to text';[207] and made a distinction between intertextuality as demarcatable allusion and the derivation of one (whole) text from another, a 'hypertext' (nothing to do with HTML) from a 'hypotext' (as the *Aeneid* from the *Odyssey* and the *Iliad*). But paradoxically, for an idea that had been used to construct meaning, intertextuality soon contributed to the destabilization of all meaning in post-structuralism (9.6.6).

9.6.6 Post-structuralism and deconstruction[208]

If structuralism had sought a meaning that could be determined without reference to the author or to the reader, what followed it – which can be vaguely entitled 'post-structuralism', and here concerns specifically 'deconstruction' – rejoiced in dismantling structuralism's entire apparatus. It takes Saussure's doctrine that words only become attached to concepts by being unlike other words; your understanding of 'red' resembles a dictionary definition in terms of other adjectives or paraphrases, themselves defined in turn – and so on. Your understanding of 'red' will therefore only be as complete as your knowledge of all other words – and your knowledge will not be the same as my knowledge, which renders language unstable. When it comes to a literary text, not only will the inherent instability of language make every reader read it differently; it will also make the text itself contain the seeds of its own contradiction, for example through irony (which exploits the ghostly presence in a word of its own opposite). The author's intention is no help, for the author too is not set on firm linguistic foundations (whence what Barthes called the 'death of the author' – *Introduction* – 2 Virgil's Life and Works). Intertextuality does not moor one text to another; all allusions are to other allusions, ramifying out but never to *terra firma*.

There are many objections to deconstruction, not least that it can itself be 'deconstructed': especially if it contains its own contradiction, will anyone ever be able to nail down what it is saying? But for those who detect in the *Aeneid* a degree of self-subversion, it is as if Virgil had arrived before the post-structuralists: he never erects an absolute positive (*pietas*, the reign of Augustus) without qualifying it; he creates characters that are not self-consistent. This is, however, deconstruction by analogy: for us to grasp that Camilla is both nymph and human, Virgil depends on language that tells us that at one point she is the first and at another the second. He requires language to have a high degree of stability if he is to set up ambivalence of his own.

9.6.7 New Historicism[209]

One consequence of deconstruction is to sever a literary work from its historical context: historical context, yet again, cannot provide any touchstone of interpretation because it is so open to interpretation itself. By contrast New Historicism, although it does not refute deconstruction root and branch, reattaches literary works to their historical moment in a different way from hermeneutics (9.6.2): literary works such as the *Aeneid* are as much part of the view of the world that belongs to their historical period as are inscriptions, graffiti, letters, or laws (not to mention other later forms of writing, such as newspapers or diaries) and exist to fulfil a social function that belonged to it as well. They are not controlled by an ideological superstructure (as a Marxist would say) but neither do they float in an intellectual bubble apart from the political realities on which they might be seen to comment. As one New Historicist has put it,[210] 'The subversive voices are produced by and within the affirmations of order; they are powerfully registered, but they do not undermine that order.'

This is clearly relevant to the debate on any 'anti-Augustan' voices in the *Aeneid*: for the New Historicists they are first and foremost, and inescapably, 'Augustan', because we hear them at all, and from then.

9.6.8 Freud, Jung and psychoanalysis[211]

Psychoanalytical criticism stands apart from the philosophical development outlined so far. The degree to which a reader finds its analysis of the *Aeneid* stimulating will depend on how amenable (s)he is to Freud's and Jung's ideas; their appeal is instinctive as well as, often rather than, evidential. (How can any assertion about the unconscious be proven?) Eagleton divides psychoanalytical literary criticism into four categories, based on its object of attention (numeration added): 'It can attend (1) to the *author* of the work; (2) to the work's *contents*; (3) to its *formal construction*; (4) or to the *reader*.'

An example of (1) is Harold Bloom, who in his 'The Anxiety of Influence: A Theory of Poetry' (1973) posits an Oedipal relationship between an author and his predecessors, whom he must supplant to make room for himself. Suddenly the author is centre-stage, reborn after death by deconstruction. Bloom's picture might be a credible one of some poets' attitude towards their models (and indeed of Virgil's towards Lucretius), but is it so of Virgil's attitude towards Homer and Ennius? His allusions only function if their targets remain common currency – the poems are cumulative, not competitive; and Virgil had no need to dislodge Homer as Rome's 'national' poet.[212]

A practical exercise in (2), Freudian analysis of content, is Oliensis' article, 'Freud's *Aeneid*' (2001).[213] It takes as its own point of departure Dido's dream (4.465 ff.) (Freud's 'Interpretation of Dreams' (1900) is his most suggestive work for literary theory: a piece of literature, like a dream, takes experience, mental dispositions, language, other literature, and packages them together, and the method of production can sometimes be teased out from these constituents). From there, Oliensis advances to Freudian preoccupations of infanticide and incest,[214] and extends them to (or 'displaces' them onto, to use a Freudian mechanism) Venus, Amata and Lavinia. The approach is one that Freud himself took when attributing an Oedipus complex to Hamlet; but insofar as dreams are a means of tapping into the unconscious,[215] whose unconscious are we tapping into – Dido's or Virgil's?

The focus on formal construction (3), can be exemplified in the system-building of Northrop Frye's *Anatomy of Criticism* (1957).[216] This creates a taxonomy of literature according to Jungian archetypes, though it leaves behind their psychological underpinning; it has much in common with structuralism (9.6.4) and, as far as the *Aeneid* is concerned, remains uncharted waters.

The focus on the reader (4), was the preoccupation of Norman Holland who in *The Dynamics of Literary Response* (1968), returned to the ancient question of why we take pleasure in reading about painful emotion. His answer,[217] that 'literature transforms our primitive wishes and fears into significance and coherence, and this transformation gives us pleasure', ascends far upstream to Aristotle's *katharsis*,[218] while uniting reader-response theory with Freud's pleasure principle. Holland later proposed[219] that a reader's ego is reinforced when the reader adapts his or her identity in the process of interpretation; this would imply that ultimately all literature is affirmative, however unsettling. But the way in which readers have sought out within the *Aeneid* the corrosion of its own Augustan vision seems to indicate something more complex than unalloyed self-affirmation.

Psychoanalytic angles on the *Aeneid* have a whiff of the esoteric – such as in the thesis title, 'Compensations for Exile: A Lacanian Analysis of Aeneas' Destiny and Dido's Tragedy in Virgil's *Aeneid*'.[220] Their attraction is precisely in their heterodoxy – even where no orthodoxy exists.

9.6.9 Feminism and gender studies[221]

Feminist criticism represents a standpoint rather than a body of theories, even though, in dismantling the patriarchy, it has found fertile soil in post-structural debate and it has needed to correct the male bias of some of psychoanalysis' major thinkers.[222] The *Aeneid*, with its patriarchal view of history (the *Aeneid* is obsessed with the male line) and yet its prominent women leaders (Dido, the founder of a city; Camilla, warrior without equal) as so often shies away from consistency. For the various reactions to the portrayal of women in the *Aeneid*, see

Introduction – 6.3.2 Women in the *Aeneid*; and for Camilla as a study in gender, see *Introduction* – 3.10 Camilla.

9.6.10 Postcolonial studies[223]

With the dismantling of empire after the Second World War, former colonies began expressing their independent identities and the effect colonial domination had had on them, in art, including literature. A highly influential document of this progression has been Edward Said's 'Orientalism' (1978), in which he pilloried the West's frequently contemptuous portrayal of the 'Orient', that is North Africa, the Middle East and Asia, an 'othering' that provided an excuse for imperialism and made more turbulent both liberation and its aftereffects, as he examines in his final chapter.

It is difficult for either the colonizers or the colonized to view dispassionately their period of intwined history; postcolonial studies are as much social as literary criticism, and of a particular era.[224] Nevertheless, some of the *Aeneid*'s themes explore in fable what could be called postcolonial experiences: emigration (the Trojans are a displaced people), cultural conflict (they are 'orientalized' by some of those they encounter[225]) and building relationships with new neighbours (Latinus, Evander, Tarchon). The *Aeneid* has a special slant on these experiences, however, because Aeneas is also returning to his 'home' (at least to that of his ancestor Dardanus); Fate is on his side and, through Latinus' prophecy, effects his welcome; and, when he finds Greeks already settled there who might be his sworn enemies (Evander and the Arcadians), they become willing allies. Thus the *Aeneid* makes the absorption of the newcomers rapid and complete, though under terms (agreed between Juno and Jupiter, 12.834 ff.) that most immigrants today would bridle at. Virgil's own society included a high proportion of non-Romans; not only, after the Social War, were Italians from outside Rome entitled to its citizenship (*Introduction* – 1.6 The late Republic (from 133 BCE onwards)), but also foreign slaves could become freedmen (*liberti* – with some political rights) and their children fully enfranchised Roman citizens. Assimilation, as much as the foundation of Rome the end-point of the *Aeneid*, had become a way of life.

CHAPTER 10
TRANSLATING THE *AENEID* (INTO ENGLISH[1])

A significant part of the history of the *Aeneid*'s reception is the history of its translation: translators in their sense of duty towards the text (or lack of it) embody their own response, whether this could be said to be of its time or not, and in turn influence the response of others. It might be supposed that the gradual exit of the author as a point of reference for interpretation would liberate the translator, or at least highlight his or her importance in bridging the gap between the reader and the original. In practice, however, to judge from the plentiful translators' prefaces, it has adjusted what constitutes 'fidelity' to within narrower boundaries.

10.1 Theory[2]

Perfect translation is manifestly impossible – hence Borges' French translator of *Don Quixote* who ended up reproducing it verbatim in Spanish.[3] So all translation is compromise, and the approach a translator can or should take to compromising has been discussed since the beginnings of translation. George Steiner remarks,[4] 'Over some two thousand years of argument and precept, the beliefs and disagreements voiced about the nature of translation have been almost the same. Identical theses, familiar moves and refutations in debate recur, nearly without exception, from Cicero and Quintilian to the present day.' Dryden's definition of a translator's options encapsulates much of what had been said before and has become a de facto standard, of particular relevance because he exemplified its application himself when translating Virgil. According to Dryden, there are three courses open:[5]

- *metaphrase*, or literal translation word for word, line for line; of this Dryden takes a dim view;[6]
- *paraphrase*, in which words are not so much followed as sense, which can be amplified but not altered;
- *imitation*, in which the translator ('if he has not lost that name') takes general hints from the original and 'runs division on the ground-work'.

Dryden himself steered, he thought, between metaphrase and paraphrase: 'I have endeavored to make Virgil speak such English as he himself would have spoken, if he had been born in England and in this present age.'[7] This presumes not only that there is only one sort of Englishman (coincidentally like Dryden) but also that this Englishman would fall instinctively into one way of expressing the Latin. Dryden's demotic proves to be itself an ideological choice. The German philosopher Friedrich Schleiermacher (1813) drew up an axis – the translator either moves the reader towards the writer ('foreignizing', in the terminology of translation studies) or the writer towards the reader ('domesticating');[8] Dryden domesticates; others do not.

For example, the late-nineteenth-century translator of the *Aeneid* into Russian, Valerii Briusov, set himself to capture as much as he could of style, imagery, meter and rhythm, the movement of the line, word play and sound play.[9] Since Russian, like Latin, is an inflected language and can be more flexible with word order than English, he had slightly more room to manoeuvre than Dryden, but the effect still provoked adverse comment: heavy, cerebral, even unintelligible. And it can be argued that Briusov's formal faithfulness to the Latin, however virtuosic, did not shift the reader towards Virgil but into a hinterland foreign to both[10]. Even so, the great benefit of foreignizing is that it averts the illusion that Virgil slots neatly into our concepts and conversation.

Not that paraphrase automatically entails domestication: the translator might paraphrase in his or her own direction, away from the average Englishman, or any particular Englishman at all. This might smack of *traduttore traditore* but can be defended if the translator feels that Virgil roused in the Romans themselves a frisson of strangeness – and, surprisingly, the one comment preserved on his style is that it was too low-brow for epic (*Introduction* – 7.7 Diction). So, contrary to Herbert Spencer's dictum, Virgil's translator does not have to 'avoid friction'.[11] The same issue, however, rears its head as with Briusov, that the reader is neither being led towards Virgil nor left at home but taken into a third place, where the *Aeneid* is at the service of the translator rather than the translator at the service of the *Aeneid*.

This is no crime, so long as the translator does not claim a direct line to Virgil. Every translator cannot help serving his or her own interests, personal, poetic or political, in some measure, or else would not undertake the task at all. In any case, if a completely self-effacing translator were conceivable; it would be because the process was mechanical rather than artistic. Burrow, observing that few of the earlier translations into English were aimed at the monarchy,[12] continues:[13]

> Most British and Irish translators of Virgil are anxious about their own standing, usually support losing political causes and often … were not 'English' but Irish or Scots, or inhabitants of the Welsh Marches. Virgil tends to be adopted into English by poets who need the consolation of his authority, or who are attracted by his manifest interest in those who are underdogs, or by the sustaining dream of his imperial vision.

There is a danger here of deducing a translator's intentions from his or her political circumstances alone; even so, the *Aeneid* cannot help carrying a political charge in a way that the *Iliad* or the *Odyssey* do not. Burrows' thesis would be stronger if it took into account the translator's audience; that target audience has influenced the style of translation particularly in the modern era, in which domestication is more commercially viable than foreignization.

There are decisions the translator makes at the outset that will affect the degree of literalness and thus of (de)familiarization:

- Prose or verse? And if verse, keeping the lineation or not, and rhymed or unrhymed? Then, if rhymed, how complex a scheme? Conington's 1866 version in the metre of Scott's 'Marmion' (see 10.2 below) is bound to domesticate; but then so, usually, does prose, which abandons poetic aura for clarity of communication.

- Mimic or abandon poetic devices? The impossibility of capturing all Virgil's word play, which ranges from alliteration and chiasmus to anagrams (e.g. 7.702, 'pulsa palus') and acrostics (7.701–4 note), is treated either as an excuse to abandon it completely or an obligation to replicate some of it. Adding word music of one's own is an option but can highlight what is not highlighted in the Latin.

- Consistent or flexible translation of key Latin words (e.g. *furor*)? This is essential if the reader is to follow Virgil's verbal threads, but (depending on the particular word) can sound awkward. This also begs the question of which words are 'key'.

- Clarify ambiguities or retain them? It might seem an obvious principle to retain ambiguities wherever possible, but this has not always been followed; and sometimes it cannot be, as when confronted with lines as untranslatable as 1.462.

It is up to you to find your own preference: *caveat lector*.

10.2 *Aeneid* in English translation[14]

The trail starts in the fourteenth century with Chaucer's paraphrases of the story of Dido in *The House of Fame* and *The Legend of Good Women* (the latter in heroic couplets, i.e. rhymed iambic pentameters – metre offers a useful basic taxonomy because it so strongly affects the language and tone of the translation). He was sensitive to the inadequacy of his own tongue and the risk that he might 'myswrite' or 'mismetre';[15] he shows due deference to his source at the same time as he departs from it:[16]

> Whan Eneas was come unto that place
> Unto the mayster temple of al the toun
> Ther Dido was in hire devocyoun,
> Ful pryvyly his weye then hath he nome.
> Whan he was in the large temple come,
> I can nat seyn if that it be possible,
> But Venus hadde hym maked invisible –
> Thus seyth the bok, withouten any les.

The first full translation of the *Aeneid*, including Maffio Vegio's Book XIII, was made by Gavin Douglas into Middle Scots (which he modestly called 'ignorant blabring imperfyte'[17]) in the early sixteenth century. Also in heroic couplets, its raw vigour is striking (here in 2. 506 ff.):

> Peraventur of Priamus wald ʒe speir [ask]
> Quhou tyd [how went] the chance. Hys fait, gif ʒe lyst, heir:
> Quhen he the cite saw takyn and downbet,
> And of his palyce broken euery ʒet [gate],
> Amyd the secret closettis eik hys fays [foes],
> The auld grayth, al for nocht, to hym tays [takes]
> Hys hawbryk quhilk [which] was lang furth of vsage,
> Set on his schulderis trymlyng than for age . . .

Douglas' rendering was of service to Henry Howard, Earl of Surrey, when in the mid-sixteenth century he translated Books II and IV, in which Aeneas and Dido suffer an isolation he himself experienced, into blank verse (its earliest use in English). This makes the first complete translation into English that of Thomas Phaer (up to halfway through Book X), abetted by Thomas Twyne (the rest, including eventually Book XIII), which was issued in 1573 (up to Book XII) and then in 1584 (complete). It is in rhymed fourteen-syllable iambic lines ('fourteeners'), the metre of Golding's *Metamorphoses* (1565–7) and Chapman's *Iliad* (1598–1611). Here is Palinurus' demise (5.854 ff.):

> Behold, the God on him a dropping braunch of Lymbo pyt
> With deadly sleeping dewe, on both his temples dashing smyt.
> And struggling to resist, his swimming eyes with sleepe opprest,
> Skant first resolvéd were his weery limes with sodeyn rest.
> And leaning noddid lowe: whan half the pup with him he drew,
> And rother, helme and all, in myds of seas he falling threw.

This bowls along without shedding its dignity. There followed, however, a fashion for using hexameters (*Introduction* – 7.8 Metre), 'with passing pitiful success' (so judged Thomas Campion);[18] perhaps their most notorious exponent was the Irishman Richard Stanyhurst, in his version of the first four books of the *Aeneid* (1584). Here is Aeneas' departure from Troy:

> When that I theese speeches deliuered, I twisted a wallet
> On my broad shoulders, my nape dyd I settle eke vnder,
> With lion his yellow darck skyn my carcase I cased,
> My father on shouldeers I set, my yoong lad lulus
> I lead with right hand , tripping with pit pat vnequal,
> My wiefe cooms after , through crosse blynd allye we iumble.

This is what Nietzsche called translation as conquest,[19] an attempt to place the *Aeneid*, metre and all, under a very personal yoke – but it is left grasping only a grotesque husk. The heroic couplet, favoured in learned circles at the end of the sixteenth century (in Donne's Satires, for example) made a merciful return among Virgil's translators in the seventeenth, which amid its constitutional turmoil produced a spate of translations, mostly by Royalists – John Ogilby published the first complete Virgil in English (1649) and repeated the feat in 1654, with much revision (not all for the better). The prevailing literary aesthetic is illustrated by a letter from one of these translators, Sir John Denham, to another, Sir Richard Fanshawe:[20]

> Nor ought a Genius less that his that writ
> Attempt translation; for transplanted wit
> All the defects of air and soil doth share,
> And colder brains like colder climates are:
> In vain they toil, since nothing can beget
> A vital spirit, but a vital heat.
> That servile path thou nobly doth decline
> Of tracing word by word and line by line . . .
> A new and nobler way thou dost pursue
> To make translations and translators too.
> They but preserve the ashes, thou the Flame,
> True to his sense but truer to his Fame.

In retrospect it is tempting to view this sequence of translators as way-markers for the 'genius', at the century's close, of John Dryden,[21] who did indeed make use of them when preserving Virgil's flame.[22] What sets Dryden apart, however, apart from talent, was the passion of his maturity:[23]

What Virgil wrote in the vigour of his age, in plenty and at ease, I have undertaken to translate in my declining years; struggling with wants, oppressed with sickness, curbed in my genius, liable to be misconstrued in all I write; and my judges, if they are not very equitable, already prejudiced against me, by the lying character which has been given them of my morals. Yet, steady to my principles, and not dispirited with my afflictions, I have, by the blessing of God on my endeavours, overcome all difficulties, and, in some measure, acquitted myself of the debt which I owed the public when I undertook this work.

He construes Virgil with unashamed reference to his own times – for 6.621 – 2 ('**Here is a man who has sold his native land for gold, and set a tyrant over it**' / '*Here's one who bartered his native land for gold, he saddled her with a tyrant*') he comes up with, 'To Tyrants others have their country sold, | Imposing Foreign Lords, for Foreign Gold' – the anaphora of 'foreign' raises the spectre of William of Orange. He makes Aeneas a model of virtue for Augustus, who is a model of sound government.[24] He erases ambiguity and amplifies at will to do so – as T. S. Eliot said,[25] 'Dryden's words … are precise, they state immensely, but their suggestiveness is almost nothing'. And to Wordsworth, Dryden in his Virgil, 'has neither a tender heart nor a lofty sense of moral dignity'.[26] Yet the grandeur is undeniable – here is Anchises' exhortation of 6.847 ff.:

Let others better mold the running Mass
Of Mettals, and inform the breathing Brass,
And soften into Flesh a Marble Face;
Plead better at the Bar; describe the Skies,
And when the Stars descend, and when they rise.
But, Rome! 'tis thine alone, with awful sway,
To rule Mankind, and make the World obey,
Disposing Peace and War thy own Majestick Way;
To tame the Proud, the fetter'd Slave to free:
These are Imperial Arts, and worthy thee.

In the eighteenth century, translators followed in Dryden's footsteps with heroic couplets, or blank verse. But none matched Dryden; Pope confined himself to Homer. So Dryden's influence, despite his critics,[27] was consolidated.

The nineteenth century saw a divergence between versions that would help the school reader construe the Latin, and a return to metrical experiment, presenting the *Aeneid* as something rich and strange but still assimilable. In the first category is Robert Singleton, first warden of Radley, who in 1855–9 published his translation of Virgil's works, marking by square brackets any clarification of his own or addition necessary for English grammar. In the second category is James Henry, a redoubtable commentator on the *Aeneid* – a classicist turned medic who was obsessed by it from an early age. His four-volume commentary *Aeneidea* was a monument of opinionated rhetoric spiced with anecdote[28] – his notes on the first fifteen lines of the poem occupy 197 pages. (His energy diminished: he covered the whole of Book XII in 66 pages.) He was also a poet, who made two partial translations of the *Aeneid*, one in his own eccentric blank verse of Books I and II (1845) and another, of Books I–VI, in short lines with two stresses (1853). From the second here is Charon (2.298 ff.):

> A férryman horrid
> Has chárge of these wáters
> Charon, térribly squálid,
> With eýes of flame stáring,
> And gréat grisly béard
> Uncáred on chin lýing ...

Contrast this with another commentator's efforts: the ballad metre used by Conington (see *Introduction* – 9.4 The sixteenth to nineteenth centuries: Resurgence and eclipse) in his 1866 version is designed for speed, a quality commended by Matthew Arnold when translating Homer[29] but jingles out of tune with Virgil. Here is Venus arriving at Caere (8.608 ff.):

> But careful Venus, heavenly fair,
> Had journeyed through the clouds of air,
>   Her present in her hand:
> Deep in the vale her son she spied
> Reposing by the river side,
>   And thus before him stands ...

A fellow-translator, Sir Charles Bowen, criticized Conington's approach for lack of majesty and argued for a linear correspondence between translation and original. This required a longer line in English, and the abandonment of rhyme. Bowen himself employed a hexameter truncated by a syllable; William Morris reverted to fourteeners and managed both to rhyme and match Virgil's lineation, adding an Anglo-Saxon tang by curious compounds (as in the last line here, when the Italians go to war, 7.620 ff.):

> Then slipped the Queen of Gods from heaven and ended their delay;
> For back upon their hinges turned the Seed of Saturn bore
> The tarrying leaves, and burst apart the iron Gates of War,
> And all Ausonia yet unstirred brake suddenly ablaze:
> And some will go afoot to field, and some will wend their ways
> Aloft on horses dusty-fierce: all seek their battle-gear.

The twentieth century operates under different imperatives, not merely of taste: imprints such as Penguin or Bantam Classics, Everyman or Oxford World Classics must offer translations of broad appeal. In general, translators weave variations on a domesticated theme, while staying recognizably close to the Latin – we have become so accustomed to this that we barely notice the balancing act this imposes. Prose is acceptable (West argues that it is preferable to unimpressive verse[30]) and verse, shorn of rhyme, can be free (Fagles has between three and six stresses in each line and, as in speech or sprung rhythm, does not count unstressed syllables);

or more tightly disciplined (so Mandelbaum's pentameters or Ahl's hexameters). Sampling is not justice, but here is a small selection of openings.

To begin with prose: as West recognizes, it must 'do honour to the richness and sublimity of the Latin'[31]. This might seem uncontentious, but it is possible to translate the *Aeneid* as flatly as a business communiqué:[32]

> This is a tale of arms and a man. Fated to be an exile, he was the first to sail from the land of Troy and reach Italy, at its Lavinian shore. He met many tribulations on his way both by land and on the ocean; high Heaven willed it, for Juno was ruthless and would not forget her anger.

Verse need not stray from the Latin more than prose – this (Mandelbaum, 1961) is in fact closer to it than what you have just read, though it abandons any tally with the Latin lineation:[33]

> I sing of arms and of a man: his fate
> had made him fugitive; he was the first
> to journey from the coasts of Troy as far
> as Italy and the Lavinian shores.
> Across the lands and waters he was battered
> beneath the violence of the High Ones, for
> the savage Juno's unforgetting anger.

Like Mandelbaum, Fitzgerald (1981) uses pentameter but regularly breaks free from it, while his language writhes with the sentence structure of the Latin:[34]

> I sing of warfare and a man at war.
> From the sea-coast of Troy in early days
> He came to Italy by destiny,
> To our Lavinian western shore,
> A fugitive, this captain, buffeted
> Cruelly on land as on the sea
> By blows from the powers of the air – behind them
> Baleful Juno in her sleepless rage.

More recent versifiers favour a more conversational, unbuttoned, style (no more iambics) – Lombardo's (2005) aims at recitation:[35]

> Arms I sing – and a man,
> The first to come from the shores
> Of Troy, exiled by Fate, to Italy
> And the Lavinian coast; a man battered
> On land and sea by the powers above
> In the face of Juno's relentless wrath ...

Something of an anomaly in the sequence is Ahl (2007), who returned to hexameters, enabling him to respect the lineation of the Latin, but in them combined his clarity with a degree of strangeness ('battered about'):

> Arms and the man I sing of Troy, who first from its seashores,
> Italy-bound, fate's refugee, arrived at Lavinia's
> Coastlands. How he was battered about over land, over high deep
> Seas by the powers above! Savage Juno's anger remembered
> Him . . .

Ruden (2008) returns to pentameters, poetically sparer than Mandelbaum or Fitzgerald and thereby, like Ahl, able to conserve the lineation of the original:[36]

> Arms and a man I sing, the first from Troy,
> A fated exile to Lavinian shores
> In Italy. On land and sea, divine will
> And Juno's unforgetting rage – harassed him.

Bartsch, in her translation of 2019, is comparable to Ruden in approach.[37]

Seamus Heaney translated only Book VI (published posthumously in 2016), his 'classics homework' to honour his old Latin teacher. He had made previous forays into that Book, rendering the portion on the golden bough as the curtain-up on 'Seeing Things' (1991), then in 'Human Chain' (2010) making his bus route (110, from Belfast to County Derry) echo several of its episodes. He captures the tensions of the modern translator when he describes himself as 'an inner literalist' or 'sixth form homunculus' who has 'nowadays . . . things other than literal accuracy on his mind and in his ear: rhythm and metre and lineation, the voice and its pacing, the need for a diction decorous enough for Virgil but not so antique as to sound out of tune with a more contemporary idiom'.[38] Here is an instance of the translator deferring to his author, in sentiments that Heaney, of Irish Catholic stock, must have found uncongenial – Anchises' exhortation again (6.847 ff.):

> Others, I have no doubt, with a more delicate touch
> Will beat bronze into breathing likenesses,
> Conjure living features out of marble,
> Argue cases more effectively, and with their compass
> Plot the heavens' orbit and predict
> The rising of the constellations. But you, Roman,
> Remember: to you will fall the exercise of power
> Over the nations, and these will be your gifts –
> To impose peace and justify your sway,
> Spare those you conquer, crush those who overbear.

But the Heaney of earthy sensibility can assert himself too: in his hypnotic Lethe, duty to the author has not obliterated the translator's 'voice' (6.703 ff.):

> Meanwhile, at the far end of a valley, Aeneas saw
> A remote grove, bushy rustling thickets,
> And the river Lethe somnolently flowing,
> Lapping those peaceful haunts along its banks.

Here a hovering multitude, innumerable
Nations and gathered clans, kept the field
Humming with life, like bees in meadows
On a clear summer day alighting on pied flowers
And wafting in mazy swarms around white lilies.

So, to return at last to Coleridge's question,[39] 'If you take from Vergil his language and metre, what do you leave him?' Coleridge did not necessarily imply, 'Nothing'; he might instead have asked in a spirit of genuine inquiry.[40] And the answer might run, 'As much as the reader is willing to detect behind the translation of possible reactions and the discussions the text has provoked'; and if, as Steiner maintains,[41] all literary reading is translation, it is not such a different starting point for modern readers of Latin; they, moreover, might stay their eyes and ears on Virgil's exquisite control of the verse and miss the turbulence of the ideas that underlie it.

MAPS

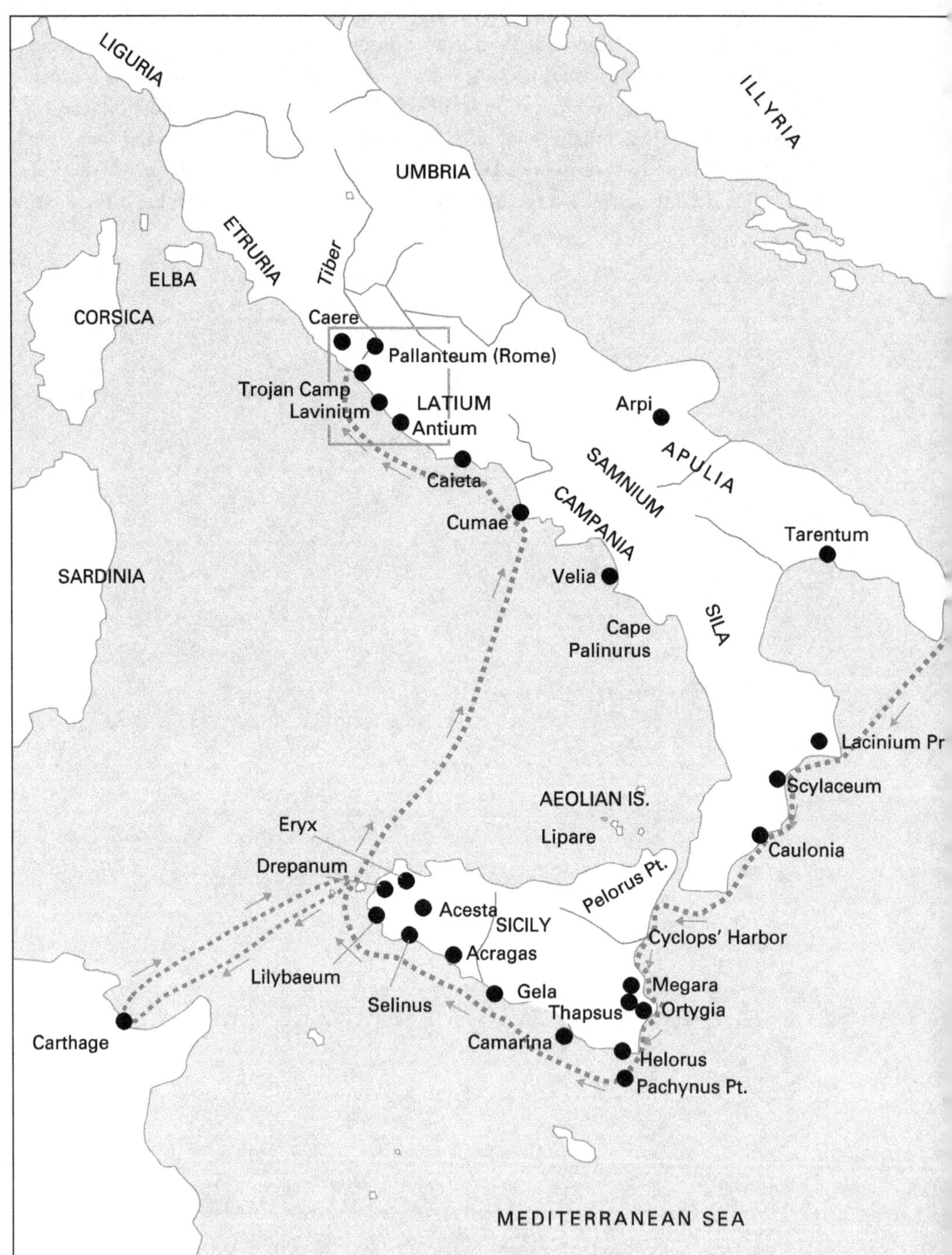

Map 1 The voyage of Aeneas; the inset marks the area for Map 2.

After F. Ahl, *Virgil* Aeneid: *A New Translation* (Oxford: Oxford University Press, 2007, 2018), lviii–lix.

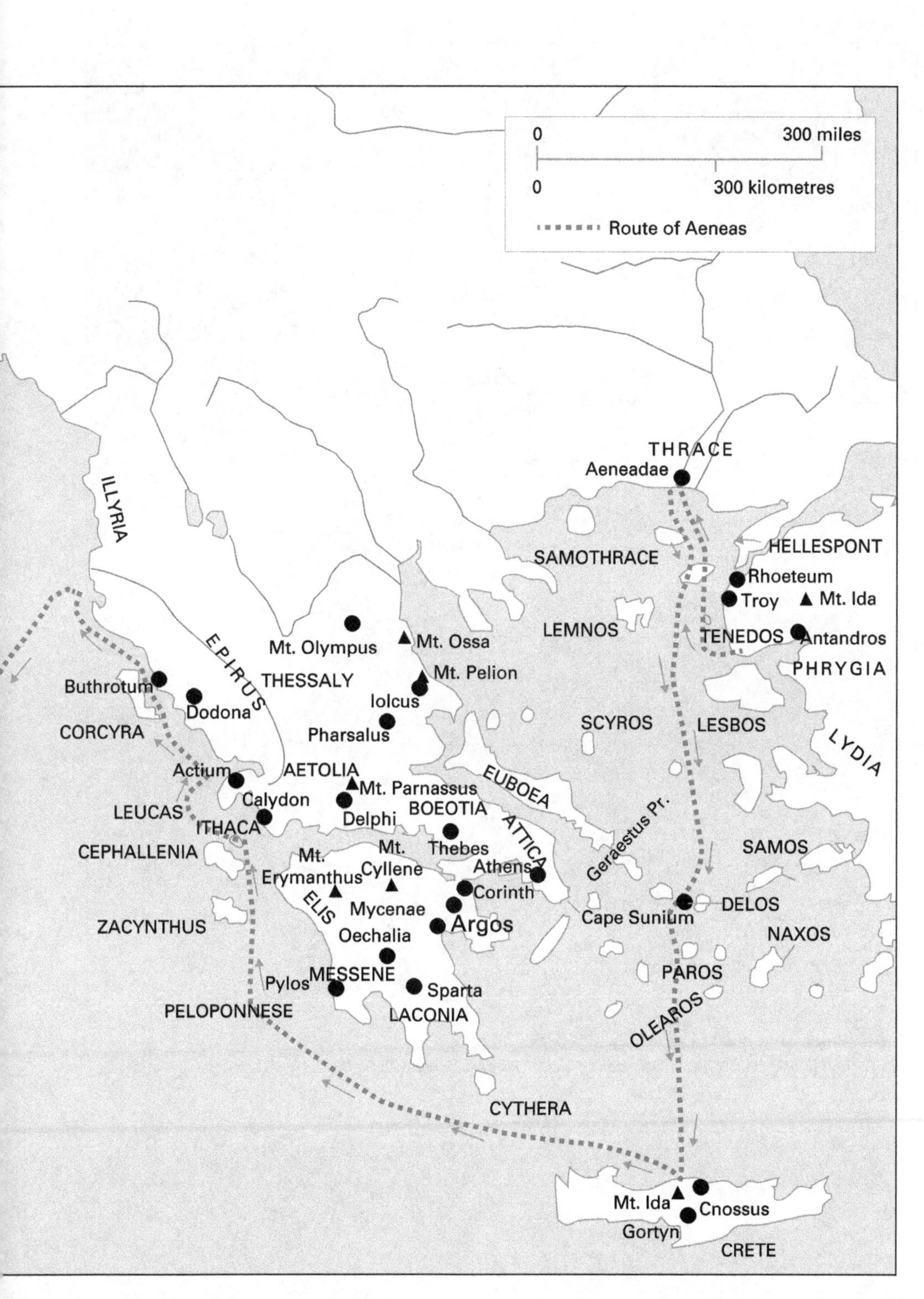

0   300 miles
0   300 kilometres
Route of Aeneas
THRACE
Aeneadae
SAMOTHRACE
HELLESPONT
Rhoeteum
Troy
Mt. Ida
LEMNOS
TENEDOS
Antandros
PHRYGIA
ILLYRIA
Mt. Olympus
Mt. Ossa
Mt. Pelion
EPIRUS
THESSALY
Iolcus
SCYROS
LESBOS
LYDIA
Buthrotum
Dodona
Pharsalus
CORCYRA
Actium
AETOLIA
Mt. Parnassus
EUBOEA
Geraestus Pr.
SAMOS
Calydon
Delphi
BOEOTIA
LEUCAS
ITHACA
Mt.
Cyllene
Mt.
Thebes
ATTICA
CEPHALLENIA
Erymanthus
Athens
Corinth
Cape Sunium
DELOS
ZACYNTHUS
Mycenae
Argos
NAXOS
ELIS
Oechalia
Pylos
MESSENE
PAROS
Sparta
PELOPONNESE
LACONIA
OLEAROS
CYTHERA
Mt. Ida
Cnossus
Gortyn
CRETE

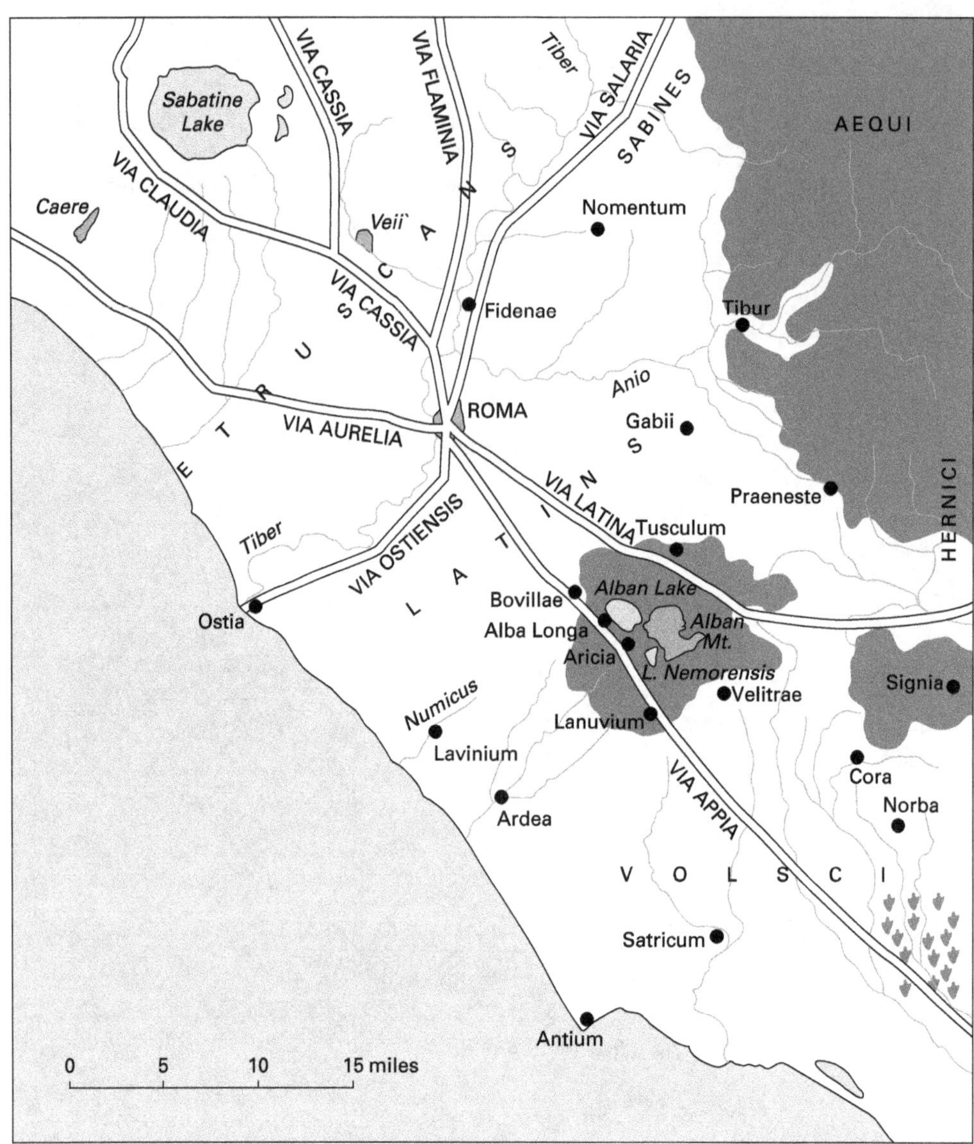

Map 2 Rome, Latium and its environs (in Virgil's time).
After F. Ahl, *Virgil* Aeneid: *A New Translation* (Oxford: Oxford University Press, 2007, 2018), lx.

FAMILY TREE OF THE ROYAL HOUSES OF GREECE AND TROY

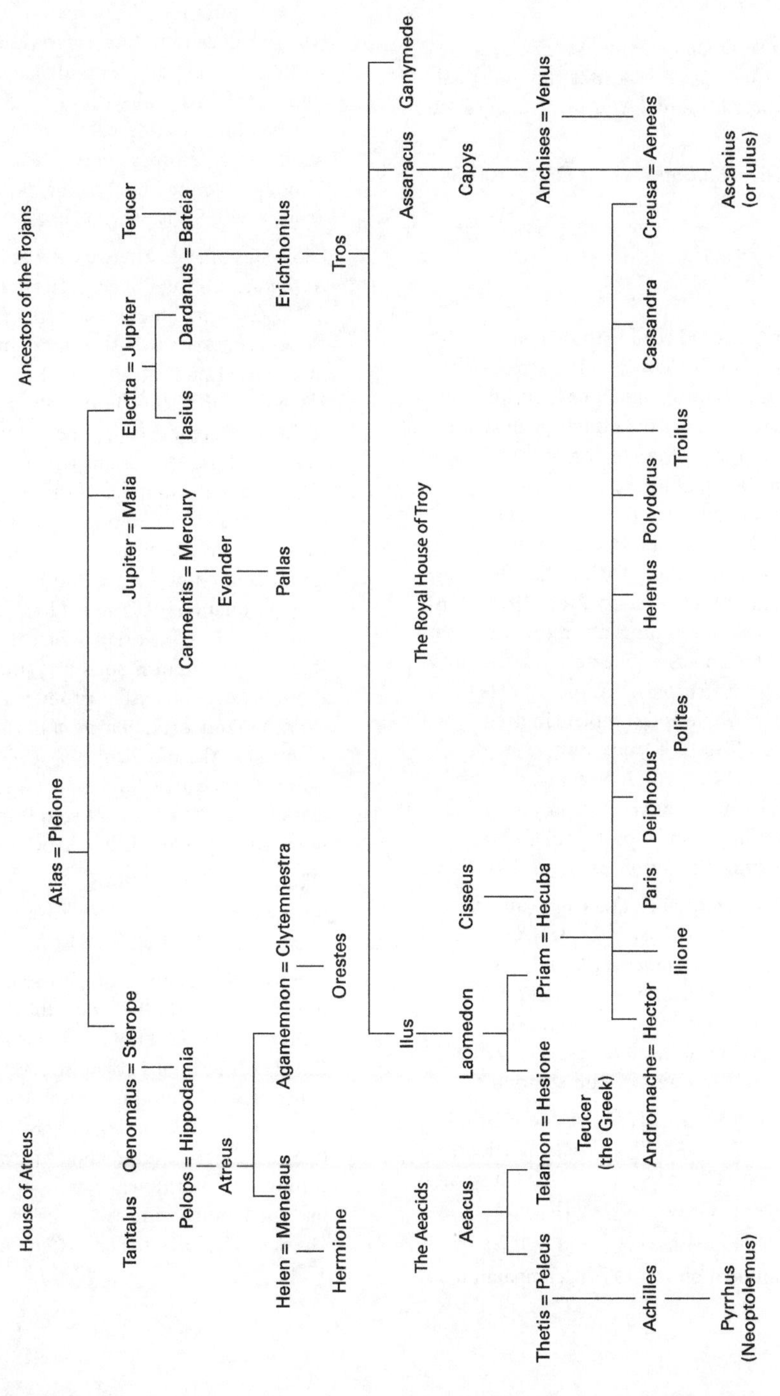

NOTES

Preface

1. *The Table Talk and Omniana of Samuel Taylor Coleridge*, 8 May 1824 (London et al.: Humphrey Milford, Oxford University Press, 1917), 56.

2. Quintilian, *Education of the Orator* 10.1.86.

Chapter 1

1. A more nuanced version of this position is expressed by R. Heinze: 'At the centre of his poem stands the eponymous hero, but it is not he who creates the unity, but an action: the migration of the Trojans, or the transportation of the Penates from Troy to Latium' (*Virgil's Epic Technique*, trans. H. and D. Harvey and F. Robertson (originally published Berlin, 1902; Berkeley, CA: California University Press, 1993), 436). Heinze's emphasis on 'unity' rather than 'hero' is Aristotelian – Aristotle declares, 'the story must be constructed ... round a single piece of action, whole and complete in itself' (*Poetics* 1459a 19 ff.), not round a single character (1451a 16). A warning: the word 'hero', although from Greek, only acquired its connotation of 'main protagonist' in the Renaissance. See *Introduction* – 7.2 The hero.

2. E. Gruen, 'Cultural Fictions and Cultural Identity', *Transactions of the American Philological Association*, (1993): 1–14, reprinted in S. Quinn, *Why Vergil? A Collection of Interpretations* (Wauconda, IL: Bolchazy-Carducci, 2000), especially 309–12 on the rival accounts of Rome's origins.

3. G. Miles, 'The *Aeneid* as Foundation Story', in C. Perkell (ed.), *Reading Vergil's* Aeneid: *An Interpretive Guide* (Norman, OK: University of Oklahoma Press, 1999), 231–50.

4. Miles (ibid.) quotes a figure of 'at least 25 basic foundation stories'; the campaign to associate Aeneas and Rome was waged by the Greek historians of Sicily, such as Alcimus (late fourth century BCE), who is said to have written at length on Italy and Sicily, and Timaeus (fourth–third century BCE) of Tauromenium (modern Taormina), who wrote a (lost) *Histories of Greece and Sicily* in 38 books. For the initial connection of Trojans with Sicily, see 5.38 note.

5. Dionysius of Halicarnassus, *Roman Antiquities* 1.72 f.; Plutarch, *Life of Romulus* 2.1 ff. also shows the free-for-all, in which Aeneas features variously; Dionysius mentions (1.72.2) an author who seems to be Hellanicus of Lesbos (fifth century BCE), saying that, 'Aeneas came into Italy from the land of the Molossians with Odysseus and became the founder of the city, which he named after Romē, one of the Trojan women' – if correctly attributed, the first extant text to link Aeneas and Rome, but a very peculiar one. Alcimus, a fourth/third century Sicilian historian, writes that Romulus was Aeneas' son by Tyrrhenia; Romulus' daughter, Alba, produced Rhomus, Rome's founder (*Fragments of the Greek Historians*, Alcimus Siculus 6, ap. Festus). This is the second-oldest extant mention – and of interest because it keeps Rome's foundation close in date to Troy's fall.

6. Dionysius of Halicarnassus, *Roman Antiquities* on Evander (1.31); on Heracles (1.41 ff.); (on waves of Greeks) 1.60.3, 1.89.1 ff.

7. The wish to establish Romanness is illustrated by Cato the Elder (third–second century BCE), most notably in his *Origins*, the first three books of whose seven concerned the founding of Rome and of other major Italian cities; he was something of a curmudgeon, addressing the Athenians through an interpreter even though he had spent much time in Athens and spoke Greek well (Plutarch, *Life of Cato the Elder* 12.4 f.).

8. Livy, *From the City's Foundation* 1.4.1.

9. Dionysius of Halicarnassus, *Roman Antiquities* 1.84.5.

10. Livy, *From the City's Foundation* 1.4.8.

11. After he was styled 'king' in earlier books, especially when described to other monarchs on an equal footing (Dido, 1.544; Latinus, 7.220), he becomes 'father' after the death of Anchises – see 1.544, 5.129–31 notes.

12. Virgil's hymn in praise of Italy in the *Georgics* begins (2.173 ff.), 'Hail! land of Saturn, you mighty mother of fruits and heroes.'

13. Augustus' inscription of his achievements, the Res Gestae, states (8.2) that his census of 28 BCE recorded 4.063 million citizens. The previous census, in 70 BCE, recorded 910,000 (Livy, *Epitome* 98.3). This is an indication of Augustus' keenness to bring the citizen body up to date and massively increase the catchment for political office (see T. Wiseman, 'The Census in the First Century B.C.', *Journal of Roman Studies*, 59, nos. 1–2 (1969): 72–5). The emperor Claudius, when advocating the expansion of citizenship to the Gauls, remarked, 'My great-uncle Augustus and my uncle Tiberius decided to admit into this Senate house the flower of the *coloniae* and the cities from all over the empire – all of them good and wealthy men of course' (CIL XIII, 1668 para 5).

14. Herodotus, *Histories* 2.145.4 gives the earliest date (mid-thirteenth century BCE); archaeological evidence from Hissarlik would suggest *c.* 1180 BCE.

15. R. Ross Holloway, *The Archaeology of Early Rome and Latium* (London and New York: Routledge, 1994), 14.

16. Lavinium, Aeneas' first city, boasts a burial of the seventh century in a tumulus; this, in the fourth century, was reconstructed as a *heroon* (hero's shrine) to Aeneas, at the time when foundation myth-making was in vogue among Greek historians. See Dionysius of Halicarnassus citing Timaeus at *Roman Antiquities* 1.67.4 and Ross Holloway, *The Archaeology*, 135–8.

17. For the much debated origins of the Etruscan civilization in today's Tuscany, see Dionysius of Halicarnassus, *Roman Antiquities* 1.26 ff., and 8.478–80 note.

18. Livy, *From the City's Foundation* 6.

19. Other estimates are 814/3 BCE by Timaeus; 748/7 BCE by Fabius Pictor (the first Roman historian, of the late third century BCE); and 751/50 BCE by Cato the Elder.

20. Plutarch, *Life of Romulus* 3.1 ff., attributes their invention to Diocles of Peparethus; it was taken up in most points, he says, by Fabius Pictor.

21. So, too, Livy, *From the City's Foundation* 1.3.8, says Silvius 'planted a number of colonies'.

22. Livy, *From the City's Foundation* 1.4.6; Moses, also found in a floating cradle, has the opposite fortune, of being adopted by pharaoh's daughter (Exodus 2.1 ff.).

23. Livy, *From the City's Foundation* 1.6.3 ff.

24. Livy calls them joint rulers, ibid. 1.13.8.

25. Ibid., 1.8.7.

26. Ibid., 1.16.2 ff.

27. Ibid., 1.17.10.

28. Ibid., 1.28.7 f.

29. Ibid., 1.39 ff.

30. Ibid., 1.58.

31. Ibid., 2.1.7 ff.

32. Ibid., 2.14.5 ff.

33. Ibid., 5.1–23.

34. Livy, whose account of this major Gallic incursion starts at ibid., 5.33, alleges they were attracted by the wine (5.33.2).

35. Ibid., 5.33 ff.

36. Plutarch, *Life of Pyrrhus* 25.

37. This is the starting point for the *Histories* of Polybius, a Greek deported to Rome in the second century, who was the first to write an account of events that explained Rome's military and political importance.

38. Polybius, *Histories* 3.10.3 f.

39. Plutarch, *Life of Cato the Elder* 27.1; Pliny, *Natural History* 15.20.74.

40. The main sources on the Gracchi are Plutarch's *Lives* of Gaius and Tiberius Gracchus, and Appian's *Civil Wars*, 1.1.9 ff.

41. For Marius' career, the main source is Plutarch's *Life of Marius*; his North African campaign is the subject of Sallust's *Jugurthine War*.

42. Appian says (*Civil Wars* 1.1.9) that Tiberius Gracchus lamented 'concerning the Italian race ... that a people so valiant in war, and blood relations to the Romans, were declining little by little in pauperism and paucity of numbers without any hope of remedy'. Velleius Paterculus writes (*Roman History* 2.15.2),

    The fortune of the Italians was as cruel as their cause was just; for they were seeking citizenship in the state whose power they were defending by their arms; every year and in every war they were furnishing a double number of men, both of cavalry and of infantry, and yet were not admitted to the rights of citizens in the state which, through their efforts, had reached so high a position that it could look down upon men of the same race and blood as foreigners and aliens.

43. Appian, *Civil Wars* 1.5.35 ff.

44. Rome's northern front was commanded in the first year by the consul P. Rutilius Rufus, with Marius as one of his generals; the southern front was commanded by the other consul Lucius Julius Caesar, with Sulla as one of his generals. The war brought into relief allegiances that would show in later patterns of support: Julius Caesar's father, Gaius Julius Caesar, was a partisan and brother-in-law of Marius (and Julius Caesar married Sulla's granddaughter to cover all the options); Pompey's father quelled rebels in the north with troops that would later be summoned by his son to aid Sulla against Marius; for geographical affiliation, see Miles, 'The *Aeneid* as Foundation Story', 240–5.

45. K. Toll, 'Making Roman-ness and the *Aeneid*', *Classical Antiquity*, 16, no. 1 (April 1997): 34–43; C. Ando, 'Vergil's Italy: Ethnography and Politics in First-century Rome', in D. Levene and D. Nelis (ed.), *Clio and the Poets. Augustan Poetry and the Traditions of Ancient Historiography* (Leiden and Boston, MA: Brill, 2002), 136–40.

46. Cicero, *Against Catiline* gives Cicero's side of the story; Sallust's *Catiline* restores some equilibrium.

47. For the period from 78 to 44 BCE, the main sources are Appian, *Civil Wars* 1.12.105–2.16.111; Dio Cassius, *Roman History* 36–44; Plutarch, *Lives* of Pompey and Caesar; Suetonius, *Life of Caesar*.

48. Plutarch, *Life of Pompey* 13.3.

49. A campaign he found time to document in his *Gallic Wars*.

50. For the period from 44 BCE to and through the reign of Augustus, the main sources are Appian, *Civil Wars* 2.16.112–15.14.145; Dio Cassius, *Roman History* 45–66; Plutarch, *Lives* of Antony and Augustus; Suetonius, *Life of Augustus*; the reign of Augustus is subjected to concentrated, if jaundiced, analysis by Tacitus in his *Annals* (1.2–3, 1.9–10); Augustus commemorated himself in his *Res Gestae*.

51. Caesar had installed her and Ptolemy XIV as co-rulers of Egypt in 47 BCE.

52. This was a project of Caesar's interrupted at his death; Antony wanted to assume Caesar's mantle; the standards lost by Crassus at the Battle of Carrhae in 53 BCE were still in Parthian hands (6.824–5 note, **Camillus**).

53. Dio Cassius, *Roman History* 49.41.1 ff.; Plutarch, *Life of Antony* 54; there is no doubt some demonizing of Cleopatra in these sources, but coins minted by Antony commemorate both the triumph over the Armenians and Cleopatra as 'Queen of kings and of her sons who are kings' (e.g. Art Institute of Chicago 1922.4855).

54. Dio Cassius, *Roman History* 53.16.6 ff.

55. *Res Gestae* 34.1.

56. *Res Gestae* 5.1, 5.3.

57. Dio Cassius, *Roman History* 53.32.5.

58. *Res Gestae* 6.2.

59. Tacitus, *Annals* 3.56.1.

60. Ibid., 1.2.1.

61. A careful reading of *Res Gestae* 26–33 indicates how much was also accomplished through diplomacy.

62. Dio Cassius, *Roman History* 51.18.1 ff.

63. Ibid., 53.25.7.

64. Tacitus, *Annals* 1.9.

65. See R. Tarrant, 'Poetry and Power: Virgil's Poetry in Contemporary Context', in F. Mac Góráin and C. Martindale (ed.), *The Cambridge Companion to Virgil* (Cambridge: Cambridge University Press, 2019), 243–62, with bibliography.

66. Polybius, *Histories* 1.4.

67. In this regard, Polybius sets out his standards at ibid., 12.25 from the third section on.

68. Ibid., 1.14.6.

69. Livy, *From the City's Foundation* 4.20.7.

70. Ibid., Proem 9.

71. Dionysius of Halicarnassus, *Roman Antiquities* 1.45–60, 1.64–5.

72. On Strabo's Latium, see *Geography* 5.3.2 ff.

73. Suetonius, *Life of Augustus* 101.4.

Chapter 2

1. The title of Roland Barthes' famous essay, *Image-Music-Text* (New York, Farrar, Straus and Giroux, 1977); it concludes, 'Classic criticism has never paid any attention to the reader; for it, the writer is the only person in literature … it is necessary to overthrow the myth: the birth of the reader must be at the cost of the death of the author.' See *Introduction* – 9.6.6 Post-structuralism and deconstruction.

2. The spelling of the poet's name in English is more correctly 'Vergil', but 'Virgil' became current in the Middle Ages by analogy with the Latin *virga*, a 'rod' / 'wand' and the link to the poet's supposed magical powers (4.613–21 note).

3. Aelius Donatus, teacher of both Servius and St. Jerome, wrote a commentary on Virgil's works, of which only this life and the prefatory remarks to the *Eclogues* remain; he is to be distinguished from Tiberius Claudius Donatus, a grammarian of the early fifth century, whose commentary on the *Aeneid* is still extant (*Introduction* – 7.6 Speeches).

4. Suetonius (see 1.8.7) in *Lives of the Poets* wrote monographs on several – Horace, Persius and Tibullus among them; biographies later than that of Aelius Donatus also exist, including one by Servius that stands at the head of his commentary (see *Introduction* - 9.2 The second to fifth centuries: Servius and Macrobius), but it is hard to argue that what they add to Donatus amounts to more than speculation – see F. Stok, 'The Life of Virgil before Donatus', in J. Farrell and M. Putnam (eds), *A Companion to Vergil's* Aeneid *and Its Tradition* (Malden, MA, Oxford and Chichester: Wiley-Blackwell, 2010), 119–20.

5. See N. Horsfall, 'Virgil: His Life and Times', in N. Horsfall (ed.), *A Companion to the Study of Virgil* (Leiden, New York and Cologne: Brill, 1995), 1–25; a marginally less sceptical investigation is Stok, 'The Life of Virgil', 107–18.

6. Aelius Donatus, *Life of Virgil* 3.

7. Ibid., 1.

8. Ibid., 11.

9. Ibid., 23 f.

10. See, for example: (unfinished sections) 2.567, the Helen episode; (inconsistencies) Nisus and Euryalus introduced at 9.176 ff. when they had already featured in the foot race (5.294 ff.) – 5.294 is an unfinished line; the highest number of incomplete lines is in Book II. How far they indicate an unfinished state is discussed in J. O'Hara, 'The Unfinished *Aeneid*', in Farrell and Putnam (eds), *A Companion*, 99–106; however effective some of them are, few critics now maintain that they would have survived revision – no other Latin epic contains such truncations.

11. Aelius Donatus, *Life of Virgil* 9 f.

12. 10.198–203, *Georgics* 3.12 ff.

13. *Catalepton* 5 – this is not universally accepted as by Virgil (see 2.1); it might be corroborated by a papyrus found in the Villa of the Papyri in Herculaneum, which almost certainly belonged to the poet, Epicurean philosopher and teacher of Siro Philodemus (first century, born 110 BCE); this contained a work of his, 'On Flattery', which addressed Virgil and L. Varius Rufus, Plotius Tucca and P. Quintilius Varus (*P. Herc. Paris* 2).

14. Aelius Donatus, *Life of Virgil* 19.

15. Ibid., 46, interpolation from Bodleian manuscript.

16. Horace, *Odes* 1.3.6 – this in an ode asking a ship to deliver Virgil safely to Athens (the journey is not otherwise recorded, though Donatus mentions Virgil's intention to sail to Athens in the last year of his life).

17. Horace, *Satires* 6.54 ff.

18. Ibid., 5.39 ff.

19. *Georgics* 3.41.

20. Servius note to 8.310.

21. Aelius Donatus, *Life of Virgil* 12, 20.

22. Horace, *Epistles* 2.1.245 ff.

23. Aelius Donatus, *Life of Virgil* 30 = Propertius, *Elegies* 2.34.65 f. Ovid, who belonged to the next generation, says ruefully, 'I only saw Virgil' – *Tristia* 4.10.51.

24. The land redistributions after Philippi (42 BCE) to deserving veterans are a recurring theme – *Eclogues* 1.71 f., 9.2 ff.; but Virgil could, of course, have begun before this.

25. Aelius Donatus, *Life of Virgil* 25.

26. Ibid.,, 22; Ovid speaks of his own facility at *Tristia* 4.10.25 f.; Cicero admired Archias' ability to extemporise verse (Cicero, *Archias* 17).

27. A fuller and more coherent version of this tale is in Aulus Gellius, *Attic Nights* 17.10.1 ff.. The image is uncomfortably close to the description of the she-wolf at 8.631 ff. – but the bear is particularly apposite because ancient zoology believed that bear foetuses were born very small and unarticulated (Aristotle, *Inquiry into Animals* 6.579a); the mother licked them into shape (Ovid, *Metamorphoses* 15.379 ff.). Quintilian, *Education of the Orator* 10.3.8, quotes Varius' remark that Virgil composed only a small number of verses each day.

28. Aelius Donatus, *Life of Virgil* 24.

29. Ibid., 23.

30. Aelius Donatus (23) cites a view, plainly nonsense, that Virgil planned twenty-four books so that he could do full justice to the deeds of Augustus.

31. Aelius Donatus, *Life of Virgil* 35.

32. Ibid., 38; Aulus Gellius, *Attic Nights* 17.10.7, says Virgil on his deathbed begged his friends to destroy the *Aeneid* because he was not satisfied with it; cf. Macrobius, *Saturnalia* 1.24.6.

33. Aelius Donatus, *Life of Virgil* 39.

34. Ibid., 40.

35. Pliny the Elder, *Natural History* 7.30.114, speaks of Augustus overriding the 'modesty' of Virgil's will to save his poems from the flames.

36. Aelius Donatus, *Life of Virgil* 36.

37. One of the sirens – washed ashore near Naples, after she had failed to lure Odysseus and flung herself into the sea (5.864–7 note), she was revered by the inhabitants; Lycophron, *Alexandra* 712 ff., Strabo, *Geography* 5.4.7.

38. Aelius Donatus, *Life of Virgil* 25; *Eclogues* 1.43 ff. has Tityrus saying he successfully petitioned 'that young man to whom our altars smoke for twelve days in the year' to keep his land – opinions differ on whether Virgil is being autobiographical here.

39. *Georgics* 1.25; 3.16, 3.46.

40. Aelius Donatus, *Life of Virgil* 27.

41. Ibid., 31.

42. Ibid., 32.

43. Macrobius, *Saturnalia* 1.24.11. The translation of the last sentence cited here is debated.

44. Tacitus speaks of the letters of Augustus as if they were widely accessible (*Dialogue on the Orators* 13.2).

45. Suetonius, in his *Life of Horace*, preserves some of the epistolary banter which took place between poet and patron – Horace appears to have taken evasive action but to have complied when pressed.

46. Ovid, *Tristia* 2.533, my emphasis.

47. A translation is available online at, www.virgil.org – though not of the *Aetna*.

48. Aelius Donatus, *Life of Virgil* 17 ff.

49. The term does not, as it appears, designate an ancient genre but came into vogue at the turn of the twentieth century to categorize short epics.

50. As in Ovid, *Metamorphoses* 8.1 ff.

51. The fourth century CE poet and teacher of rhetoric Ausonius asked, 'What might the Catalepta of Virgil mean?' (*Grammaticomastix* 5).

52. From the poems' name in Latin, *Bucolica*.

53. Though the genre as such was not identified until late antiquity, possibly the Middle Ages – see C. Martindale, 'Green Politics: The *Eclogues*', in Mac Góráin and Martindale (eds), *The Cambridge Companion*, 174, and 190–2 provide a bibliography *raisonné*.

54. Certain names recur across the poems – but it is not inevitable that they refer to the same person (e.g. Menalcas, in Eclogues 3, 5 and 9 and mentioned in 2 and 10.

55. Who Virgil meant by the 'boy' is much debated; Servius reports that Asinius Gallus claimed it was him. Perhaps the most widespread theory is that he was to be the offspring of the marriage between Antony and Octavia, Octavian's sister. The Christian interpretation probably originates with Lactantius (Divine Institutes 7.24), a Christian author who became adviser on religious matters to the emperor Constantine. Constantine himself delivered a sermon, 'Speech to the Assembly of the Saints', in the early 320s CE that quotes the fourth Eclogue and explicitly puts this interpretation on it (Chapter 19). Augustine of Hippo, *City of God* 10.27, understands the wiping away of guilt in *Eclogues* 4.13 f. to refer to Christ.

56. So, for example, D. Ross, *Virgil's Aeneid: A Reader's Guide* (Malden, MA, and Oxford: Blackwell, 2007), 127–31.

57. Polybius, *Histories* 4.20.1–21.1 discusses the importance of music to the Arcadians – and attributes it to the harshness of their lives; the idyllic pastoral associations of Arcadia date from Sannazaro's work of that name, published in the early sixteenth century.

58. Horace, *Satires* 1.10.44 f., written in 35 BCE or earlier.

59. Theocritus was from Sicily.

60. Apollo.

61. Alfenus Varus, consul suffect (= replacement) for 39 BCE, a notable jurist who served on the land commission of 41 BCE.

62. As does Aelius Donatus, *Life of Virgil* 18: 'Asinius Pollio, Alfenus Varus and Cornelius Gallus . . . kept him from being penalized in the distribution of lands after the victory at Philippi, when the lands on the other side of the Po were being divided amongst the veterans by order of the triumvirate.' This is pure extrapolation from Eclogues 1 and 9; it 'makes sense' but is unwarranted. Virgil makes Tityrus old and a slave, as if to caution against Servian impetuosity.

63. Horace (*Odes* 1.6), Propertius (*Elegies* 1.7), Ovid (*Amores* 1, which has Cupid take the place of Virgil's Apollo) are more resolute in declining to write epic.

64. See further *Introduction* – 8.4.4 Alexandrian poetry and epic: Callimachus, Theocritus, Apollonius of Rhodes, Lycophron.

65. C. Cornelius Gallus, politician and influential composer of elegies, as Prefect of Egypt in 26 BCE disgraced himself and committed suicide (so Dio Cassius, *Roman History* 53.23.5 ff.).

66. 3.32 ff. seem to refer to the triple triumph of 29 BCE, 4.560 f. certainly refer to Octavian's campaigns after Actium in 30–29 BCE – they underline the dangers of hard-and-fast 'end' dates.

67. Seneca, *Letters* 86.15, observes, 'Virgil sought, however, not what was nearest to the truth, but what was most appropriate, and aimed, not to teach the farmer, but to please the reader.'

68. M. Terentius Varro (first century BCE – born some forty years before Virgil), one of Rome's greatest polymaths, claimed in his old age that he had written 7 x 70 books (Aulus Gellius, *Attic Nights* 3.10.17), many lost already during his lifetime. When he was eighty he produced *On Farming*, ostensibly as a guide for his wife Fundania who had just bought a farm. Its three books take the form of (rambling) dialogues, which suggests a wider intended readership.

69. This can be taken as a crow of genuine victory, or a lament for man's lot.

70. See 2.610 and 2.642–3 notes.

71. A *makarismos*, or declaration of blessedness – 1.94–101 note.

72. Apollo, who had killed the Cyclops because his son Asclepius had been struck by Zeus with a thunderbolt of their manufacture, was forced by Zeus to serve the mortal Admetus as a herdsman – Euripides, *Alcestis* 1 ff.

73. Debate continues over whether this would be a historical epic very different from the *Aeneid*, or something very like the actual *Aeneid* but viewed as a metaphor for Augustus' struggles.

74. Literally 'ardent' – not *furor* here; the epic projected would be a more historical one than the *Aeneid* turned out to be – unless Aeneas' battles are also Augustus'.

75. Priam's brother, so a figure from the distant Trojan past; 4.584–5 note.

76. Aristaeus, son of Apollo, was the tutelary deity of herdsmen and of vine and olive plantations; he was credited with the introduction of beekeeping.

77. The Old Man of the Sea; the *Odyssey*'s story (4.435 ff.) of Menelaus extracting information from him is the origin for Virgil's account here.

78. According to Apollodorus, *Library* 1.3.2, he was the son of a Thracian king Oeagrus and the Muse Calliope – he could move stones and trees by his singing; according to Strabo (*Geography* 7, Fragment 18) he was a human wizard-minstrel.

79. Sometimes called a '*sphragis*' (= 'seal').

80. The Euphrates stands for the east: Octavian followed up his victory at Actium with a foray into Syria and negotiations with the Parthians (Dio Cassius, *Roman History* 51.18).

81. B. Otis, *Virgil: A Study in Civilised Poetry* (Oxford: Oxford University Press, 1964), 189–90.

82. D. Ross, *Virgil's* Aeneid, 137; also D. Ross, *Virgil's Elements: Physics and Poetry in the* Georgics (Princeton, NJ: Princeton University Press, 1987), reviewed by P. Hardie, '*Virgil's Elements*', *Classical Review*, 38, no. 2 (1988): 242.

83. See W. Batstone, 'Virgilian Didaxis', in Mac Góráin and Martindale (eds), *The Cambridge Companion*, 213; and 213–15 provide a bibliography *raisonné*.

84. Cato the Elder (second century BCE) wrote *On Agriculture*, which still survives.

85. Theophrastus (fourth–third century BCE) succeeded Aristotle as head of the Peripatetic School at Athens; his interests were similarly wide, but of relevance here are his two works on botany, *Inquiry into Plants* and *Explanations of Plants*.

86. Virgil's debt to Lucretius is clearest in his passages on sexual desire (3.209 ff.; compare Lucretius, *On the Nature of Things* 4.1058 ff.) and on plague (3.478 ff.; compare *On the Nature of Things* 6.1138 ff.), but Lucretius' example of detailed observation is all-pervading.

87. Horsfall (ed.), *A Companion*, on the sources for the *Georgics*, 77–89, cites (79–80) Eratosthenes, Nicander, Callimachus and Aratus.

88. Catullus 64 tells the story of Theseus and Ariadne within a description of the marriage of Peleus and Thetis.

89. Of John of Garland, see E. Theodorakopoulos, 'Closure and the Book of Virgil', in Mac Góráin and Martindale (eds), *The Cambridge Companion*, 227.

90. Milton in his passage from *Lycidas* (a pastoral poem of mourning, cf. Eclogue 5) to epic in *Paradise Lost*; Spenser similarly, from *The Shepheardes Calendar* to *The Faerie Queen*.

91. Theodorakopoulos, 'Closure', 229.

Chapter 3

1. It is therefore not merely a question of a modern audience, whose tastes have been formed by the conventions of the novel and the whole field of psychology, feeling dissatisfied with epic convention, whether Homer's or Virgil's – though the modern novel has set up very different expectations.

2. R. Lyne, *Further Voices in Vergil's* Aeneid (Oxford: Clarendon Press, 1987), 44–5.

3. For a book-length alternative view, see C. Mackie, *The Characterisation of Aeneas* (Edinburgh: Edinburgh University Press, 1988), in which the author offers a detailed examination of every speech of Aeneas, on the grounds that selective quotation is misleading; and contends (among much else) that, while *pietas* comes across from those speeches, Aeneas' behaviour in the narrative is not always consistent with it.

4. Heinze, *Virgil's Epic Technique*, 279–80; Jenkyns says, 'There is psychological acuity, certainly – keen observation of how people act and think – but not much individuation, the creation of different personalities who, once met, can be recognized again in different circumstances' (R. Jenkyns, *Virgil's Experience: Nature and History, Times, Names, and Places* (Oxford: Clarendon Press, 1998), 306.

5. Continued from citation in note 2.

6. Otis, *Virgil*, 89.

7. Aristotle, *Poetics* (imitation) 1448a; (what is said about tragedy can apply to epic) 1449b; (primacy of plot) 1450a; (appropriateness) 1454a.

8. *Il.* 6.119.

9. Heinze, *Virgil's Epic Technique*, 410–12; cf. D. Feeney, 'The Taciturnity of Aeneas', *Classical Quarterly*, NS 33 (1983), reprinted in S. Harrison (ed.), *Oxford Readings in Virgil's Aeneid* (Oxford: Clarendon Press, 1990), 179, 'the healing and unifying power of dialogue is a constant feature of the Homeric poems'.

10. *Il.* 1.58–305; the sequence of speakers runs Achilles – Calchas – Achilles – Calchas – Agamemnon – Achilles – Agamemnon – Achilles – Agamemnon – [Achilles – Athene, audible only to each other] – Achilles – Nestor – Agamemnon – Achilles. Of the three assemblies in the *Aeneid*, the Trojans in Book IX, the gods in Book X and the Latins in Book XI, that in Book IX (9.230–302) is by far the most intricate, at which Ascanius invites Nisus to speak, after which the order runs Nisus – Aletes – Ascanius – Euryalus – Ascanius.

11. *Od.* 14.52–408. The *Aeneid's* longest exchanges are between Aeneas and the disguised Venus (1.321–409), and Aeneas and the ecstatic Sibyl (6.45–155) – three speeches for each speaker; but the two meetings are notable for the peculiarity of their communication. The most common form of interchange is one utterance and one response, sometimes with the first speaker coming back again. Nisus and Euryalus have two speeches each in 9.184–221. Virgil can stitch together a series of duologues (as in 2.638 ff. – Anchises: Aeneas, Creusa: Aeneas, Anchises: Aeneas) but does not have three- or more-way dialogue (the nearest to that is at 12.10–80, where Turnus, Latinus, Amata and the silent Lavinia are together but the others only address Turnus). For this and for a comparison with the more varied Homer, see Heinze, *Virgil's Epic Technique*, 404–5; or at greater length D. Beck, *Homeric Conversation*, Hellenic Studies Series 14 (Washington, DC: Center for Hellenic Studies, 2005).

12. In the *Iliad*, when Achilles addresses his horses (19.400 ff.), they reply – unlike Polyphemus' ram (10.833–71 note); those in

Virgil's audience who knew their Homer might have wondered which precedent would be followed.

13. Venus' request of Vulcan (8.374 ff.), precisely because of its intimacy, comes across as sheer manipulation.

14. Achilles' reproach to Patroclus (*Il.* 16.7 ff.), 'Patroclus, why are you in tears, like a little girl running along beside her mother and begging to be carried …' is amusing because it is incongruous.

15. *Il.* 16.80 ff.

16. Epithets are not straightforward – they can take on a questioning, almost ironic, ring, as when Aeneas, possessed by *furor* after Pallas' death and laying waste all round him, is called *pius* (10.591).

17. The Romans were very used to thinking in terms of *exempla*, 'examples' for themselves to follow (e.g. Cicero, *In Defence of Murena* 66, of Cato; for Livy, see *Introduction* – 7.2 The hero); it is a short step to seeing literary characters in terms of the *exempla* they provide. See J. Griffin, 'The Creation of Characters in the *Aeneid*', in B. Gold (ed.), *Literary and Artistic Patronage in Ancient Rome* (Austin, TX: University of Texas Press, 1982), 125–6.

18. See also H. Lovatt, 'Character in Virgil', in Mac Góráin and Martindale (eds), *The Cambridge Companion*, 388; she refers to the work of C. Gill on the ancient notion of an 'objective-participant' self, built up from its social interactions and not dictating them as our 'subjective individualist' self would.

19. See further Griffin, 'The Creation of Characters', 127–30.

20. *Homeric Hymn to Aphrodite* (5) ll. 196 f.

21. Such as Agamemnon, *Il.* 2.243.

22. So, e.g., 2.268–79 note.

23. See S. Casali, 'The Development of the Aeneas Legend', in Farrell and Putnam (eds), *A Companion*, 37–51; N. Horsfall, 'The Aeneas Legend and the *Aeneid*', *Vergilius*, 32 (1986): 8–17.

24. Xenophon (fifth–fourth century BCE), *On Hunting* 1.15.

25. Lycophron (fourth century), *Alexandra* 1261 ff.; some claim that this part of the poem is a later interpolation.

26. *Rhetorica ad Herennium* (author unknown) 4.34.46.

27. So the note of a scholiast on 7.123 (cf. Naevius, *Punic Wars*, Fragments 2–4).

28. DServius' note to 3.10 cites lines of Naevius (= *Punic Wars*, Fragments 5–7), 'The wives of both were passing out from Troy by night; their heads were veiled, and both were weeping many tears, as they went away.'

29. Macrobius, *Saturnalia* 6.2.31 – see 1.223–53 note.

30. DServius, note to 1.273 – he also quotes Eratosthenes' rival claim, that Romulus was the son of Ascanius; the earliest Greek accounts put the foundation of Rome at most three generations after Troy's sack (see *Introduction* – 1.1 Rome's origins).

31. Ennius, *Annals*, Fragments 18–19.

32. Ibid., 22–3.

33. Ibid., 21.

34. Ibid., 31.

35. Also from DServius, note to 1.273.

36. Servius, note to 8.631.

37. Ibid., note to 1.128, says that only during the second Punic War was she placated.

38. See S. Farron, '*Aeneid* VI, 826-835 (The Vision of Julius Caesar and Pompey) as an Attack on Augustan Propaganda', *Acta Classica*, 23 (1980): 59–62.

39. British Museum, R.8922.

40. Octavian himself between 32 and 29 BCE minted coins showing Venus on the obverse and his youthful figure in armour on the reverse ('Caesar son of the deified (Caesar)'), British Museum, R.6161 – he may have been adopted, but he was no less part of the divine lineage. He nevertheless remained coy of being declared a god himself – see *Introduction* – 6.4.5 Deification.

41. Suetonius, *Life of Caesar* 6.1.

42. Appian, *Civil Wars* 2.11.76 (Pharsalus); 2.15.104 (Munda).

43. Dio Cassius, *Roman History* 43.43.2 f.

44. Appian, *Civil Wars* 2.10.68.

45. Ibid., 2.15.102; *Corpus of Latin Inscriptions* I² 215.

46. *Res Gestae* 20.3.

47. Dio Cassius, *Roman History* 53.23.6.

48. See N. Horsfall, 'Virgil and the Conquest of Chaos', *Antichthon*, 15 (1981): 141–50, reprinted in Harrison (ed.), *Oxford Readings in Virgil's* Aeneid, 466–77, especially 471–3.

49. Quoted in C. Bowra, 'Aeneas and the Stoic Ideal', *Greece & Rome*, 3, no. 7 (1933): 8–21, reprinted in Harrison (ed.), *Oxford Readings in Virgil's* Aeneid, 363; 365 f. look at early criticism (and defence) of Aeneas.

50. R. Graves, 'The Cult of Virgil', *Virginia Quarterly Review*, 38, no. 1 (1962): 28.

51. These two books, by far the longest speech in the *Aeneid*, give the lie to any claim that Aeneas is temperamentally tongue-tied; besides, they include (e.g. in the narration of Creusa's words to him, 2.675 ff. and 2.776 ff.) instances of his failure to communicate; he is aware of it, even if he masks his emotions (2.792ff.).

52. Venus' hug at 8.615 seems almost perfunctory – the weapons are the thing: Aeneas says nothing to her, at least so far as Virgil reports.

53. The relationship between Anchises and Aeneas is respectful, but there is no room for warmth – in the underworld, Anchises slips out of his son's attempted embrace (6.700 ff.).

54. Lyne, *Further Voices*, 181–3, proposes that Virgil is offering a critique of Stoic inhibition.

55. Dryden, however, was impatient with French critics who 'make Aeneas little better than a kind of St. Swithin hero, always raining' (*Discourse on Epick Poetry*).

56. Ezra Pound reports a favourite anecdote of W. B. Yeats, on an Irish sailor who, having studied the *Aeneid*, declared 'Ach, him a hero? Bigob, I t'ought he waz a priest.' (E. Pound, *ABC of Reading* (London: George Routledge and Sons, 1934), 29). Hardie wonders if this is simply because he is so often called 'Father Aeneas' after the death of Anchises. Pound himself declares of Virgil, 'His hero is a stick who would have contributed to the *New Statesman*' (*Literary Essays of Ezra Pound*, ed. T. S. Eliot (London: Faber, 1954), 215).

57. Cicero, *Tusculan Disputations* 4.69; W. Camps, *An Introduction to Virgil's* Aeneid (London: Oxford University Press, 1969), 29–30, examines the Roman attitude to the 'compulsive element' of love; Virgil's own

examination of love in the *Georgics* (3.242 ff.) condemns it as 'fiery madness', alike in man and other animals.

58. E.g. Achilles at *Il.* 20.254 ff.

59. Caesar could write coldly of the massacre by his men of thousands of Gauls, including women and children hounded by his cavalry (*Gallic Wars* 4.14.3–4.15.3).

60. So most famously A. Parry, 'The Two Voices of Virgil's *Aeneid*', *Arion: A Journal of Humanities and the Classics*, 2 (1963): 66–80, reprinted in Quinn, *Why Vergil?*, see p. 165; also Feeney, 'The Taciturnity of Aeneas', 189.

61. D. Butterfield, 'Aeneas – The Empty Protagonist', *Omnibus*, 83 (March 2022): 6.

62. For further detail, see Lovatt, 'Character in Virgil', 394–7.

63. Heinze, *Virgil's Epic Technique*, 271, 273, his analysis continues to 279.

64. Otis, *Virgil*, 223.

65. Camps, *An Introduction*, 25–6.

66. V. Pöschl, *The Art of Vergil: Image and Symbol in the* Aeneid (Ann Arbor, MI: University of Michigan Press, 1970), 59.

67. The Roman concept of character is mostly taken for granted by Roman authors; the two words for it (*ingenium* and *indoles*) come from *gigno* (I beget) and (probably) *alo* (I nourish) and so correspond to 'nature' and 'nurture', respectively, but that tells us little about its being static or mutable. However, one rare occasion when the concept is examined is in Plautus' play *Mostellaria*: Philolaches (1.2, ll. 84 ff.) compares at length a person to a house built by parents but then occupied by offspring on their first salary; as Philolaches puts it, 'I immigrated into my own character' – and by it brought the building to near-collapse; for him, character is static. See Ross, *Virgil's* Aeneid, 26–31; Lucretius observes (*On the Nature of Things* 3.307 ff.), 'By schooling many achieve an equal gloss but the character they're born with still remains.'

68. Strabo, *Geography*, 14.5.14.

69. Suetonius, *Life of Augustus* 89.1.

70. Plutarch, *Sayings of Kings and Commanders* 92.

71. Heinze considers Aeneas a Stoic hero because he follows Fate (*Virgil's Epic Technique*, 301 f.); Bowra measures the Aeneas of Books I–VI against the four Stoic cardinal virtues and finds him wanting; but from Book VII onwards considers him transformed into a Stoic model, his *furor* a departure from traditional Stoicism that Augustus approved ('Aeneas and the Stoic Ideal', 366 ff.).

72. Augustine (*City of God* 9.4) ascribes a Stoic character to Aeneas when he is unmoved by Anna's pleas (4.449).

73. Pöschl, *The Art of Vergil*, 50–7, raises this in discussing the extent to which Aeneas could be considered Stoic.

74. Seneca, *On Mercy* 2.4.5.

75. It does not seem too much to assume that Turnus loved Lavinia before Allecto arrived (12.70); we hear of Amata's support for Turnus' suit at 7.56 f. and 7.344 f., admittedly briefly; whether Turnus presumed that Lavinia was his bride-to-be (e.g. 9.138) pre-Allecto is an open question, though given Amata's favour it is a tempting supposition.

76. Lyne, *Further Voices*, 66–9, speaks of gods 'working with' existing emotions: the responsibility for an action lies on a sliding scale between totally divine and totally human. But if Turnus would have declared war anyhow, what is the point of Allecto's intervention? (See *Introduction* – 4.2 Olympian gods in Homer.)

77. For others' view of him, see 7.473 f.

78. See M. Gale, 'The Shield of Turnus (*Aeneid* 7.783-92)', *Greece & Rome*, 44, no. 2 (1997): 176, 182–5.

79. Virgil never mutes the *furor* with which Turnus is imbued – 12.8 (the bloody maw is also *furor*'s), 12.101 ff., 12.331 ff. (where he is compared to Mars); and Turnus recognizes it in himself (12.680).

80. Pöschl, *The Art of Vergil*, p. 110 ff. – see 12.1–53 and 12.676–80 notes. Dido is also powerfully recalled by Amata (12.57 ff., 12.593 ff.): as in Book VII, her trajectory seems parallel to and slightly ahead of Turnus'.

81. The relationships are, however, contrasted: Anna is sincere with Dido, not Dido with Anna; Turnus is truthful with Juturna, not she with him.

82. For examples of Turnus' *pietas*, see 9.22 ff. (9.22–4 note); 10.619 f.

83. Pöschl, *The Art of Vergil*, 95, speaks of 'the contrast of his noble nature with the demoniacal passion which robs him of insight and sanity'.

84. Aristotle's *Poetics* speak of completeness of action (a beginning, middle and end – 1450b; for epic, 1459a), scale of action (able to be retained in the audience's memory – 1451a) and unity of action (the play moves towards a single deed – also 1451a); Aristotle is perhaps over-prescriptive, but Virgil (knowingly or not) meets his requirements.

85. *Poetics* 1453a, for the underlying cause of the central tragic figure's reversal of fortune.

86. This is the term used by Aristotle for one of the necessary components in a tragic plot (*Poetics* 1452a).

87. Another component of Aristotle's tragic plot (*Poetics* 1452a).

88. Such a contest is a regular feature of old (fifth–fourth century BCE) comedy but the term can also be applied in tragedy – e.g. Jason and Medea's exchange in Euripides' *Medea* 446 ff.. The term is not Aristotelian.

89. The third of Aristotle's components (*Poetics* 1452b).

90. Aristotle (*Poetics* 1453a) speaks of the tragic hero/heroine as 'one of those people held in great esteem' who enjoys 'great good fortune', in whose case 'the change to bad fortune is not due to any moral defect or depravity but to an error of some kind'.

91. 'Tragedy . . . effects through pity and fear the purification (*katharsis*) of such emotions' (Aristotle, *Poetics* 1449b); post-Aristotelian critics speak more generally, of 'shaking' (*ekplēxis*) the audience in a pleasurable way – so Longinus (*On the Sublime* 15.2), 'The aim of poetry is to <u>shake</u> the audience; that of prose is vividness' (my emphasis); cf. Strabo, *Geography* 1.2.17, Plutarch, 'How a Young Man Should Listen to the Poets' 17a.

92. 'Poetry', says Aristotle (*Poetics* 1451b), 'tends to express universals . . . The universal is the kind of speech or action which is consonant with a person of a given kind in accordance with probability or necessity'.

93. In Euripides' *Medea*, Jason abandons the heroine for a younger woman; she is forced into exile but prior to leaving kills their children – Jason curses her with the blood she has shed. The parallels between Dido and Apollonius' Medea make it a looming possibility that Dido might turn into a Euripidean woman scorned.

94. For Euripides' *Hippolytus*, see 6.445–9 note; Dido resembles Hippolytus in her vow of chastity and Phaedra in being made by Aphrodite to fall passionately in love, both of them eventually doomed.

95. P. Hardie, 'Virgil and Tragedy', in Mac Góráin and Martindale (eds), *The Cambridge Companion*, 328.

96. Explored in J. Dyson, 'Dido the Epicurean', *Classical Antiquity*, 15, no. 2 (1996): 203 ff.

97. For a full-length study of Ascanius see A. Rogerson, *Virgil's Ascanius: Imagining the Future in the* Aeneid (Cambridge: Cambridge University Press, 2017); she brings out the uncertainty of his prospects despite the prophesied generations of his descendants (e.g. 8.628 f.).

98. To accept Dido's 'seventh summer' from 1.755 f.

99. S. Casali, 'The Theophany of Apollo in the Vergil, *Aeneid* 9: Augustanism and Self-reflexivity', in L. Athanassaki, R. Martin and J. Miller (eds), *Apolline Politics and Poetics* (Athens: Hellenic Ministry of Culture, European Cultural Centre of Delphi, 2009), 318, available online, University of Rome, 'Tor Vergata', available online: https://art. torvergata.it/bitstream/2108/58574/103359/ Casali-The%20Theophany%20of%20Apollo. pdf (accessed 6 May 2024).

100. As argued by R. Lloyd, 'The Character of Anchises in the *Aeneid*', *Transactions and Proceedings of the American Philological Association*, 88 (1957): 44–55.

101. This is the title of the oldest living male in the family, with total authority over the other members of the household but with responsibility also for their well-being (moral, religious and social); he would be expected to take on civic duties (political and religious) for the honour of his wider clan. See *Introduction* – 6.2.1 *Familia*.

102. He seizes the opportunity that the Trojans present to marry off his daughter sight unseen (7.259 ff.); unused to conflict (7.46 f.), when he is confronted by a hawkish mob he makes his stand by shutting himself away (7.599 f.); he re-emerges twice to promote the cause of peace (11.302 ff., 12.161 ff.) and, though thwarted on these occasions, watches (12.707 ff.) as the single combat (which he had opposed – 12.19 ff.) brings it about.

103. Remembering an encounter with Anchises, he welcomes Aeneas and the Trojans outright (8.154 ff.); he tells the story of Hercules' encounter with Cacus, which he never witnessed himself, with relish for violence and gruesome detail (8.190 ff.); he has an appetite for battle if not the capacity (8.508 ff., 11.160 f.); his advice, to rely on an alliance with the Etruscans (8.511 f.), bears fruit; he takes a risk in sending Pallas with a small contingent (8.514 ff. – he knows the danger, 8.578 ff.), particularly before he can be certain what the Etruscans will do; he does not blame Aeneas for Pallas' death (11.164 f.), instead imposing the duty of revenge (11.178 f.).

104. Latinus' loss of his turbulent queen might not be considered tragic; but the loss of a war he always opposed surely is.

105. For Dido, first at 4.69; in Amata's case, 7.377.

106. See also 12.54–80, 12.54, 12.55–6, 12.59 notes.

107. Which does not imply that Turnus felt for Amata as she for him.

108. The blank is filled in by Ursula Le Guin in her *Lavinia* (London: Weidenfeld and Nicholson, 2008).

109. The *filia familias* would live at home until matched with a husband by her parents (see *Introduction – 6.2.1 Familia*); her legitimate membership of a well-born family and her virginity were her assets. For Heinze, this is all there is to Lavinia (*Virgil's Epic Technique*, 460).

110. R. Williams, 'The Function and Structure of Virgil's Catalogue in *Aeneid 7*', *Classical Quarterly*, 11, nos 3–4 (1961): 149.

111. T. Becker, 'Ambiguity and the Female Warrior: Vergil's Camilla', *Electronic Antiquity*, 4, no. 1 (1997), available online: https://scholar.lib.vt.edu/ejournals/ElAnt/V4N1/becker.html (accessed 6 May 2024).

112. L. Fratantuono, *Madness Unchained: A Reading of Virgil's* Aeneid (Lanham, MD: Lexington, 2007), 228.

113. B. Boyd, 'Virgil's Camilla and the Traditions of Catalogue and Ecphrasis (*Aeneid* 7.803-17)', *American Journal of Philology*, 113, no. 2 (1992): 213–21; Boyd emphasizes the visual qualities of both catalogue and *ekphrasis*, in this case accentuated by the spectators.

114. Mezentius in Books VIII, IX and X, Turnus in Books IX, X and XII (he does not fight in XI).

115. He already showed his esteem for her when he cited her presence to the assembly as a reason for continuing to fight (11.432).

116. Tarchon's words are a reproach to his men – and thus a tribute to Camilla by the back door.

117. E. Pyy, 'Decus Italiae virgo: Virgil's Camilla and the Formation of Romanitas', *Arctos*, 44 (2010): 188; the thesis would be more striking if the defeated nation were not led by the woman in question – but Hecuba, Creusa (if alive), Andromache and Lavinia are not similarly emblematic.

118. This is argued by B. Xinyue, '*Imperatrix* and *bellatrix*: Cicero's Clodia and Vergil's Camilla', in D. Campanile, F. Carlà-Uhink and M. Facella (eds), *TransAntiquity: Cross-Dressing and Transgender Dynamics in the Ancient World* (London and New York: Routledge, 2017), 169–78, https://www.docdroid.net/KF4ld5P/domitilla-campanile-transantiquity-crossdressing-and-transgender-dynamics-in-the-ancient-world-1-1.pdf↑ge=179 (accessed 6 May 2024).

119. In Book XI, ll. 507. 508, 604, 664, 676, 718, 762, 778, 804 and 808 – the last two incidents of the word (or rather the adjective from it) are at her death.

Chapter 4

1. This book refers to the gods by their Latin names unless in a Greek context, or when citing a Greek author.

2. V. Warrior, *Roman Religion* (Cambridge: Cambridge University Press, 2006), 62–6.

3. The process can be seen in action when Naevius (Fragment 16), has Venus address her father 'the highest and best', where 'highest' corresponds to an epithet of Zeus in Homer (*Od.* 1.45) and 'best' is part of Jupiter's cult title at Rome, 'Jupiter Greatest and Best'.

4. This mapping did not have to be complete – Dionysius of Halicarnassus, Roman Antiquities 2.18.3 speaks of Romulus excising unbecoming elements of Greek myth so that (2.19.1), 'Indeed, there is no tradition among the Romans . . . of Saturn destroying his own offspring to secure himself from their attempts or of Jupiter dethroning Saturn and confining his own father in the dungeon of Tartarus, or, indeed, of wars, wounds, or bonds of the gods, or of their servitude among men.' Virgil does, however, refer to Saturn's deposition – 8.320; and on the adjective 'Saturnian', see 1.23 note.

5. A god or goddess could be worshipped in a particular aspect or with a particular geographical association – 'Mars Ultor' = 'Mars the Avenger'; 'Lacinia' relates to one Lacinius, whom Heracles slew when Lacinius tried to steal the cattle of Geryon with which Heracles was returning (Diodorus Siculus, *Library of History* 4.24.7).

6. See D. Feeney, *The Gods in Epic* (Oxford: Oxford University Press, 1991), chapter 1, 'The Critics: Beginnings, and a Synthesis', 5–56.

7. Pindar, *Olympian* 1.30 ff.

8. In his *Theogony*, composed in the late eighth century BCE, on the origin and genealogy of the gods.

9. Herodotus, *Histories* 2.53: '<Homer and Hesiod> are the ones who taught the Greeks the descent of the gods, and gave the gods their names, and determined their spheres and functions, and described their outward forms.'

10. When wounded, Aphrodite (*Il.* 5.330 ff.) and Ares (*Il.* 5.855 ff.) both behave like children who have hurt themselves and run squealing for instant relief.

11. Hephaestus tells of one between Zeus and Hera when he, interposing himself, was flung from heaven (*Il.* 1.590 ff.).

12. Demodocus sings of the adultery between Aphrodite and Ares, trapped in a net by Hephaestus while the gods look on and laugh (*Od.* 8.266 ff.).

13. *Il.* 1.601 ff.

14. And even then there is an element of slapstick in the gods' brawling as they engage with human conflict at *Il.* 21.388 ff., while Zeus laughs in delight.

15. Xenophanes, Fragment B11.

16. Xenophanes, Fragments B25 and B26.

17. Allegorization is attributed by the commentators on Homer (the scholiasts) to Theagenes of Rhegium; rationalization is exemplified by the geographer, Hecataeus of Miletus.

18. A method to be seen in action at Plato's *Cratylus*, 396a ff.

19. See Plato, *Phaedrus* 229c-e on the latter method of exegesis; its most celebrated exponent was Euhemerus, who gave his name to the term 'Euhemerism'.

20. So G. Williams, *Technique and Ideas in the Aeneid* (New Haven, CT: Yale University Press, 1983), 17–39, chapter 2, 'The Gods in the *Aeneid*'.

21. Plato, *Republic* 378b, 378d–e.

22. Aristotle, *Poetics* 1449b – this concerns tragedy, but just before it Aristotle declares that what goes for tragedy also goes for epic.

23. Aristotle, *Poetics* 1460b.

24. Ibid.

25. *Il.* 9.702 f.

26. So P. Jones, *Homer's* Iliad: *A Commentary on Three Translations* (London: Bristol Classical Press, 2003), 32.

27. R. Lyne, *Further Voices in Vergil's* Aeneid (Oxford: Clarendon Press, 1987), 66–9.

28. Did Aeneas really have a deep-seated urge to leave Carthage when Mercury visited him (4.279 ff.)? Feeney, *The Gods in Epic*, 173–4, acknowledges Aeneas' 'conscience' (his thoughts for his son, the apparitions of his father (4.351 ff.) but opposes 'working with'. In Book V, the Trojan women, although they have mixed feelings about their onward voyage (5.644 ff.), penetrate Iris' disguise with almost comical ease and have to be awed into insurrection.

29. *Il.* 3.381 ff.; this passage is discussed by W. Johnson, *Darkness Visible: A Study of Vergil's Aeneid* (Berkeley, CA: University of California Press, 1979), 37–45, in which he sets it against the erotic compulsion afflicting Dido at 1.657 ff. – a more flickering, impressionistic depiction – 'divine intervention and psychological realism are merged together implausibly'.

30. See Feeney, *The Gods in Epic*, chapter 4, 'Vergil's *Aeneid*', 129–87.

31. Ross, *Virgil's* Aeneid, 62–7, outlines this development.

32. Cotta in Cicero, *On the Nature of the Gods* 3.21.60.

33. Servius is an Aristotelian in principle (note on 9.74): 'In poetry certain things are not to be made to conform with exact interpretation or with truth.'

34. R. Hexter, 'On First Looking into Vergil's Homer', in Farrell and Putnam (eds), *A Companion*, 28–9.

35. For example, the Neo-Platonist philosopher Porphyry (third century CE) wrote a work, *Homeric Questions*, which survives, following on from a work of the same title by Aristotle, which does not. He develops Aristotle's argument: 'It is on the basis of a certain convention that it is conceded to poets and painters and sculptors to represent the gods as having human characteristics, and to tell of their battles against each other, their periods of servitude and their metamorphoses' (Porphyry 2.226.10 ff., not available online).

36. Virgil almost implies, 'the gods are what you make of them' – Nisus makes precious little, until he turns belatedly to the moon (9.207–18 note).

37. J. Duffy, 'Homer's Conception of Fate', *Classical Journal*, 42, no. 8 (1947): 477–85, does not hesitate to make Fate the will of Zeus; H. Shakeshaft, 'Cruel Fate and the Beginning of the End in *Iliad* 16', *Omnibus*, 86 (September 2023): 2, endorses an exception.

38. Prophecy is linked to fate when Evander receives the warning from the soothsayer that a foreigner must lead his army (described at 8.499 ff.) and he then describes Aeneas' arrival to satisfy that requirement as 'fate' (8.477).

39. E.g. 5.95, where the narrative is focalized through Aeneas as he sacrifices to his father and a snake appears – the spirit of the place, or Anchises himself?

40. *Od.* 13.287 ff.

41. Servius, note on 10.628, 'Fate is the utterance of Jupiter'.

42. The Parcae, or personifications of Fate (1.22 note), are concerned with life's duration rather than its course.

43. The 'fate of the gods' is not something that features in the *Aeneid*, even if it were theoretically possible.

44. Individuals have Fates and communities likewise (e.g. 1.22, Rome's eventual sack of Carthage); the former must comply with the latter – or the latter are brought about by the former. Although Jupiter is in principle implicated in the Fate of Carthage as much as of Rome, the *Aeneid* is Rome-centred and Jupiter the god of the Capitol.

45. So Cicero, *On Fate* 28: '"He will come," when true, is as immutable as "He has come."' (Cicero's monograph examines the arguments for hardline physical determinism – certainly not Virgil's position.)

46. Williams, *Technique and Ideas*, 5–9, speaks of Fate as 'a synecdoche for the historical process'.

47. Dido's death was not fated (4.696); the concessions that Juno seeks from Jupiter are not governed by any law of Fate (12.819).

48. The Stoics were more submissive, speaking of either being lead or dragged by Fate – 5.21–5 note.

49. Sometimes characters in the poem speak as if it did, each to make a point – so Evander's, **'Fortune . . . and Fate . . . set me here in this place'** / *'Fortune . . . and Fate . . . have planted me in this place'* (8.333 ff.), is a stronger way of saying, 'I'm here through the guidance of Fate'; or Nautes', **'Let us follow the Fates, whether they lead us on or lead us back'** / *'Whether the Fates will draw us on or draw us back, let's follow where they lead'* (5.709), is much more persuasive than, 'Let's go with the flow.' They do not impose a Stoic view of Fate on the poem.

50. As in English, the Latin word can also mean 'luck' – this is how Nisus and Euryalus use it at 9.240 and 9.282, and Turnus at 10.284, all characters who seem insensitive to Fate. The opposite extreme of *Fortuna*'s range is represented by Cicero, explaining in a dialogue with Atticus the Stoics' materialism (*Academica* 1.29), of the force that governs everything, 'they sometimes also term it Fortune, because many of its operations are unforeseen and unexpected by us on account of their obscurity and our ignorance of causes'. Cicero could run with the more popular definition – in his dialogue *On Divination* (2.7.18), he remarks to Quintus:

> Surely nothing is so at variance with reason and stability as *fortuna*? Hence it seems to me that it is not in the power even of God himself to know what event is going to happen accidentally and by chance. For if He knows, then the event is certain to happen; but if it is certain to happen, *fortuna* does not exist. And yet *fortuna* does exist, therefore there is no foreknowledge of things that happen by chance.

There was a goddess Fortuna, who was worshipped at many shrines in Rome (Cicero, *Laws* 2.28).

51. Evander (8.334) distinguishes between '*fortuna* that governs everything and *fatum* that cannot be avoided' – Servius says that Evander speaks as a Stoic, but at the same time admits that for Stoics *fortuna* is opposed to *fatum*; in fact, for Stoics, *fortuna* does not exist. It is therefore more consistent to see *fortuna* as 'what governs all outcomes', including those unforeseen; unlike *fatum*, it is within *fortuna*'s rights to be fickle (e.g. 5.604).

52. Other views of this sequence of encounters are of course possible: they have been viewed even as psychotherapeutic.

53. A version of the Euthyphro dilemma (Plato, *Euthyphro* 10a): 'Is that which is holy loved by the gods because it is holy, or is it holy because it is loved by the gods?' For Stoics, the second option was correct – Seneca wrote, 'An irrevocable course of events carries along human and divine affairs equally. The founder and controller of all things himself although he wrote down what is fated, also follows it; he always obeys, he ordained just the once' (On Providence, *Dialogues* 1.5.8).

54. Williams, *Technique and Ideas*, 9; in the *Iliad*, Zeus at least considers altering the path of destiny, only to be dissuaded (to save his son Sarpedon, 16.431 ff.; to save Hector, 22.167 ff.).

55. See *Introduction* – 3.2.2 Aeneas between the *Iliad* and the *Aeneid*: The Aeneas legend.

56. Eliot called him, 'The man without a destiny' – *What is a Classic?* (London: Faber, 1945), 21.

57. Were the victims of the war in Italy fated to die? Juno, through Allecto, sparked off the conflict; but Jupiter had also predicted it (1.263); Virgil's laments for those killed do not decide the matter, but, for example, the epitaph on Umbro (7.750 ff.) has greater pathos if his death was not inevitable, if the conflict Jupiter had foreseen might have spared him.

58. For a picture of a Jupiter motivated entirely by power and reputation, see J. Hejduk, 'Jupiter's *Aeneid*: Fama and Imperium', *Classical Antiquity*, 28, no. 2 (2009): 279–327; it should be said that his prophecy to Venus and his settlement with Juno indicate their preoccupation with the same things – Venus at 1.235 f., Juno at 12.828.

59. His thunderbolt is described at 8.431 f.; his authority over the gods is in evidence at the divine assembly of Book X10 (especially ll. 9, 104), but so is the other gods' willingness to flout it.

60. 10.473, 10.606 ff. and by implication 10.758 ff., when all the gods, Venus and Juno included, are spectators of the battle.

61. Anchises attributes pity to him at 5.725 after the burning of the fleet – but this sounds like a mortal's imputation.

62. *Il.* 14.157 f., 15.18 ff. and 24.527 ff., respectively.

63. And Jupiter is not alone: Aeneas' bitter comment on the death of Rhipeus, the most just and most observant of righteousness among all the Trojans, is, 'The gods thought otherwise' (2.426 ff.).

64. Servius makes this identification in his note to 1.78; Virgil does not confine her, however – she can spy Aeneas' fleet from high in the *aether* at 7.288.

65. 4.120, 10.634, 12.792, 12.796.

66. His contribution to the siege of Troy, invigorating the Greeks and egging on the other gods (2.617 f.) does not necessitate his presence.

67. This can also be viewed as Jupiter trying officially to contain the support she had shown for Turnus in Book IX.

68. Diodorus Siculus, *Library of History* 23.5.1.

69. *Il.* 1.400 ff., 14.292 ff., 15.36 ff., respectively.

70. Ibid., 22.582 ff.

71. So Neptune, when he declares his duty to help Venus in Book V, insists on a price – one life in return for many (5.815); that life is Palinurus', who has done nothing to deserve being sacrificed.

72. Not just of the family of Aeneas – Lucretius, *On the Nature of Things* 1.1 f.: 'O mother of the Roman race, delight of men and gods, Venus most bountiful.'

73. *Il.* 18.432 ff.; Apollonius of Rhodes, *Argonautica* 4.865 ff., adds a different account of the mésalliance.

74. E.g. *Il.* 3.424.

75. *Homeric Hymn to Aphrodite* ll. 45 ff.: Zeus makes her desire Anchises in requital for the many mortal loves she has inflicted on him and other gods.

76. See E. Gutting, 'Venus' Maternity and Divinity in the *Aeneid*', in R. Ferri, J. Mira Seo and Katharina Volk (eds), *Callida Musa: Papers on Latin Literature: In Honor of R. Elaine Fantham*, Materiali e discussioni per l'analisi dei testi classici 61 (Pisa and Rome: Fabrizio Serra editore, 2009), 41–55.

77. Recognizing a god(dess) at the instant of departure is the norm in Homer (e.g. *Od.* 1.319 ff.) but Virgil makes this recognition a twist of the knife.

78. This is one of Juno's preoccupations – 1.48 f.

79. M. Silk, 'Heracles and Greek Tragedy', *Greece & Rome*, 32, no. 1 (1985): 6.

80. Livy, *From the City's Foundation* 1.7.3.

81. So a silver didrachm from Rome dated 269–266 BCE: British Museum 1867,0101.31.

82. Livy, *From the City's Foundation* 1.7.15.

83. Diodorus Siculus, *Library of History* 4.21.3.

84. Both Pompey and Mark Antony issued coins depicting the lion-skin and club with or without Hercules himself.

85. For Hercules in the *Aeneid*, see G. Galinsky, 'Hercules in the *Aeneid*', in *The Heracles Theme* (Oxford: Basil Blackwell, 1972), reprinted in Harrison (ed.), *Oxford Readings in Virgil's* Aeneid, 277 ff.

86. Augustus surpasses Hercules in the extent of his travels at 6.801 ff.; at Actium, on Aeneas' shield (8.678 ff.) he is the all but divine opponent of Egypt's alien forces and animal gods. Octavian's triple triumph was celebrated on the three days following the feast of Hercules (8.102–25 note).

87. Aeneas' *labores* ('trials') are an ostinato in the poem (1.8–11 note; one of them, the descent to the underworld, Aeneas shares with Hercules (6.122–3 note); like Hercules, in the underworld his bright armour disperses the shades (6.489 note); Evander sits Aeneas on a lion-skin (8.177) before narrating the tale of Hercules and Cacus – later Aeneas' horse will be caparisoned in (another) lion's skin (8.552 f.); Hercules also had entered Evander's palace (8.362 ff.).

88. For Lucretius, Hercules was the measure of Epicurus – the latter far greater because he had brought a permanent solution to men's mental woes, whereas the twelve labours solved a few local problems that most people could avoid anyhow (*On the Nature of Things* 5.22 ff.).

89. Horace, *Odes* 3.3.9 ff.; at the start of his *Epistles* 2.1, he also praises Augustus for his military and moral strength and his legal reform, actions which earn him a place among the gods, like Romulus, Castor and Pollux – and Hercules.

90. Apollodorus, *Library* 2.7.7.

91. Cicero, *Tusculan Disputations* 1.32.

92. Aristotle, *Politics* 1253a 27–9.

93. So argues Feeney, *The Gods in Epic*, 159–61.

94. The Greek name 'Heracles' ironically means 'glory of Hera'.

95. The same phrase, 'hostile Juno' (*Iunonis iniquae*), is used in relation to both Aeneas and Hercules (1.668 and 8.292).

96. Euripides, *Heracles* 922 ff.: Heracles imagined his victims to be the tyrant

Eurystheus, who assigned his labours, and Eurystheus' family; his sanity restored, he is overcome with remorse and is only saved from suicide by the friendship of Theseus and the offer of refuge in Athens.

97. Apollodorus, *Library* 2.4.12.

98. Seneca, *Letters* 41.3 vividly captures this sense of the divine in landscape.

99. Horace famously promises to sacrifice a goat to a spring at Bandusia, possibly on his Sabine farm (*Odes* 3.13).

100. Ovid, *Metamorphoses* 6.392 f., 'fauns and satyrs, their brothers'.

101. Ovid, *Heroides* 5.135 ff.; *Fasti* 4.761 f.

102. Nymphs are strictly speaking not full-blown goddesses – the Homeric Hymn (5), to Aphrodite (ll. 259 ff.) says of the mountain nymphs who would bring up the infant Aeneas, 'Long indeed do they live, eating the food of heaven and dancing among the gods …', but describes their death as well as their birth; Cicero's *On the Nature of the Gods* 3.17.43 enters the controversy, his speaker declaring them not to be gods; the *Georgics* (later in this paragraph) beg to differ (cf. 9.102).

103. *Georgics* 2.493 f.

104. A corresponding protecting spirit, a *juno*, for the *mater familias*, the mother of the house, might also be venerated.

105. Its shrine, the *lararium*, was sometimes in the main entrance hall of the house (the *atrium*) but more commonly in the kitchen area.

106. Their identity and number were a matter of debate (Macrobius, *Saturnalia* 3.4.6 ff.) – or unknown (so Varro, cited in Arnobius, *Against the Heathen* 3.40).

107. A custom referred to in Livy, *From the City's Foundation* 26.36.6 and Cicero, *On Ends* 2.7.22.

108. Thus Ovid, or at least his wife, on his leaving Rome – *Tristia* 1.3.41 ff.; Demipho returning from abroad in Terence's *Phormio*, line 311 / 2.1.82 (lineation varies).

109. Plautus, *The Merchant* 834 f. / 5.1.5 f.

110. The public Lares (plural of Lar) were placed at crossroads (*compita*), marking the division between Rome's neighbourhoods (*vici*) – it was their festival, the Compitalia, that Augustus reinvigorated after it had fallen into disuse during the civil wars; we are told (Scholiast on Horace *Satires* 2.3.261) that he restored the shrines, adding a statue in each to his own *genius* (Ovid, *Fasti* 5.129 f., 5.143 ff.), and set up an order of priests in his own honour to maintain worship at them; this process began some time after 12 BCE and culminated in 7 BCE (P. Goodman, 'In omnibus regionibus? The Fourteen Regions and the City of Rome', *Papers of the British School at Rome*, 88 (2020): 123).

111. Under the Laws of the Twelve Tables of *c.* 450 BCE that began the corpus of Roman legislation, the dead had to be interred outside the city walls.

112. Cicero, *On the Laws* 2.22.

113. Though possibly even a majority held that death was the end: on many tombstones appear the letters 'nf f ns nc' (*non fui, fui, non sum, non curo* = 'I didn't exist, I did exist, I don't exist, I don't care').

114. Studies on individual deities in the *Aeneid* (Mars, Mercury, Iris and Aurora) by L. Fratantuono can be consulted on www.academia.edu; they can seem to put ingenuity under strain.

115. Apollo has a Greek title, 'leader of the Muses' (*Mousēgetēs*) – Plato, *Laws* 2 653d.

116. Cicero, *On the Laws* 2.19: 'No individual shall have gods for himself, either new or alien ones, unless they have been recognized by the state. Privately they shall worship those gods whose worship they have received from their ancestors.'

117. On Cybele in the *Aeneid*, see R. Wilhelm, 'Cybele: The Great Mother of Augustan Order', *Vergilius*, 34 (1988): 77–101.

118. On Isis, see Warrior, *Roman Religion*, 88–91.

119. Isis Capitolina is mentioned in two inscriptions, CIL VI.2247 and 2248, not available online.

120. Dio Cassius, *Roman History* 40.47.3; for the exclusion of temples to foreign gods beyond the city boundary, compare Juno, brought from Veii and lodged on the Aventine Hill (see 2.348–54 note).

121. Dio Cassius, *Roman History* 47.15.4.

122. Ibid., 53.2.4.

123. Ibid., 54.6.6.

124. Catullus 63.

125. Livy, *From the City's Foundation* 29.14.13 f.

126. Aulus Gellius, *Attic Nights* 2.24.

127. Livy, *From the City's Foundation* 38.18.9 f.

128. Plutarch, *Life of Marius* 17.5 f.

129. E.g. an *aureus* in the British Museum: 1964,1203.75.

130. *Res Gestae* 19.2.

131. On Cybele's representation on the Prima Porta statue, see J. Reeder, 'The Statue of Augustus from Prima Porta, the Underground Complex, and the Omen of the Gallina Alba', *American Journal of Philology*, 118, no. 1(1997): 109.

132. A sardonyx cameo in the Vienna Kunsthistorisches Museum shows Livia wearing Cybele's mural crown; a first-century CE statue, thought to be of Livia, in the J. Paul Getty Museum likewise.

133. Cicero, *On the Replies of the Soothsayers* 12.24 – this is an attack on Clodius for disrupting the Megalesia, so Cicero plays up the desecration.

134. Dionysius of Halicarnassus, *Roman Antiquities* 2.19.3 ff.

135. See notes to 1.50–63; 3.578–82; 4.178–9; 4.238–58; 5.116–23; 5.362–86; 6.258–9; 6.580; 7.784–802 **fire like Etna's**; 8.184–279; 8.236–40; 8.691–5; 9.441–2; 9.691–716; 10.317–22; 10.565–70; 10.689–716; 11.351; 12.921–3.

136. The *gigantes* in Greek – they formed a specific group; other giants existed apart from them.

137. Hesiod, *Theogony* ll. 116 ff.

138. So are they illustrated in art – most spectacularly on the altar at Pergamon (third century BCE).

139. Hesiod, *Theogony* ll. 453 ff.

140. Hesiod, *Theogony* ll. 617 ff.; distilled in Apollodorus, *Library* 1.2.1.

141. The term 'Gigantomachy' is sometimes allowed to include the 'Titanomachy', e.g. P. Hardie, *Virgil's* Aeneid: *Cosmos and Imperium* (Oxford: Clarendon Press, 1986), 85.

142. Apollodorus, *Library* 1.6.3.

143. The Gigantomachy is most fully described in Apollodorus, *Library* 1.6.1 ff.; Typhon's story is also told by Hesiod, *Theogony* ll. 820 ff.; for different versions of Typhoeus' fate, see 3.578–82 note.

144. Lucretius, *On the Nature of Things* 5.110 ff.

145. Horace, *Odes* 3.42 ff., whose ll. 65–7 runs, 'Strength without control crashes under its own momentum; controlled strength the gods reinforce' – *furor* is not mentioned, but the thought is on the same lines.

146. For a reconstruction of Orphic beliefs, see R. Parker, 'Early Orphism', in A. Powell (ed.), *The Greek World* (London: Routledge, 1995), 483–510. O. Kern's 1922 collection of Orphic Testimonies and Fragments is available online, with translation. (It has been superseded by Bernabe's collection of 2007, not available online.) An early discussion of the evidence is M. Nilsson, 'Early Orphism and Kindred Religious Movements', *Harvard Theological Review*, 28, no. 3 (1935): 181–230.

147. In the Greek world, the Eleusinian and Samothracian mysteries (at Athens and on the island of Samothrace) were the most famous other examples; in the Roman world, Mithraism spread widely – there is a temple to Mithras on Hadrian's Wall; the worship of Cybele was, in its original location, a mystery.

148. Aristotle thought he never existed – Cicero, *On the Nature of the Gods* 1.38.107; but Aristotle is in a small minority: Euripides' chorus in the *Alcestis* sings of 'the Thracian tablets that the voice of Orpheus filled with writing' (ll. 967 ff.).

149. The Derveni papyrus, unearthed from a Macedonian tomb in 1962, is a major find that dates from the fourth century BCE; as well as being possibly the oldest Greek manuscript in existence, it provides a commentary on one of these Orphic theogonies, dating from the late fifth century – and suggests an allegorical interpretation of it R. Janko, 'The Derveni Papyrus (Diagoras of Melos, *Apopyrgizontes Logoi*?): A New Translation', *Classical Philology*, 96, no. 1 (2001): 1–32, column XIII); Plato's Socrates, *Timaeus* 40d f., refers

ironically to the origins of gods as declared by their descendants – such as Orpheus.

150. Orpheus travelled with Jason – see Apollonius of Rhodes, *Argonautica* 1.28.

151. Orphic Testimonies 221–5 (Kern) mention a variety of other Orphic writings – a Physics, a work on Astronomy, a Rape of Kore, Divination by Sand, Divination by Eggs, poems called 'Mixing Bowls', 'Robe', 'Net' – the last three probably allegories of cosmic processes or structures.

152. 'Those dark mysteries with their torch processions were revealed by Orpheus' (*Rhesus* 943 f.); 'Continue then your confident boasting, take up a diet of greens and play the showman with your food, make Orpheus your lord and engage in mystic rites, holding the vapourings of many books in honour' (*Hippolytus* 952 ff.).

153. Diodorus Siculus imputes Egyptian influence as well – according to *Library of History* 1.96.2 ff., Orpheus borrowed from burial rituals in honour of Osiris; Herodotus (*Histories* 2.123.2 f. – quoted in footnote 171) avows that the notion of metempsychosis came from the Egyptians to Greece, but there is no evidence to support belief in the transmigration of souls among the Egyptians (see L. Žabkar, 'Herodotus and the Egyptian Idea of Immortality', *Journal of Near Eastern Studies*, 22, no. 1 (1963): 59).

154. See Parker, 'Early Orphism', 494–5; it must be said that the only ancient source for the genesis of mankind from the Titan remains is the sixth-century CE Neoplatonist Olympiodorus – Orphic Fragments 220 (Kern); a much more sceptical account of the evidence comes in R. Edmonds, 'Tearing Apart the Zagreus Myth: A Few Disparaging Remarks on Orphism and Original Sin', *Classical Antiquity*, 18, no. 1 (1999): 35–49; see also R. Edmonds, *Redefining Ancient Orphism: A Study in Greek Religion* (Cambridge: Cambridge University Press, 2013), part 3.

155. Diodorus Siculus, *Library of History* 3.62.6; Orphic Fragments 220 (Kern).

156. Orphic Fragments 210 (Kern); this allows Dionysus to be born again from Semele.

157. Ibid., 220 (Kern).

158. Plato, *Laws* 701b f., has the Athenian stranger describe men in anarchy as 'displaying the old Titanic nature'; Christian terminology carries the wrong connotations, but the analogy between Orphic and Christian thought explains the interest church fathers took in Orphism.

159. A gold ivy leaf found in a fourth-century BCE grave at Pelinna in Thessaly carries an inscription beginning: 'Now have you died and now have you been born, thrice blessed, on this day. Say to Persephone that Bakkhios has released you.' See Parker, 'Early Orphism', 497–8.

160. Proclus explains this rebirth in terms that do not imply punishment – Orphic Fragments 224 (Kern); Socrates in Plato's *Cratylus* (400c) attributes the origin of the Greek word for 'body' to the Orphic poets, saying that it means 'safe' (i.e. confinement) for the soul while it is being punished; he does not, however, link this meaning with multiple reincarnations. It is impossible to know from the evidence if Orphics believed in punishment in the underworld (as in Plato) additional to that on earth.

161. Apollodorus, *Library* 1.3.2 says specifically Dionysian; other authors speak simply of 'mysteries' (e.g. Demosthenes [fourth century BCE], 25.11).

162. Plato (*Laws* 782c) says those living by Orphic precepts neither eat nor sacrifice animals; according to Herodotus (*Histories* 2.81), 'they do not bring wool into temples nor are they buried with it, as is the rule for Bacchics, Egyptians and Pythagoreans'. It is a surprise that a sect that shrank from animal sacrifice should centre on the mysteries of Dionysus, whose ecstatic devotees tore live animals apart (*sparagmos* – Euripides, *Bacchae* 735) – the death of Orpheus, torn apart by Bacchants (*Georgics* 4.520 ff.), possibly reflects a punishment for diverging from Dionysiac worship; the plot of Aeschylus' lost play, the *Bassarae*, centres on Orpheus paying the penalty for turning from Dionysus to the sun god / Apollo.

163. Adeimantus, in Plato's *Republic* (363d f.), mockingly calls it 'a state of eternal inebriation'; Socrates looks forward to conversing with Orpheus, Musaeus, Homer

and Hesiod, with or without a drink
(*Apology* 41a).

164. Plato, *Republic* 364e.

165. Plato, *Meno* 81 f.

166. Aristophanes, *Frogs* 1032 f., has Aeschylus
paying tribute to both and demarcating
their roles: 'Orpheus taught us rites and to
refrain from killing, and Musaeus taught the
cures of illness and oracles.'

167. Plato, *Republic* 600b – Socrates remarks,
'Pythagoras was himself especially
honoured for <transmitting to posterity a
certain way of life>, and his successors,
even to this day, denominating a certain way
of life the Pythagorean, are distinguished
among their contemporaries.' Isocrates'
(fourth century BCE) *Busiris* adds detail
(28 f.):

> Pythagoras of Samos . . . more
> conspicuously than others seriously
> interested himself in sacrifices and in
> ceremonial purity, since he believed that
> even if he should gain thereby no greater
> reward from the gods, among men, at any
> rate, his reputation would be greatly
> enhanced. And this indeed happened to
> him. For so greatly did he surpass all others
> in reputation that all the younger men
> desired to be his pupils, and their elders
> were more pleased to see their sons staying
> in his company than attending to their
> private affairs. And these reports we cannot
> disbelieve; for even now persons who
> profess to be followers of his teaching are
> more admired when silent than are those
> who have the greatest renown for eloquence.
> (Trans. Norli)

168. Sadly, Aristotle's *On the Pythagoreans* has
been lost. Much of the familiar anecdote,
such as his originating the theorem named
after him, is open to doubt; the prohibition
on beans is better attested (Aristotle in
Diogenes Laertius, *Life of Pythagoras* 8.34)
– see C. Huffman, 'Pythagoras', *The Stanford
Encyclopedia of Philosophy* (*Spring 2024
Edition*), ed. Edward N. Zalta and Uri
Nodelman, available online: https://plato.
stanford.edu/archives/spr2024/entries/
pythagoras/ (accessed 6 May 2024).

169. Aristotle, *Meteorology* 342b 30 f.

170. Porphyry, *Life of Pythagoras* 19; he is (most
probably) citing Dicaearchus, a fourth-
century BCE member of Aristotle's Lyceum.

171. Herodotus (*Histories* 2.123.2 f.) attributes
the doctrine of the immortal soul to the
Egyptians:

> The Egyptians were the first who maintained
> . . . that the human soul is immortal, and at
> the death of the body enters into some other
> living thing then coming to birth; and after
> passing through all creatures of land, sea,
> and air, it enters once more into a human
> body at birth, a cycle which it completes in
> three thousand years. There are Greeks who
> have used this doctrine, some earlier and
> some later, as if it were their own; I know
> their names, but do not record them.
> (Trans. Godley)

172. *Od.* 11.34 ff.

173. Diogenes Laertius, *Lives of the Eminent
Philosophers* 8.36.

Chapter 5

1. See S. Braund, 'Virgil and the Cosmos' in Mac
Góráin and Martindale (eds), *The Cambridge
Companion*, 279–83.

2. Servius remarks (his note to 10.467), 'Poets
exploit philosophical sects so far as they are
relevant to their own business.'

3. In the sense of the word coined by Claude
Lévi-Strauss (*The Savage Mind* (London:
Weidenfeld and Nicholson, 1962), chapter 1,
16–18), to mean the activity of the myth-
maker who (felicitously) turns to his own
purposes whatever comes to hand.

4. C. Nash, 'Philosophical Readings in Virgil's
Aeneid', DPhil thesis (University of Oxford,
Oxford, 2017), 8–16, argues for the
importance of reading the *Aeneid* with
philosophical awareness, available online:
https://ora.ox.ac.uk/objects/uuid:0a5a33f4-
fe6b-4e7e-a712-41731a7ac42c/files/
mc60c1893720b2dd9be764c01096bf812
(accessed 7 May 2024).

5. Plato, *Republic* 620a ff.

6. Horace (*Epistles* 2.2.41 f.) reminisces: 'I
happened to be brought up at Rome and

taught how much wrathful Achilles had harmed the Greeks.'

7. So it turned out: Juvenal (*Satires* 7.227 ff.) describes the pupil 'breathing in the stench of as many lamps as boys, while your Horace grows wholly discoloured, and soot clings tight to your blackened Virgil'.

8. See also *Introduction* – 4.2 Olympian gods in Homer.

9. Virgil seems in sympathy with Livy's Proem (section 10): 'In history . . . you can find for yourself and your country both examples and warnings: fine things to take as models, base things, rotten through and through, to avoid' (trans. De Selincourt).

10. Three eras are spoken of: the Old Academy (from Plato to *c*. 266 BCE), the Middle Academy (*c*. 266–155 BCE) and the New Academy (155–86 BCE).

11. Cicero, *Academica* 1.12.44 ff., on Arcesilaus – Cicero is our main source on the thinking of the 'New Academy'; 1.4.15 ff. of the same dialogue reprises the history of philosophy at Athens.

12. Heinze, *Virgil's Epic Technique*, 436–8.

13. Aristotle, *Poetics* 1459a.

14. Also ibid.

15. Ibid., 1451b.

16. Ibid., 1459a–60b; they are much briefer than his analysis of tragedy, but he declares (1449b) that anything epic has is present in tragedy.

17. So the first four books of the *Odyssey* document what Telemachus is doing during Odysseus' confinement on Ogygia.

18. Aristotle, *Poetics* 1460a.

19. Epicurus was himself reacting to Aristotelian physics (which supported infinite divisibility – *On Generation and Corruption* 1.2) and developing the atomism of Democritus and Leucippus (ibid.)

20. Or worse – Cicero, *On the Nature of the Gods* 1.92 f., portrays thoroughly ill-humoured competitiveness on both sides.

21. Seneca, *Letters to Lucilius* 1.2.5; Seneca quotes Epicurus often and sometimes favourably, though he departs from much of Epicurean doctrine; see M. Graver, 'Seneca and Epicurus', in P. Mitsis (ed.), *Oxford Handbook of Epicurus and Epicureanism* (Oxford: Oxford University Press, 2020), 250–83.

22. Diogenes Laertius, *Lives of the Eminent Philosophers* 10.6; Epictetus, though impassioned, falls short of insults in his attacks on Epicurus in his own *Discourses*, e.g. 1.23, 2.20 and 3.7.

23. Marcus Aurelius, Meditations 7.64, 9.41, 11.26

24. Horace, *Epistles* 1.4.15 f.

25. Cicero, *In Defence of Murena* 62.

26. Diogenes Laertius, *Lives of the Eminent Philosophers* 10.9 ff.

27. Listed in ibid., 10.27 ff.

28. Fragments of *On Nature* have been recovered from the Villa of the Papyri, supposed by some to have belonged to Philodemus, in Herculaneum.

29. Diogenes Laertius, *Lives of the Eminent Philosophers* 10.35 ff.

30. The most extended analysis of Lucretius' influence on the *Aeneid* is in Hardie, *Virgil's Aeneid*, 156–240.

31. For the poem's contents, see further *Introduction* – 8.4.6 Lucretius.

32. For example, Lucretius, *On the Nature of Things* 3.1–30.

33. For contradiction (sometimes more overt than others), see 1.42–5; 1.52–63; 1.723–56; 2.604–5; 4.31–53 (Epicureanism rather than specifically Lucretius, as 4.208–10, 4.376–80); 4.173–97; 4.613–21; 6.274–81; 6.285–9; 6.440–4; 6.548–627; 6.585–94 (though you might take Aeneas' underworld visit as a vast fantasy, endorsing Lucretius); 6.724–55; 6.847–53; 7.445–74; 8.293–300; 9.630–1; 10.175–8; 12.921–3 notes.

For sympathetic echo of ideas (rather than merely language) often in the mouths of characters other than the narrator, see 1.712–4 (love as disease); 1.723–7 (Iopas' cosmology that does not mention gods); 2.105–44 (human sacrifice); 4.1–2 (love as wound and fire); 6.237–42 (cave of Avernus); 8.306–36 (golden age of Saturn and the evolution of society); 8.349–50 (local atmosphere on the Capitol inspiring religious awe / superstition); 8.370–406 (Venus and Vulcan corresponding to Lucretius' Venus and Mars); 9.671

(origins of thunder); 12.908–12 (the effects of fear) notes. For Virgil sitting on the fence, see 3.570–7; 10.636–42 note.

34. Heinze, *Virgil's Epic Technique*, 475.

35. Lucretius, *On the Nature of Things* 1.271 ff.

36. Ibid., 5.1194 ff.; Lucretius relishes the cataclysm that breaks up the old order (1.77 ff.).

37. For those prepared to tackle the Latin, see Hardie, *Virgil's Aeneid*, 237–40.

38. Lucretius, *On the Nature of Things* 2.112 ff.

39. 4.402 ff., 1.148 ff., 7.718 ff., respectively.

40. Hardie, *Virgil's Aeneid*, 171–2.

41. To be distinguished from Zeno of Sidon, a prominent Epicurean of the first century BCE.

42. A school of philosophy initiated, it is said, by Socrates' pupil Antisthenes – Diogenes Laertius, *Lives of the Eminent Philosophers* 6.10 f.

43. According to the Suda, a tenth-century Byzantine encyclopaedia that preserves much information from more ancient sources.

44. Other than the sources cited, information here is taken from D. Konstan, 'Epicurus', *The Stanford Encyclopedia of Philosophy (Fall 2022 Edition)*, ed. Edward N. Zalta and Uri Nodelman, available online: https://plato.stanford.edu/archives/fall2022/entries/epicurus/ (accessed 7 May 2024); the fount of wisdom here is A. Long and D. Sedley, *The Hellenistic Philosophers*, 2 vols (Cambridge: Cambridge University Press, 1987).

45. See M. Durand, S. Shogry and D. Baltzly, 'Stoicism, *The Stanford Encyclopedia of Philosophy (Spring 2023 Edition)*, ed. Edward N. Zalta and Uri Nodelman, available online: https://plato.stanford.edu/archives/spr2023/entries/stoicism/ (accessed 7 May 2024); the jigsaw of original sources is complex and many of the pieces hard to locate – see Long and Sedley, *The Hellenistic Philosophers*.

46. Diogenes Laertius, *Lives of the Eminent Philosophers* 10.42, 45, Letter to Herodotus; 'galaxy' is defined at 10.88; more on the formation of galaxies at 10.73–4, 10.89, Letter to Pythocles.

47. Aetius (second century BCE) 1.7.33 (not available online).

48. Diogenes Laertius, *Lives of the Eminent Philosophers* 7.134.

49. Eusebius (third–fourth century CE), *Evangelical Preparation* 15.18.2.

50. Diogenes Laertius, *Lives of the Eminent Philosophers* 10.61 f., Letter to Herodotus.

51. Lucretius, *On the Nature of Things* 2.216 ff.

52. Ibid., 5.107.

53. Diogenes Laertius, *Lives of the Eminent Philosophers* 10.63, Letter to Herodotus.

54. Cicero, *Academica* 1.39.

55. Diogenes Laertius, *Lives of the Eminent Philosophers* 7.135–6.

56. Ibid., 7.142, 156.

57. Ibid., 10.46, Letter to Herodotus.

58. For the Stoics, perception was a part of logic / epistemology rather than physics.

59. Cicero, *On the Nature of the Gods* 1.16.43.

60. Diogenes Laertius, *Lives of the Eminent Philosophers* 10.123 f., Letter to Menoeceus.

61. Diogenes Laertius, *Lives of the Eminent Philosophers* 10.134, Letter to Menoeceus.

62. Cicero, *On the Nature of the Gods* 1.24.65 ff.

63. Lucretius, *On the Nature of Things* 5.1168 ff. – though he can also imply that visions of the divine come from outside (6.76 f.).

64. Ibid., 3.18 ff.; cf. Cicero, *On the Nature of the Gods* 1.17.45.

65. Ibid., 7.142.

66. Origen (second century CE), *Against Celsus* 4.14.

67. Anna (4.34 – on the obliviousness of the dead, though she goes on to talk of appeasing the gods); Iarbas (4.205 ff, on divine indifference); Dido (4.379 f., similarly – though she goes on to talk of the mindfulness of the dead, herself in particular); Nisus (9.184 f., on gods as, possibly, the construct of human desires).

68. Diogenes Laertius, *Lives of the Eminent Philosophers* 10.133, Letter to Menoeceus: Epicurus rather confusingly simply asserts that destiny is ridiculous because only some things happen by necessity; others happen by chance or our agency. He does not explain how.

69. Cicero, *On Fate* 22; the Stoic Chrysippus attacked the idea of swerve because it is uncaused; the sceptic Carneades said (*On*

Fate 23) it is sufficient for voluntary action that it be caused not by the movement of atoms but instead by some power in the voluntary agent. Some see a shadow of this idea in Epicurus' *On Nature*, Book 25 – see D. Russell, 'Epicurus and Lucretius on Saving Agency', *Phoenix*, 54, nos 3–4 (2000): 233–4.

70. Diogenes Laertius, *Lives of the Eminent Philosophers* 10.135.

71. Cicero, *On Divination* 1.125: Quintus, putting forward the Stoic position, says,

> Now by Fate I mean ... an orderly succession of causes wherein cause is linked to cause and each cause of itself produces an effect. That is an immortal truth having its source in all eternity. Therefore nothing has happened which was not bound to happen, and, likewise, nothing is going to happen which will not find in nature every efficient cause of its happening.

72. Cicero, *On the Nature of the Gods* 1.15.39:

> Chrysippus ... says that divine power resides in reason, and in the soul and mind of the universe; he calls the world itself a god, and also the all-pervading world-soul, and again the guiding principle of that soul, which operates in the intellect and reason, and the common and all-embracing nature of things; beside this, the fire that I previously termed aether; and also the power of Fate, and the Necessity that governs future events ...

73. Cicero, *On Fate* 41.

74. Cicero, *On Divination* 1.3.6.

75. As Cicero argues in *On Divination* 2.8.20 ff.

76. Diogenes Laertius, *Lives of the Eminent Philosophers* 10.128-32, Letter to Menoeceus.

77. Diogenes Laertius, *Lives of the Eminent Philosophers* 10.128-32, Letter to Menoeceus.

78. Ibid., 7.92.

79. Cicero, *Stoic Paradoxes* 1 and 2; *Tusculan Disputations* 5; Diogenes Laertius, *Lives of the Eminent Philosophers* 7.102 ff.

80. Cicero, *Tusculan Disputations* 5.24.53.

81. So, for example, Cicero, *Stoic Paradoxes* 5.

82. Cicero, *On Ends* 3.6.20 f.

83. Diogenes Laertius, *Lives of the Eminent Philosophers* 10.129, Letter to Menoeceus.

84. Ibid., 10.127, Letter to Menoeceus; cf. 149, one of the Sayings.

85. Philodemus (first century BCE), *On Anger* 27 ff. This is the best Epicurean discussion we have of any emotion – see J. Annas, 'Epicurean Emotions', *Greek, Roman and Byzantine Studies*, 30, no. 2 (1989): 145–64, available online: http://www.chartes.it/images/attachment/Annas,%20Emotions.pdf (accessed 7 May 2024).

86. As set out by Pseudo-Andronicus (first century BCE), *On the Emotions* 1.1 ff. – not available online; Cicero, *Tusculan Disputations* 4.5.11-4.9.22 expounds the Stoic position (especially 4.5.11-4.6.13) – he attributes the fourfold division to Zeno, who uses it to classify 'commotions of the mind repugnant to reason and against nature'. He lists the breakdown of each class, for example, 'Under fear are comprehended sloth, shame, terror, cowardice, fainting, confusion, astonishment.'

87. Anger is one of these – Cicero, *Tusculan Disputations* 4.9.21: 'the passion for punishing someone who seems to have inflicted hurt unjustly'.

88. Cicero, *Tusculan Disputations* 4.7.14.

89. Hume, *Treatise on Human Nature* 2.3.3.4 414–5.

90. Lucretius, *On the Nature of Things* 5.925 ff.; this long excursus appears to have followed Epicurus' *On Nature*; it is a secular version of the progress and decadence Evander charts for Latium at 8.313 ff.

91. Diogenes Laertius, *Lives of the Eminent Philosophers* 10.119.

92. Cicero, *On Ends* 1.20.65 ff.

93. Diogenes Laertius, *Lives of the Eminent Philosophers* 7.121.

94. Cicero, *On Ends* 3.21.70.

95. Virgil passes over in silence what Ascanius and Pallas made of each other.

96. A conveniently accessible summary of Cicero's philosophy can be found in R. Woolf, 'Cicero', *The Stanford Encyclopedia of Philosophy (Spring 2022 Edition)*, ed. Edward N. Zalta, available online: https://plato.

stanford.edu/archives/spr2022/entries/cicero/ (accessed 7 May 2024).

97. Cicero, *On the Nature of the Gods* 1.3.6.

98. The years 54–51 BCE and 45–4 BCE, the first of which came after Caesar, Pompey and Crassus had extended their stranglehold on Roman politics (at the Conference of Lucca, 56 BCE) and the second of which when Caesar had reached the zenith of his personal power and after Cicero's daughter Tullia had died following the birth of her son.

99. In addition to works on rhetoric, not considered here.

100. Cicero, *On the Nature of the Gods* 1.3.7; he says the same thing in greater detail in *On Divination*, 2.2.4 ff.

101. Cicero, *On the Nature of the Gods* 1.3.9.

102. Cicero, *On the Nature of the Gods* 1.3.11; he is called upon to defend the Academic standpoint as an adherent at *Academica* 2.20.64.

103. Cicero, *On Duties* 2.8.

104. Aristotle's dialogues have not survived; Cicero described them as 'a golden stream of eloquence' (*Academica* 2.38.119), so very different from the dry lecture notes that have come down to us.

105. E.g. for Aristotle, *On Duties* 2.56; for the Peripatetics, *On Ends* 3.12.41.

Chapter 6

1. J. Reed, 'Vergil's Roman', in Farrell and Putnam (eds), *A Companion*, 66–79, points out the way in which Virgil 'problematizes' Romanness; although it is made less vague by its juxtaposition to other nationalities (e.g. the 'exotic' army at Actium – the notion of 'exotic' is hardly exact, either), the mixing of origins (Corythus, home of Dardanus, and Troy for Aeneas; Argos and Latium for Turnus) obscures its significance.

2. J. Reed, *Virgil's Gaze: Nation and Poetry in the Aeneid* (Princeton, NJ: Princeton University Press, 2007), argues that in the *Aeneid* the sense of Roman identity is unstable and constantly shifting.

3. See N. Horsfall, 'Virgil and the Poetry of Explanations', *Greece & Rome*, 38, no. 2 (1991): 203–5.

4. DServius says that Ennius and Naevius both made Aeneas grandfather of Romulus – waiving chronology. See *Introduction* – 3.2.2 Aeneas between the *Iliad* and the *Aeneid*: The Aeneas legend.

5. See, for example, 7.733–43 on the Teutons; the mustering Latins are compared to the Nile and Ganges at 9.30 ff.; some leaders are reallocated from their normal ethnic allegiance to a new one – Messapus from the Messapians to the Faliscans (7.691–705 note); Halaesus from the Faliscans and Oebalus from Sparta both to the Campanians (7.723–32, 7.733–43 notes, respectively); Turnus' father Daunus has nothing to do with the Daunians (8.146 note).

6. This would not be the case in Greek colonies (*ktiseis*), where loyalty and ties to the mother-city trumped all others – both the observance and the breach of this can be seen in the relationship between Epidamnus, its mother-city, Corcyra, and Corcyra's mother-city, Corinth; Epidamnus in its travails of 433 BCE appealed to Corcyra but received help from Corinth, upset that Corcyra had been neglecting it (Thucydides, *History of the Peloponnesian War* 1.24 f.).

7. Aeneas mentions to Evander that Dardanus came from elsewhere to Troy (8.134).

8. There are other Greek Italians – Tiburtus and his brothers are Argive (7.672), Halaesus is associated with Agamemnon (7.723) and Virbius is the son of Hippolytus (7.761).

9. An example of the social mobility that followed is Publius Ventidius who, taken prisoner during the Social Wars, walked with his mother in the triumph of Pompeius Strabo of 89 BCE; he later secured the patronage of Caesar, rising to become a general and, uniquely, himself to celebrate a triumph over the Parthians, in 38 BCE (Aulus Gellius, Attic Nights 15.4; Plutarch, *Life of Antony* 34.5).

10. Gaul illustrates the process: Caesar had completed the conquest of Gaul (58–*c.* 50 BCE) but the territory gained only became a Roman province under Augustus in 27 BCE; he subdivided that territory into three (Gallia

Aquitania, Belgica and Lugdunensis) in 22 BCE; he also granted certain colonies in Gaul citizenship (under the Italic law, *ius Italicum*) – Lugdunum (Lyon), Forum Julii (Fréjus) and Narbo (Narbonne); Claudius, who was born at Lugdunum, in 48 CE secured the right of wealthy inhabitants from the three more recent provinces to enter the senate; Gauls, along with all free-born in the Roman Empire, were fully enfranchised in 212 CE under an edict of the emperor Caracalla, likewise born in Lugdunum.

11. As Aeneas promises the Latins at 12.189 ff.

12. All three visions chart the path from Romulus (1.292; 6.778; 8.631 f., also 8.638 and 8.654) to civil war (suggested at 1.291; dreaded at 6.828; evoked at 8.675 ff., though as an east–west conflict) to peace under Augustus (1.293 ff.; 6.791 ff.; 8.714 ff.).

13. So, too, Apollo, 3.97 f.; Faunus, 7.98 ff. and 7.256 f.

14. This is far more than the prophecy of a prosperous foundation; it has been compared to the Hebrew Bible narrative in which 'a national hero leads his people back to a former homeland with much trouble from the indigenes, stimulated by the divine injunction to kindle a light unto the nations' (Reed, 'Vergil's Roman', 74).

15. See 1.254–96, 6.756–853, 8.626–728 notes; see also J. Zetzel, 'Rome and Its Traditions', in Mac Góráin and Martindale (eds), *The Cambridge Companion*, 272–7.

16. In Hardie, *Virgil's* Aeneid, 362–6.

17. Ovid, *Fasti* 2.683 f.

18. The Latin puns on *urbs* (city) and *orbis* (world), as in the Papal address *urbi et orbi*.

19. For *familia*, see R. Saller, '"Familia, Domus", and the Roman Conception of the Family', Phoenix, 38, 4 (1984): 337–42; for *gens*, see Cicero, *Topics* 6.29, defining (after the jurist Scaevola) it as: (1) bearing the same name, (2) born of free citizen parents, (3) not numbering an ex-slave in their ancestry and (4) not deprived of any of their legal rights.

20. So Ulpian (second/third century CE) in the great sixth-century legal compendium the *Digest*, 50.16.195.1–4, which shows how *familia* might include slaves; on women as *pater familias*, and on the asymmetry with the term *mater familias*, see R. Saller, 'Pater Familias, Mater Familias, and the Gendered Semantics of the Roman Household', *Classical Philology*, 94, no. 2 (1999): 187.

21. In the prologue to Plautus' *Crock of Gold* (ll. 15 ff.) the Lar complains of neglect by first the father and then, after his death, the son of the house.

22. Whether she did or did not change her name depended on the form of marriage she had undergone: so-called *cum/in manu* marriage made her part of her husband's *familia*, but in late Republican times most marriages were not of this type.

23. When adopted by Caesar, Augustus became Gaius Julius Caesar Octavianus (having been Gaius Octavius before). The process of adopting an adult is described in brief by Aulus Gellius (*Attic Nights* 5.19.8 f.) and includes the candidate submitting to the adopting father's right of life and death over him.

24. Table IV of the Twelve Tables, the oldest set of Roman laws, promulgated in 449 BCE (Livy, *From the City's Foundation* 3.57.10).

25. *Digest* 48.5.23 – an extract, possibly paraphrased, from the original; the severity of the law on adultery might have been an attempt to recriminalize what had become commonplace (6.3.1 below) and to restore old values.

26. Cicero, *Against Piso* 3.6.

27. After the Battle of Munda, 45 BCE – Suetonius, *Life of Julius Caesar* 85; Dio Cassius, *Roman History* 44.4.4.

28. *Res Gestae* 35.1.

29. Seneca, *On Benefits* 3.33.4.

30. Horace, *Odes* 3.6.46 ff., 'Our father's generation, worse than their fathers, has borne us, who are still baser, and will soon bring forth progeny who are baser again.'

31. In the Julian laws on the marriage of the orders (18 BCE) and on adultery (17 BCE), already mentioned, and the *Lex Papia Poppaea*, of 9 CE, which instituted a form of child benefit (*ius liberorum*), in the form of privileges rather than subsidy; Augustus was appointed 'supervisor of laws and morals' in 19, 18 and 11 BCE (*Res Gestae* 6.1), after Virgil's death, but the need for action was visible before it.

32. What are portrayed as happy marriages between Aeneas and Creusa, and between Sychaeus and Dido, are truncated; for a particularly dim view of marriage in the *Aeneid*, see E. Fantham, H. Foley, N. Kampen, S. Pomeroy and H. Shapiro, *Women in the Classical World* (New York and Oxford: Oxford University Press, 1994), 297–9.

33. A Roman man's name was made up of *praenomen*, *nomen* and *cognomen*, of which the *nomen* represented the *gens*: Gaius Julius Caesar belonged to the Julii, the Julian *gens*.

34. Table V of the Twelve Tables.

35. On this section, see R. Lyne, *The Latin Love Poets from Catullus to Horace* (Oxford: Clarendon Press, 1980), chapter 1, 'Traditional Attitudes to Love: The Moral and Social Background' (a male perspective); S. Pomeroy, *Goddesses, Whores, Wives and Slaves* (London: Pimlico, 1995), chapter 8, 'The Roman Matron'; Fantham et al., *Women in the Classical World*, chapter 10: 'The "New Woman": Representation and Reality', and chapter 11: 'Women, Family and Sexuality in the Age of Augustus and the Julio-Claudians', 294–306 and 322–7.

36. Valerius Maximus, *Memorable Deeds and Sayings* 6.7.2.

37. Eulogy of Turia (*Laudatio Turiae*), left column 30 (Wistrand), ll. 35 ff. in the Latin. A shorter eulogy, of one Murdia, survives from about the same period – she was twice married, but the eulogy was delivered by one of her sons. He says: 'the funerary speech for all good women is wont to be simple and similar, because their natural qualities preserved under their own charge do not require variations of phraseology … in <u>modesty, honesty, chastity, obedience, wool-working, diligence and trustworthiness</u> she was the equal and model of other upstanding women, nor did she fall behind any in *virtus*.' The underlined qualities are comparable to Turia's; 'affection' does not feature.

38. Appian, *Civil War* 1.3.20; Plutarch, *Life of Romulus* 27.4 shows that speculation about the cause of his death was rife.

39. Plutarch, *Life of Tiberius Gracchus* 1.4 f.; *Life of Gaius Gracchus* 4.2 ff.

40. How? In addition to fatherly authority, women were also placed under the watchful eye of a guardian (Ulpian, *Rules* 11.1), unless exempted by bearing three children, or four if a freedwoman (*Rules* 11.28a). Ovid suggests that absence on military service was the cause:

> Maybe in the days when Tatius ruled, the grubby Sabine women refused to be taken by more than one man; now Mars puts men through their paces in foreign wars and Venus reigns in the city of her Aeneas. The lovely ladies play, and the only chaste ones are those nobody has propositioned; or, if rustic simplicity doesn't forestall her, she asks for herself.
>
> (*Amores* 1.8.38 ff.)

But the guardians / husbands could apparently be present and complicit – Horace (*Odes* 3.6.25 ff.) imagines a dinner party given by a host with a young wife: 'Soon she's pursuing young philanderers over her husband's wine-cups … she rises from her place to order and openly – her husband can't be unaware.'

41. Sallust, *Catiline* 25.

42. It recoiled upon him: his daughter Julia, married first to Marcellus (6.854–92 note) without issue, then to Agrippa, by whom she had five children, and lastly to Tiberius (and offered to others, too – Suetonius, *Life of Augustus* 63.2), used to boast that she knew her children were legitimate because she only took a lover when already pregnant – 'I never put a passenger on board unless the ship is full' (Macrobius, *Saturnalia* 2.5.9). Her marriage to Tiberius, was unhappy from the start; they separated, though did not divorce, after less than six years (before 6 BCE). When Julia, in 2 BCE, was drunk and disorderly (and worse) in the Forum, it fell to the fatherly authority of Augustus to discipline her. He banished her, according to his own law, to the island of Pandateria (Dio Cassius, *Roman History* 55.10.12 ff.); he subsequently (8 CE) banished his granddaughter, also Julia, for the same alleged reasons, to the island of Trimerus (Tacitus, *Annals* 4.71.1).

43. Aulus Gellius (*Attic Nights* 10.23.5) quotes Cato's words: 'If you should take your wife in adultery, you may with impunity put her to death without a trial; but if you should commit adultery or indecency, she must not

presume to lay a finger on you, nor does the law allow it.' Seneca (*Epistle* 94.26) is much fairer – if the wife cannot have an adulterer, the husband cannot take a mistress.

44. Cicero makes it all part of youth's romps – *In Defence of Caelius* 28; he is careful to stipulate that no reputations should be damaged in the process. He has in mind brief liaisons with unmarried women (though those of his own class tended to be married off young) and most likely the *demi-monde* (actresses, courtesans), freedwomen or slaves; since Clodia, the object of Cicero's client Caelius' passion, was married, Caelius was on sticky ground; so Cicero makes sure she had no (good) reputation to lose.

45. The examples of such marriages are ubiquitous – Ovid (*Tristia* 4.10.69 f.) also illustrates the ease of divorce: 'When I was just a boy I was made to marry a good-for-nothing wife I didn't respect – it didn't last long.' Pompey's union with Caesar's sister Julia, some thirty years younger than him, is remarkable for the love he showed her (Plutarch, *Life of Pompey* 48.5) – and the love she showed him was 'notorious' (53.2). The hungry Antony (Cicero guys his infatuation with a boy and with the actress Cytheris in *Philippics* 2.44 and 2.58) was married four times; to a freedwoman, then Antonia Hybrida whom he threw out for adultery, then to Fulvia who died in 40 BCE, then to Octavian's sister Octavia, whom he cuckolded for Cleopatra. The sources unsurprisingly idealize Octavia – Plutarch paints her as virtuous and long-suffering (*Life of Antony* 53-7); she brought up all of Antony's surviving children by his other wives.

46. Though their like inhabits the love elegy of Tibullus and Propertius, who at one point protests of Cynthia, 'No ancient beauty had a house as full of men as yours' (*Elegies* 2.6.1).

47. Cicero, *In Defence of Caelius* 38.

48. These make a fascinating chronicle of an affair from which, if taken at face value, Catullus had much higher expectations than Lesbia – he claims it as eternal because she says so (poem 109), a sort of marriage (poem 68.70 ff., where she enters like a bride crossing the threshold); and when she rejects him he is wounded and reviles her (poem 58). Why does Catullus exalt this liaison as he does, and why do other elegists so submit themselves to their fickle loves (e.g. Propertius, *Elegies* 4.8.71 f.)? It is a curious reversal – Fantham et al., *Women in the Classical World*, chapter 10, 289, speculates on the possible reasons for it.

49. On Sulpicia, see Fantham et al., *Women in the Classical World*, 323–6; it is possible that these poems were ghost-written by a man, but most scholars accept them as by a woman – and either way the impact depends on 'Sulpicia's' feelings being no different from a man's.

50. Sulpicia, *Poems* 1.1 f.

51. Plutarch, *Life of Antony* 10.3; Dio Cassius gives an example of what Plutarch claims at *Roman Histories* 48.4.1 ff.; Fulvia was the first mortal woman to be portrayed on a coin (examples can be found in the Palazzo Massimo alle Terme collection), albeit garbed in the wings of Victory.

52. This is what Asconius (first century CE) claims in his summary of Cicero's defence speech of Milo (section 32).

53. Velleius Paterculus, *Roman History* 2.74.2 f.

54. Dio Cassius, *Roman History* 47.8.4.

55. Typology in the sense from biblical exegesis, where a subsequent event (or person) is seen to fulfil a past prophecy – so here the Roman women of Virgil's own day would be seen as prefigured by types in the *Aeneid*.

56. Livy, *From the City's Foundation* 34.7.8.

57. Servius refused to be impressed by Camilla; his note on 7.803, Camilla's first appearance, runs: 'Wisely [the poet] moves on to women after full commemoration of the men … Clearly there is already the hint of an unlucky outcome in the fact that among these very beginnings even women are mobilised under arms.' G. Arrigoni, *Camilla, amazzone e sacerdotessa di Diana* (Milano: Cisalpino-Goliardica, 1982), 628 (not available in English), is fairer: Camilla from her first appearance is portrayed as 'an ironic antithesis to the Roman lady, especially the Augustan version, idealised as weaver and domestic Minerva'.

58. Heinze curiously endorses Mercury despite the obvious counterexamples, *Virgil's Epic Technique*, 366–9.

59. E. Oliensis, 'Sons and Lovers: Sexuality and Gender in Virgil's Poetry', in Mac Góráin and Martindale (eds), *The Cambridge Companion*, 435. Augustus is said in 17 BCE to have quoted Quintus Caecilius Metellus Macedonicus, censor in 131 BCE, to the Senate in support of his own legislation encouraging marriage and childbearing: 'If we could survive without a wife, citizens of Rome, all of us would do without nuisance; but since nature has so decreed that we cannot manage comfortably with them, nor live in any way without them, we must plan for our lasting preservation rather than for our temporary pleasure' (Livy, *Periochae* (Summaries) 59.8–9).

60. A. Keith, *Engendering Rome: Women in Latin Epic* (Cambridge: Cambridge University Press, 2000), 75.

61. Ibid., 78.

62. See S. Nugent, 'The Women of the *Aeneid*: Vanishing Bodies, Lingering Voices', in C. Perkell (ed.), *Vergil's* Aeneid: *An Interpretive Guide* (Norman, OK: University of Oklahoma Press, 1999), 251–70.

63. Oliensis, 'Sons and Lovers', 435.

64. Edgar Allan Poe, 'The Philosophy of Composition', *Graham's American Monthly Magazine of Literature and Art* (April 1946): 163; Poe continues that a bereaved lover is the most suited to the topic – and in Dido and Camilla, Virgil appears fascinated by his own creations.

65. Keith, *Engendering Rome*, 113–14.

66. Ibid., 14, 29.

67. Quintilian, *Rhetorical Education* 1.8.2.

68. Servius, note to 5.5; cf. 11.782 note.

69. E. Giusti and V. Rimell, 'Vergil and the Feminine', *Vergilius*, 67 (2021): 14.

70. Cicero, *On the Nature of the Gods* 2.3.8, glosses *religio* as 'attending to (the worship of) the gods'; Polybius, *Histories* 6.56, remarks, 'I conceive that what in other nations is looked upon as a reproach, I mean a scrupulous fear of the gods, is the very thing which keeps the Roman commonwealth together.'

71. Cicero, *On Divination* 2.4.10 f.

72. Cicero's Epicurean advocate caricatures this in *On the Nature of the Gods* 3.21.53 ff.

73. Varro, in the Divine Affairs section of his *Antiquities of Human and Divine Matters*, as reported by Augustine of Hippo (*City of God* 6.5.1 f.), divides divinity into distinct theologies – the mythical (as in the poets), the physical (as in philosophers) and the civic (as in state religion). Augustine attributes this split to Q. Mucius Scaevola, *pontifex maximus* from 89–82 BCE, who held that there are three views of the gods – one of the poets, another of philosophers and another again of the city authorities (*City of God* 4.27).

74. For example, the basic ambiguity between 'belief in their existence' and 'trust in their benevolence'; see Feeney, *The Gods in Epic*, 171–2.

75. Cicero, *On the Nature of the Gods* 1.1.2.

76. Cicero, *On the Nature of the Gods* 1.6.14.

77. Cicero, *On Divination* 2.12.28; specifically on augury, he says the same (2.33.70): 'Out of respect for the opinion of the masses and because of the great service to the State we maintain the augural practices, discipline, religious rites and laws, as well as the authority of the augural college.'

78. Cicero, *On the Responses of Soothsayers* 19.

79. For example, Cicero, *Philippics* 2.32.79 reports how Antony used his powers as augur to obstruct a consular election; Dionysius of Halicarnassus, *Roman Antiquities* 2.72.4 speaks of the important role the Fetial priests played in obtaining a successful outcome to war.

80. The four main colleges in Virgil's day were: (1) 16 pontiffs (including the Vestal virgins), (2) 16 augurs, (3) 7 *epulones*, who organized the feasts at festivals and games and (4) The *quindecimviri sacris faciundis* ('15 men in charge of performing rites') responsible for the Sibylline books and the worship of foreign deities. Over them all was the chief priest (*pontifex maximus*). There were other colleges of priests also – the *flamens* were dedicated to individual deities; their most important member was the *flamen Dialis* (Jupiter's man – to him various privileges were accorded, such as a seat in the senate,

but on him also strict rules were imposed – Aulus Gellius, *Attic Nights* 10.15); the Salii, dedicated to Mars (8.280–305 note); the Fetial priests, devoted to Jupiter, who advised the senate on international treaties or declarations of war; and the Arval brethren, a body revived by Augustus that made offerings to a goddess of fertility.

81. Velleius Paterculus, *Roman History* 2.43.1; Suetonius, *Life of Julius Caesar* 1.1, 13.1.

82. Cicero, *On His House* 1.1.

83. A mysterious group established by Titus Tatius (8.635–8 note) 'to retain the rites of the Sabines' (Tacitus, *Annals* 1.54).

84. Suetonius, *Life of Augustus* 31.4, *Res Gestae* 7.3; the Secular Games were games held every *saeculum*, or maximum span of human life (100 / 110 years); the Compitalia was a festival in honour of the Lares of the crossroads (see *Introduction* – 4.5.5 Gods local, domestic and minor).

85. *Res Gestae* 7.3; he had been elected a pontiff, augur and *quindecimvir* all before he was thirty.

86. Ibid., 10.2.

87. Macrobius, *Saturnalia* 3 is largely an encomium of Virgil's expertise on matters or religious ritual.

88. This section owes much to V. Panoussi, 'Aeneas' Sacral Authority', in Farrell and Putnam (eds), *A Companion*, 52–65.

89. Respectively, the pontiffs, augurs, *epulones*, *quindecimviri* and Fetial priests.

90. Altars always stood in the open air, partly because of the messiness of sacrifice but also for the spectacle: temples were dark and confined spaces, entered only by priests.

91. As reflected in, e.g., Livy, *From the City's Foundation* 4.7.3 – three tribunes resigned the consular powers to which they had been elected, 'because Caius Curtius, who had presided at the election, had not selected his tent with due regard to ceremony'. The requirements were exacting, so restarts were common – Livy has Camillus remark (5.52.9), 'Call to mind, I pray you, how often ceremonies are repeated, because through negligence or accident some detail of the ancestral ritual has been omitted.'

92. One religious formula applied in sacrifices for fruitfulness was *do ut des* – 'I give so you will give.'

93. Pliny the Elder, *Natural History* 28.3.10 f.

94. A prayer, vow, oracular consultation, burial, foundation of a city, truce, expiation, marriage – all are (or can be) occasions of sacrifice.

95. Ovid, *Fasti* 2.533 ff.

96. Curses (*defixiones* or *devotiones*, but not the *devotio* of 6.824–5 note) scratched into sheet lead, rolled up and sometimes pierced with a nail or nails, have been found all over the Roman Empire. Placed underground in graves, wells or springs, they are suitably blood-curdling – for examples, see Warrior, *Roman Religion*, 99–103. Betting men (or women) were particularly prone to submit them: 'I call on you, demon, whoever you are, and ask that from this hour, from this day, from this moment, you torture and kill the horses of the Green and White teams, and that you kill and crush the drivers Clarus, Felix, Primulus and Romanus, and that you leave not a breath in their bodies' (ILS (= 'Selected Latin Inscriptions') 8753).

97. Ovid, *Art of Love* 2.106 f.

98. Horace, *Epodes* 5.15 ff.

99. As listed by Cicero, *On Divination* 1.6.12.

100. The skill of interpreting dissected victims was Etruscan; experts in the art were regularly summoned from Etruria and were established at Rome before the end of the third century BCE (Livy, *From the City's Foundation* 27.37.6; Cicero, *On Divination* 1.2.3) but they remained solo operators, consulted by senate and private citizens alike, until the emperor Claudius formed them into a college in 47 CE (Tacitus, *Annals* 11.15). Unlike priests, they were paid for their services.

101. At the time *decemviri* (there were 10); their number was later increased to 15 (*quindecimviri*), though when is unknown.

102. Livy, *From the City's Foundation* 22.1.8 ff.

103. Ibid., 22.9.7. A notorious example of disdaining the auspices was the jest of Publius Claudius Pulcher in 249 BCE, during the First Punic War: when he heard that the sacred chickens had refused food,

he ordered them to be thrown into the sea with the words, 'If they won't eat, then let them drink' (Cicero, *On the Nature of the Gods* 2.3.7; Valerius Maximums, *Memorable Deeds and Sayings* 4.3). He promptly lost the sea battle of Drepana.

104. Cicero, *On Divination* 1.2.3.

105. 'Astrologers who haunt the circus grounds' (as Ennius called them – Cicero, *On Divination* 1.58.132) seem to have occupied a hinterland between prophecy and magic. Valerius Maximus (*Memorable Deeds and Sayings* 1.3.3) reports that, in 139 BCE, the praetor C. Cornelius Hispallus 'by edict commanded the Chaldeans to depart out of Italy, who by their false interpretations of the stars cast a profitable mist before the eyes of shallow and foolish characters.' Tacitus (*Histories* 1.22) was justified, however, when he classified astrologers as 'a breed of men untrustworthy for the powerful and deceitful for the ambitious, a breed that will always be both forbidden and retained in our state.' Augustus, says Suetonius (*Life of Augustus* 94.12), consulted an astrologer in the company of Agrippa, who asked first and received such a glowing forecast that Augustus himself hesitated to ask in his turn; when he did he was so pleased that he published his horoscope and minted silver coin with Capricorn on the reverse (e.g. a denarius in the British Museum 1865,0809.3); at the same time, according to Dio Cassius (*Roman History* 56.25.5 f.) he banned astrological predictions regarding death or to those who were alone. Presumably he wanted to make manipulation harder for those who wanted to follow his example.

106. Cicero, *On Divination* 2.24.52 f.

107. J. O'Hara, *Death and the Optimistic Prophecy in Vergil's* Aeneid (Princeton, NJ: Princeton University Press, 1990), 3–4; see, in reply to many of the arguments, the review by A. Schiesaro, 'Death and the Optimistic Prophecy in Vergil's Aeneid', review, *Classical Philology*, 88, no. 3 (1993): 258 ff.

108. Questions as open-ended as Venus' **'What end do you set to their labours'** / . . . *ordeals?'* (1.241), and answers as wide-ranging as Jupiter's, or visions as broad as that of future Romans in the underworld

and future conflicts on the shield, are not the norm. Aeneas never asks about his long-term prospects; Venus does not tell him. Cicero (*On Divination* 2.9.22 f.) suggests that nobody wants to know their future misfortunes in full in case the foreboding that resulted would taint, or significantly alter, the passage of their lives.

109. If the source is a god – hence Aeneas' faith in Apollo (6.343); a human can err (*Tolumnius* 12.263 f.), or use inaccurate prophecy to his own advantage: Odysseus, already on Ithaca and in disguise, predicts his own return to distract from himself (*Od.* 18.143 ff., 20.226 ff.).

110. Homer, *Od.* 11.602 ff. (sometimes considered a late addition), and Hesiod, *Theogony* 950 ff.; the story of Heracles' death is told in Sophocles' *Trachiniae*, though it stops short of the apotheosis.

111. Plutarch, *Life of Alexander* 28; the legends of Alexander's birth, which he presumably encouraged, are also recounted by Plutarch (*Life of Alexander* 2, 3), as is that of his encounter with the priest of Zeus Ammon (*Life of Alexander* 27.8 ff.).

112. Suetonius, *Life of Caesar* 76.1 ff.

113. Ibid., 88; Cicero did not approve, especially because Antony became Caesar's priest (*Philippic* 2.110); the ways in which this new god was revered, largely defined by the triumvirate, are listed by Dio Cassius, *Roman History* 47.18.4 ff.

114. Livy, *From the City's Foundation* 1.16.

115. Several designs of denarii of Octavian were minted that feature Venus, on the obverse or reverse, and the inscription CAESAR DIVI F(ILIUS).

116. *Eclogue* 1.6 ff.; some speculate (but this is the only evidence) that Virgil's land had been confiscated but then returned to him by the triumvirate; Aelius Donatus' *Life of Virgil* 61 ff. embroiders colourfully.

117. Dio Cassius, *Roman History* 51.20.1.

118. Dio Cassius, *Roman History* 51.20.7 f.; Suetonius, *Life of Augustus* 52, adds that he only allowed dedications to himself and Rome in combination (as at the Maison Carrée, Nîmes); nevertheless, Horace, *Epistles* 2.1.15 ff., declares hyperbolically,

'We … load you while here with timely honours, set up altars, to swear our oaths at, by your godhead, acknowledging none such has risen or will arise.'

119. Horace, *Odes* 4.5.33 ff.; more famously, the poet looks forward to a rosy-lipped Augustus drinking nectar with Hercules and Pollux (*Odes*, 3.3.11 f.).

120. Ovid, *Fasti* 4.950 ff.

121. Tacitus, *Annals* 1.10 – Tacitus quotes Augustus' detractors accusing him of stealing worship from the gods by his temples and priesthoods; the *Res Gestae* are of 'deified Augustus'.

122. Suetonius, *Life of Claudius* 11.2.

123. See M. Willcock, 'Battle Scenes in the *Aeneid*', *Proceedings of the Cambridge Philological Society*, 209 (1983): 87–99; and his, 'Virgilian Battle Scenes', a review of *Forme e significati della narrazione bellica nell' epos virgiliano. I cataloghi degli uccisi e le morti minori dell'Eneide* by P. Mazzocchini, *Classical Review*, 52, no. 1 (2002): 61–3; for Homeric battle scenes, see Jones, *Homer's* Iliad, 39–43.

124. Calculated by H. van Wees as 5,500 of 15,000 lines – cited in Jones, *Homer's* Iliad, 39.

125. The night raid of Nisus and Euryalus in Book IX; the assembly of the gods and Etruscan catalogue in Book X; the burial of the dead and assembly of the Latins in Book XI; and the ceremonial of the truce in Book XII. (The combat scenes of Book II do not make up this difference.)

126. F. Sandbach, 'Anti-Antiquarianism in the *Aeneid*', *Proceedings of the Virgil Society*, (1965–6), reprinted in Harrison (ed.), *Oxford Readings in Virgil's* Aeneid, 455–60.

127. 2.440–4, 9.170, 9.503–24 notes; 12.673 ff.

128. *Il.* 9.588 f., the siege of Calydon.

129. Ibid., 15.355 ff.

130. There are five, possibly six, instances of combat from a chariot in the *Iliad*: 5.13, 8.118 ff., 11.532, 15.386, 16.377 ff. and possibly 16.809.

131. The occasional Trojan does appear as well – Orsilochus and Butes (11.690) and, spectacularly, Chloreus (11.768).

132. It gains significance because it was prepared for in the *lusus Troiae* at the end of the games in Book V (5.545 ff.), and because Pallas cannot use his horsemen in Book X, nor does Camilla participate in it.

133. 'like a tower', *Il.* 7.219.

134. *Il.* 15.676 ff.

135. So Agamemnon, *Il.* 11.43.

136. Pallas' appearance in a dried-up gully (10.362 ff.) is a rare allusion to the geography, but he is not there by design.

137. On archery as less estimable, see 9.569–76 note, **Asilas** – but Ascanius distinguishes himself with the bow, 9.621 ff.

138. *Il.* 5.302 ff.

139. The scenes of the injured Mezentius recouping his strength (10.833 ff.) and of Aeneas being treated by Iapyx, the field doctor (12.383 ff.), must have been replicated any number of times in reality.

140. Homer in the *Iliad* uses this technique primarily for Menelaus (e.g. 4.127) and Patroclus (16.692).

141. Respectively, *Iliad* Book 5; 11.91 ff.; 20.158 ff., up to 22.404, the duel with and defeat of Hector.

142. *Il.* 13.361 ff.; 16.284 ff., respectively; Patroclus' onslaught is not such a catalogue of victims as normal for an *aristeia*; he influences the whole battlefield. The spacing of *aristeiai* in the *Iliad* is careful: Diomedes in Book 5 enjoys the greatest success before Achilles, and the intervening aristeiai form a catenary up to Achilles' climax.

143. *Il.* 4.446 ff.

144. *Il.* 5.1 ff.

145. *Il.* 5.9 ff.

146. For example, at *Il.* 8.273 ff.

147. Willcock, 'Battle Scenes', 89.

148. Heinze, *Virgil's Epic Technique*, 194.

Chapter 7

1. The word 'structure' is used here in a non-technical sense, i.e. without structuralist connotations, for the relationship between

books and the relationship between parts within a book.

2. Heinze, *Virgil's Epic Technique*, 458.

3. See G. Duckworth, 'The *Aeneid* as a Trilogy', *Transactions and Proceedings of the American Philological Association*, 88 (1957): 2, citing Conway (1928) and, for the refinement, Stadler (1942).

4. So Aelius Donatus, *Life of Virgil* 21, 'Last of all he began the *Aeneid*, a varied and complicated theme, and as it were a mirror of both the poems of Homer'; and Macrobius, *Saturnalia* 5.2.6, 'And surely the *Aeneid* itself borrowed for its own purposes first the wanderings from the *Odyssey* and then the battles from the *Iliad*?'

5. For example, Otis, *Virgil*, 217.

6. F. Cairns, *Virgil's Augustan Epic* (Cambridge: Cambridge University Press, 1989), chapter 8, argues for the *Odyssey* as a complete structural model for the *Aeneid*.

7. For others, see 1.441–93 (the scenes on Juno's temple) and 2.453–68 notes (the reminiscence of Hector and Andromache).

8. G. Duckworth, 'The Architecture of the *Aeneid*', *American Journal of Philology*, 75, no. 1 (1954): 1–15, from which extracts are reprinted in Quinn, *Why Vergil?*, 148–54; he credits Conway (1928) with the basic matching pattern.

9. Pöschl, *The Art of Vergil*, 171–2.

10. Duckworth, 'The *Aeneid* as a Trilogy', 1–10; the table is adapted from his.

11. Book V – the games from *Iliad* Book 23; Book VI – the underworld from *Odyssey* Book 11; Book VII – the catalogue from *Iliad* Book 2; and Book VIII – the shield from *Iliad* Book 18.

12. Duckworth, 'The *Aeneid* as a Trilogy', 9.

13. Thus when Otis says, of Book XI, 'the best clue to its meaning is its structure' (*Virgil*, 361), his claim is hard to understand: since the structure is in itself a perceived principle of arrangement, there is a risk of a circular argument, of defining or explaining the structure in such a way that it conforms to a previous interpretation of the text.

14. Pöschl sees it as 'the harmonious blending of opposites', *The Art of Vergil*, 173.

15. G. Duckworth, 'Tripartite Structure in the *Aeneid*', *Vergilius*, 7 (1961): 2–11; he has developed from this a theory that Virgil, who Donatus tells us (*Life of Virgil* 15) was in youth a keen mathematician, incorporated the golden mean ratio into the proportions of the *Aeneid*, see Duckworth, 'Mathematical Symmetry in Vergil's *Aeneid*', *Transactions and Proceedings of the American Philological Association*, 91 (1960): 184–220.

16. A brief but concentrated example is Nestor's speech at *Il.* 7.132 ff.: 'I would I were young again' – Ereuthalion – Areithous' armour – Maceman – Lycurgus killing Areithous – Maceman – Areithous' armour – Ereuthalion – 'I would I were young again,' in some 28 lines.

17. For example, *Il.* 2.110.

18. Ibid., 6.445 f.

19. Ibid., 7.89 ff.

20. Ibid., 9.412 ff.

21. *Od.* 5.171, 21.274.

22. Ibid., 9.19 f.

23. See R. Williams, *Aeneas and the Roman Hero* (London: Bristol Classical Press, 1973), 28–31.

24. So the opening of David Copperfield: 'Whether I shall turn out to be the hero of my own life, or whether that station will be held by anybody else, these pages must show.'

25. As *Vanity Fair* parodied in its subtitle, *A Novel without a Hero*.

26. D. Feeney, 'Epic Hero and Epic Fable', *Comparative Literature*, 38, 2 (1986): 138–9, 143–4; the article traces the transition from the ancient to the modern concept of 'hero'.

27. This Greek word refers to the chief actor, who might play more than one part in a drama.

28. Aristotle, *Poetics* 1451a.

29. DServius, note to 1.1.

30. J. Dryden, 'A Parallel betwixt Painting and Poetry', Preface to *De Arte Graphica: The Art of Painting, by C.A. Du Fresnoy with Remarks*, trans. J. Dryden (London: Printed by J. Heptinstall for W. Rogers, 1695).

31. Plato, *Hippias Minor* 363b.

32. Livy, *From the City's Foundation* 1 Preface, 9.

33. What follows is largely drawn from I. de Jong, *Narratology and Classics: A Practical Guide* (Oxford: Oxford University Press, 2014).

34. The term was coined in 1969 by Tzvetan Todorov in his *Grammaire du Décameron*.

35. T. Eagleton, *Literary Theory: An Introduction* (Oxford: Blackwell, 1983), 90–2.

36. I. de Jong, *A Narratological Commentary on the* Odyssey (Cambridge: Cambridge University Press, 2001).

37. This commentary is not scrupulous in distinguishing 'Virgil' from 'the narrator' – mainly to avoid the resulting ponderousness.

38. The rhetorical term for this is *apostrophe*, a turning aside from an audience to an individual; the narratological term for this is *metalepsis*, when the narrator enters the world of the characters.

39. Thus it is possible to take 'the man and the weapons' of the first line to be Augustus (so D. Fowler, 'Virgilian Narrative: Storytelling', in Mac Góráin and Martindale (eds), *The Cambridge Companion*, 410).

40. Odysseus in the *Odyssey* can be convicted of unreliability even when telling his own story: notoriously he claims he fell asleep before his crew opened the sack of winds from Aeolus, yet he records their conversation (*Od.* 10.31 ff.).

41. The narratological term is *analepsis*.

42. This is how Genette poses the problem – in *Narrative Discourse: An Essay in Method* (1972), trans. J. Lewin (New York: Cornell University Press, 1980), 186.

43. Horsfall (ed.), *A Companion*, 110; for Conte, this elusiveness prevents the text from being tagged with any ideological label (G. Conte, *The Rhetoric of Imitation: Genre and Poetic Imitation in Virgil and Other Latin Poets*, ed. Charles Segal (Ithaca, NY, and London: Cornell University Press, 1986), 182–3).

44. This is what Fowler, quoting Conte, contends, see D. Fowler, 'Deviant Focalisation in Virgil's *Aeneid*', *Proceedings of the Cambridge Philological Society*, 36 (1990): 51 ('the moral evasion that the transfer of focalisation embodies'), 58.

45. Servius, note on 1.23: Juno recalls the **war … fought long since / *old campaign*** at Troy; Servius says the Latin, 'old war', could mean 'war of long ago' from Virgil's point of view, or 'long-lasting war' from Juno's; the operative point of view is either the speaker's, or if there is no speaker, the narrator's (which it is, he says, in this case). He gives a second example that goes against what he has just said: when the Tyrians admire (in speech or at least thought) the Trojan gifts (1.709 f.), and at the same time admire the **glowing face of the god**, this is partly the narrator interpolating himself, since the Tyrians do not know that Cupid is impersonating Ascanius. Note the 'partly'.

46. Heinze, *Virgil's Epic Technique*, 362–3, cf. 370–3 and, on the games, 169.

47. Otis, *Virgil*, 49, 'The Subjective Style' is at 41–96.

48. Such is the view taken of Otis by A. La Penna in, 'Sul cosidetto stile soggetivo e sul cosidetto simbolismo di Virgilio', *Dialoghi Archeologia*, 1 (1967): 220–44, quoted in Fowler, 'Deviant Focalisation', 55.

49. This is not uncommon in normal conversation, see Fowler, 'Deviant Focalisation', 44.

50. Magus appeals to Aeneas' sense of family(10.524 ff.); Latinus to Turnus' growing awareness that he will lose to Aeneas (12.43) – but in both cases the impact of their arguments is dissipated by slips that offend the hearer: an offer of wealth to Aeneas, a loss of heroic status foretold to Turnus.

51. K. Quinn, *Virgil's Aeneid: A Critical Description* (London: Routledge, 1968), 94.

52. From the first departure from Sicily to establishment in Latium.

53. Battlefield speeches in Homer are of an even more implausible length – Achilles taunts Aeneas as if nothing were going on and Aeneas in retort lectures Achilles on his (Aeneas') ancestry (*Il.* 20.177–258).

54. Hardie, *Virgil's* Aeneid, 314; Hardie views physical space as 'politicised and moralised … On the human level this expansion is the historical growth of Rome, and is presented fairly realistically in terms of the horizontal axis; but it may also, more fantastically, be understood as expansion along the vertical axis' (p. 268).

55. 2.222, 2.338, 2.488, 5.140, 5.451, 11.832 ff., 11.878, 12.409, 12.724.

56. For example, *Il.* 2.153, 12.338, 14.60, 17.424 f.

57. So the shepherd's carved drinking cup in Theocritus, *Idylls* 1.27-56; Jason's cloak at Apollonius of Rhodes, *Argonautica* 1.721-67; Europa's flower basket in Moschus, *Europa* 44-61, the coverlet on Ariadne's marriage bed at Catullus 64.50–264. In the *Iliad*, Achilles' shield is described from the point of view of Hephaestus as he makes it (Il. 18.478 ff.).

58. M. Putnam, *Virgil's Epic Designs; Ekphrasis in the* Aeneid (New Haven, CT: Yale, 1998), 2, 'All of Virgil's notional ekphrases are in consequential ways metaphors for the larger text which they embellish . . . [They] represent the poem itself and afford us deeper ways of reading which we may plumb only through the actuation of sight into insight.'

59. A convenient summary can be found at Jones, *Homer's* Iliad, 38–9; at the time of writing, a catalogue of Homeric similes is available online: https://johnstoniatexts. x10host.com/homer/homericsimiles.html (accessed 8 May 2024).

60. For example, *Il.* 16.156 ff.; cf. Juturna compared to a swallow, 12.473 ff.

61. For example, ibid., 12.421 ff.; cf. Mnestheus compared to a dove, 5.213 ff.

62. For example, in delight, ibid., 21.347 and in awe or dismay *Il.* 4.452 ff.; cf. 2.304 ff.

63. At ibid., 17.737 ff., four similes follow one hot on the heels of another as the Greeks withdraw the body of Patroclus; the *Aeneid* never stacks up more than two and those are not extended, e.g. 10.134 ff., 10.272 ff.

64. *Il.* 13.586 ff.

65. For the statistics and a useful summary of the similes themselves, see E. Wilkins, 'A Classification of the Similes in Vergil's *Aeneid* and *Georgics'*, *Classical Weekly*, 14, no. 22 (18 April 1921): 170–4.

66. D. West, 'Multiple-Correspondence Similes', *Journal of Roman Studies*, 59, nos 1–2 (1969): 40–9, reprinted in Harrison (ed.), *Oxford Readings in Virgil's* Aeneid, especially 429–35.

67. For this simile, see also ibid., 443.

68. Thus R. Hornsby, 'The Vergilian Simile as Means of Judgement', *Classical Journal*, 60, no. 8 (1964): 337–44, reprinted in Quinn, *Why Vergil?*, 80–9, draws attention to the links and then concludes from them that Dido is responsible for her own downfall; this leaves no role for the gods.

69. The attempt to weave a skein of connections between similes is rejected by G. Williams in, '*Patterns of Action in the Aeneid: An Interpretation of Virgil's Epic Similes* by Roger A. Hornsby – Review', *Classical Review*, 22, no. (1972): 276.

70. 9.668 ff., 12.451 ff.

71. 10.405 ff., 12.521 ff.

72. Figures taken from the tables on the University of Ghent website, 'Direct Speech in Greek Epic Poetry', available online: https://www.dsgep.ugent.be/ (accessed 27 January 2023); it counts Odysseus' narrative of his journey as a single speech. To prove that statistics are also contestable, P. Jones gives seventy-seven speakers for the *Iliad*, occupying 43 per cent of the poem (*Homer's* Iliad, 13–14).

73. For example, it ignores the use of indirect speech as a substitute.

74. These figures are taken or derived from G. Highet, *The Speeches in Virgil's* Aeneid (1972; Princeton, NJ: Princeton University Press, 2016), 19–20, appendix 1; Aeneas' monologue to Dido is not included as a speech, but speeches within it are.

75. Highet offers a classification into apostrophes, commands, diplomatic or political, encouragements, farewells, greetings, legal, narrative/descriptive, oracular/interpretive, persuasions, questions, responses to commands or questions, soliloquys, taunts/threats, vituperations (the latter uniquely instantiated by Numanus Remulus) (*The Speeches*, 19–20, appendix 2).

76. There are six speeches in the *Iliad* that are longer, three in Book IX.

77. Heinze, *Virgil's Epic Technique*, 406.

78. Ibid., 414.

79. *Il.* 11.670–762.

80. So Hector facing Achilles, ibid., 22.98 ff.; Odysseus cast from his raft, *Od.* 5.298 ff.

81. For example, on *apostrophe*, Quintilian (*Education of the Orator* 9.3.25 f.) cites 3.56 f., 4.595 and 8.643.

82. Macrobius, *Saturnalia* 4.2.3 ff.

83. Eusebius, at Macrobius, *Saturnalia* 5.1.5.

84. Tiberius Claudius Donatus, *Interpretations of Virgil*, pp. 2 and 4 (not available in translation) – see Highet, *The Speeches*, 5–6; R. Starr, 'An Epic of Praise: Tiberius Claudius Donatus and Vergil's *Aeneid*', *Classical Antiquity*, 11, no. 1 (1992): 159–74.

85. Highet, *The Speeches*, 287.

86. *Il* 20.248 ff.: Aeneas to Achilles, 'Man's tongue is glib. There are words of all sorts at its command. They cover a wide range one way and another. You get the kind of answer you have asked for.'

87. Quintilian, *Education of the Orator* 2.17.21; Cicero, *On Oratory* 2.214 f., implies that where arguments cannot be met by reason, the speaker needs to work up a froth of emotion.

88. Servius, note on 9.134, though his remark seems off target in that context.

89. On 'diction', see further L. Wilkinson, 'The Language of Virgil and Horace', *Classical Quarterly*, 9, no. 3–4 (1959): 181–92, reprinted in Harrison (ed.), *Oxford Readings in Virgil's* Aeneid, 413–28.

90. Quintilian, *Education of the Orator* 1.7.18.

91. Quintilian compliments Virgil on his discretion in using archaisms, a device that if overused quickly becomes irksome (*Education of the Orator* 8.3.24, 1.6.40).

92. Aelius Donatus, *Life of Virgil* 44.

93. The sheer unlikelihood of Agrippa the military man of 8.682 commenting on the poet is slightly in favour of identifying him with this M. Vipsanius (otherwise unknown). Agrippa might well have taken against the *Aeneid's* spotlight on Marcellus, preferred to him as Augustus' successor – 6.854–92 note.

94. Quoted by Wilkinson, 'The Language' (see n. 89), 418–19; the same judgement is made by V. Moul, 'Virgil as a Poet', in Mac Góráin and Martindale (eds), *The Cambridge Companion*, 347–50.

95. Catullus 64.

96. J. Henry, Aeneidea, *or Critical, Exegetical and Aesthetical Remarks on the Aeneis* (1883; New York: Burt Franklin, repr. 1972), 3.39.

97. Aristotle, *Rhetoric* 1404b 5; an alternative translation goes, 'Art is cleverly concealed when a speaker chooses his words from ordinary language …'

98. Horace, *Art of Poetry* 46 f.

99. Macrobius, *Saturnalia* 6.6.1 ff.

100. 'Seize the day' (or better, 'pluck' it; Horace, *Odes* 1.11.8) is one of countless instances.

101. Literally rendered, 'falsified weapons' (2.422); 'to arm the spear-point with poison' (9.773; 'driven deep it drinks the virgin blood' (11.804); 'the silent wound lives beneath her breast'; 'the tow lives belching thick smoke beneath the hard oak' (5.681); 'the barking of dogs rages to the winds' (5.257); 'father Inachus pouring forth a stream from an embossed urn' (7.792).

102. Macrobius, *Saturnalia* 5.14.5, adducing examples from both Homer and Virgil; the second one from Virgil is 'Love conquers all things, and we too should yield to love' (*Eclogues* 10.69).

103. Wilkinson, 'The Language' (see n. 89), 428.

104. A book-length exploration of Virgil's diction is R. Lyne, 'Words and the Poet' [Oxford: Clarendon Press, 1989]; it presupposes a grasp of the Latin.

105. See J. O'Hara, 'Virgil's Style', in Mac Góráin and Martindale (eds), *The Cambridge Companion*, 374–5.

106. On ambiguity, see ibid., 376–9.

107. Quoted in K. Gransden (ed.), *Virgil in English* (London: Penguin, 1996), xxv.

108. If the second consonant is a liquid, 'l' or 'r', the poet has the option of treating a preceding short vowel as long.

109. A spate of experiments followed Launcelot Shadwell's translation (1844) of the *Iliad* into hexameters: notably Longfellow's *Evangeline* (1847) and two narrative poems by Clough, *The Bothie of Toper-Na-Fuosich* (1848) and *Amours de Voyage* (1849). After Landor in 1850 (quoted here) came out against the English hexameter, Kingsley came out in favour, with the publication of his own contributions in *Andromeda and Other Poems* (1858) and a fictionalized debate on the English hexameters in *Westward Ho!*, chapter 9 (1855). Tennyson wrote hexameters in protest against hexameters (*On Translations of Homer*,

1863). Of modern translators, Frederick Ahl has used the metre (see the extract in 7.5).

110. See further Moul, 'Virgil as a Poet', 356–7; O'Hara, 'Virgil's Style', 372.

111. Because of its inflection, Latin word order is far more flexible than English.

112. One of the most valiant attempts before Ahl was by Robert Bridges, in Ibant Obscuri: *An Experiment in the Classical Hexameter* (Oxford: Clarendon Press, 1916), his version of Aeneas' descent into the underworld, from Book VI and the first use of the metre in translating Virgil since the sixteenth century. He captures some of the clash between the quantitative metre and word stress. Here is an extract – to be read once in strict hexameter rhythm and a second time as English (*Ibant Obscuri* ll, 28–34 = *Aeneid* 6.295–301):

> Hence is a road that led them a-down to the Tartarean streams,
> Where Acheron's whirlpool impetuous, into the reeky
> Deep of Cokytos disgorgeth, with muddy burden.
> These floods one ferryman serveth, most awful of aspect,
> Of squalor infernal, Chāron: all filthily unkempt
> That woolly white cheek-fleece, and fiery the blood-shotten eyeballs:
> On one shoulder a cloak knotted up his nudity vaunteth.

113. Aelius Donatus, *Life of Virgil* 32.

Chapter 8

1. Quintilian, *Education of the Orator* 10.2.1 f.: 'For there can be no doubt that in art no small portion of our task lies in imitation, since, although invention came first and is all-important, it is expedient to imitate whatever has been invented with success. And it is a universal rule of life that we should wish to copy what we approve in others.'

2. Aelius Donatus, *Life of Virgil* 44 ff.

3. Q. Asconius Pedianus was a historian of the first century CE; the other authors mentioned are unknown but presumably earlier in date.

4. Macrobius, *Saturnalia* 6.1.5.

5. Heinze, *Virgil's Epic Technique*, 458.

6. Quintilian (*Education of the Orator* 9.2.65) examines, under *emphasis* (= 'meaning more than we say') a figure 'wherein through a certain innuendo we intend something unspoken to be communicated not as an opposite, as in "irony," but some "other" meaning which lies hidden and is as it were to be found by the reader … It is used in three circumstances: first if speaking openly is unsafe, second, if doing so is unseemly, and thirdly it is employed for the sake of elegance, and brings more pleasure through its novelty and variety than it would if directly spelled out' (trans. Thomas). But for Virgil, allusion is more than the addition of 'novelty' or 'variety'. See further R. Thomas, *Virgil and the Augustan Reception* (Cambridge: Cambridge University Press, 2001), 7–11.

7. That the Roman audience did pick them up is evident from the ancient commentaries and from Macrobius; Seneca, *Moral Letters* 108.34, has Seneca quoting Virgil quoting Ennius quoting Homer. To what extent Virgil expected his hearers then (or us now) to do so, or to understand their use, is impossible to say; in that sense, the *Aeneid* remains a private poem cast in a public form.

8. So D. Kennedy, 'Virgilian Epic', in Mac Góráin and Martindale (eds), *The Cambridge Companion*, 223.

9. For a brief introduction to the nature of oral poetry, see Jones, *Homer's Iliad*, 15–18.

10. *Il.* 23.299, 23.316–7.

11. So Odysseus retails (*Il.* 9.264–98) Agamemnon's terms (*Il.* 9.122–56), thirty-four lines in which the only change is from the first person in Agamemnon's speech to the first person in Odysseus'.

12. See Lyne, *Further Voices*, chapter 3, 'Allusion', 100–44, provides a detailed discussion and worked examples.

13. So in Farrell's two articles in the two editions of the *Cambridge Companion to Virgil*; the first, J. Farrell, 'The Virgilian Intertext', in C. Martindale (ed.), *The Cambridge Companion to Virgil* (Cambridge: Cambridge University

Press, 1997), 222–38, makes a very good introduction; J. Farrell, 'Virgil's Intertextual Personae', in Mac Góráin and Martindale (eds), *The Cambridge Companion*, 299–325, builds on that introduction and concludes with a valuable bibliography on intertextuality. For an alternative view, see E. Giusti, 'Virgilian Criticism and the Intertextual *Aeneid*', *Mnemosyne*, 76 (2023): 871–95.

14. Lyne, *Further Voices*, 12.

15. Cairns, *Virgil's Augustan Epic*, 195.

16. Macrobius, *Saturnalia* 6.1.7: 'I shall show that Virgil himself did not borrow some of the material taken from Homer, but rather that other earlier authors borrowed from Homer, and he in turn took it from those authors, whom he'd doubtless read.' (Similarly at 6.3.1.) Other commentators left it open whether the latest author was aware of the accumulating echoes – a second century CE scholion (annotation) on Persius (5.161) details how Menander offers a model to Terence, Terence to Horace and Horace to Persius (see Cairns, *Virgil's Augustan Epic*, 194–5).

17. For other such two-tier allusions, see 1.498–502, 5.382–6 (a three-tier allusion) and 6.692 notes.

18. Triton, previously in the poem a mildly benevolent figure, prising ships off rocks at 1.144 and escorting Neptune ceremonially at 5.824 there are, however, many precedents for gods being touchy about their distinctive prowess – Marsyas (Apollodorus, *Library* 1.4.2), Arachne (Ovid, *Metamorphoses* 6.1).

19. Camps, *An Introduction*, 1969, 106.

20. Lyne, *Further Voices*, 103.

21. Camps, *An Introduction*, 1969, 109.

22. Now something of a period piece on this is N. Coffee, J.-P. Koenig, S. Poornima, R. Ossewaarde, C. Forstall and S. Jacobson, 'Intertextuality in the Digital Age', *Transactions of the American Philological Association*, 142, no. 2 (2012): 383–422.

23. The thread of this section follows Otis, *Virgil*, 6–40, chapter 2, "The Obsolescence of Epic".

24. Macrobius, *Saturnalia* 5.17.4.

25. D. Nelis, 'Virgil's Library', in Farrell and Putnam (eds), *A Companion*, 13–17.

26. Ibid., 20; Hexter, 'On First Looking, 26–36.

27. G. Knauer, 'Vergil's *Aeneid* and Homer', *Greek, Roman and Byzantine Studies*, 5, no. 2 (1964), reprinted in Harrison (ed.), *Oxford Readings in Virgil's* Aeneid, 393 of 390–412. Knauer acknowledges the work of many collectors of Homeric quotations, from Servius and Macrobius on – and above all in the sixteenth century – but found much still unnoticed.

28. Ibid., 408: 'the last books of the *Odyssey*, 16–24, defied transformation'.

29. Aristotle, *Poetics* 1459b.

30. Hesiod, *Works and Days* 35 ff., 396 f., 633 ff.

31. Identified in the notes; also collected in D. Sider, 'Vergil's *Aeneid* and Hesiod's *Theogony*', *Vergilius*, 34 (1988): 15–24.

32. Aristotle, *Poetics* 1449a.

33. Choerilus of Samos, in the second half of the fifth century, tried to reclaim history for epic when writing his *Persica* (? – its title is unknown), on the Persian Wars; Antimachus of Colophon, towards the end of the century, retained a mythological subject (presumably with divine machinery) in his *Thebais* but innovated in style and diction. Little of either work survives, but their example lived on in, for example, the work of the third-century Cretan Rhianos: he followed Choerilus in writing a *Messeniaca*, about the second Messenian War, between Sparta and Messenia in the seventh century BCE, with its hero Aristomenes as his Achilles; he wrote other 'regional' poems (*Achaica*, *Thessalica*, *Eliaca*) but he also followed Antimachus in composing (another) fourteen-book *Heracleia* – stoutly mythological, and like his other work, all but lost. A third strand of epic, the panegyric-historical, came in the wake of Alexander the Great. Its most famous, but far from only, exponent was Choerilus of Iasos, who is the butt of Horace's mockery – 'Alexander the Great liked him, and for his crude ill-conceived verses he received pieces of Philip, royal coin' (*Epistles* 2.1.232 ff.); Horace (*Art of Poetry* 357 f.) is pleasantly surprised if he finds two or three redeeming lines in him.

34. They are categorized by the festivals at whose games the patrons won their laurels – the Olympian, Pythian and Nemean.

35. See R. Balot, 'Pindar, Virgil, and the Proem to *Georgic* 3', *Phoenix*, 52, nos 1–2 (1998): 83–94.

36. Athena in Aeschylus' *Eumenides* is no mere *dea ex machina*, but inaugurates the trial by jury that forms the climax to the play and the whole trilogy which it closes. Sometimes the gods set the drama in motion in the first place (so Apollo's prophecy in Sophocles' *Oedipus Tyrannus*, or Aphrodite in Euripides' *Hippolytus*) or bring about a *dénouement* (so Poseidon in Euripides' *Hippolytus*); only exceptionally is a god part of the action (as in Aeschylus' *Eumenides* previously mentioned, or Dionysos in Euripides' *Bacchae*). Sometimes, too, the gods are present but indifferent – Poseidon who laments the destruction of Troy at the start of Euripides' *Trojan Women* is quickly persuaded by Athena to turn his attention to punishing the Greeks.

37. Macrobius, *Saturnalia* 5.18.21.

38. Martial, *Epigrams* 5.5.8, 7.63.5.

39. Hardie, 'Virgil and Tragedy', 326–41.

40. There is as yet no inventory of allusions to tragedy in the manner of Knauer for Homer or Nelis for Apollonius.

41. In particular the following passage:

> The original essence of tragedy consists then in the fact that within such a conflict each of the opposed sides, if taken by itself, has justification; while each can establish the true and positive content of its own aim and character only by denying and infringing the equally justified power of the other. The consequence is that in its moral life, and because of it, each is nevertheless involved in guilt.

(G. W. F. Hegel, *Aesthetics: Lectures on Fine Art*, trans. T. Knox (Oxford: Oxford University Press, 1975), 1196).

42. G. Conte, 'The Strategy of Contradiction', in G. Conte, *The Poetry of Pathos: Studies in Virgilian Epic*, ed. S. Harrison (Oxford: Oxford University Press, 2007), 160–3.

43. Hardie, 'Virgil and Tragedy', 328–9.

44. Quoted by Hardie, ibid., 327.

45. Conte, *The Rhetoric*, 161.

46. Its nearest rival, though a later starter and never as large, was at Pergamum, built by Eumenes II in the first half of the second century BCE. Libraries had a long history before the Hellenistic period; the Royal Library of Ashurbanipal, for instance, at Ninevah, dates from the seventh century BCE and contained, among more than 30,000 texts and fragments, the *Epic of Gilgamesh*. Closer to home, Aristotle's Lyceum collected texts for the researches that went on in it. For a short introduction to the library of Alexandria, see L. Reynolds and N. Wilson, *Scribes and Scholars: A Guide to the Transmission of Greek and Latin Literature* (Oxford: Oxford University Press, 2013), 5–8.

47. Callimachus, *Aetia* 1, Fragment 1.21 ff.

48. Ibid., *Aetia* 3, Fragment 75.

49. In his hymns, Callimachus again eschews straightforward narrative or aretalogy – his anecdotes of gods and heroes dive off in unexpected directions while the gods and heroes themselves are viewed from a quirky, almost comical, angle – e.g. in Hymn 3, Artemis is a little girl asking Zeus for all her attributes and Heracles a paunchy glutton who cannot understand why she would hunt deer instead of boar.

50. See R. Thomas, 'Callimachus Back in Rome', in M. Harder, R. Regtuit and G. Wakker (eds), *Callimachus* (Groningen: Egbert Forsten, 1993), 1.205–9, available online: https://www.academia.edu/25466839/Callimachus_Back_in_Rome (accessed 8 May 2024); there is still no inventory for allusions to Callimachus in the *Aeneid*.

51. The Alexandrians did not invent literary allusion: more than a century before them, Aristophanes (*Frogs* 943) had twitted Euripides for adding to his verse 'the juice of chatterboxes strained from books'. But the habit of allusion as a 'good in itself' is peculiarly Alexandrian.

52. The story of a falling-out between Callimachus and Apollonius is now treated as apocryphal. In his Proem to *Georgics* 3, Virgil announces that he is moving away from the topics favoured by the Hellenistic poets while at the same time importing their Muses (ll. 1-12).

53. Servius even goes too far, in his preamble to Book IV, in attributing the whole of it to Apollonius' *Argonautica* Book 3 (see

Introduction – 9.2 The second to fifth centuries: Servius and Macrobius). For a more exact approach, see, for example, references in Heinze, *Virgil's Epic Technique*, 76, 110, 112.

54. Above all through the work of D. Nelis in his, 'Vergil's *Aeneid* and the *Argonautica* of Apollonius Rhodius (Cambridge: Francis Cairns, 2001); it contains a detailed inventory of references to Apollonius; its chapter 10, 'Vergil and the Apollonian Experiment', 382–402, presents a summary of his findings.

55. Biographies of Apollonius are part of the scholia to two manuscripts of the *Argonautica*; his name is mentioned on a list of heads of the Library at Alexandria (*Oxyrhyncus Papyrus* 1241).

56. Pindar, *Pythian* 4.184 ff.

57. For one such see R. Hunter, '"Short on Heroics": Jason in the *Argonautica*', *Classical Quarterly*, 38, no. 2 (1988): 436–53.

58. Apollonius of Rhodes, *Argonautica* 1.648 f., 1.1220.

59. Ibid., 4.1673 ff.; my italics.

60. For the gods in Apollonius, see D. Feeney, *The Gods in Epic* (Oxford: Oxford University Press, 1991), chapter 2, 'Apollonius' *Argonautica*', 57–98.

61. Figure taken from the table on the University of Ghent website, 'Direct Speech in Greek Epic Poetry', available online: https://www.dsgep.ugent.be/ (accessed 27 January 2023).

62. Slightly adapted from Nelis, 'Vergil's *Aeneid* and the *Argonautica*', 405.

63. Examples abound – e.g. in one short stretch of the *Argonautica* 1.1061 f., 1.1075 ff., 1.1138 f., 1.1148 f.

64. Herodotus, *Histories* 4.153 ff.

65. Nelis, 'Vergil's *Aeneid* and the *Argonautica*', 397.

66. Apollonius of Rhodes, *Argonautica* 1.1153 ff. and 2.1 ff., respectively.

67. Otis, *Virgil*, 13–15.

68. Probably not Lycophron of Chalcis, a third-century BCE grammarian and tragedian in charge of comedies at the Library of Alexander, but a homonym of the early second century.

69. For example, S. West, 'Lycophron Italicised', *Journal of Hellenic Studies*, 104 (1984): 130–7.

70. Lycophron, *Alexandra* 1226–80, 1446–50.

71. Cicero (*Brutus* 72) dates the first production of one of his plays to 240 BCE.

72. Ibid., 71.

73. Ibid., 75.

74. Scholiast on Persius, *Satire* 6.9 f.: 'Ennius states in the beginning of his *Annales* that in the course of a dream he saw a vision of Homer who said that he was once a peacock and from it, according to a rule laid down by the philosopher Pythagoras, his soul had been conveyed into Ennius.' On what Ennius might have wanted to convey by this dream, see P. Aicher, 'Ennius' Dream of Homer', *American Journal of Philology*, 110, no. 2 (1989): 227–32.

75. W. Clausen, 'Callimachus and Latin Poetry', *Greek, Roman and Byzantine Studies*, 5, no. 3 (1964): 185–7.

76. *Greek Anthology* 7.42 (an anonymous poem on Callimachus' source of inspiration for the *Aetia*); Callimachus, *Aetia*, Fragment 2 is a small shard.

77. Horace ridicules those for whom this is desirable (*Satires* 1.10.74 f.): 'What, would you be such a fool as to be ambitious that your verses should be taught in shabby schools?' Such, however, was also Horace's fate (*Introduction* – 9.1 The first 150 years after Virgil).

78. Ennius, *Annals*, Fragments 21.

79. Many are indicated in the commentary – e.g. 1.64, 1.223–6, 1.254 notes.

80. See N. Goldschmidt, *Shaggy Crowns: Ennius' Annales and Virgil's Aeneid* (Oxford: Oxford University Press, 2013), 'Introduction: Fragments'; the book also contains an inventory of Ennian citations.

81. Ovid, *Tristia* 2.259.

82. Horace, *Epistles* 2.1.50 ff.

83. Horace, *Satires* 1.10.54 f.

84. Horace, *Satires* 1.4.62.

85. Catullus 95.3.

86. Cicero, *Letters to His Brother Quintus* 2.15.4 f.

87. = 'coals to Newcastle', i.e. something of which Quintus has no need.

88. About Caesar's campaign against Ariovistus.

89. 'What age will be ignorant of Varro and his first boat, or of its commander Jason in quest of the golden fleece?' – Ovid, *Amores* 1.15.21 f.; Quintilian more mundanely says that Varro obtained his reputation as 'an interpreter of others' work' and is 'not to be despised' (*Education of the Orator* 10.1.87).

90. According to Diogenes Laertius, *Lives of the Eminent Philosophers* 8.77, Empedocles (fifth century BCE) wrote two poems, *On Nature* and *On Purifications*, of 5,000 lines in total.

91. Aratus' *Phaenomena* (third century BCE), on constellations and the heavens more generally, is still extant.

92. Lucretius says his purpose is 'to shine clear light before your mind | To let you see into the heart of hidden things' (*On the Nature of Things* 1.144 f.); e.g. 'But liquids in their fluid composition | Must consist more of atoms smooth and round. | You can pour poppy seeds as easily as water, | The tiny spheres do not hold each other back, | And if you knock a heap of them they run | Downhill in the same way as water does.' (2.451 ff., Trans. Melville).

93. Lucretius, *On the Nature of Things* 1.68 ff.

94. For a dose of caution, see N. Crowther, 'Parthenius and Roman Poetry', *Mnemosyne*, 29 (1976): 65–7.

95. What we know of Parthenius comes from the *Suda*, the tenth-century Byzantine encyclopaedia. On Parthenius' impact, see Otis, *Virgil*, 26–7; Clausen, 'Callimachus', 187–93.

96. Macrobius, *Saturnalia* 5.17.18.

97. Aulus Gellius, *Attic Nights* 9.9.3: 'Virgil therefore showed skill and good judgment in omitting some things and rendering others, when he was dealing with passages of Homer or Hesiod or Apollonius or **Parthenius** or Callimachus or Theocritus, or some other poet.'

98. Gallus was likely to be receptive to Parthenius' recommendations, since he composed poetry on his passion for Lycoris – admired by Propertius (*Elegies* 2.34.91 f.); nine lines is all that has been recovered of Gallus' works. Virgil praises him warmly in

his sixth and addresses him in his tenth Eclogue; Servius tells us (note to *Eclogues* 6.72) that Gallus translated poems of Euphorion, an Alexandrian disciple of Callimachus and one of Parthenius' sources, into Latin.

99. Parthenius, *Erōtika Pathēmata* (*Love Romances*), Preface.

100. This is the sort of territory occupied by Parthenius' eleventh love story, on Byblis, the incestuous love of (or for) her brother and the metamorphosis of her into an owl or her tears into a river.

101. Catullus 95.

102. A river in Cyprus linked to legend of Adonis – so Catullus predicts the poem will be cherished by those local to its subject.

103. An epic, of which we know nothing, in the tradition of Ennius' *Annals*; it was clearly a plentiful fund of waste paper – Catullus called it elsewhere (35.1) 'papyrus shat out'.

104. Presumably Volusius' home town.

105. His (hypothetical) dates are 84–54 BCE (Jerome says he died in his thirtieth year – *Chronicon* B58); he was born in Verona (his parents had a home at nearby Sirmio) but moved to Rome and lived there for the rest of his life, except for a year in Bithynia as one of C. Memmius' entourage (57–6 BCE); he moved in high society (Suetonius has him lampooning, apologizing and going to dinner with Julius Caesar – *Life of Julius Caesar* 73) as well as in his circle of fellow poets.

106. Horace links Catullus and Calvus at *Satires* 1.10.19; Catullus addresses or mentions Calvus in poems 14, 50, 53 and 96.

107. So-called by Cicero in a letter to Atticus (7.2.1) and at *Orator* 161.

108. E.g. Catullus 29, on Caesar and Pompey.

109. Catullus 1.

110. Because of its narrative component it is commonly referred to as Catullus' *epyllion*.

111. Catullus 64.69 ff.

112. See 4.20–3, 4.215–18, 4.314–19, 4.365–7, 4.437–9, 4.532, 4.584–629, 4.657–8 notes.

113. Propertius, *Elegies* 4.1.64.

114. Cicero, *Tusculan Disputations* 3.45.

Chapter 9

1. See P. Hardie, *The Last Trojan Hero: A Cultural History of Virgil's* Aeneid (London: I. B. Tauris, 2014); Farrell and Putnam (eds), *A Companion*; N. Horsfall, 'Virgil's Impact at Rome: The Non-literary Evidence', and W. Barnes, 'Virgil: The Literary Impact', in Horsfall (ed.), *A Companion*, 249–55 and 257–92, respectively; R. Tarrant, 'Aspects of Virgil's Reception in Antiquity', in Mac Góráin and Martindale (eds), *The Cambridge Companion*, 43–62.

2. See Hardie, *The Last Trojan Hero*, chapter 9, 'Art and Landscape'; Farrell and Putnam (eds), *A Companion*, 'Part Three: The *Aeneid* in Music and the Visual Arts'.

3. Velleius Paterculus, *Roman History* 2.36.3; cf. Ovid, *Art of Love* 3.337 f., 'exiled Aeneas, begetter of lofty Rome, than whom no work in Latium is more famous'.

4. Ovid, *Remedies for Love* 395.

5. The date is implied by Jerome, *Chronicon*, B16.

6. Tacitus, *Dialogue on Orators* 13.2.

7. Suetonius, *On Grammarians and Teachers* 16.3.

8. Quintilian (first century CE), *Education of the Orator* 1.8.5.

9. The teacher would give an example, the children follow – Macrobius, *Saturnalia* 1.24.5.

10. Juvenal, *Satires* 7.226 f.

11. M. Geymonat, 'The Transmission of Virgil's Works in the Antiquity and the Middle Ages', in Horsfall (ed.), *A Companion*, 298.

12. Treatises on grammar abounded – one scholar has reckoned that, had the text itself been lost, it would be possible to reconstruct the *Aeneid* from citations of it in grammatical textbooks (Hardie, *The Last Trojan Hero*, 7–8.

13. Probus, critic of the simile in Book I, was a grammarian (1.498–502 note).

14. Servius, note on 10.18.

15. Aelius Donatus, *Life of Virgil* 26.

16. Macrobius, *Saturnalia* 5.17.5.

17. Suetonius, *Life of Nero* 54.

18. Augustine, *Sermons* 241.5.

19. See 1.1–7 note; Horsfall claims 46 of the 62 ('at most 64') Virgilian graffiti at Pompeii are from the *Aeneid* – Horsfall (ed.), *A Companion*, 252.

20. Petronius (first century CE), *Satyricon* 68.4 – the line in question is 5.1.

21. Aelius Donatus, *Life of Virgil*, 43; for a survey of these critical voices down the centuries, see J. Farrell, 'Virgil's Detractors', in Farrell and Putnam (eds), *A Companion*, 435–48.

22. This is an allusion to Zoilus of Amphipolis, called 'Scourge of Homer' for his obsession with Homeric 'blunders'.

23. Seneca, *Apocolocyntosis* 1.2.

24. Juvenal, *Satires* 11.180 ff.

25. Juvenal, *Satires* 6.434 ff.

26. Suetonius, *Life of Nero* 47.2 recounts how one of Nero's retinue asked him, as he faced death with horror, 'Is it so wretched to die?' (Turnus at 12.646).

27. Ovid, *Remedies for Love* 379 ff.: 'Let charming elegy … lightly sport in kindly mood at her own pleasure. Achilles must not be told of in the metres of Callimachus.' Epic (at this point, *c.* 2 CE) is not for Ovid; he had claimed Cupid was responsible for stealing him away from it (see *Introduction* – 2.3 *Eclogues* (or *Bucolics*), on *recusatio*).

28. Ovid, *Metamorphoses* 14.116–19.

29. Ibid., 14.120 ff.

30. Ovid, *Heroides* 7.133 ff.

31. Ovid, *Fasti* 3.545 ff.

32. Ibid., 3.623.

33. He was a member of the Pisonian conspiracy against Nero; Tacitus tells of his final moments in *Annals* 15.70.1.

34. Lucan, *Pharsalia* 1.33 ff.; cf. *Georgics* 1.24 f.

35. Lucan's Book 1 Proem is a seven-line counterblast to Virgil's Book I Proem, also of seven lines; it then asks, 'What *furor*, what freedom with the sword poured out Roman blood for foreign enemies?'

36. Lucan, *Pharsalia* 9.961 ff.

37. Pliny the Younger, *Letters* 3.7.8.

38. *Punic Wars* 3.573 ff., 9.346 ff., 10.657 ff., 15.125 ff.

39. Barnes, 'Virgil', 273.

40. Ibid., 276–7.

41. Statius, *Thebaid* 12.816; at 10.445, he promises immortality to his duo of dead heroes, Hopleus and Dymas, hoping that Nisus and Euryalus will be their companions among the shades.

42. Dante, *Purgatorio* 22.64 ff.

43. So by Thierfelder in W. Rutz (ed.), *Lucan* (Darmstadt: Wissenschaftliche Buchgesellschaft, 1970), 63.

44. For the *Aeneid* and Christianity, see Hardie, *The Last Trojan Hero*, chapter 6, 127–47.

45. A phrase of Tertullian's, in his *Apology*, chapter 17.

46. For his disapproval see Jerome, *Letters* 22.29: 'How can Horace go with the psalter, Virgil with the gospels, Cicero with the apostle?'; for a citation of Virgil, see *Commentary on Ezekiel* ch. 40, where he quotes 2.755 to evoke the darkness of the catacombs.

47. G. Clark, 'Augustine's Virgil', in Mac Góráin and Martindale (eds), *The Cambridge Companion*, 77–87.

48. Augustine of Hippo, *City of God* 1.3.

49. It is less in the tradition of philosophical dialogue than an extended conversation piece, like Plato's *Symposium* or Aulus Gellius' *Attic Nights*.

50. Generally supposed to be based on a previous one by Aelius Donatus, the author of the *Life of Virgil* and tutor of St. Jerome, a century earlier.

51. See D. Fowler, 'The Virgil Commentary of Servius', in Mac Góráin and Martindale (eds), *The Cambridge Companion*, 88–94.

52. Servius, preface to his commentary on the *Aeneid*; the translation of this and the next two extracts is taken from R. Williams, 'The Purpose of the *Aeneid*', *Classical Quarterly*, NS 10 (1960): 145–51, reprinted in Harrison (ed.), *Oxford Readings in Virgil's* Aeneid, 21.

53. Aelius Donatus, *Life of Virgil* 21.

54. Tiberius Claudius Donatus, *Proem to* Aeneid I.

55. I.e. with notes by different commentators.

56. Hardie, *The Last Trojan Hero*, 8.

57. For example, by the learned Irish, some of whose annotations on the *Eclogues* and *Georgics* were collected in the tenth-century *Scholia Bernensia*.

58. On the commentaries after Servius, see S. Casali and F. Stok, 'Post-classical Commentary', in Mac Góráin and Martindale (eds), *The Cambridge Companion*, 95–108.

59. The Camuldensian disputations of *c.* 1473; see Hardie, *The Last Trojan Hero*, 36, 89.

60. Servius appears on the frontispiece of Petrarch's fourteenth-century codex of Virgil, now in the Biblioteca Ambrosiana, Milan – Plate 1 in Hardie, *The Last Trojan Hero*.

61. See ibid., 87–8.

62. Claudian, *Against Rufinus* 1.25 f.

63. Ibid., 1.51 f.

64. Claudian, *On the Third Consulship of Honorius* 96 ff.

65. Tertullian, *On the Prescription of Heretics* 39.

66. For a translated example, see Hardie, *The Last Trojan Hero*, 177–8; such source material suits the associations sex has in the *Aeneid* (e.g. for Dido, 4.169 ff.; at the death of Camilla, 11.803 f.).

67. Hardie, *The Last Trojan Hero*, 11; he mentions the improbable heir to Proba, the Aberdonian and Laudian clergyman Alexander Ross, who composed a thirteen-book *Christiad of the Evangelising Virgil*, published in 1638 (p. 132).

68. *Life of Alcuin* 5 – not available online.

69. Alcuin, *Poems* 45.67 f., not available online; see further Hardie, *The Last Trojan Hero*, 103–4.

70. This was adapted into German (dialect) by Heinrich von Veldeke, in his *Eneide* (late twelfth century), contrasting the destructive passion of/for Dido with the chaste and enduring love of/for Lavinia.

71. Dante, *Inferno*, 1.85 ff.; on Dante and his successors up to and including Milton see C. Burrow, 'Virgils from Dante to Milton', in Mac Góráin and Martindale (eds), *The Cambridge Companion*, 128–40.

72. Dante, *Purgatorio* 22.67 ff.

73. Ibid., 30.43 ff.

74. *Georgics* 4.525 ff.

75. Dante, *Inferno* 20.113.

76. Cacciaguida's evocation of Florence's innocent tranquillity is at *Paradiso* 15.97 ff.

- it is not the same as the primitive simplicity of Evander's *Pallanteum*. Dante compares Cacciaguida to Anchises at 15.25, as if Cacciaguida's recollection of the past replaces Anchises' vision of the future.

77. Dante, *Paradiso* 6.80 f.

78. Augustine of Hippo, *Confessions* 8.12.29.

79. Precedent for this is to be found in the *Historia Augusta*, the deeply suspect biographies of thirty emperors from Hadrian onwards, in which the *Lives* of Hadrian (2.8) and Alexander Severus (14) refer to the practice (among others).

80. From H. Thrale, *Thraliana* (Oxford: Clarendon Press, 1942), 1.560–1, cited by C. Martindale in his 'Introduction', to Mac Góráin and Martindale (eds), *The Cambridge Companion*, 7.

81. On the Christiad, see Hardie, *The Last Trojan Hero*, 139–40; he also cites (p. 6) Vida's, *Art of Poetry*, a book of instruction on how to write Virgilian Latin verse.

82. E.g. each has its own take on the descent into the underworld and prophecy of Anchises in Book VI – Ariosto (*Orlando Furioso* 3.5–3.63 has the lady knight Bradamante fall into a subterranean church where, at the tomb of Merlin, the witch Melissa presents a parade of Bradamante's descendants, the d'Este family, ending on two traitors (instead of Marcellus); and Spenser in his Faerie Queen has the heroine Britomart meet Merlin in a deep delve (3.3.7); the wizard prophesies her future lineage, up to Queen Elizabeth (the 'royall virgin', 3.3.49), but then breaks off as if dismayed by some ghastly spectacle (3.3.50). Spenser also gives Britain a back-history as far as the Trojan War, with Trojans founding Troynovant (= 'new Troy') on the Thames, i.e. London (3.9.33 ff.).

83. Ariosto's opening canto emulates the *Aeneid* in 'I sing', but stops short at the Muse.

84. Tasso, *Gerusalemme Liberata* 19.25 f.

85. Ibid., 20.141 ff.; in his *Discourse on Heroic Poetry*, however, Tasso defended Aeneas' killing of Turnus for three reasons: (1) the threat Turnus would still pose if left alive, (2) Aeneas' promise to Evander and (3) religious obligation.

86. Ariosto, in his rewrite of Nisus and Euryalus (*Orlando Furioso* 18.165.1 ff.) also has the captor sparing the captive, moved by *pietade* (= 'pity', not *pietas*). Burrow, however, sees a recoil from Christian pity back towards Roman *pietas* in both *Orlando Furioso* and *Gerusalemme Liberata* – Burrow, 'Virgils', 133.

87. Although he had trodden a self-consciously Virgilian path from his *Shepheardes Calendar*, via a translation of the *Culex* ('Gnat', from the *Virgilian Appendix*) as far as the *Faerie Queen* itself (forced, he says, 'for trumpets sterne to chaunge mine Oaten reeds', *Faerie Queen* Prologue 1.4).

88. See L. Svensson, 'Remembering the Death of Turnus: Spense's *Faerie Queene* and the Ending of the *Aeneid*', *Renaissance Quarterly*, 64, no. 2 (2011): 430–71, especially 451 ff.

89. Spenser says as much – in his Letter to Sir Walter Raleigh, he sums up his aims in the *Faerie Queen*:

The generall end therefore of all the booke, is to fashion a gentleman or noble person in vertuous and gentle discipline . . . In which I have followed all the antique poets historicall: first Homer . . . then Virgil, whose like intention was to doe in the person of Æneas: after him Ariosto comprised them both in his Orlando: and lately Tasso dissevered them againe, and formed both parts in two persons, namely, that part which they in philosophy call *Ethice*, or vertues of a private man, coloured in his Rinaldo: the other named *Politice*, in his Godfredo.

90. *The Tempest*'s opening storm is an acknowledgement of the *Aeneid*'s, and it too symbolizes turbulence in the order of things; Ferdinand greets Miranda with the words, 'Most sure, the goddess | On whom these airs attend' (I.ii.489 f.), as Aeneas his mother, **'Surely you must be a goddess?'** / *'Oh, a goddess, without a doubt!'* (1.328); the banter on the 'widow Dido' (II.i.62 ff.) resembles a parody on the variant accounts of Dido, as chaste (non-Virgilian) and unchaste (Virgilian).

91. Milton, *Paradise Lost* 1.26.

92. The Portuguese poet Camões' *Lusiads* (1572 – see 9.4.1), on the voyages of Vasco da Gama round the Cape of Good Hope to India, finds an unlikely echo in Milton's lines on Satan arriving at Eden, (*Paradise*

Lost 4.159 ff.), 'As when to them who sail | Beyond the Cape of Hope, and now are past | Mozambic, off at sea north-east winds blow | Sabaean odours from the spicy shore.'

93. Milton, *Paradise Lost* 1.77, 2.933 and 4.390; when Satan reaches Eden, he beholds, 'A sylvan scene, and as the ranks ascend | Shade above shade, a woody theatre| Of stateliest view' (Paradise Lost, 4.140 ff.) – just as the harbour where the Trojans moor on the north African coast has **a backcloth of shimmering trees, a dark wood with quivering shadows, looming over the water /** *as a backdrop looms a quivering wood, above them rears a grove, bristling dark with shade* (1.164 f.).

94. Milton, *Paradise Lost* 12.451 ff.

95. *Paradise Regained* could therefore have followed a more *Aeneid*-like plot – but it is a retelling of the Temptation of Christ (as in Luke's Gospel), and its four books are not on remotely the same scale as *Paradise Lost.*

96. See Hardie, *The Last Trojan Hero*, 42–4; Burrow, 'Virgils', 136–9.

97. This provoked, in the mid-seventeenth century, a fashion for travesties of the *Aeneid* throughout Europe – at the lowest level of vulgarity lay Paul Scarron's *Le Virgile travesty en vers burlesques* (published in instalments between 1648 and 1653), in which according to one critic, 'Dido and Aeneas spoke like fishwives and porters.' Charles Cotton produced an English equivalent in 1670, *Scarronides: or Virgil Travestie*, in rhyming octosyllabics; here is Mercury to a drunken Aeneas (4.557 ff., sort of): 'But Mercury, though he slept profoundly, | Made bold to beat up's quarters roundly, | And thus 'gan rattle him: 'Thou lousie, | Mangie, careless, drunken, drowsie | Coxcomb! How oft must I be sent | Hither from Jove to complement | Your worship to a reverent care | Of the young Bastard here, your heir? | Whilst fast thou ly'st tipled, or tipling; | Nor ar'st what danger the poor stripling | Lies open to. Y'had best snore on, | Somebody will be here anon …'

98. Thomas Hughes, *The Misfortunes of Arthur*, 5.2.

99. Dekker, *The Magnificent Entertainment* (1604).

100. *Eclogues* 4.6.

101. This ostensible Royalist had, in 1658, ten years before he was made the first Poet Laureate, penned verses honouring Cromwell at his death: 'Heroique Stanzas Consecrated to the Glorious Memory of his Serene and Renowned Highness Oliver, late Lord Protector &c.'

102. Pope, *Windsor-Forest*, 42; he nevertheless prided himself on not making up to royalty – his epitaph runs, 'HEROES and KINGS! your distance keep: | In peace let one poor Poet Sleep, | Who never flatter'd Folks like you: | Let Horace blush, and Virgil too.'

103. *Georgics* 3.37 ff.

104. Scaliger, *Poetices* 5.3.

105. By at least 125 different authors – Casali and Stok, 'Post-classical Commentary', 100.

106. Ibid.

107. Ibid., 102–7.

108. La Cerda, *Commentary on Virgil, To the Reader* – quoted in A. Laird, 'Juan La Cerda and the Predicament of Commentary', in R. Gibson and C. Shuttleworth (eds), *The Classical Commentary: Histories, Practices, Theory* (Leiden and Boston, MA: Brill, 2002), 180 (available as ebook), 171–203 offer a warm appreciation of La Cerda's achievement.

109. Gibbon called Heyne, 'The last and best Editor of Vergil' (*Memoirs of My Life*, ed. G. Bonnard (New York: Funk and Wagnalls, 1966).

110. Virgil's position was more stable in France – Voltaire wrote a historical epic on Henry IV of France, *Henriade* (1723), in whose Appendix he observed that, if Virgil was the creation of Homer, he was his finest work; the same could not be said of the *Henriade.*

111. Dryden, *Introduction to Virgil's* Aeneid (1697), pp. xxi and xx, respectively; Gibbon observed in the slaying of the dictator Mezentius, 'the daring pretensions of the people, to punish as well as to resist a tyrant … the minds of Romans were still Republican' (*Critical Observations on the Sixth Book of the* Aeneid (London: Printed for P. Elmsley, 1770), 13).

112. *Plain Truth, or Downright Dunstable* (London: Printed for J. Roberts, 1740),

12–13 (available online in facsimile, Google Books, accessed 8 May 2024); the subtitle runs, *A poem containing the author's opinion of the sale of poetic and prose performances with some critical thoughts on Horace and Virgil together with a few hints on the Author's amours, as well as his private and uncommon sentiments on government*; quite a pot pourri.

113. Chapman, Letter in dedication, etc. of *Achilles Shield*.

114. Dryden, Preface to *Fables Ancient and Modern*.

115. Burke, *A Philosophical Inquiry into the Origin of Our Ideas of the Sublime and the Beautiful* 2.1; his fundamental principle (1.7) runs,

Whatever is fitted in any sort to excite the ideas of pain, and danger, that is to say, whatever is in any sort terrible, or is conversant about terrible objects, or operates in a manner analogous to terror, is a source of the sublime; that is, it is productive of the strongest emotion which the mind is capable of feeling. When danger or pain press too nearly, they are incapable of giving any delight, and are simply terrible; but at certain distances, and with certain modifications, they may be, and they are delightful, as we every day experience.

116. Longinus (first century CE), *On the Sublime* 2.1, 2.3.

117. J. Warton, postscript to vol. 4 , 305–6 of C. Pitt, *The Works of Virgil in English Verse* (London: Printed for R. and J. Dodsley).

118. Byron, Letter to Mr Moore, 11 April 1817.

119. Schlegel, 'Geschichte der klassischen Literatur', ed. Edgar Lohner, *Kritische Schriften und Briefe 3* (Stuttgart: Kohlhammer, 1964), 166.

120. Hegel, *Lectures on the Philosophy of Religion*', ed. W. Jaeschke (Hamburg: Meiner, 1983–5), 2.402.

121. Virgil was still held in esteem by Goethe and Schiller, even if they preferred Homer.

122. Arnold enunciated his view on Virgil in his inaugural lecture as Professor of Poetry at Oxford in 1857, 'The Modern Element in Literature' – over the *Aeneid* 'there rests an ineffable melancholy … This suffering, this graceful-minded, this finely gifted man … is not the adequate interpreter of the great period of Rome.' See N. Vance, 'Virgil and the Nineteenth Century', in C. Martindale (ed.), *Virgil and his Influence* (London: Bristol Classical Press, 1984), 186–7; also Johnson, *Darkness Visible*, 5.

123. On Sainte-Beuve's thesis and the unfortunate fate of his lecture series, see Vance, 'Virgil', 175–7.

124. C. Sainte-Beuve, *Study on Virgil* (Paris: Garnier-frères, 1857), p. 1.

125. Hardie, *The Last Trojan Hero*, 15.

126. Tennyson, 'To Virgil', ll. 21 ff. – this follows Tennyson's tribute to the *Georgics* and the *Eclogues* (in that order) and references Aeneas' comment on the Trojan War scenes depicted on Dido's temple, 1.462.

127. A. Kerney, 'Making Tennyson a Classic: Churton Collins' *Illustrations of Tennyson* in Context', *Victorian Poetry*, 30, no. 1 (1992): 75.

128. J. Seeley, *The Expansion of England* (London: Macmillan & Co., 1883; Cambridge: Cambridge University Press, 2010), 135.

129. J. Bryce, *The Ancient Roman Empire and the British Empire in India* (London et al.: Humphrey Milford, Oxford University Press, 1914), 66.

130. Hardie, *The Last Trojan Hero*, chapter 6, 149–72.

131. One theory of the source of syphilis is that it was brought back from the Americas.

132. D. Quint, *Epic and Empire* (Princeton, NJ: Princeton University Press, 1993), 99–210, 'Part Two: Epic and the Losers'.

133. T. Jones, 'The Classics in Colonial Hispanic America', *Transactions and Proceedings of the American Philological Association*, 70 (1939): 41–3.

134. See M. Reinhold, 'The Americanization of Vergil, from Colonial Times to 1882', reprinted in Quinn (ed.), *Why Vergil?*, 316–24, and a multifaceted exploration in 'The American Aeneid', Part Four of Farrell and Putnam (eds), *A Companion*, 356–417.

135. Cited by Reinhold, ibid., 319.

136. Ibid., 322; Reinhold also mentions John Adams' grandson, Charles Francis Adams,

who in 1832 read all the major works of Virgil in the original and approved of them.

137. *annuit coeptis* ('he agreed the undertakings') is adapted from *Georgics* 1.40 (recycled at *Aeneid* 9.625); *novus ordo seclorum* ('a new order of the ages') is adapted from *Eclogues* 4.5; *e pluribus unum* ('from many, one') comes from the Moretum ('Salad', more accurately a sort of garlic paste), l. 102 – this poem, a description of a poor farmer preparing his meal and once part of the *Virgilian Appendix*, has been, but is no longer, attributed to Virgil.

138. The American Caleb Alexander published a literal translation of the *Aeneid* in 1796, but it paled by comparison.

139. Reinhold, 'The Americanization', 318.

140. Its jaunty couplets start with: 'Aeneas finish'd here his ditty | Of old King Priam and his city: | The Trojans at a tale so deep, | And wondrous roving, fell – asleep | But not the Queen …'

141. On the Columbiad, see Hardie, *The Last Trojan Hero*, 168–70.

142. Ibid., 169.

143. J. Dexter, 'A Nineteenth-Century American Interpretation of the *Aeneid*', *Classical World*, 105 (2011): 42–3.

144. After a deliberately stilted rendition of the first seven lines, the text (in hexameters) suddenly lifts off:

> O Muse! Relate me the facts, if you happen to know 'em,
>   Concerning the hero of this astonishing poem;
>   Explain why the queen of the gods was so terribly eager
>   So clever and pious a man at each step to beleaguer; –
>   Why with wrath she pursued him, – with shipwreck and tempest and thunder:
>   Do they cultivate such reprehensible morals up yonder?

145. The idea of a canon of great books has been heavily criticized – hence the 'canon wars' in America of the 1980s and 1990s: M. Witt, 'Are the Canon Wars Over? Rethinking Great Books', *The Comparatist*, 24 (May 2000): 57–63.

146. S. Braund and M. Torlone (eds), *Virgil and his Translators* (Oxford and New York: Oxford University Press, 2018) provides essays on the cultural settings as well as the translations themselves in a wide range of countries; F. Mac Góráin, 'Virgil: The Future?', in Mac Góráin and Martindale (eds), *The Cambridge Companion*, 474, cites articles on (sometimes specific periods in) Mexico, Ireland, India and Africa.

147. What follows is taken from Liu Jinyu, 'Virgil in China in the Twentieth Century', *Sino-American Journal of Comparative Literature*, 1 (2015): 67–105, consulted online: www.academia.edu.

148. For example, Euclid's *Elements*, Aristotle's *On the Soul*, Cicero's *On Friendship*, Epictetus' *Handbook*, Aesop's *Fables*.

149. Zhou Zuoren, 'History of European Literature', originally lecture notes at Peking University in 1917–18, see Zhou Zuoren and Zhi An, *History of European Literature* (Ouzhou Wenxueshi) (Shijiazhuang: Hebei Jiaoyu Chubanshe), 55–7, cited in Jinyu, 'Virgil in China', 14–15.

150. This article is not easily accessible online and is little discussed. Erskine's original article was published in *Harper's Magazine*, August 1930, 280–6.

151. Jinyu, 'Virgil in China', 25.

152. Quoted in ibid., 27, from W. Sellar, *Roman Poets of the Augustan Age: Vergil* (1877; repr. Cambridge: Cambridge University Press, 2011), 87.

153. Jinyu, 'Virgil in China', 35.

154. For the twentieth- and twenty-first-century period, see S. Harrison, 'Some Views of the *Aeneid* in the Twentieth Century', in Harrison (ed.), *Oxford Readings in Virgil's Aeneid*, 1–20; C. Perkell, 'Editor's Introduction', in Perkel (ed.), *Reading Vergil's Aeneid*, 14–28; K. Haynes, 'Classic Vergil', in Farrell and Putnam (eds), *A Companion*, 421–34; Hardie, *The Last Trojan Hero*, 16–19. The most recent book dedicated purely to modern reception is T. Ziolkowski, *Virgil and the Moderns* (Princeton, NJ: Princeton University Press, 1993).

155. Heinze, *Virgil's Epic Technique*, 473.

156. E. Pound, 'How to Read' (1931), in *Literary Essays*, ed. T. S. Eliot (London: Faber, 1954;

repr. 1985), 28, available online: https://archive.org/details/in.ernet.dli.2015.504260/page/n7/mode/2up (accessed 9 May 2024).

157. T. Haecker, *Vergil: Father of the West* (London: Sheed and Ward, 1934), 78.

158. In the second of these, Eliot discusses Vergil as 'prophet', as Haecker, *Vergil*, 77; see T. S. Eliot, 'Vergil and the Christian World', *Sewanee Review*, 61, no. 1 (Winter 1953): 3. Analysis in Johnson, *Darkness Visible*, 6–8; D. Kennedy, 'Modern Receptions and Their Interpretative Implications: The Case of T.S. Eliot', in Mac Górain and Martindale (es), *The Cambridge Companion*, 23–42, is a meditation on Eliot's contribution to interpretation in general.

159. Eliot's ideas on a classic also go back to Sainte-Beuve: 'The idea of the classic implies in itself something that has consequence and stability, that makes a cohesive tradition, that is self-composed and self-transmitted, and that endures' 'The idea of a classic implies something that has continuance and consistence, and which produces unity and tradition, fashions and transmits itself, and endures' ('"What is a Classic" (1850), *Causerie du Lundi*, III', in C. Sainte-Beuve, *Essays by Sainte-Beuve*, trans. Elizabeth Lee (London: Walter Scott, 1890), 2).

160. T. S. Eliot, *What is a Classic?* (London: Faber and Faber, 1945) 31.

161. W. Auden, 'Shield of Achilles' and 'Secondary Epic', in *W. H. Auden: Collected Poems*, ed. E. Mendelson (London: Faber, 1976), 596 and 598, respectively.

162. Here is a sample:

> Why Virgil's poems have for the last two thousand years exercised so great an influence on our Western culture is, paradoxically, because he was a renegade to the true Muse. His pliability; his subservience; his narrowness; his denial of that stubborn imaginative freedom which the true poets who preceded him had prized; his perfect lack of originality, courage, humour, or even animal spirits : these were the negative qualities which first commended him to government circles, and have kept him in favour ever since.

There is much more where this comes from: see R. Graves, 'The Virgil Cult', *Virginia Quarterly Review* 38, no. 1 (1962): 13–35.

163. Pöschl, *The Art of Vergil*, 18, 12.

164. Above all in the large-scale studies by the Germans Karl Büchner (1955 entry for 'Vergil' in the encyclopaedia Pauly-Wissowa) and Friedrich Klingner, in his book on Virgil's works, *Virgil*: Bucolica, Georgica, Aeneis (Zurich: Artemis Verlag, 1967).

165. Otis, *Virgil*, 384.

166. Probably by W. Johnson; see W. Clausen, Appendix to Horsfall (ed.), *A Companion*, 313.

167. Parry, 'The Two Voices'.

168. W. Clausen, 'An Interpretation of the Aeneid', *Harvard Studies in Classical Philology*, 68 (1964): 146.

169. M. Putnam, *The Poetry of the* Aeneid (Cambridge, MA: Harvard University Press, 1965), 196; earlier (p. 193) he comments, 'It is Aeneas who loses at the end of Book XII, leaving Turnus victorious in his tragedy'.

170. The privileging of the 'private' is not necessarily Latin – the word *privatus* originally meant 'deprived' (of public office).

171. W. Camps, *An Introduction*, 110, argues that the communal goal elevates individuals: 'The human action and suffering is . . . part of a process leading to an end in history which is felt to matter more than the fortunes of the individual humans, yet so as to enhance rather than diminish their value.' He acknowledges that this notion might be more than some can stomach, and in doing so admits the 'private voice': 'Those who cannot enter with sympathy into Virgil's conception of Rome may find in the meaning of his poem for themselves in its complementary theme, the impact of world forces and world movements on the lives of individuals and the human qualities displayed in their response.'

Hardie, *Virgil's* Aeneid, turns Pöschl's symbolism into a more complicated structure – the forces that assert order in nature are analogous to those that do so in politics and state-craft and are mythologically represented by the gods defeating the giants (Gigantomachy); this is reflected by the cosmic and gigantomachic imagery of the poem, and is encapsulated in the Shield of Aeneas, on which Rome (*urbs*) becomes a microcosm of the world (*orbs*). Hardie has since reflected the *Aeneid's* critical aspect – e.g. in *The Epic Successors of Virgil: A Study in the Dynamics of a Tradition* (Cambridge: Cambridge University Press, 1993).

172. Johnson, *Darkness Visible*, 130.

173. Ibid., 1–22.

174. Lyne, *Further Voice*, 2; it is always worth asking, and not always clear, what exactly the further voice is saying.

175. Conte, 'The Strategy', 151. His examples (pp. 154 ff.) are, on purpose, obvious ones: is killing Turnus vengeance, a violation of the duty to spare the defeated, or the execution of divine will? Is Turnus an arrogant thug or a tragic hero of independence? Is Mezentius a case of barbarous bestiality or paternal love? The answer to these questions is, 'All of the above' (which might make them 'contraries' rather than 'contradictories'); but no less important is the degree to which similar questions can be multiplied: Are the Trojans colonizers or invaders? Is Neptune a bringer of order (Book I) or disrupter of it (destroying Laomedon's Troy, demanding the sacrifice of the innocent Palinurus)? Is Pallas a boy or a heroic warrior? Is Latinus strong or weak? Is Jupiter?

176. Whitman, 'Song of Myself' 51, in Hardie, *The Last Trojan Hero*, 19.

177. For a recent, moderately pessimistic, position on the ending, see R. Gaskin, 'On Being Pessimistic about the End of the *Aeneid*' (University of Liverpool, 2021), available online: https://livrepository. liverpool.ac.uk/3146177/1/On%20being%20 pessimistic%20about%20the%20end%20 of%20the%20Aeneid.pdf (accessed 10 May 2024).

178. Homeric cinema is, most recently, *O Brother, Where Art Thou?* (2000) and *Troy* (2004); earlier *The Odyssey* (1997), *The Fury of Achilles* (1962), *Helen of Troy* (1956) and *Ulysses* (1954).

179. Hardie, *The Last Trojan Hero*, 18.

180. See K. Kirchwey, 'Vergil's *Aeneid* and Contemporary Poetry' in Farrell and Putnam (eds), *A Companion*, 465–81.

181. Ibid., 467; by comparison the *Iliad* is more favoured – Alice Oswald's *Memorial: An Excavation of the* Iliad (London: Faber and Faber, 2013) is one recent example.

182. F. Cox, *Sibylline Sisters: Virgil's Presence in Contemporary Women's Writing* (Oxford: Oxford University Press, 2011), she mentions novels by such as Margaret Drabble, A. S. Byatt and Ursula Le Guin, as well as poetry by Ruth Fainlight, Carol Anne Duffy and U. A. Fanthorpe, in addition to women poets already mentioned.

183. In a further Virgilian contradiction, it is the innocent victims who are commemorated in the memorial, but Virgil's words are about those on the aggressive mission.

184. S. Harrison, 'The *Aeneid* in the 20th Century', in Harrison (ed.), *Oxford Readings in Virgil's* Aeneid, 17.

185. T. Schmitz, *Modern Literary Theory and Ancient Texts: An Introduction* (Malden, MA: John Wiley & Son, 2007; first published in German, 2002), 5.

186. T. Eagleton, *Literary Theory: An Introduction*, 2nd edn (Malden, MA, and Oxford: Blackwell, 1996), ix; in *After Theory* (London: Penguin, 2004), he has issued not a recantation but an adjustment of perspective. Take p. 103: 'No idea is more unpopular with contemporary cultural theory than that of absolute truth . . . Let us begin, then, by seeking to defend this remarkably modest, eminently reasonable notion.'

187. The name was taken from John Crowe Ransom's book, *The New Criticism* (New York: New Directions, 1941).

188. Eagleton, *Literary Theory*, 2nd edn, 42.

189. Ibid. 61–4; J. Zimmermann, *Hermeneutics: A Very Short Introduction* (Oxford: Oxford University Press, 2015), 41–66; both discussing the thought of Gadamer (and, in Zimmermann's case, Ricoeur).

190. In its broadest sense, everything in literary theory – and much outside it (our

understanding of the world and each other) – can be considered 'hermeneutic'; but here the term can keep its original application, to literary texts and the theories concerning them that are labelled 'hermeneutic'.

191. What is given here is one version of it; the 'hermeneutic circle' itself is open to interpretation.

192. Eagleton, *Literary Theory*, 2nd edn, 62.

193. Ibid., 64–77, looking at Iser, Barthes, Sartre and Fish; C. Martindale, *Redeeming the Text : Latin Poetry and the Hermeneutics of Reception* (Cambridge: Cambridge University Press, 1993), chapters 1 and 2; Schmitz, *Modern Literary Theory*, 86–97.

194. Martindale, *Redeeming the Text*, 3.

195. As in A. Zanker and G. Thorarinsson, 'The Meanings of "Meaning" and Reception Studies', *Materiali e discussioni per l'analisi dei testi classici*, 67 (2011): 9–19.

196. Quoted by Zimmermann, *Hermeneutics*, 59; matters are not that simple – a reader, unlike someone in a conversation, lacks the signals of facial expression, intonation or gesture (emphasized by Bakhtin – 9.6.4); and a text is the same for all readers and can be returned to, whereas a conversation is for its participants only and perishes.

197. Eagleton, *Literary Theory*, 2nd edn, 82–90, taking in Formalism, the Prague School and Semiotics.

198. Schmitz, *Modern Literary Theory*, 2.

199. The prototype of such a 'system' is Claude Lévi-Strauss' structural analysis of myth, in his *Structural Anthropology* (New York: Basic Books, 1963), from the French of 1958.

200. Schmitz, *Modern Literary Theory*, 38–40.

201. Eagleton, *Literary Theory*, 2nd edn, 40.

202. Ibid., 92.

203. The closest I can find is J. Farrell, 'The Narrative Forms and Mythological Materials of Classical Epic', in C. Christiane Reitz and S. Finkmann (eds), *Structures of Epic Poetry* (Berlin, Munich and Boston, MA: De Gruyter, 2019), 51–80, but this whole project is confined to Greek and Latin epic and therefore cannot claim applicability to epic as a whole. A broader

analysis can be found in C. M. Bowra, *Heroic Poetry* (London: Macmillan and Co. 1952) but it is not explicitly structuralist.

204. See the last paragraph on structure within individual books, *Introduction* 7.1.2.

205. Schmitz, *Modern Literary Theory*, chapter 5, 77–85.

206. J. Kristeva, *Desire in Language: A Semiotic Approach to Literature and Art* (New York: Columbia University Press, 1980), 66, cited by Schmitz, *Modern Literary Theory*, 78.

207. Michael Riffattere in 1966, quoted in Schmitz, *Modern Literary Theory*, 80.

208. Eagleton, *Literary Theory*, 2nd edn, chapter 4, 110–30, above all on Derrida and Barthes; Schmitz, *Modern Literary Theory*, chapter 8, 113–39, also on De Man, Hirsch and Fish.

209. Schmitz, *Modern Literary Theory*, chapter 10, 159–75, also the preceding chapter on Foucault, pp. 141–5.

210. S. Greenblatt, *Shakespearean Negotiations: The Circulation of Social Energy in Renaissance England* (Berkeley, CA: University of California Press, 1988), 52, quoted by Schmitz, *Modern Literary Theory*, 170.

211. Eagleton, *Literary Theory*, 2nd edn, 131–68, above all on Freud, Lacan, Althusser, Holland, Bloom and Kristeva; Schmitz, *Modern Literary Theory*, chapter 12, 195–204, also on Jung.

212. Goldschmidt, *Shaggy Crowns*, argues for rivalry; Hardie, *The Epic Successors*, chapter 4, for a Bloomian view of first-century Roman epic.

213. E. Oliensis, 'Freud's "Aeneid"', *Vergilius*, 47 (2001): 39–63; her article begins with a survey of how Freud has hitherto been applied to the poem.

214. Ibid., 51; for greater detail, see Oliensis, 'Murdering Mothers', chapter 2 of her *Freud's Rome: Psychoanalysis and Latin Poetry*, Roman Literature and Its Contexts (Cambridge: Cambridge University Press, 2009), 57–91.

215. 'The interpretation of dreams is the "royal road" to a knowledge of the unconscious element in our psychic life', in S. Freud, *The Interpretation of Dreams* (Ware: Macmillan, 1997), 441.

216. N. Frye, *Anatomy of Criticism: Four Essays* (Princeton, NJ: Princeton University Press, 1957).

217. N. Holland, *The Dynamics of Literary Response* (Oxford: Oxford University Press, 1968), 30.

218. Aristotle, *Poetics* 1449b.

219. N. Holland, *5 Readers Reading* (New Haven, CT: Yale, 1975), 209.

220. J. Hayes, MA thesis, University of California, San Bernardino, 2008.

221. Schmitz, *Modern Literary Theory*, chapter 11, 176–94, mentioning Iragaray, Cixous, Kristeva, Fetterley, de Beauvoir and Millett.

222. See Eagleton, *Literary Theory*, 2nd edn, 162–6.

223. Schmitz, *Modern Literary Theory*, 206–7.

224. See Eagleton, *Literary Theory*, 2nd edn, 205–6.

225. From resentment (Iarbas, 4.215 ff.), bravado (Numanus Remulus, 9.614 ff.) or self-exhortation (Turnus, 12.99 f.).

Chapter 10

1. For articles on translation into other languages, see *Introduction* 9.4.3 Diaspora: The *Aeneid* in China.

2. A comprehensive survey of the theory of literary translation up to 1998, and advocacy of translation as both possible and desirable, is to be found in G. Steiner, *After Babel: Aspects of Language and Translation*, 3rd edn (Oxford: Oxford University Press, 1998), chapter 4, especially 248–83. He quotes Goethe (p. 262), writing in a letter to Carlyle in July 1827: 'Say what one will of the inadequacy of translation, it remains one of the most important and valuable concerns in the whole of world affairs.'

3. J. Borges, 'Pierre Menard, Author of the *Quixote*', *Sur* (May 1939).

4. Steiner, *After Babel*, 251.

5. As set forth in his Preface to Ovid's *Epistles Translated by Several Hands* (London: for Jacob Tonson, 1680).

6. J. Dryden, Dedication to his translation of the *Aeneid* (1697), in *Virgil's* Aeneid, trans. John Dryden (New York: P. F. Collier, 1909), 62, available online: https://oll.libertyfund.org/titles/dryden-the-aeneid-dryden-trans (accessed 10 May 2024).

7. Wordsworth, after translating *Aeneid* Books I–III during the early 1820s, also reached a position beyond metaphrase: 'Having been displeased in modern translations with the additions of incongruous matter, I began to translate with a resolve to keep clear of that fault, by adding nothing; but I became convinced that a spirited translation can scarcely be achieved in the English language without admitting a principle of compensation.' Cited in C. Burrow, 'Virgil in English Translation', in Mac Góráin and Martindale (eds), *The Cambridge Companion*, 121–2.

8. From F. Schleiermacher, 'On the Various Methods of Translation' (1813), quoted in M. Reynolds, *Translation: A Very Short Introduction* (Oxford: Oxford University Press, 2016), 53.

9. S. Braund, 'Mind the Gap: On Foreignizing Translations of the *Aeneid*', in Farrell and Putnam (eds), *A Companion*, 452–3.

10. Ibid., 460, though on the French translator Pierre Klossowski.

11. Quoted by Steiner, *After Babel*, 282.

12. The first translation dedicated to a reigning monarch (Prince Albert) was by Rann and Charles Rann Kennedy, published in 1849 – though Thomas Phaer had dedicated his translation of the first seven books to Mary I a few months before her death in 1558, and Richard Fanshawe had dedicated his version of *Aeneid* Book IV to Prince Charles in 1648, when Charles I was under imprisonment: it was a form of literary protest against the Commonwealth.

13. Burrow, 'Virgil', 109.

14. The Gransden (ed.), *Virgil in English*, sadly hard to obtain, with plentiful extracts from translations down the ages, is an invaluable compendium; Burrow (previous note) examines the background of many translators.

15. Chaucer, *Troilus and Criseyde* 5.1795 f.

16. Chaucer, 'The Legend of Dido' (from *The Legend of Good Women*), ll. 1016 ff.

17. Gavin Douglas, *The XIII bukes of Eneados of the famose poete Virgill* (1553), 1.46.

18. Thomas Campion, *Observations in the Art of English Poesie* (1602).

19. F. Nietzsche, *The Gay Science* (Chemnitz: Verlag von Ernst Schmeitzner, 1882), 83.

20. Sir John Denham, verse letter to Sir Richard Fanshawe, 1648, on the latter's translation of Guarini's *Il pastor fido*; cited by Gransden (ed.), *Virgil in English*, 331.

21. For a comprehensive examination of Dryden's translation, see R. Thomas *Virgil and the Augustan Reception* (Cambridge: Cambridge University Press, 2001), chapter 4, 122–53.

22. Dryden's 1687 rendition of the episode of Nisus and Euryalus borrowed wholesale from that of Richard Maitland, Earl of Lauderdale; Dryden rewrote it for his 1697 version. Not all of Dryden's immediate predecessors could serve as models – some branched off in their own direction, as did Sir Richard Fanshawe himself with his Spenserian stanzas.

23. J. Dryden, 'Postscript to the Reader' (1697), opening.

24. 'Virgil, who designed to form a perfect prince, and would insinuate that Augustus, whom he calls Æneas in his poem, was truly such, found himself obliged to make him without blemish, thoroughly virtuous.' Dryden's Dedication to his translation (1697).

25. T. S. Eliot, 'John Dryden', in *Homage to John Dryden* (London: Leonard and Virginia Woolf at the Hogarth Press, 1924).

26. Wordsworth, letter to Scott, 7 November 1805.

27. Luke Milbourne, another translator of the *Aeneid*, wrote censoriously of his predecessor in his *Notes on Dryden's Virgil* (1698); for Alexander Pope, Milbourne exemplified how 'Pride, malice, folly against Dryden rose' (*Essay on Criticism* ll. 458 ff.).

28. See R. Williams, 'James Henry's *Aeneidea*', *Hermathena*, 116 (1973): 27–43; and for a sample, *Introduction* 7.7 Diction.

29. M. Arnold, *On Translating Homer* (1861): the four cardinal virtues in translating Homer for Arnold are rapidity, directness of thought, plainness of expression and nobility.

30. D. West, *Virgil: The Aeneid* (London: Penguin, 1991), xlv.

31. Ibid., xlvi.

32. W. Jackson Knight, The Aeneid (London: Penguin, 1956).

33. A. Mandelbaum, The Aeneid *of Virgil* (New York: Bantam, 2004).

34. R. Fitzgerald, *Virgil:* The Aeneid (London: Everyman, 1981).

35. S. Lombardo, *Virgil:* Aeneid (Hackett, 2005).

36. S. Ruden, The Aeneid: *Virgil* (New Haven, CT: Yale, 2008).

37. S. Bartsch, The Aeneid: *A New Translation – Vergil* (London: Profile Books, 2020).

38. S. Heaney, Aeneid: *Book VI* (London: Faber, 2016), xv.

39. See Preface.

40. So O'Hara, 'Virgil's Style', 368.

41. Steiner, *After Babel*, 28.

SELECT BIBLIOGRAPHY

A. Principles: Books, journals and classical source texts

What follows is a select or, more precisely, a personal bibliography of the books to which I have referred most often and most generally in this *Companion*, or which are complementary to it. Several of them at least would be found in any academic library with holdings on Virgil's *Aeneid*. Many other books are cited, along with articles, in the *Companion's* discussions of particular topics, and their details are given in full at that point in the *Introduction* or *Commentary*. They might be harder to obtain.[1]

I would recommend readers new to Virgil or to the *Aeneid* to start from one of the introductions (sections B and C); they are short but far from basic. Once embarked on the *Companion* commentaries, readers might want to pursue discussion of an individual book in one of the book-by-book guides (section D). After reading the whole poem, they could turn to collections of essays (section E), or to the longer examinations by individual authors (also in E). I would put in a plea that students, however short of time, at some point brave the footnotes and follow up, even for no more than a single episode in the poem, Virgil's allusions and the relevant ancient and modern criticism. This will take them, as I have found, on a fascinating journey into Virgil's literary laboratory and thence to the debate it has generated, made pungent by the characters of the commentators. The latter's bibliographies will lead further into the scholarly fission.[2] For any reader wanting closer proximity with the Latin, I have appended the commentaries that I consulted (section F).

To avoid congesting this bibliography I have not listed the journal articles mentioned in the body of the *Companion*. They are without exception available online; the journals database that I used was JSTOR. (A small minority of articles were found by searching on the internet directly). As far as I could I favoured content that was not trammelled for a non-Latinist by extended analysis of Latin (or Greek) language, and where quotations were translated.

For ancient texts cited, an internet search for the author 'in English' or 'in translation' will quickly yield (at the time of writing) one or more of the resources listed below:

- https://www.perseus.tufts.edu/hopper/collections, Greek and Roman collections – many texts can be found here, in both English and the original language (though Servius' *Aeneid* commentary is given only in Latin);

- https://penelope.uchicago.edu/Thayer/E/Roman/Texts/, 'Lacus Curtius', for a selection of Latin and Greek works, sadly not all translated (Macrobius, Aulus Gellius, Suetonius, Plutarch);

- https://topostext.org/texts, for a comprehensive catalogue of Greek literature, all translated (Hyginus can only be found here);

- https://www.attalus.org/poetry/, for a selection of Greek and Roman authors not on Perseus (fragments of Ennius and Naevius);

- https://www.theoi.com/Library.html, for a useful selection of Greek literature (*Epic Cycle*, Lycophron, Pausanias);

- https://www.poetryintranslation.com/, for modern translations of many Greek and Roman works.

The drawback to consulting online translations is that they, or the editions from which they were made, are often antiquated. This has additional repercussions for the fragments of Ennius, where the available online translation (on the Attalus site), to which this *Companion* refers, is by Warmington (1935);[3] the numbering in the edition that he used differs from that of Skutsch (1985),[4] referred to by many modern commentaries. Online accessibility, however, seemed to me paramount. For more up-to-date renderings and scholarship, readers may seek online access to the Loeb Classical Library.

Anyone with world enough and time to pursue historical fragments will find that I have used, for Roman historians, Hermann Peter's collection of 1883 (https://archive.org/details/historicorumrom 02petegoog) and for Greek historians the digital collection available at: https://www.dfhg-project.org/.

B. Introductions to Virgil

Griffin, J. *Virgil*, Oxford Past Masters Series (Oxford: Oxford University Press, 1986; reprinted London: Bristol Classical Press, 2001).
Hardie, P. *Virgil*, Greece and Rome: New Surveys in the Classics (Oxford: Oxford University Press, 1998; reprinted Cambridge: Cambridge University Press, 2010).

C. Introductions to the *Aeneid*

The following examine the text, aspect by aspect:

Camps, W. *An Introduction to Virgil's* Aeneid (London: Oxford University Press, 1969; reprinted 2010).
Gransden, K. *Virgil*, The Aeneid: *A Student Guide* (Cambridge: Cambridge University Press, 2004; 2nd edn by S. Harrison, 2010).
Ross, D. *Virgil's* Aeneid: *A Reader's Guide* (Malden, MA, and Oxford: Blackwell, 2007).

For those wishing to look at the *Aeneid* alongside Homer:

Jenkyns, R. *Classical Epic: Homer and Virgil* (London: Bristol Classical Press, 1998).

A *vade mecum* through the books of the poem, discussing major themes and narrative techniques:

Anderson, W. *The Art of the* Aeneid (Hoboken, NJ: Prentice-Hall, 1969; reprinted London: Bristol Classical Press, 2004).

D. Longer guides to the *Aeneid*

The following offer a more extended treatment of the individual books of the *Aeneid* and much more besides:

Fratantuono, L. *Madness Unchained: A Reading of Virgil's* Aeneid (Lanham, MD: Lexington, 2007).
Horsfall, N. (ed.) *A Companion to the Study of Virgil* (Leiden, New York and Cologne: Brill, 1995).
Otis, B. *Virgil: A Study in Civilised Poetry* (Oxford: Oxford University Press, 1964).
Perkell, C. (ed.) *Reading Vergil's* Aeneid: *An Interpretive Guide* (Norman, OK: University of Oklahoma Press, 1999).
Putnam, M. *The Poetry of the* Aeneid (Cambridge, MA: Harvard University Press, 1965), Books II, V, VIII and XII.
Quinn, K. *Virgil's* Aeneid: *A Critical Description* (London: Routledge, 1968).

E. The *Aeneid* in modern criticism

These are the single works to which the *Companion* returns most frequently. They have laid the foundation for much subsequent criticism; age does not diminish the freshness of their insights. They might furnish a basic reading list:

Hardie, P. *Virgil's* Aeneid: *Cosmos and Imperium* (Oxford: Clarendon Press, 1986).
Heinze, R. *Virgil's Epic Technique*, trans. H. and D. Harvey (first published Berlin, 1902; London: Bristol Classical Press, 2004).[5]
Johnson, W. *Darkness Visible: A Study of Vergil's* Aeneid (Berkeley, CA: University of California Press, 1979; reprinted Chicago, IL: University of Chicago Press, 2015).

Lyne, R. *Further Voices in Vergil's* Aeneid (Oxford: Clarendon Press, 1987).

Pöschl, V. *The Art of Vergil: Image and Symbol in the* Aeneid (Ann Arbor, MI: University of Michigan Press, 1962; reissued in paperback 1970).

Collections of significant essays and journal articles:

Farrell, J. and M. Putnam (eds) *A Companion to Vergil's* Aeneid *and Its Tradition* (Malden, MA, Oxford and Chichester: Wiley-Blackwell, 2010).

Harrison, S. (ed.) *Oxford Readings in Virgil's* Aeneid (Oxford: Clarendon Press, 1990).

Mac Góráin, F. and C. Martindale (eds) *The Cambridge Companion to Virgil*, 2nd edn (Cambridge: Cambridge University Press, 2019).

Quinn, S. *Why Virgil? A Collection of Interpretations* (Wauconda, IL: Bolchazy-Carducci, 2000).

F. Commentaries on the individual books

When working from the Latin, I tried where possible to use one older and one more recent single-volume commentary on each book, because tastes and emphases change – earlier commentators could remain idiosyncratic while their successors are more aware of the ever-growing corpus of Virgilian criticism. I did not do this for Book VIII because three new commentaries appeared almost simultaneously (in 2017–18); and Books IX, X and XII have only relatively recently been accorded single-volume commentaries in English.

Book I   Austin, R. Aeneidos: *Liber Primus* (Oxford: Clarendon Press, 1971; reprinted 1984).
             Ganiban, R. *Vergil:* Aeneid *Book 1* (Indianapolis, IN: Focus, 2008).

Book II   Austin, R. Aeneidos: *Liber Secundus* (Oxford: Clarendon Press, 1964; reprinted 1980).
             Horsfall, N. (ed.) *Virgil,* Aeneid *2: A Commentary* (Leiden and Boston, MA: Brill, 2008).

Book III   Heyworth, S. and Morwood, J. *A Commentary on Vergil:* Aeneid *3* (Oxford: Oxford University Press, 2017).
             Horsfall, N. *Virgil,* Aeneid *3: A Commentary* (Leiden: Brill, 2006).
             Williams, R. Aeneid *III* (Oxford: Clarendon Press, 1962; reprinted London: Bristol Classical Press, 2003).

Book IV   Austin, R. Aeneidos: *Liber Quartus* (Oxford: Clarendon Press, 1955; reprinted 1983).
             O'Hara, J. *Vergil:* Aeneid *Book 4* (Indianapolis, IN: Focus, 2011).

Book V   Williams, R. Aeneidos: *Liber Quintus* (Oxford: Clarendon Press, 1960; reprinted London: Bristol Classical Press, 1991).
             Farrell, J. *Vergil:* Aeneid *Book 5* (Indianapolis, IN: Focus, 2014).

Book VI   Austin, R. Aeneidos: *Liber Sextus* (Oxford: Clarendon Press, 1977; reprinted 1986).
             Horsfall, N. *Virgil,* Aeneid *6: A Commentary* (Berlin and Boston, MA: De Gruyter, 2013).

Book VII   Fordyce, C. Aeneidos: *Libri VII–VIII* (Oxford: Published for the University of Glasgow by Oxford University Press, 1977; reprinted London: Bristol Classical Press, 1991).
             Horsfall, N. *Virgil,* Aeneid *7: A Commentary* (Leiden and Boston, MA: Brill, 2000).
             (A commentary by R. Ganiban (ed.) *Vergil,* Aeneid *Book 7* (Indianapolis, IN: Focus, 2021) has become available and is to be preferred to Fordyce.)

Book VIII   Maclennan, K. (ed.) *Virgil:* Aeneid *Book VIII* (London: Bloomsbury, 2017).
             O'Hara, J. *Vergil:* Aeneid *Book 8* (Indianapolis, IN: Focus, 2018).
             (At the time of writing, I was unable to consult L. Frantantuono, *Virgil,* Aeneid *8* (Leiden and Boston, MA: Brill, 2018), which is a major contribution here.)

Book IX   Hardie, P. (ed.) *Virgil:* Aeneid *Book IX* (Cambridge: Cambridge University Press, 1994).

Book X   Harrison, S. (ed.) *Vergil:* Aeneid *10* (Oxford: Clarendon Press, 1991).
             (A commentary by A. Rossi (ed.) *Vergil:* Aeneid *10* (Indianapolis, IN: Focus, 2023) has become available.)

Book XI   Horsfall, N. *Virgil,* Aeneid *11: A Commentary* (Leiden: Brill, 2003).
             McGill, S. (ed.) *Virgil:* Aeneid *Book XI* (Cambridge: Cambridge University Press, 2020).

Book XII   Tarrant, R. (ed.) *Virgil:* Aeneid *Book XII* (Cambridge: Cambridge University Press, 2012).

Select Bibliography

The Focus series of commentaries is reaching completion (Books IX, XI and XII still to go, at the time of writing). They offer a level of notes and a presentation of criticism old and new that are suited to a reader in English.

Select Bibliography

1. Because I myself had difficulty accessing them, I have not cited the *Virgil Encyclopedia*, ed. R. Thomas and J. Ziolkowski, 3 vols (Malden, MA: Wiley-Blackwell, 2013) or the monumental collection of articles in P. Hardie, *Virgil: Critical Assessments* (London: Routledge, 1999).

2. It can be tempting to transfer William Hazlitt's dictum ('On the Ignorance of Learned Men', in *Table-Talk; or, Original Essays* (London: John Warren, 1821), 159–78) from Shakespeare to Virgil: 'If we wish to know the force of genius, we should read Shakespeare; if we wish to see the insignificance of human learning, we may study his commentators.' Yet Hazlitt himself was one of them – Heinrich Heine, clearly a kindred spirit, called him the only one of any consequence (*Shakespeare's Mädchen und Frauen* (Paris: Delloye, 1839). Readers can quickly judge for themselves whether or not a piece of criticism is sharpening their appreciation of the poem.

3. Quintus Ennius, *Remains of Old Latin, Volume I: Ennius. Caecilius*, trans. E. Warmington, Loeb Classical Library 294 (Cambridge, MA: Harvard University Press, 1935).

4. Quintus Ennius, *The Annals of Quintus Ennius*, ed. O. Skutsch (Oxford: Oxford University Press, 1985).

5. A useful review of Heinze's enduring value, and of his limitations, is P. Hardie, 'Virgil's Epic Techniques: Heinze Ninety Years On', *Classical Philology*, 90, no. 3 (1995): 267–76.

INDEX

The index has been compiled from the text of the poem, the introductory essays, the commentary and the most significant endnotes ('endn.' in the locators).

References to the introduction are simple page numbers (with 'endn.' where they refer to endnotes). References to the text and its commentary are of the form 1.111 where the initial numeral is the book number, followed by the line number(s). If a locator is of the form 1.111 n. then the reference is to the commentary notes and not to the text of the *Aeneid*.

Names that occur in the poem are indexed using bold type (in contast with figures referred to but not named in the text (Cleopatra, Pompey), or figures referred to only in the commentary notes.

I-LS, II-LS, III-LS (etc.) refers to the section on Literary sources at the start of the commentary on Book I, II, III (etc.); similarly I-D (etc.) refers to the section describing the book at the start of each chapter.

Abaris 9.344

Abas

    (1) **Trojan 1.121**

    (2) **Greek 3.286**, 3.287–8 n.

    (3) **Etruscan 10.170, 10.427**

Abella 7.740

academic scepticism 65

Academy 65

Acamus 2.262

acanthus 1.647–55 n.

Acarnania 5.298

Acca 11.820, 11.823, 11.897

Accius, Lucius 9.622 n. (Ascanius akin to Philoctetes)

Acesta 5.36 n. (alliance with Rome), **5.718**

Acestes 1.195, 1.550, 1.558, 1.570; 5.30, 5.36, 5.37 n. (on appearance), 5.38 n. (on ancestry), **5.61, 5.73, 5.106, 5.301, 5.387** (boxing match), **5.418, 5.498** (archery contest), **5.519, 5.531, 5.540, 5.573, 5.630, 5.711** (gives name to city), **5.746–57, 5.771; 9.218, 9.286** (mentioned as king)

Achaean 1.283–5 n. (creation of province Achaea)

Achaean War 6.836–7 n.

Achaemenides 3.614–91

Achates 1.120, 1.174 (meaning of name), **1.188** (Aeneas' armour-bearer), **1.312, 1.459** (addressed by Aeneas), **1.513–19, 1.579–85** (addresses Aeneas), **1.644–5, 1.656, 1.696; 3.523** (hails Italy); **6.34–5, 6.158–60** (conversing with Aeneas);

8.466 , 8.520–2, 8.586; 10.332 (fights beside Aeneas), **10.344** (grazed); **12.384, 12.459**

Acheron 5.99; 6.107, 6.132 n. (meaning, rivers listed), **6.295; 7.91, 7.312, 7.569; 11.23**

Achilles 1.1–7 n. (as type of hero), **1.30, 1.458** (on temple of Juno), **1.468, 1.484, 1.752; 2.29, 2.197, 2.275, 2.476, 2.540** (remembered by Priam), **2.548** (in Pyrrhus' taunt); **3.87, 3.326; 5.804–11** (Neptune saves Aeneas from him); **6.89, 6.168, 6.839; 9.742** (Turnus as another Achilles); **10.581; 11.404, 11.438** (weapons by Hephaestus); 12.90–1 n. (invulnerability), 12.350–2 (his horses), **12.545**

Acidalia 1.720

aclys 7.723–32 n.

Acmon 10.128

Acoetes 11.30, 11.85 (in mourning)

Aconteus 11.612, 11.615

Acragas 3.703

Acrisius 7.372, 7.410

Acron 10.719, 10.730

acrostic 7.601–3 n.

Actium 9; 3.276 n., **3.280; 8.675** (sea battle against Antony and Cleopatra), **8.704** (Apollo's epithet)

Actor

    (1) **Trojan 9.500**

    (2) **Auruncan from Capania 12.94 , 12.96**

Adamastus 3.614

annals *see* Ennius, Tacitus
ant 107 and 4.402–7 (Trojans compared to them)
Antaeus 10.561
Antandros 3.6
Antemnae 7.631
Antenor 1.242; 6.484
Antheus 1.181, 1.510; 12.443
Antiphates 9.696
Antony: Marcus Antonius 8–9, 56 (adopts Hercules as image); 6.621–2 n. (apparently referred to in the underworld); 8.359–61 n. (house on Esquiline), 8.675–713 n., 8.685 (dependency on Cleopatra, Battle of Actium), 8.724–8 n. (Parthian campaign)
Antores 10.778, 10.779 n.
Anubis 8.698
Anxur
  (1) Volscian 10.545
  (2) Volscian name for Tarracina in Latium 7.799
Apennines 12.697–727 n., 12.703
Aphidnus 9.702
Aphrodite 5.759–61 n. (worshipped on Mt. Eryx)
Apollo 45 (particular domains); 2.21–3 n. (Sminthian Apollo), 2.114–21 (consulted by Greeks, says Sinon); 2.319 (his priest, Panthus), 2.429; 3.69–83 n. (preeminence in Book III), 3.75–7 (tethering Delos), 3.84–101 (consulted by Aeneas), 3.119, 3.154–63 (interpreted by Helenus), 3.188, 3.251–2 (quoted by Celaeno), 3.274–5 (temple on Leucate), 3.359, 3.369–462 (prophecy delivered through Helenus), 3.474, 3.479, 3.637; 4.6, 4.58 (Dido's sacrifice), 4.143–9 (simile describing Aeneas), 4.345–6 (Grynean Apollo), 4.376 (Dido's sarcasm); 6.9–13, 6.35 (Sibyl, priestess at Cumae), 6.18–33 (temple built by Daedalus), 6.56–76 (Aeneas' prayer and promise of temple), 6.69–74 n. (patron deity of Augustus, Apolline games), 6.77–80, 6.100–1 (Sibyl possessed), 6.343–7 (prophecy about Palinurus); 7.62 (Latinus' sacrifice), 7.241 (quoted by Ilioneus), 7.773 (Asclepius); 8.336 (directing Evander), 8.704 (bending his bow over Actium), 8.720–1 (Augustus enthroned in temple); 9.638–63 (blocks Ascanius from entering battle) ('nothing in excess'), 9.654 n. (kills Python at
Delphi); 10.171 (as ship's figurehead), 10.316 (baby Lichas dedicated but killed), 10.537 (priest killed), 10.875; 11.785–95 (Apollo Soranus, who hears only half Arruns' prayer), 11.913; 12.392 (rewards Iapyx with medical skills), 12.392–7 n. (particular domains), 12.402–6 (to no avail), 12.516
Apollonius of Rhodes 18 and 24 (influence on early Virgil), 127–30 (synopsis of *Argonautica),* 130 (influences on *Argonautica),* 130–1 (two-tier allusion in *Aeneid),* 131 (as foundation story); I-LS, 1.657–94 n. (Cupid parallels Eros), 1.723–56 (Orpheus sings of the world's creation); III-LS; 3.13–68 n. (curse of Hamadryad), 3.202 n. (helmsman Tiphys), 3.209–67 and 3.251–2 nn (Phineus and Harpies), 3.225–6 n. (Birds of Ares), 3.374–462 n. (Phineus' prophecy to Argonauts), 3.548–87 n. (Scylla and Charybdis); IV-LS, 4.9 n. (Medea on her love), 4.24–7 n. (Medea on shame), 4.54–89 n. (Medea as fawn), 4.90–128 (Hera and Athena ask for Aphrodite's help), 4.143–50 n. (Apollo simile), 4.160–72 n. (wedding of Jason and Medea), 4.327–30 n. (Hypsipyle wanting Jason's child), 4.412 n. (apostrophising Eros), 4.474–7 n. (Medea and her sister Chalciope), 4.480–2 n. (on Oceanus), 4.483–6 (Medea's use of drugs), 4.487–91 n. (Medea's power over nature), 4.509–11 n. (Medea going to temple of Hecate), 4.522–52 n. (Medea awake thinking), 4.584–629 n. (Medea's curse), 4.657–8 n. (Medea's lost happiness); V-LS (boxing match), 5.8–41 (visit to Circe), 5.213–7 n. (Argo as hawk), 5.225–43 n. (Athena propels Argo), 5.253–3 n. (Athena's embroidery for Jason), 5.362–86, 5.371–4, 5.376–7 5.424–60, 5.426–7, 5.434–6 nn (boxing), 5.410–11 n. (Hercules' effect on morale); 6.422–3 n. (Medea lulls dragon), 6.453–4 n. (simile of moon through clouds), 6.707–9 n. (bee simile); 7.37–40 n. (invocation to Erato),, 7.212–48 n. (Argus requests golden fleece from Aeetes), 7.511–39 n. (babies terrified by dragon's hiss, sown warriors), 7.691–705 n. (flock of sea-birds simile), 7.706–22 n. (waves simile), 7.808–11 n. (Euphemus runs on surface of sea); 8.18–35 n. (sunlight

(2) tactics 2.440–4 n. (interlocking shields/ mantelet; ladders – cf. 11.505–7), 2.491–5 (battering ram); 10.238–40 n. (plans for deployment not followed through); 11.511–14 (pincer movement on city of Latinus), 11.515–16 (ambush on Aeneas)

(3) taunts 9.560–2 n., 9.590–620 n. (Numanus Remulus); 10.531–4 and 10.557–60 and 10.592–4 (Aeneas), 10.649–50 (Turnus), 10.811–12 (Aeneas), 10.491–5 (Turnus), 10.897–8 (Aeneas to Mezentius); 11.686–9 (Camilla to Ornytus), 11.715–7 (Camilla to son of Aunus); 12.359–61 (Turnus to Trojans), 12.889–93 (Aeneas to Turnus)

Batulum 7.739
bear 5.37 and 8.366–8 nn (Libyan bearskin)
Bebrycia 5.362–86 n., 5.373
bee 22–3 (in *Georgics*); 1.430–6 (simile); 6.707–9 (simile); 7.64–7 (omen); 9.182–3 n. (unanimity); 12.587–92 (shepherd smokes out swarm)
Bellerophon 5.116–23 n.
Bellona 58; 7.319; 8.703
Belus
    (1) ancestor of Dido 1.729
    (2) Dido's father 1.621; 2.81
Benacus 10.205
Benedict, Saint: Benedict of Nursia 7.706–22 n.
Beowulf 145
Berecynt(h)ian 2.788 n.; 6.784 ; 9.82, 9.619
Berenice *see* Catullus (Book VI citations)
Berlioz, Hector IV-D (opera *Les Troyens*)
Bernardus Silvestris 143 (allegorical commentary on *Aeneid*)
Beroe 5.620, 5.646–52
birds *see also* crane, dove, eagle, geese, hawk, swan, swallow 6.239–40 n. (cannot fly over Sibyl's cave), 6.310–12 (simile of migrating birds); 10.185–8 n. (crests of birds' feathers)
bireme *see* ships
Bitias
    (1) Phoenician or Trojan 1.738
    (2) Trojan 9.672 (defends Trojan camp), 9.703–9 (slain by Turnus); 11.396 (boasted of by Turnus)
Bloom, Harold 163
blushes 12.54–80 n.
boar 4.159 (desired prey of Ascanius); 10.707–18 (Mezentius like boar at bay), 10.730–1 n. (ferocity described by Lucretius)

boasting 10.545–9 n.
boat race 5.114–285; *see also* games
Bola 6.775
bonnet, Phrygian 4.215–18 n.; 9.614–18 n.
Bononia 10.198–203 n.
Borges, Jorge Luis 165
Bowen, Sir Charles 170
boxing 131 (in Theocritus); 5.64–70 and 5.364 nn (in army, gloves, procedure), 5.362–484 (at the games), 5.362–86 n.,
breastplate *see* armour, chain mail
Briareus 3.578–82 n. (under Etna); 6.287
Bridges, Robert 116 endn. 112 (*Aeneid* translated into hexameters)
Briusov, Valerii (Bryusov, Valery) 165–6
Broch, Hermann 158
Brontes 8.425
Brutus, Lucius Junius 4; 6.818; *see also* Brutus, Marcus Junius
Brutus, Marcus Junius 8; 6.817–23 n.
Bucolics see Virgil
bull 120 (linked similes); 12.103–6 n. (Turnus in simile), 12.715–19 (Aeneas and Turnus in simile); *see also* religion: sacrifice, animals for
burial 2.506–58, 4.613–21, 6.505, 9.486–9, 10.491–5 and 11.865–5 nn (importance of burial); 3.62–8 (ritual); 4.239–44 and 10.745–6 nn (closing eyes of dead), 4.457–61 n. (burial at home); 5.42–103 n. (9–day period; memorial for Anchises), 5.652 n. and 11.35 (role of women); 6.177–8 (pyre as place of tomb), 6.212–35 (details of cremation ceremony for Misenus), 6.325 n. (coin in mouth), 6.756–853 n. (Roman funeral processions); 7.1–4 n. (not for glory); 9.485–6 n. (corpses as carrion); 11.29–31 n. (position of body on bier), 11.59–99 n. (funeral procession for Pallas), 11.142 n. (torches), 11.184–199 (cremations of battle dead), 11.204–9 n. (inhumation and mass burial), 11.851 n. (trees round tombs)
Burke, Edmund 150 (on the sublime)
Bushnell, John 2.15–16 n.
butcher lists 10.747–54 n.
Butes
    (1) Trojan, famous boxer, son of Amycus 5.372
    (2) armour-bearer of Anchises, guardian of Ascanius 9.647

Buthrotum 3.293, 3.294–355 n.
Byron, George Gordon Lord 151 (on Virgil), 154 (in China); 7.641–817 n. (parodies catalogue)
Byrsa 1.367

Cacus 8.184–279 n., 8.194–201 (described), 8.205–8 (theft of Hercules' cattle), 8.218 (betrayed by lowing cow), 8.222–7 (flees and takes refuge), 8.241–2 (cave ripped open), 8.259–61 (throttled), 8.303–4 (in the song of the Salii)
Caeculus 7.681; 10.544
Caedicus
    (1) friend of Remulus 9.362
    (2) Rutulian 10.747
Caeneus
    (1) = Caenis, a woman changed into a man by Neptune 6.448
    (2) Trojan warrior 9.573
Caere 7.652 (1,000 men with Lausus); 8.479, 8.597; 10.183 (300 men with Astur and Aeneas); 12.281
Caesar
    (1) Gaius Julius Caesar 8 (rivalry with Pompey), 20 (in Georgics), 85 (priesthoods); 6.830 (against Pompey, invading Italy, clemency); 2.692–704 n. (Caesar's comet); 5.545–603 n. (performing *lusus Troiae*); 6.772 n. (awarded Civic Crown); 7.99–101 (statue dominating the world), 7.317–22 n. (evoked by 'father-in-law'); 8.646–51 n. (coinage showing *libertas*); 9.128–9 n. (management of morale)
    (2) Gaius Julius Caesar Octavianus (later Augustus) 6.792 (Augustus, founding golden age); 8.678–81 (Octavian at Actium), 8.714–6 (Octavian receiving tribute at triumph after Actium)*; see also* **Augustus**
    (3) unclear whether 1 or 2 above 1.286 (Julius Caesar's eastern campaigns, Augustus' settlement with Parthians); 6.789
Caesar, Lucius Julius 31
Caesar, Sextus Julius 31
Caesarion 9
Caicus 1.183; 9.35
Caieta
    (1) town in Latium 6.124–55 n. (link to Elpenor in *Odyssey*), 6.900
    (2) nurse of Aeneas 57; 7.2

Calchas 2.100, 2.122–9 (requires death of Sinon), 2.176–82 (requires Greek return to Argos), 2.185 (orders wooden horse)
Cales 7.728
Callimachus 19, 126–7 (poetic manifesto); 3.13–68 n. (Erysichthon, Hymn to Demeter), 3.73–7 n. (Hymn to Delos), 3.181 n. (Cretans as liars), 3.578–82 (Briareus under Etna), 3.692–718 n. (origins of Sicilian cities); 7.378–83 n. (simile of spinning-top), 7.435–6 n. (Erysichthon in Hymn to Demeter); VIII-LS (Hecale for poverty welcoming greatness), 8.416–22 n. (Lipare as Hephaestus' forge), 8.449–53 (Cyclops at work); Calydonian boar 7.304–7 n.
Calliope 9.525
Calybe 7.419
Calydon 7.306 ; 11.270
Calypso *see* Homer: *Odyssey*
Camerina 3.701
Camers 10.562 (son of Volcens, killed by Aeneas); 12.224 (Juturna in disguise)
Camilla 42–3 (character, womanliness), 81–2 (womanliness); 7.803 (entry at end of catalogue); 11.432 (mentioned by Turnus), 11.498–506 (presents her cohort), 11.499 n. (gap in her biography), 11.517–9 (given command by Turnus), 11.535–94 (described by Diana), 11.604 (joins with Latin cavalry), 11.648–63 n. (exemplars for her fighting methods), 11.649–63 (with her comrades compared to Amazon), 11.664–724 (*aristeia*), 11.759–67 (stalked by Arruns), 11.778–82 (attracted by gaudiness of Chloreus), 11.796–7 (Apollo grants her death), 11.803–4 (struck by spear), 11.816–27 (expires in Acca's arms, last instructions for Turnus), 11.831 n. (linked with Turnus by line describing death), 11.833 (loss revitalises Trojan side), 11.839 (death seen by Opis), 11.856, 11.868, 11.892 (watched by the women of the city), 11.898 (Acca reports death to Turnus)
Camillus, Marcus Furius 2.348–54 n. (*evocatio*); 3.537–8 n. (triumph); 6.825
camp, Trojan 9.8 n., 9.150–2 n., 9.468–72 n.; 10.25–7 n.; 11.36 n.
Campion, Thomas 168
Campus Martius 58
Capaneus 7.647–54 n. (impiety)

(sailing round Leucate), 3.359–61 n. (types
of prophecy, astrology), 3.500–5 endn. 288
(Segesta and Rome), 3.694–6 (on fountain
of Arethusa); 4.215–18 n. (hair), 4.232–4
endn. 125 (glory), 4.586–90 endn. 251
(expressions of mourning); 5.759–61 n.
(deified Julius Caesar's honours), 5.762–78
n. (storm gods); VI-LS and 6.703–23 n.
(*Dream of Scipio*), 6.621–2 n. (Antony's
arbitrariness). 6.623 and 8.666–70 nn
(Catiline), 6.724–6 n. (single pervading
spirit), 6.824–5 n. (Drusi),, 6.841–6 n.
(Gracchi), 6.878 n. (*fides*); 8.370–406 n.
(*suasio*), 8.485–8 n. (Etruscan pirates);
9.19–21 n. (apparent division of the skies),
9.47–76 n. (Hannibal hurls javelin over
gates of Rome), 9.310–11 (youth of
Octavian), 9.464 and 12.107–8 nn (Stoic
and Peripatetic views on anger and
courage)9.614–16 n. (dancing); 10.907–8
n. (gladiators' bravery in death); 11.122–4
n. (on an ambitious and divisive speaker),
11.197–9 n. (pig sacrifed on grave),
11.336–75 n. (caricatured in Drances);
12.414–15 n. (goats taking dittany)
Cimin(i)us, lake 7.697
Cincinnatus, Lucius Quinctius 9.609–11 endn.
287 (return from war to farming)
cinema *see* narratology: visual narration,
reception: book and film
Cinna, Gaius Helvetius 136
**Circe 3.386 (on the route foretold by Helenus);
7.10 (island skirted), 7.20, 7.191 (wife of
Picus), 7.282 (horses bred by her), 7.799;
see also Homer: *Odyssey*, Apollonius of
Rhodes: *Argonautica***
Circus Maximus 5.286–90 n.
Cisalpine Gaul *see* Gauls
Cisseus
> **(1) King of Thrace, father of Hecuba 5.537 ;
7.320 ; 10.705**
> **(2) Latin warrior 10.317**
Cithaeron 4.143–50 n., 4.303
Civic Crown 6.772 n.
civil war 8 (Marius and Sulla; Caesar and
Pompey); 1.124–56 n.; 6.832–5; 7.335–40
n., 7.545, 7.601–40, 8.698–703 and 12.313
nn (*discordia*); 9.598–9 (Caesar and
Pompey, Octavian and Antony)
Claros 3.360
Clarus 10.126
Claudian, Claudius Claudianus 144
Claudius 7.708

Clausen, Wendell *see* 'Harvard School'
Clausus 7.707
Cleanthes 68
Cleopatra 8–9; 1.494–519 and 4.643–4 nn
(comparison with Dido); 6.696 n.;
8.688–713 (at Actium and afterwards);
11.532–96 n. (contrasted with Camilla),
11.734 n. (Rome cowed by her threats)
**Cloanthus 1.222 (thought lost), 1.510, 1.612;
5.122–3 (boat race contestants), 5.152,
5.167, 5.225–48 (prays and wins boat
race)**
Clodia 80
Cloelia 8.651
Clonius 9.574; 10.749
Clonus 10.499
Cluentius 5.122–3
Clusium 10.167, 10.655
Clytius
> **(1) Trojan 9.774; 10.129; 11.666**
> **(2) Rutulian 10.325**
**Cnossos 3.115; 5.306; 6.23, 6.566; 9.305; *see
also* Crete**
**Cocles, Quintus Horatius 8.650; 9.815–18 n.
(Turnus also dives into Tiber)**
**Cocytus 6.132 (rivers listed), 6.297, 6.323;
7.562 and 7.479 (home to the demon
Allecto)**
Coeus 4.179
coins 31 (Venus portrayed), 56 (Hercules
portrayed), 59 (Cybele portrayed), 81
endn. 51 (Fulvia portrayed), 93 endn. 115
(Augustus as DIVI FILIUS); 1.291–6 n.
(Temple of Janus depicted), 1.443 n. (horse
on Carthaginian shekel); 2.707–11 n.
(Aeneas departing from Troy); 3.424–8 n.
(Scylla portrayed), 3.694–6 n. (Arethusa
on Syracusan coins); 6.808–12 n.
(Octavian on restoring laws); 8.646–51 n.
(*libertas* on coins of Caesar and Augustus),
8.682–4 n. (Agrippa depicted with Naval
Crown); 12.856–9 n. (Parthian depiction
of bowman)
Coleridge, Samuel Taylor viii, 173
Collatia 6.774
Collins, John Churton 151
colonization 2 (Greek *diaspora* – 3.399–402 n.)
and endn. 17 (colonies as source of
citizens), 131 (dispersal of heroes from
Troy), 152 (as process), 164 (Postcolonial
Studies); 3.19–21 n. (gods consulted),
3.692–718 n. (in Sicily); VIII-D
(Pallanteum), 8.51–4 n.; *see also* empire

Cybele (Cybebe) 58–9 and 76 (acceptance at
    Rome and worship), 77 (embodiment of
    Rome); 2.788 (becomes Creusa's
    protectress); 6.784–7 (wearing mural
    crown and mother of gods); 8.698–703
    n. (Bellona's worship similar); 9.82–92
    (asks to protect Aeneas' fleet), 9.107–17
    (changes ships to nymphs), 9.253–4
    (thanked by Aeneas as goddess of cities),
    9.619 (instruments); 10.156–8 n.
    (chariot, arrival in Rome), 10.220,
    10.234 (mentioned by Cymodocea)
Cybele (Cybelus) 3.111; 11.768
Cyclades 3.127; 8.692
Cyclops 60; 1.201 (recalled by Aeneas); 3.569,
    3.588–654 n., 3.616–39 (Achaemendides'
    ordeal), 3.644 and 3.647 (community of
    Cyclops), 3.675–81 (gathered on shore);
    6.630 (as wall-builders); 8.416–38
    (smithy under Etna), 8.440
    (commissioned by Vulcan); 11.263
    (Diomedes recalls Odysseus' adventure);
    see also Brontes, Steropes, Pyracmon
Cycnus 7.691–705 n. (invulnerable son of
    Neptune); 10.189
Cydon 10.325
Cydonian 12.858
Cyllene 4.252, 4.276; 8.139
Cymodoce, Cymodocea 5.826; 10.225
Cymothoe 1.144 (clears up after storm)
Cynics 68
Cynthus 1.498; 4.147
Cypria 123
Cyprus 1.622
Cyrene 22
Cythera 1.257, 1.657, 1.680; 4.128; 5.800; 8.523,
    8.615; 10.51, 10.86

da Gama, Vasco 152
Daedalus 6.14, 6.29
Dahae 8.728
Dalmatia 9; 8.714–6 n. (triple triumph)
Danaë 7.365–72 n.; 7.410 (foundress of Ardea)
Danaids 10.497–9 n.
Danaus 3.287–8 n.; 10.497–9 n.
dancing 9.614–16 n.
Dante Alighieri 146 (Virgil's influence); 2.424–30,
    3.41–8, 3.56–7 nn; VI-D
Dardania 2.281, 2.325; 3.52, 3.107–9 n., 3.156;
    6.65; 8.120
Dardanus 3.94–6 n., 3.107–9 n., 3.167 (as
    Italian), 3.503 (ancestral founder of Troy
    common to Helenus and Aeneas); 4.365;

6.650; 7.207 (route from Etruria to
    Troy), 7.240; 8.134 (son of Electra,
    grandson of Atlas)
Dares
    (1) Trojan boxer 5.368–483, 5.368 n.
    (2) Trojan warrior, possibly the same person
    12.363
Daucus 10.391
Daunus 8.146; 10.616, 10.688; 12.22, 12.90
    (sword made by Vulcan), 12.934
Davidiad see Marulić, Marko
dawn and dusk, descriptions of 1.306 n.; 3.521 n.;
    4.129 n., 4.584–5 n.; 7.25–8 n.; 9.459–60
    n.; 10.257 n.; 11.1 n., 11.182–3 n., 11.913–4
    n. (dusk); 12.113–5 n.
Dawn *see* 'Aurora'
de Camões, Luís 152
de la Cerda, Juan Luis 149; 9.703–9 n.; 12.919–52
    n.
de Saussure, Ferdinand 160, 161
de Villerias y Roelas, José 152
Death 11.197
deceit 2.57–75 n. and endn. 50, 2.610 and 2.642–3
    nn (Laomedon); 9.153 n. (Turnus)
Decii 6.824
deconstruction *see* literary theory
deer 1.184–93 (deer hunt); 4.69–73 (Dido as
    wounded hind); 7.483–8 (Sylvia's pet stag);
    12.749–55 (simile of dog hunting stag)
deification *see* gods
Deiopea 1.72
Deiphobe 6.36
Deiphobus 2.310 (house collapses); 6.494–547
    (meets Aeneas in the underworld)
Dekker, Thomas 148
Delos 3.69–83 n. (early history), 3.73–7 n.
    (once floating, now tethered), 3.84–98
    (oracle there consulted), 3.162 and 4.144
    and 6.12 (birthplace of Apollo and
    Diana)
Delphi 3.90–2 n., 6.347
Demeter *see* Ceres
Demodocus 1.441–93 n., 1.723–56 n.
Demodocus 10.413
Demoleos 5.260–5
Demophoon 11.675
Denham, Sir John 168
deprecatio 3.602–6 n.
Dercennus 11.850
Destiny *see* Fate
Deucalion and Pyrrha 8.314–18 n.
devotio 6.824–5 n. (Decii); 11.376–444 n.
    (Turnus' near-*devotio*); 12.693–5 n.

Diagoras 84

dialogue 26 (importance for characterisation), 113 (speeches), 1.113, 120–1 n. (rarity between Aeneas and his men), 1.530–3 (information passed from Aeneas to his men); 5.17–20 n. (Aeneas with Palinurus); 6.158–9 n. (Aeneas with Achates), 6.372 n. (Aeneas cut short with dead spirits); 9.176–223 n. (Nisus and Euryalus); 12.1–80 (Turnus, Latinus, Amata – but not Lavinia)

Diana 45 (particular domain); 1.329 (Aeneas trying to identify his mother), 1.499 (as comparison for Dido); 3.681; 4.511 (as moon and Hecate); 6.69–74 n. (effigy in Temple of Apollo); 7.306 (sender of Calydonian boar), 7.761–80 (story of Virbius and Hippolytus); 9.403 (prayed to by Nisus); 11.534–94 (on Camilla); 11.652 (Camilla carries 'weapons of Diana'), 11.843, 11.857; see also Hecate, Phoebe

dictator 5; 6.824–5 n. (Camillus)

Dicte 3.171; 4.73

diction 114–6, 115 (everyday language), 115–6 (sentence structure, ambiguity);

Dido 25 (characterisation), 35–6 (recalled by Turnus), 36–7 (tragic portrayal), 81 (womanliness), 87 (personal religion); 1.299 (Mercury sent to ensure Dido allows Trojans into Carthage), 1.340–68 (Venus tells Dido's history), 1.352–9 n. (her treasure at Tyre), 1.446–9 (builder of Juno's temple), 1.496–504 (arrives at temple like Diana), 1.561–78 (welcomes Trojans), 1.594–610 (addressed by Aeneas), 1.613–30 (answers Aeneas), 1.670 (maligned by Venus), 1.683–8 (to be poisoned by Cupid), 1.697–8 (reclines at feast), 1.712–4 n. ('unhappy'), 1.712–22 (effects of Cupid as Ascanius); 1.728–37 (libation and prayer), 1.749–56 (invites Aeneas to tell his story); Book IV throughout; 4.8 n. (mental states), 4.10–11 n. (as hostess), 4.13–4 n. (unawareness of Fate), 4.15–19 n. (meaning of name), 4.24–7 n. (neglected by gods), 4.54–89 n. (sacrifices), 4.65 and 4.69, 4.101, 4.238–58 n. (relationship with gods), 4.259–64 n. (Aeneas dressed by Dido), 4.283, 4.298, 4.376, 4.433, 4.465, 4.474, 4.501, 4.548, 4.646, 4.697 (*furor*), 4.86–9 n. (Dido as embodiment of Carthage), 4.474–503 (resort to magic), 4.651–2 n. (finally understands role of Fate); 5.571–2 (horse given to Ascanius); 6.450–74 (meets Aeneas in underworld), 6.453–4 n. (link to moon); 9.266 (cup promised to Nisus); 11.72–5 (twin cloaks, one used to cover Pallas); 12.54–80 n. (echoed by Turnus, Latinus and Amata)

Didymaon 5.359

Dindyma 2.788 n.; 9.618; 10.252

Dio Cassius *see* Cassius Dio Cocceianus, Lucius

Diodorus Siculus 11 (thumbnail sketch)

Diogenes Laertius 66–7 (on Epicurus),

Diomedes 26; 1.96–7 (combat with Aeneas), 1.471 (on temple of Juno), 1.752 (horses); 2.163–8 (with Ulixes seizes Palladium), 2.197; 4.425–7 n. (exhumes Anchises' bones); 8.1–17 and 11.269–70 nn (fortunes after Troy), 8.9 (Latin envoys sent); 10.29 (mentioned by Venus, ancestry), 10.581 (in battlefield taunt); 11.213–42 and 11.243–99 nn (change since Troy), 11.225–30 (response to Latin envoys in sum), 11.252–90 (speech to envoys, men changed into birds), 11.404; 12.351 (kills Dolon)

Dione 3.19

Dionysius of Halicarnassus 11 (thumbnail sketch); III-LS (Aeneas' itinerary from Troy to Drepanum), 3.189–91 n. (losses and additions to expedition), 3.389–93 n. (Aeneas' visit to Dodona), 3.531 n. (fleet divided); IV-LS, 4.613–21 n. (Aeneas' 3 years in Italy); V-LS, 5.604–63 (burning of the boats); VI-LS (stop-offs in Italy), 6.760–6 and 7.483–92 nn (Iulus as son, Silvius brother, of Ascanius), 6.767–790 n. (Alban kings); 7.45–80 n. (account of Aeneas' arrival); VIII-LS (Evander), 8.104–6 n. (Pallas), 8.184–279 n. (Cacus story), 8.328–9 n. (Greek immigration to Italy before Aeneas); 9.630–1 n. (thunder at siege of Lavinium); 10.672–5 n. (Roman military oath); 12.821–8 n. (name 'Latins' given to merged peoples)

Dionysus 4.143–50 n. (Aeneas implicitly compared to him)

Diores 5.297, 5.324 (in fourth place), 5.339–47 (protests at no third prize); 12.509 (killed by Turnus)

Dioscuri *see* Castor; Pollux

ekphrasis
  (1) geographical 110
  (2) artefacts 110–1; 1.441–93 (Temple of
    Juno); 5.250–7 (cloak inwoven with
    Ganymede), 5.536–8 (Anchises' mixing
    bowl); 6.20–31 (Daedalus' designs on
    Temple of Apollo, Cumae) and 6.14–41 n.
    (interpretations as allegory); 7.785–8
    (Turnus' helmet); 8.630–728 (shield of
    Aeneas); 10.497–9 (Pallas' baldric)
Elba (Latin 'Ilva') 10.173
Electra 8.135–7
elegy 135–7; 4.74–6 n. (influence on language of
    Dido episode); 9.312–3, 9.444–5 and
    9.446–502 nn (Nisus and Euryalus
    episode); 12.392–7 n. (Apollo and Iapyx),
    12.800–2 n. (Jupiter to Juno)
Eleusinian mysteries 61 endn. 147
Eliot, Thomas Stearns 156 (*Aeneid* as classic), 169
    (on Dryden); 6.450–76 n. (Aeneas' reunion
    with Dido)
Elis 3.694; 6.588
Elissa 1.340–1 n.
Elymi 5.38 n.
Elysium 5.735; 6.535–7 n., 6.743–7
Emathion 9.571
embassy 7.153–5, 7.237 (Ilioneus to Latinus; olive
    branch wrapped in wool – cf. 8.116, 8.128,
    11.101); 8.9–17 (Latins to Diomedes;
    misinformation), 8.126–151 (Aeneas'
    speech to Evander); 11.100–5 (Latins to
    Aeneas)
embroidery 1.637–42 n.; 3.483–5 n.
Empedocles 6.760–6 n.
empire 8–9 (growth of Roman Empire), 77
    (Rome's mission), 151–2 (*Aeneid* as
    exemplary imperial text), 152–4 (Age of
    Exploration), 153 (North American
    aversion to *Aeneid*)
Enceladus 3.578; 4.179
Eneasroman XII-D
Eneti 1.248 n.
Ennius 31 (Aeneas legend), 114 (diction), 132–3
    (innovator in Roman epic, *Annals*, impact
    on Virgil), 137 (detractors); 1.272–7 n.
    (chronology), 1.278–83 n. (end of Juno's
    wrath); II-LS, 2.500–5 n. (fragment from
    Andromache), 2.265 n. (sunk in wine and
    sleep) 2.687–8 (Anchises as prophetic);
    3.692–718 n. (importance of Sicily);
    4.465–73 n. (dream sequence); 6.179–82 n.
    (tree-felling), 6.841–6 and 9.781–7 nn (Q.
    Fabius Maximus); 7.122–7 n. (Anchises as

prophetic), 7.294–6 n. (imperishability of
    Troy), 7.516–7 n. (on river Nar), 7.601–40
    and 8.698–703 nn (breaking open temple
    of War); VIII-LS (shield of Aeneas), 8.72 n.
    (Father Tiber), 8.90–3 n. (spectators,
    greased hulls), 8.150 (pledge from
    Romulus to Numitor), 8.241–6 n. (hollow
    cavern), 8.642–5 n. (vulture scavenges
    Mettus); IX-LS, 9.316–19 n. (deep sleep
    after celebration), 9.486–9 n. (failure to
    bury the dead), 9.503–4 n. (trumpet
    sound), 9.525–9 n. (scroll of war), 9.630–1
    n. (thunder as omen), 9.672–90 n. (Istrian
    sally causes chaos among Romans),
    9.806–14 n. (Roman tribune beaten back);
    10.11–13 n. (Juno's support for Carthage
    in Second Punic War), 10.101–3 n.
    (calming of the elements), 10.395–6 n.
    (dying head described), 10.531–4 n. (war
    as trade), 10.783–832 n. (missiles like
    rain); 11.425–7 n. (fickleness of fortune),
    11.468–97 n. (simile of escaped horse),
    11.597–647 n. (as source for cavalry
    battle), 11.601–2 n. (plain flashing with
    spears); 12.68–9 n. (simile for blushing),
    12.234–5 n. (afterlife in the speech of
    men), 12.565–73 n. (for victory the
    conquered must admit defeat)
Entellus 5.382–6 n., 5.387–484 (boxing match)
Epeus 2.264
ephebeia 8.514–17 n.; 9.176–223 n. (Euryalus),
    9.621–37 n. (Ascanius)
Epic Cycle 123–4; 1.457–8 n. and 1.474, 1.489,
    1.491 nn (scenes on Juno's temple); II-LS
    (*Sack of Troy*), 2.15–16 n. (*Sack of Troy* on
    Trojan horse), 2.403–6 and 2.572–3 nn
    (*Sack of Troy, Little Iliad* on rape of
    Cassandra), 2.456–7 endn. 201 (*Little Iliad,
    Sack of Troy* on death of Astyanax),
    2.506–58 n. (*Little Iliad, Sack of Troy* on
    death of Priam); 5.311–12 n. (*Aethiopis* on
    Penthesilea); 6.56–60 (*Aethiopis* on death
    of Achilles); 6.494–534 n. (*Little Iliad* and
    Sack of Troy on Deiphobus and Helen);
    7.475–510 n. (*Cypria*, Agamemnon shoots
    a stag at Aulis); epic, history of 123–4
    (Homer and immediate successors), 124
    endn. 32 (later Greek epic), 126
    (Callimachus), 127 (Apollonius of
    Rhodes), 132–3 and 136 (development of
    Roman epic), 140–2 (successors to Virgil),
    144–5 (era of early Christianity), 145–6
    (Middle Ages and Renaissance), 147–8

gaze 4.331–3 n. (Aeneas does not look at Dido); 4.467–9 and 6.469 nn (Dido looks away from Aeneas); 12.1–4 n., 12.151 n. (turning eyes away), 12.684–91 and 12.697–727 nn (attention shifts to the single combat), 12.915 (Turnus looks at the Rutulians), 9.920–1 (Aeneas aims his spear), 12.930–1 (Turnus towards Aeneas), 12.938–41 n. (Aeneas's eyes settle on Pallas' baldric), 12.945–7 n. (Aeneas stares at the baldric)

geese 8.652–62 (sound alarm against Gauls)

Gela 3.701

Geloni 8.725

gender XI-D, 11.39–41 n., 11.59–99 n. (Pallas), 11.494–835 n. (Camilla's death), 11.893 n. (mothers as combatants); *see also* hero, women, effeminacy, transgender

gender studies *see* literary theory

genius loci see spirit of the place

gens see family

geography 75 (importance for Roman identity), 109 (adds human specificity); 3.553, 3.554–7 and 6.201 nn (altered by Virgil); 4.151–5 n. (vast perspective conjured up); 6.8 n. (invented), 6.9–12 n. (familiar sites recalled), 6.295 and 6.366 nn (vague); VII-D (reverence for Italy), 7.641–817 n. (role in catalogue); geographical looseness *passim*

Georgics see Virgil: *Georgics*

Gerusalemme Liberata see Tasso, Torquato

Geryon 6.289; 7.662; 8.202

Getae 3.35; 7.604

Gibbon, Edward 154

gifts 1.647–55 (Aeneas to Dido); 3.464–71 (Helenus to Trojans), 3.483–5 (Andromache to Ascanius); 7.152–5 and 7.243–8 nn (embassy to Latinus), 7.274–83 (Latinus to Trojans); 8.166–8 (Anchises to Evander); 11.333–5 (Latinus to Aeneas); *see also* Dido: gifts

Gigantomachy 60–1, 77 (Rome's subjugation of other nations); 3.578–82 n. (Etna); 8.184–279 and 8.236–40 nn (Cacus story), 8.691–5 n. (Battle of Actium); 9.691–716 n. (Turnus against Pandarus and Bitias); 10.565–70 n. (Aeneas as Aegaeon), 10.689–716 n. (Aeneas killing Mezentius)

Glaucus
- **(1) sea deity 5.823; 6.36**
- **(2) son of Antenor 6.483**
- **(3) son of Imbrasus 12.343**

glory 103 and 4.232–4 n. and V-D (hero's goal); 6.703–23 n. (given civic interpretation), 6.899 (Aeneas inspired by future renown); 7.4 (empty glory of toponym); 10.606–88 n. (relationship to disgrace)

gods
- (1) general 45 (Greek and Roman equivalence, syncretism), 46 (family tree), 46–7 (Homeric gods and the reaction to them), 48 (determining human action), 48–9 (gods in the Aeneid), 56–8 (local and minor), 58–60 (foreign); 1.253 (should reward piety); 4.217–8 and 11.50 (useless sacrifices), 4.509–11 (of underworld); 6.322–4 (swearing by Styx – *see also* oaths); 10.659–60 (pity aggression and struggles of mortals); *see also under individual gods' names*
- (2) belief in 83–4; 4.205–18 (Iarbas); 9.207–18 n. (Nisus)
- (3) consultation of 3.84–101 (Apollo on Delos); 6.62–97 (Sibyl at Cumae); 7.81–106 n. (Faunus, by incubation); *see also* oracles
- (4) deification 56 (Hercules), 93–4 (others, including Alexander the Great, Augustus and Livia); 6.788–94 n. (Augustus, Caesar)

golden age 20, 148 (in Tudor and Stuart ceremonial pomp); 6.788–94 (restored by Augustus); 7.202–4 n. (Latinus' revival); 8.319–25 and 8.306–36 n. (described); 11.252–4 n. (mentioned by Diomedes)

golden bough 6.124–55 n., 6.136–48 , 6.406, 6.636

Gorgon 2.616; 6.289; 7.341; 8.438

Gortyn 11.773

Gracchi 7; 6.824–5 n. (Drusi)

Gracchus 7; 6.824–5 n. (Drusi), 6.842 (reforming activities)

Gradivus 10.541–2 n.

graffiti 140; 1.1–7 n.; 2.1 n.

Grattius Faliscus 12.749–57 n.

Graves, Robert 156

Graviscae 10.184

Greeks 2 and 8.328–9 n. (early contact with Italy), 7 (Greece conquered by Rome); 6.847–53 and 9.602 nn (Roman attitude towards Greeks)

Grynia 4.345

Guadelupe see de Villerias y Roelas, José Antonio

Gyaros 3.76

Gyas
  (1) Trojan commander, captain of the Chimaera in the boat race 1.222 (thought lost), 1.612; 5.118 (boat race), 5.160–77 (throws helmsman overboard), 5.184, 5.223; 12.460 (in action)
  (2) Latin 10.318
Gyges 9.762
Gylippus 12.272

Haecker, Theodor 155–6
Haedi 9.668 n.
Haemon 9.685
Haemonides 10.537
hair 1.404–5 (Venus' scented locks), 2.277 n. (Hector's), 2.682–4 (Ascanius' on fire); 3.62–8 n. (unbound in mourning), 3.369–73 (untied for worship); 4.215–18 n., 12.99–100 (effeminate); 7.73–7 (Lavinia's on fire); 10.137–8 (Ascanius' as he leads defence of camp), 10.831–2 n. (Lausus' soiled with blood), 10.844 (Mezentius' white hair fouled in grief – cf. 12.611); 11.77 (Pallas' covered in death), 11.640–2 n. (blonde hair makes conspicuous); 12.97–100 n. (Turnus threatens to soil Aeneas' scented curls), 12.605 (torn in grief), 12.611 (Latinus' white hair soiled in mourning1)
Halaesus 7.724; 10.352, 10.411–25 (falls to Pallas)
half lines *see* incomplete lines
Halius 9.767
Halys 9.765
hamartia see Aristotle (analysis of tragedy)
hand, right 1.408 (Aeneas and Venus), 1.514 (expressing reunion); 2.592 (Aenes and Venus), 2.723 (Iulus takes Aeneas'); 4.307–8 n. and 4.597 (Dido's and Aeneas'); 5.443 and 5.457 and 5.479 (at the boxing); 6.695–8 n.; 7.234 (Aeneas' offered by Ilioneus to Latinus), 7.266 (sought by Latinus), 7.366 (Amata says given by Latinus to Turnus); 8.124 (Aeneas and Pallas), 8.169 (Aeneas and Evander), 8.467 (morning greeting), 8.558 (Evander and Pallas); 9.289 (Euryalus citing Ascanius'); 10.517 (Aeneas remembers), 10.773 (Mezentius prays to his, as weapon-wielder); 11.164–5, 11.172 and 11.178 (Evander demands vengeance at Aeneas' hand), 11.292 (Diomedes urges union of Trojans and Latins), 11.408 (Turnus raises his on Drances); 12.14 (Turnus imagines dispatching Aeneas), 12.579 (Aeneas extends it against Latinus' city), 12.659 (Amata turns hers on herself), 12.930 (Turnus extends his in supplication), 12.939 (Aeneas checks his before dealing the deathblow to Turnus)
Hannibal 6–7; 4.219 and 4.622–9 nn (oath of hostility to Rome); 10.11–13 n. (crosses Alps)
Harpalyce 1.317; 7.803–17 n.
Harpalycus 11.675
Harpy 3.212, 3.226, 3.249, 3.365; 6.289
haruspex 88; 4.60–4 n.; 8.498 n.
'Harvard School' 154, 156–7
hawk 11.664–724 (Camilla in the attack)
Heaney, Seamus 172–3; VI-D
Hebrus
  (1) river in Thrace 1.317 ; 12.331
  (2) Trojan 10.696
Hecale see Callimachus
Hecate 4.511, 4.609; 6.118, 6.247, 6.564
Hector 1.99; 1.273, 1.483, 1.750; 2.270–85 (appears to Aeneas at Troy), 2.522, 2.543; 3.304 (honoured by Andromache), 3.312, 3.319, 3.343, 3.488; 5.190, 5.372, 5.634; 6.166; 9.155 (prolonged the Trojan war); 11.289 (Diomedes compares Aeneas with him); 12.440
Hecuba 2.501, 2.515–25 (urges Priam to seek sanctuary); 7.312–22 n. (dreams of birth of Paris)
Hegel, Georg Wilhelm Friedrich 125 (theory of tragedy), 151 (view of Virgil)
Heinze, Richard 155
Hekatoncheir 60; 3.578–82 endn. 332 (different accounts of their allegiance)
Helen 1.650; 2.567–88 (at temple of Vesta – episode doubted), 2.601; 7.634
Helen episode 2.567–88 n.
Helenor 9.544
Helenus 3.295, 3.329, 3.334, 3.346, 3.374–462 (instructions for Aeneas), 3.380 (forbidden by Juno to tell everything), 3.546, 3.559, 3.684, 3.712
Helicon 7.641; 10.163
Hellanicus of Lesbos II-LS; 7.205–11 n. (Dardanus' route from Etruria to Troy)
helmet 2.412 n. (crests); 5.673 (Ascanius discards his helmet); 5.490–1 n. (used for drawing lots), 5.673 (Ascanius discards his in front of Trojan women); 6.779–80 (7.785–8, 9.50 and 9.732–3 (Turnus' described);

of Aeneas), 7.647–54 n. (epithet 'tamer of horses'); 9.49–50 (Turnus on horseback), 9.269–71 n. (Turnus' horse as prize), 9.359–60 n. (decorative plaques); 10.858–9 (closeness of Rhaebus to Mezentius); 11.89–90 (Pallas' Aethon weeps), 11.571–2 (mare's milk food for Camilla); 12.82–4 (Turnus' described), 12.333–4 (Mars' wind-swift team)

hospitality 1.525 and 1.613–42 nn (Dido), 1.539–40 n. (owed to sailors); 2.74–5 n.; III-D (good and bad), 3.15 , 3.80 n. (Anius on Delos), 3.353–5 (Helenus to Aeneas); 4.10–11 n. (Aeneas' transformation from guest) and endn. 43 (*xenia*); 8.112–14 n. (Evander to Aeneas), 8.362–3 and 10.460–3 n. (Evander to Hercules)

household gods 57; 1.1–7 n. (shrine at Lavinium), 1.68, 1.378, 1.527, 1.704 (at Carthage); 2.293 (Hector's instructions), 2.514 (at Priam's altar), 2.717 (carried by Anchises), 2.747; 3.12, 3.15, 3.148 (in a vision to Aeneas), 3.603; 4.21, 4.598 (Dido's sarcasm); 5.62 (at sacrifice to Anchises), 5.632, 5.744 (Lar); 6.68 (referred to by Sibyl); 7.121 (saluted by Aeneas in Italy); 8.11, 8.39, 8.123 and 8.543 (of Pallas and Evander), 8.679 (at Actium); 9.258–9 (invoked by Ascanius); 11.264

Housman, Alfred Edward 12.55 n.

Howard, Henry, Earl of Surrey 167

hundred-hander *see* Hekatoncheir

hunting 1.180–209 n. (connotations within *Aeneid*); 4.69–73 n. (simile of hunting shepherd), 4.129–59 (Dido's royal hunt), 4.120–2 and 10.707–18 nn (Roman methods); 5.252–3 n. (Ganymede); 7.475–510 and 7.477–8 nn (Ascanius shoots stag); IX-D and 9.176–8 n. (Nisus and Euryalus), 9.551–3 (simile of hunted beast at bay), 9.590–2 and 9.605–6 n. (Ascanius' transition from hunter to warrior); 12.749–57 n. (cordon of feathers to hem in prey)

Hyades 1.744; 3.516

Hydaspes 10.747

Hydra 6.287, 6.576; 7.658; 8.300 (killed by Hercules)

Hyginus, Gaius Julius 6.122–3 n. (Theseus inconsistency)

Hylaeus 8.294

Hyllus 12.535

Hypanis 2.340, 2.428

hyperbole 68, 114; 3.563–7 n. (storms), 3.672–4 n. (with pathetic fallacy); 6.625 –7 and 7.167 nn (increasing from epic to epic)

Hyrcanians 4.367; 7.605

Hyrtacus

    (1) father of Hippocoon 5.492, 5.503

    (2) father of Nisus 9.177, 9.234, 9.319, 9.406

hysteron proteron 4.120–2 endn. 81; 10.477 n.; 12.924–6 n.

Iaera 9.673

Iapyx

    (1) Cretan coloniser of Apulia 8.710; 11.247, 11.678

    (2) son of Iasus, a physician 12.391 (obtains gift of healing from Apollo), 12.405–6 (fails to extract arrow from Aeneas' leg), 12.420. 12.425

Iarbas 4.36, 4.196, 4.198 n., 4.326

Iasius

    (1) brother of Dardanus, and son-in-law of Teucer (1) 3.94–6 n., 3.168

    (2) (or Iasus) father of Palinurus 5.843

    (3) father of Iapyx 12.392

Ibycus 2.572–3 n.

Icarus 6.31

Ida

    (1) mountain near Troy 2.696, 2.788 n. Cybele connection), 2.801; 3.6, 3.112; 5.252–4 (site of Ganymede's abduction), 5.449; 7.139, 7.207, 7.222; 9.80, 9.112, 9.620; 10.158, 10.230, 10.252, 10.285

    (2) a mountain in Crete 3.105 (cradle of Jupiter); 12.412

    (3) the mother of Nisus 9.177

Idaeus

    (1) Priam's charioteer 6.485

    (2) Trojan 9.500

Idalium 1.681, 1.693; 5.760; 10.52, 10.86

Idas

    (1) Trojan 9.575

    (2) Thracian 10.351

Idmon 12.75

Idomeneus 3.121–3 n., 3.122, 3.401; 11.265

Ilia 1.274; 6.778

Iliad see Homer

Ilione 1.653

Ilioneus 1.120, 1.521–59 (addresses Dido), 1.611; 7.212–49 (addresses Latinus); 9.501, 9.569

Iliou Persis see Epic Cycle

Ilium *see* Troy

Ilua/Ilva *see* 'Elba'

Ilus

    (1) son of Tros, and King of Troy 6.650

    (2) earlier name for Iulus 1.268

    (3) Rutulian 10.400

Ilyria 1.243

Imaon 10.424

Imbrasus 10.123; 12.343

imitation 165

immigration 76 (before Aeneas' arrival); 6.86–7
    n. (hostility prophesied); 8.306–36 n. (after
    golden age); *see also* integration

imperium 77 (Rome's mission)

impietas see pietas

Inachus

    **(1) first king of Argos; 'Inachian' = Argive,
    Greek 7.286 , 7.372; 11.286**

    (2) river in Argos 7.792

Inarime 9.716

incomplete lines 2.622–3 n.; 3.337–43 n.

inconsistencies Book III Inconsistencies; 5.626 n.
    (still seven years on), 5.750–1 n.
    (discrepancy on women left in Sicily),
    5.827–71 n. (Palinurus' death); 6.122–3 n.
    (Theseus trapped in or escaped from
    Hades), 6.146–8 n. (golden bough),
    6.494–534 n. (Deiphobus and Helen),
    6.760–6 n. (Iulus / Silvius as head of Alban
    line; Aeneas as long-lived); 7.107–47 n.
    (Celaeno's prophecy attributed to
    Anchises), 7.170–91 n. (Picus' family);
    11.911 n. (cavalry in Aeneas' ambush);
    12.834–5 n. (Trojans to take on Latin
    customs)

India(ns) 6.794; 7.605; 8.705; 12.67

Indiges 1.259 n.; 12.794

Ino 5.823

integration 7.531–3 n.; VIII-D, 8.635–8 n.
    (Sabines); 12.835–7 (Trojans absorbed by
    Italians)

intertextuality 117 (quest for literary sources),
    118–20; 120–1 (two-tier allusion /
    contamination); *see also* subjectivity,
    allusion, literary theory

intratextuality 118–20 (allusion to the Aeneid
    itself, or to other works of Virgil)

inversion 6.88–90 n. (Aeneas and Turnus) and
    endn. 55 (Dido and Camilla)

invocation 1.8–11 (Muse); 6.264–7 (underworld
    powers); 7.1–4 (Caieta), 7.37–40 (Erato),
    7.41 n., 7.641–6 (Muses); 9.77–9 (Muses),
    9.525–8 (Calliope); 10.163–5 (Muses);
    12.500–4 (gods)

Io 7.789

Iollas 11.640

Ionia 3.211, 3.671; 5.193

Iopas 1.740

Iphitus 2.435

**Iris 58; 4.693–705 (sent by Juno to the dying
    Dido); 5.606–58 (sent by Juno to the
    Trojan women); 9.2–15 (sent by Juno to
    Turnus), 9.18 (recognised by Turnus),
    9.803–4 (sent by Jupiter to Juno); 10.38,
    10.73**

Isis 58

Ismarus

    **(1) mountain/town in Thrace also called
    Ismara 10.351**

    (2) Lydian 10.139

'it is said…' 1.12–33 n. (poet distances himself)

Italus 1.533; 7.178

Italy 3; 76 (Italianness and Romannness)

Ithaca 2.104, 2.122, 2.128; 3.272, 3.613, 3.619

itinerary III-LS (to Drepanum); 3.531 n. (single
    landing point in Italy)

Itys 9.574

Iulus *see* **Ascanius**

Ixion 6.601

Janiculum 8.337–69 n. (map), 8.358

**Janus 57; 1.291–6 n.; 7.180, 7.610 (guardian of
    gates of War); 8.357; 10.228–9 n. (his
    priest); 12.198 (with two faces)**

Jason 37; 3.8–11 n. (cries as leaves home);
    4.143–50 n. (compared to Apollo), 4.307–8
    n. (right hand offered or given to Medea);
    5.8–41 n. (atones for murder of Apsyrtus
    in Sicily); 7.167 and 12.899–900 nn (lifts
    stone quoit that would need Ares or four
    lesser men), 7.212–48 n. (claims
    harmlessness and Destiny); 8.589–90 and
    10.272–3 nn (like Sirius)

Jerome (St. Jerome) 142 (familiarity with Virgil);
    2.755 n. (visiting catacombs)

Jesuits *see* missionaries

Jocasta 12.593–611 n.

Johnson, William 157

Julia

    (1) aunt of Julius Caesar 31 (Caesar's lineage)

    (2) daughter of Julius Caesar 8 (marriage to
    Pompey)

    (3) daughter of Augustus 9–10 (marriages),
    80 endn. 42 (her behaviour)

Julian dynasty 31

**Julii 31 (Venus connection); 1.288, 1.267–71
    (link to 'Ilium')**

Jung *see* literary theory

Juno 31 (in Ennius), 45 (particular domain and Juno Lucina of childbirth), 52–4 (character in Aeneid; provides poem's structure; Fate; wrath), 81 (womanliness); 1.4 (her wrath), 1.15–32 (love of Samos, Carthage, Argos but hostility to Troy), 1.44–75 (stirs up storm), 1.73–5 (particular domain and Juno Lucina of childbirth), 1.278–83 (end of wrath), 1.279 (Jupiter promises her placation to Venus), 1.446–9 (Temple of Juno at Carthage), 1.662–72 (Venus acts against Juno's wrath), 1.734 (invoked by Dido); 2.348–54 n. (invited to leave Veii in *evocatio*), 2.612–4 (participates in sack of Troy), 2.761 (temple warehousing Greek loot); 3.380 (limits Helenus' revelations), 3.437–9 (Helenus enjoins sacrifice to her), 3.547 (that sacrifice carried out), 3.552 (Temple of Juno Lacinia); 4.59 (Dido sacrifices to her), 4.90–128 (marriage pact with Venus), 4.166–7 (present at the cave), 4.371 and 4.608 (spoken of by Dido), 4.693–5 (sends Iris to end Dido's pain); 5.606–8 (sends Iris to stir up Trojan women), 5.679, 5.781–2 (Venus complains of her to Neptune); 6.90–1 (Sibyl forecasts her shadowing Trojans), 6.138 (Proserpina as 'Juno of the underworld'); 7.286–322 (soliloquy on her frustration; moves in 'lower air'), 7.323–40 (summons Allecto), 7.419, 7.428 ('Calybe' claims Juno sent her), 7.438–9 (mentioned by Turnus), 7.544–60 (discharges Allecto), 7.592, 7.622 (breaks open gates of War), 7.682–3; 8.60 (Tiberinus tells Aeneas to sacrifice to Juno), 8.84–5 (Aeneas sacrifices sow), 8.292 (unfairness to Hercules); 9.2–3 (sends Iris to Turnus), 9.745–6 and 9.764 (protects and boosts Turnus), 9.802–3 (Jupiter sends Iris to stop her); 10.1–117 n. (in debate), 10.62–95 (speaks to the assembled gods); 10.606–32 (asks Jupiter to extend Turnus' life), 10.633–42 (shapes decoy 'Aeneas'), 10.659 (casts off boat), 10.760 (watches the battle along with the gods); 12.134–60 (incites Juturna to intervene), 12.791–842 (final accord with Jupiter; nn: end of wrath); *see also* Fate

Jupiter 20 and 21 (in Georgics), 45 (particular domain), 50–1 (Fate), 51–2 (character in Aeneid), 53 (responses to Juno); 1.42 (thunderbolt against Ajax), 1.78, 1.223–53 (addressed by Venus), 1.224–96 (prophesies to Venus), 1.297–300 (dispatches Mercury to Carthage), 1.380–1, 1.522, 1.665; 2.326, 2.617–8 (abets destruction of Troy), 2.689 (invoked by Anchises); 3.20–1, 3.102–5 n. (hidden as baby on Crete), 3.104, 3.116, 3.171 (denies Crete to Trojans), 3.223, 3.279, 3.681; 4.91, 4.110–3 (Venus speculates on his plans), 4.198–218 (rebuked by Iarbas), 4.219–37 (sends Mercury to Aeneas), 4.269–76 (paraphrased by Mercury), 4.331, 4.356 (authority invoked by Aeneas), 4.372 (invoked as just by Dido), 4.377, 4.590, 4.614; 5.17, 5.255 (his eagle snatches up Ganymede), 5.687–99 (prayed to by Aeneas to save ships), 5.726 (sends vision of Anchises), 5.747, 5.784; 6.123, 6.129–30 (deifies few), 6.272, 6.580–4 (plotted against by sons of Aloeus), 6.585–6 (impersonated by Salmoneus); 7.110 (guides Trojan picnic), 7.133, 7.139, 7.219–20 (ancestor of Aeneas), 7.287 and 7.308 (Juno as 'wife of Jupiter'), 7.799; 8.301, 8.319–20 (ousts Saturn), 8.353 (seen on ancient Capitol), 8.381, 8.427–8 (thunderbolts being manufactured), 8.560, 8.573 (prayed to by Evander), 8.640; 9.82–106 (allows Cybele to save Trojan fleet), 9.128–9 (Turnus construes this omen), 9.208–9 (spoken of by Nisus), 9.564, 9.624–31 (prayed to by Ascanius), 9.670–1, 9.673, 9.716 (buries Typhoeus), 9.803–4 (sends Iris to stop Juno); 10.1–117 (assembly of gods; n.: interventions after gods told not to intervene), 10.112–3 (promises impartiality, fate to take its course); 10.466–73 (asserts fate's primacy to Hercules), 10.567–8 (fought by Aegaeon), 10.606–27 (grants Juno an extension for Turnus); 11.725–8 (mobilises Tarchon), 11.901 (ordains Turnus should leave ambush); 12.140–1 (has raped Juturna), 12.200 (as god of oaths), 12.247, 12.503–4 (questioned by the poet), 12.565, 12.725–7 (weighs fates of Aeneas and Turnus in scales),

Little Iliad 123

Livia Augusta 7.706–22 n. (of *gens Claudia*)

Livius Andronicus, Lucius 132

Livy 10–11 (thumbnail sketch), 81 (on women's appetite for adornment), 104 (on the purpose of his history); 1.247 n. (Antenor), 1.259 n. (Aeneas' death), 1.267–71 n. (Ascanius as son of Lavinia), 1.272–7 and 6.781–4 nn (story of Romulus and Remus), 1.291–6 n. (shutting Temple of Janus); 2.105–44 n. (human sacrifice), 2.246 n. (fall of Veii), 2.685–6 n. (Servius Tullius); 3.13–16 n. (corn bloodied by scythe); 6.760–6 n. (Silvius son of Ascanius), 6.813–5 n. (Tullus Hostilius, sack of Alba), 6.815–16 n. (Ancus Martius), 6.817–23 n. (Tarquins, Lucius Junius Brutus and his sons); 7.45–80 n. (story of Aeneas' arrival), 7.202–4 n. (Numa's religious reforms); VIII-LS (details of Pallanteum, early Roman history on Aeneas' shield), 8.179–83 and 8.268–72 nn (entrails eaten at festival of Hercules), 8.184–279 n. (Cacus story), 8.225–7 n. (portcullis), 8.268–72 n. (Potitius and Pinarii), 8.342–4 n. (creation of 'asylum' for immigrants), 8.407–53 n. (Lucretia weaving), 8.475–6 n. (12 Etruscan cities), 8.635–8 n. (rape of Sabine women), 8.641 n. (oath before a treaty), 8.642–5 n. (Mettus Fufidius), 8.646–51 n. (Horatius Cocles), 8.646–51 n. (*libertas*), 8.652–62 n. (Gauls repelled; Manlius executed), 8.665–6 n. (women donate jewellery to war effort), 8.724–8 n. (Dahae); 9.25–6 n. (uselessness of decorated weapons), 9.310–11 n. (youth of Scipio Africanus), 9.505–6 n. (Volscians attacking Roman camp), 9.609–11 n. (Camillus in old age); 10.163–214 n. (cities of Etruria), 10.891 n. (cavalryman attacks another's horse); 11.19–20 n. (ignoring omens when striking camp), 11.508 n. (Cloelia), 11.522–9 n. (Caudine Forks); 12.107–8 n. (anger and courage), 12.232 n. (religiosity of Etruscans), 12.509–12 n. (Gauls decorating horses with decapitated heads), 12.821–8 n. (name 'Latins' given to merged peoples), 12.821–8 n. (Hannibal threatened to wipe out name of Rome), 12.865–8 n. (story of M. Valerius)

Locrians 3.399; 11.265

locus amoenus 6.638–9 n.

Lombardo, Stanley 171

Longinus 150; 6.450–76 n. (Ajax's silence to Odysseus); 7.37–45 n. (genius and fairy-tales)

Lorrain, Claude 8.81–101 n. (*Aeneas' Arrival at Pallanteum*)

Lowell, Robert 11.139–81 n. (imagines Aeneas at Pallas' funeral)

Lucagus 10.575–7, 10.586 (charioteer for his brother), 10.592 (taunted by Aeneas)

Lucan 141; 6.49–50 and 6.98–101 nn (description of Sibyl's ecstasy); 8.696–7 n. (Cleopatra's sistrum); 12.856–9 n. (Parthian poisoned arrows)

Lucas 10.561

Lucetius 9.570

Lucian 6.384–416 n. (on Charon), 6.412–16 n. (Charon's boat), 6.426–49 n. (categories of prematurely dead), 6.545 n. (roster of dead)

Lucifer 2.801; 8.589

Lucilius, Gaius 7.750–60 n. (Marsian destroying snakes)

Lucretia 4; IV-LS

Lucretius 24, 61 (Gigantomachy), 66 (Epicureanism), 67–8 (influence on Virgil, *Aeneid* as corrective), 67 endn. 33 (relevant passages of *Aeneid*), 114 (use of archaism), 133–5 (*On the Nature of Things*, synopsis, *Aeneid* as anti-Lucretian); 1.52–63 n. (on thunder), 1.712–4 n. and 4.672–92 endn. 293 (on love); 2.105–44 and 2.116–9 nn (sacrifice of Iphigeneia), 2.604–5 (detachment of gods); 3.135–46 n. (plague) 3.199 n. (lightning), 3.570–7 n. (Etna); 4.1–2 endn. 36 (love), 4.173–97 n. (thunderbolts), 4.693–5 n. (death as loosening bond of soul to body); 5.759–61 n. (Romans as descendants of Venus); 6.237–42 n. (Avernus), 6.268–73 n. (darkness and colour), 6.274–81 n. (suffering personified outside doors of death), 6.285–9 n. (mythical creatures), 6.440–4 n. (permanence of death), 6.548–627 n. (Tityus, Tantalus, Sisyphus), 6.577–9 n. (reflection in a puddle), 6.585–94 n. (Salmoneus as riposte to Lucretius), 6.724–55 n. (reincarnation affirmed against Lucretius), 6.847–53 n. (quiet obedience); 7.445–74 n. (iron filings jumping to a magnet); 8.22–5 n. (mirrored stars), 8.293–300 n. (on not being able to explain), 8.306–36 n. (origins of society); 8.349–50 n. (on *religio*), 8.370–406 and

8.403–6 nn (Venus and Mars at start of poem), 8.388–92 n. (pleasure of love-making), 8.388–92 n. (lightning); 9.83–92 n. (strictness of Cybele), 9.226 n. (sacrifice of Iphigenia recalled), 9.411–15 n. (death of a calf), 9.444–5 n. (bodies piled in plague), 9.586–9 n. (slingshot melting as it flies), 9.603–4 n. (hardiness of primitive man), 9.630–1 n. (no thunder from clear sky), 9.671 n. (explanation of thunder); 10.175–8 n. (Etruscan divination by lightning), 10.217 n. (release of sleep), 10.252–3 n. (Cybele's associated symbolism), 10.636–42 n. (explains apparitions), 10.689–716 n. (redefines *pietas*), 10.730–1 n. (wounded boars); 111.615–17 n. (siege engine in simile); 12.331–6 n. (black face of fear), 12.416–19 (panacea), 12.614–96 n. (rocks dislodged by time), 12.903 n. (plague-induced amnesia), 12.908–12 n. (effects of fear), 12.921–3 n. (simile of missile from catapult)

Lucrine lake 3.386 and 3.441–2 nn

Luna 9.403

Lupercal 8.343

Lupercalia 85

Luperci 8.663

Lusiads, The see de Camões, Luís

lusus Troiae see Game of Troy

luxury and simplicity 1.637–42 and 1.728–30 nn (Carthage); 4.133–5, 4.136–9 and 4.259–64 nn (Dido and Aeneas); 5.8–41 n. (Acestes); 8.98–100 n. (Evander's kingdom), 8.337–69 n. (poverty not to be despised), 8.347–8 n. (gilded ceilings), 8.685–8 n. (barbarian wealth); 9.590–620 n. (Numanus Remulus)

Lyaeus *see* **Bacchus**

Lycaeus 8.344

Lycaon

    (1) Cretan metal worker 9.304

    (2) Trojan/Arcadian 10.749

Lyceum 65

Lycia, Lycians 1.113; 4.143, 4.346, 4.377; 6.334; 7.721, 7.816; 10.126, 10.751; 11.773; 12.344, 12.516

Lycophron 18, 24, 30 (on Aeneas), 131–2 (parallels between *Alexandra* and the *Aeneid*); III-LS; 8.506 n. (Tarchon's alliance with Aeneas); 11.243–99 (foundation of Argyripa/Arpi), 11.269–70 n. (Diomedes' wife plots against him)

Lyctos 3.401

Lycurgus 3.14

Lycus 1.222; 9.545, 9.556 (killed by Turnus)

Lydia 2.781; 8.479; 9.11; 10.155

Lynceus 9.768

Lyne, Oliver 157

lyric 118 (in allusion), 124–5 (Pindar), 135–7 (Latin lyric before Virgil); 9.176–449 n. (Nisus and Euryalus episode)

Lyrnes(s)us 10.128; 12.547

Lyssa 7.323–40 n.

Macedonia 1.283–5 n. (creation of Roman province)

Macedonian War, Third 6.836–40 n.

Machaon 2.263

Macrobius, Ambrosius Theodosius 113–4 (analysis of rhetoric), 115 (new usages), 117 (Virgil's borrowing), 121 (on 'contamination'), 122–3 (wide range of literary sources), 125 (Virgil and tragedy), 142 (*Saturnalia*), 143 (Virgil's aim); 1.223–53 n. (Naevius' precedent for storm), 1.723–56 n. (criticises Iopas' documentary song); 2.15–17 n. ('Trojan pork'); IV-D (popularity of Dido episode), IV-LS (falsity); 7.323–40 and 475–510 nn (censures Virgil on causes of war), 7.641–817 n. (lack of organisation in catalogue); 8.175–6 n. (sitting to feast Hercules), 8.276–9 n. (Hercules crosses sea in wine cup)

Maecenas 16; 8.475–6 n. (Etruscan origins)

maenad *see* bacchant

Maeon 10.337

Maeonia 4.216; 8.499; 9.546; 10.141; 11.759

Maeotis 6.799

magic 88; 4.512–18

Magnalia Christi Americana see Mather, Cotton

Magus 10.521, 10.523–36 (supplicates Aeneas in vain)

Maia 1.297; 8.138, 8.140 (in Aeneas' relation of himself to Evander)

makarismos 1.94–101 n.; 9.337–8 n., 9.446–9 n.; 11.252–4 n., 11.416–8 n.

Malampus 10.320

Malea 5.193

Mandelbaum, Allen 171

Manilius, Marcus 3.359–61 n.; 6.847–53 n.

Manlius 8.652

Manto 10.199

Mantua 15

Marcelli 9, 10; 6.756–853 n., 6.855, 6.858 n., 6.879–81 n., 6.883; 7.706–22 n. (of *gens*

priests
> (1) at Rome 84–5 (link with politics,
> priesthoods revived by Augustus), 84
> endn. 80 (catalogued); 6.69–74 n.
> (*quindecimviri*); 7.187–91 n. (shield of
> Salii); 8.280–305 (Salii); 9.52–3 n. (*fetiales*
> declare war); 12.169–71 n. (*fetiales* strike
> sacrificial victim)
>
> (2) in the *Aeneid* 86; 2.429–30 and 10.538–41
> nn (killing of priests: Panthus,
> Haemonides); 11.768 (Chloreus once
> priest of Cybele), 11.785–8 n. (Arruns
> priest of Apollo on Mt. Soracte); *see also*
> Salii

Pristis 5.116, 5.154–7, 5.187, 5.218–26

Privernum 11.540

Privernus 9.576

prizes *see* games

Probus, Marcus 1.498–502 n.; 11.552–5 n.

Procas 6.767

Prochyta 9.715

Procne 12.468–99 n.

Procris 6.445

Prometheus 6.595–600 n.

Promolus 9.574

propemptikon 11.45–8 n.

Propertius, Sextus 16; 5.77–9 n. (roses for the
dead); 6.854–92 and 6.855–6 nn (elegy for
Marcellus); 8.696–7 n. (Cleopatra's
sistrum); 10.195–7 n. (prows in form of
centaurs); 11.734 (Rome cowed by
Cleopatra's threats); 12.68–9 n. (lily-
whiteness), 12.845–8 n. (Cupid's wings)

prophecy
> (1) at Rome 88–9; 10.175–8 n. (Etruscan skill)
>
> (2) in the *Aeneid* 90–93; 3.251–2 n. and
> 3.379–80 (bound to be incomplete);
> 4.613–21 n. (predictions of dying);
> 7.107–47 n. (ingredient of foundation
> legends); 10.862–5 n. (in the face of death)

**Proserpina 2.712–6 n.; 4.698; 6.122–3 n.
(kidnap attempt by Theseus and
Pirithous), 6.142, 6.251 (sacrificed to by
Aeneas), 6.402**

Protagoras 84

Proteus 22

Proteus 11.262

Prytanis 9.767

psychoanalysis *see* literary theory

pudor 4.24–7, 4.169–72 and 4.321–3 nn; 5.453–7;
10.670–86 (Turnus' sense of heroic
disgrace)

Punic *see* Carthage *and* Phoenician

Punic Wars 6–7, 10 (recorded by Polybius); 1.13
n.; 4.622–9 n.; 6.841–6 n. (Cato, Scipios,
Serranus, Fabii); 10.11–13 n. (predicted by
Jupiter); 12.34 n. (announcement of defeat
at Trasimene)

Punica see Silius Italicus

Purcell, Henry IV-D (opera *Dido and Aeneas*)

purple, Tyrian 1.336 n. (manufacture) and endn.
203 (use on toga), 1.637–42 n. (luxury);
4.133–5 n. (Aeneas and Dido in purple
and gold); 5.132–3 (boat captains in
purple and gold); 7.814 (Camilla sports
purple and gold); 9.514–6; 10.722 (attracts
attention on battlefield); 11.72–7 n. (Dido's
cloak bestowed on Pallas), 11.772
(Chloreus in purple and gold), 11.819
(colour in Camilla's cheeks); 12.67–8 (as
dye for ivory – Lavinia's blush), 12.126
(with gold, ceremonial wear for leaders)

Putnam, Michael *see* 'Harvard School'

**Pygmalion 1.347, 1.364; 4.325 (still feared by
Dido)**

Pyracmon 8.425

Pyrgi 10.184

Pyrgo 5.645

Pyrrhus of Epirus 6 (Pyrrhic War); 6.841–6 n.
(Decii, Fabricius); 11.552–5 n. (as a child
flees Epirus)

Pyrrhus *see* Neoptolemus

Pythagoreanism 62–3, 6.724–55 n.
(reincarnation)

queen *see* kingship

Quercens 9.684

quindecimviri 84 endn. 80, 88

Quintilian: Marcus Fabius Quintilianus ix
(assessment of *Aeneid*), 83 (on reciting
Homer and Virgil), 139 (use in education);
6.847–53 n. (Roman versus Greek
oratory); 10.1–117 n. (keeping calm in
debate)

**Quirinus 1.292 (with Remus); 6.859; 7.187
(Picus assimilated to him), 7.612**

Quirites 7.710

radiate crown 12.162–4 n.

rainbow 4.700–1; 5.658; 9.15

Rapo 10.747

rationalization 47; 9.184–5 n. (Nisus)

reader response theory *see* literary theory

reception 139–42 (first 150 years), 160 (distinct
from reception theory), 142–5 (second to
fifth centuries), 145–7 (Middle Ages and